The Great American Mission

—————————————

AMERICA IN THE WORLD

SVEN BECKERT AND JEREMI SURI, *series editors*

Also in the Series

Martin Klimke, *The Other Alliance: Student Protest in West Germany and the United States in the Global Sixties*

Andrew Zimmerman, *Alabama in Africa: Booker T. Washington, the German Empire, and the Globalization of the New South*

Ian Tyrell, *Reforming the World: The Creation of America's Moral Empire*

Rachel St. John, *Line in the Sand: A History of the Western U.S.–Mexico Border*

The
Great American Mission

MODERNIZATION AND THE
CONSTRUCTION OF AN
AMERICAN WORLD ORDER

David Ekbladh

PRINCETON UNIVERSITY PRESS

PRINCETON AND OXFORD

Second printing, and first paperback printing, 2011
Paperback ISBN 978-0-691-15245-5

The Library of Congress has cataloged the cloth edition of this book as follows

Ekbladh, David, 1972–
The great American mission: modernization and the construction
of an American world order / David Ekbladh
p.   cm.—(America in the world)
Includes bibliographical references and index.
ISBN 978-0-691-13330-0 (hardcover : acid-free paper)
1. Economic development—United States—History. 2. Economic assistance,
American—History. 3. Industrial policy—United States—History. 4. United States—
Foreign economic relations. 5. United States—Foreign relations. I. Title.
HC110.E44E43   2010
338.91′73—dc22   2009014451

British Library Cataloging-in-Publication Data is available

This book has been composed in Sabon

Printed on acid-free paper. ∞

Printed in the United States of America

5   7   9   10   8   6   4

For Leah

CONTENTS

ILLUSTRATIONS

ACKNOWLEDGMENTS

INDEBTEDNESS makes the scholarly world go round. No project is ever fully the work of a single scholar. Therefore, it is a pleasure to owe as much as I do to the many who have helped this book become a reality. I knew when I started how important the help of others would be to my scholarship, but I was pleasantly surprised to learn how racking up such debts would enrich my professional and personal life.

A collection of institutions was instrumental to this project's completion. Grants from the Eisenhower Institute, John F. Kennedy Institute, Lyndon Baines Johnson Foundation, National Endowment for the Humanities Summer Stipend program, Princeton University's Library Fellows program, Rockefeller Archive Center, Smith Richardson Foundation, and Truman Library Institute made vital research and writing possible. The Earhart Foundation was particularly flexible, contributing a series of timely awards. The International Development Program and the Foreign Policy Program at the Paul H. Nitze School of Advanced International Studies of Johns Hopkins University generously provided a year in an invigorating interdisciplinary environment. There, Grace Goodell took an early interest in my work and has been a model of the complements teaching offers scholarship. She is also a peerless professional example and a trusted friend.

An Olin Postdoctoral Fellowship with International Security Studies at Yale University not only provided a wonderful perch to finish the bulk of the initial manuscript but also provided a lesson in scholarly community. While in residence there, my home was badly damaged by a fire. Immediately upon learning of this, Paul Kennedy and Ted Bromund offered their support. I am forever in their debt for the considerable resources that helped undo a nightmare of destroyed research materials and smoke-damaged books.

Like every scholar, I was spoiled by the professionalism of the staff of the libraries and archives that were culled for this project. I am grateful to all, but I owe special thanks to Dan Linke and the staff at the Seeley G. Mudd Library; Tom Rosenbaum at the Rockefeller Archive Center; and Jonathan Green and Idelle Nissila at the Ford Foundation Archives.

This book grew out of my dissertation at Columbia University. The guidance and support I received from Anders Stephanson, Alan Brinkley, and Charles Armstrong marked the early contours of this project and my career. Frank Ninkovich was a model outside reader and has continued to offer beneficial advice. Michael Adas with his expansive scholarship and generous nature quickly outgrew the limited role of outside reader to become a valued friend and mentor.

An opportunity to work with the Carnegie Corporation of New York brought new perspectives and some valued relationships that continue to shape my views. David Hamburg provided a model for how scholarship leads to engagement with the issues in the world around us. David Speedie has been an abiding supporter. An unexpected delight was the fond concern Patricia Rosenfield took in my work and career. Her faithful attention and omnivorous mind have enriched me greatly.

Jim Mooney deserves special mention. At a difficult moment, he reached out to a young colleague, providing tricks of the trade, good humor, and sincere concern. Jim grew gravely ill as this book approached its final stages. Even so, he kept tabs on it and its author. It was a sign of the interest he took in all his students. His delight in teaching, in all forms, fostered life-long curiosity among those who learned from him. His death was a great loss. But Jim left a living memorial in his students, and I am honored to call myself one of them.

I have also been the recipient of vast professional largess. The input of David Armitage, Robert Beisner, Mark Berger, Nick Cullather, David Brion Davis, Bill Douglas, Lynn Eden, David Engerman, Frank Fukuyama, John Gaddis, Hiroshi Hori, Akira Iriye, Alan Kraut, Michael Latham, Mark Lawrence, Charles Maier, Erez Manela, Ernest May, Bruce Mazlish, David Painter, Tom Robertson, John Sewell, Brad Simpson, Frank Sutton, and Marilyn Young came in various forms and forums and refined my work considerably.

My students have extended my thinking in remarkable ways. Members of a seminar at Yale helped clarify some of my analysis. Other students have formally aided my research, and my thanks go to Vinny Intondi, Eden Knutsen, and Lindsay Schakenbach for the good work they provided. Jordan Segall deserves special mention for his incomparable thoroughness and enthusiasm as a research assistant.

My new home at Tufts University has brought a rapid addiction to the collegial atmosphere sustained by the history department and the campus community generally. Ina Baghdiantz-McCabe, Jeff Berry, Ben Carp, Annette Lazzara, Gary Leupp, Howard Malchow, Beatrice Manz, Andrew McCellan, Jeanne Penvenne, Alisha Rankin, Tony Smith, and Ichiro Takayoshi, among others, remind me that a supportive environment is more than worth the considerable individual efforts devoted to its maintenance.

Great thanks rightly belong to the series editors Jeremi Suri and Sven Beckert, as well as to Brigitta von Rheinberg and Clara Platter at Princeton University Press. They were flexible with deadlines upended by fire and patient with a new author.

Friends inside and outside the guild of history were invaluable. I learned to depend on the good humor and support of Chris Capozzola, Matt Raffety, Thea Hunter, Michelle Dhanda, Erika McEntarfer, Susan Brewton, Leah Werchick, Rosalind Glatter, Lisa Foulda, Kerr Houston, Karen Stern, Ezra Gabbay, and Mike Williamson. My obligations are steep to Eric Yellin, a superb friend who has shown surprising and reverential talents. He has a match in another dear friend and exceptional scholar, Nicole Sackley.

For everything these people and institutions gave to me for this project, in the end, the conclusions are entirely my own.

It is unlikely that any of these conclusions would have been reached without my family. The whole extended clan of my sisters, brothers-in-law, mother- and father-in-law, niece and nephew, and parents did the simplest yet most important of things—they never entertained a doubt about this project or my career. They were also the deepest reservoirs of support, concern, and good cheer.

Above all there is my wife, Leah. We met on a rooftop in Washington and discovered common interests and affection on an evening that neither of us wanted to end. I have since learned that the light of her mind is equal to the incandescence of her smile. As our lives blended together she became the greatest partisan, critic, and muse for my work. The humor, richness, and joy she has brought to my life have made me realize that wonderful night never did end. It is to her that this book, as well as myself, is dedicated.

—Cambridge, Massachusetts, 2009

ABBREVIATIONS

ACVA	American Council of Voluntary Agencies
ARP	Asian Recovery Program
CAP	Community Action Plan
CARE	Cooperative American Remittances to Europe [later Everywhere]
CDF	Comprehensive Development Framework
CENIS	Center for International Studies
CFR	Council on Foreign Relations
CIFRC	China International Famine Relief Commission
CORDS	Civilian Operations and Revolutionary Development Support
D&R	Development and Resources Corporation
DRV	Democratic Republic of Vietnam
ECA	Economic Cooperation Administration
ECAFE	Economic Commission for Asia and the Far East
ECLA	Economic Commission for Latin America
ECOSOC	Economic and Social Council
ERP	European Recovery Program
FAO	Food and Agriculture Organization
FOA	Foreign Operations Administration
GMD	Guomindang [Chinese Nationalist Party]
IBRD	International Bank for Reconstruction and Development
ICA	International Cooperation Agency
IIAA	Institute for Inter-American Affairs
IMF	International Monetary Fund
IPR	Institute of Pacific Relations
IVS	International Voluntary Service
JCRR	Joint Commission on Rural Reconstruction
JDG	Joint Development Group
MDDA	Mekong Delta Development Authority
MEM	Mass Education Movement
MIT	Massachusetts Institute of Technology
MSA	Mutual Security Agency
MVP	Millennium Village Project
NCCRR	North China Council for Rural Reconstruction
NGO	Nongovernmental Organization
NLF	National Liberation Front

NSS	National Security Strategy
OEO	Office of Economic Opportunity
OWI	Office of War Information
PUIFRC	Peking Union International Famine Relief Commission
PUMC	Peking Union Medical College
ROK	Republic of Korea
RVN	Republic of Vietnam
SCAP	Supreme Command Allied Powers
SEADAG	Southeast Asia Development Advisory Group
SUNFED	Special United Nations Fund for Economic Development
TCA	Technical Cooperation Administration
TVA	Tennessee Valley Authority
UNC	United Nations Command [Korea]
UNDP	United Nations Development Program
UNESCO	United Nations Economic, Social, and Cultural Organization
UNKRA	United Nations Korean Reconstruction Agency
UNRRA	United Nations Relief and Rehabilitation Agency
USAID	United States Agency for International Development
USAMGIK	United States Army Military Government in Korea
VISTA	Volunteers in Service To America
VOLAGS	Voluntary Groups
WHO	World Health Organization

The Great American Mission

INTRODUCTION

Make no little plans: they have no magic to stir men's
blood . . . Make big plans: aim high in hope and work.
—*Daniel Burnham, 1908. Quoted by Eugene Staley*

THROUGHOUT HIS LONG CAREER, Eugene Staley often quoted Daniel
Burnham and his maxim of "make no little plans." Unintentionally, Staley
was revealing much about himself and the ideas with which he surrounded himself during the mid-twentieth century. An economist by training, Staley ranged the globe working on the stirring and critical mission
of international development when its resonance on the world scene was
at its height. On the surface, Staley might not seem a peer of Burnham,
the architect responsible for the dramatic Chicago Exhibition of 1893.
But both men shared a faith in modernity, particularly its American example. Burnham, too, carried this faith abroad. It is no surprise that Staley,
who believed in development as both a humanitarian need to adjust societies to the pressures of an all-encompassing modern world and a critical
means to contain ideologies that would pull peoples away from the
healthy means to achieve progress, found a kindred spirit in Burnham.

Nothing about the ideas and policies that Staley and ranks of others
flung into the world was little. Their ambitions and goals were as vast as
the process to which they committed. To ensure that their methods to
achieve a future brightened by the hallmarks of modernity were chosen
by other peoples, they did indeed have to "stir men's blood." Pulses would
be quickened by standards of living raised by the application of technology. Power plants, dams, roads, bridges, and a host of other massive ex-
pressions of applied science offered revolutionary commodities that
would change how people lived. New ways of living would emerge as
people bent their personal existences to the opportunities and the boundaries marked by these forces. Change would be constant and it would be
as intimate as it was vast.

Guiding progress was not a new concept when Staley took up the task.
For Americans the concept went well back into their history. But, unintentionally, Burnham's words evoke the qualitative difference in the efforts
during the twentieth century. Behind them lay the "big plan." For Burnham, plans meant ambitions, but for his successors, planning in relation
to development implied the marshalling and management (often by government authorities) of resources for a particular goal. The concept of

planning and assumptions about the role of the state and society lay behind the approaches to development promulgated in the period. It mattered under what political regimes these large-scale projects claiming the imprimatur of planning would be implemented. Politics and ideology were at the center because these decided where development would lead and where societies would be delivered at the end of their journey. Particular projects might claim dispassionate, objective origins with technical or social scientific analysis to ease implementation and quiet dissent, but the larger ideological framework in which any program delivered is always present.[1] Because of the deep roots of politics in development, it has long been an electric topic (as has scholarship on it) with passionate judgments on the efficacy of one doctrine or another being the currency of debate.

Development reflects the political milieu from which it springs. Accordingly, it was instrumental in the ideological struggles of the twentieth century. Liberalism, communism, and fascism—those systems with broad prescriptions for the organization of political, social, cultural, and economic life—were impelled to demonstrate to their home populations as well as to the international public that they could deliver on the promises of a better life, brought about by the technologies and the outlooks of the modern world. Here development becomes crucial to understanding how the United States confronted other ideological systems when they emerged as threats. It has particular relevance to the Cold War, which now dominates scholarship in modern international history. As scholarship on the Cold War heaves from a focus on origins to a more nuanced discussion of how it was waged, a clutch of historians have seen the importance of development to a struggle that is characterized as being a struggle between two ideological systems—liberal capitalism and state communism. Proving the efficacy of their respective ideologies was a necessity and drove each side to intervene across the globe.[2] These interventions varied. Among the many ways the powers sought to exert control over the newly categorized "Third World" was development. Both sides sought transformation in the new states as a way to demonstrate that their ideologies were best suited to deliver the benefits of modern life. Scholars have rightly seen that while modernization shared a lineage with colonialism, its application in the twentieth century held distinctions from modern empire. It was not driven by unalloyed "exploitation and subjection" but rather sought "control and improvement." However, this hardly meant it was pure. Modernization is deeply implicated in what has more aptly been described as the establishment of American global hegemony.[3] The project that modernization served in the twentieth century was not always humanitarian, but strategic. Vigorous new scholarship has demonstrated how modernization served as a powerful lens, justification, and weapon for the United States in a vast cold war.[4] This meant the scope, goals, and even promise of modernization were constrained and sometimes compromised by the demands of policies cut for global combat. Promises of a better life were mixed with actions that could be coercive and, sometimes, blisteringly violent. It is a reality that has persisted as development has persisted in global affairs beyond the Cold War. This is not to call into question the motives or actions of many individuals who were honestly committed to supporting the ambitions of others to improve their lot. What it does do is describe the framework that shaped how modernization was conceived and applied.

If development was a weapon in the ideological combat that was the Cold War, then its proximate origins must be understood. Much scholarly work on the topic remains firmly rooted in the Cold War and does not demur to accepted narratives of development in the era. Development as it is presently understood, as well as the foreign aid offered by various countries to foster it, is regularly given origins in the years after 1945 by a diverse chorus of voices. It is linked to the start of official aid programs tied to the Truman Doctrine in 1947.[5] Several have even picked a specific date, January 20, 1949, when President Harry Truman announced his global "Point Four" assistance program. With that speech, the United States abruptly defined much of the world freeing itself of colonial rule as "underdeveloped." In this schema, emergence from this historical status could only be accomplished through American aid. Such a simple and easily definable takeoff point has led a number of scholars to declare the late 1940s the starting line for inquiry. This beginning is a simple and (for some) politically palatable means of demarcation. Freed from fetters of the past, all else becomes a "prehistory."[6]

This is not to impugn fine scholarship but to remind that the concept of development has no clear beginning in the U.S. case or internationally. As scholars often acknowledge, pinpointing the absolute, single beginning of any broad historical issue is a difficult task.[7] Elements of the faith in guiding change that constitutes the core development have been in play in some form for quite some time. In fact, the term "modernization" has been used, albeit to convey different meanings, at least since the late 1700s. The assertion here is not that modernization, as a conscious set of policies to promote improvement and progress, began in the 1930s, but that a vital new formulation crystallized. This shift was critical in reshaping thinking, policy, and action on development in ways that continue to resonate in the present. It is important to explicate the changes that mark departures and refine our understanding of how such a broad theme emerges and operates on the global stage. The type of modernization that played such a powerful role in the Cold War waged by the United States was not actually specific to it. The grand plans that endeavored to lay down great technological monuments, alter nature, and, most important, to transform human perceptions had firm links to the years before the conflict. Ideas and methods that would play vital roles in U.S. policy formed in the 1930s and 1940s, with a set of emerging approaches to foster development through, as contemporaries sometimes referred to it, the "reconstruction" of modern societies. In those crisis years, liberals came to a new consensus on development. There was another crucial shift—that development, seen as worldwide in its scope, had a direct, strategic rationale. Liberals were also prepared to counter threats posed by other ideological systems that also had programs of global development. These ideas had immediate use as a means to tamp the appeal of fascism and communism, by demonstrating liberalism's ability to deliver the benefits of the modern world to people at home and abroad. Concepts necessary to actually implement such development emerged from a collection of sources, particularly New Deal reform and nongovernmental activity. These approaches were mobilized and integrated into strategy and official policy. What some began to label "modernisation" was integrated into a globalism itself based in the necessity of American world leadership.

Nominating an approach to development that privileged large-scale transformation as a means to contain ideological threats to liberal society marked a crucial moment of departure. Modernization ideas worked their way into Cold War policies, they were not created by them. A struggle that is increasingly remembered as a global competition between two ideological systems required each to demonstrate its ability to promote social and economic progress.[8] This was especially true for the United States, a nation believing itself the archetype of modern technological society and a pillar of liberalism—ideas that easily segued into long held views that it was a city on the hill for others to emulate.[9] But the template for using development as part of an ideological struggle had been laid down during the crisis years of the 1930s and 1940s. While the Cold War is vital to understanding the maturation and extension of many of these concepts, the fact that many methods and institutions had a defined role before the confrontation reveals new avenues to explore the increasing global influence of the United States in the last century.

A consensus (as contemporaries sometimes referred to it) on development during the mid-twentieth century accepted that development be broadly conceived, embracing whole countries and regions if need be, and based on large-scale planning. It held great affection for technology—particularly grand industrial edifices—as both the means and ends of the process. The aim was to have extensive and profound impacts on societies. Technologies were sought to provide material benefits, but these were also means to promote human change. For example, dams and power plants were sought after because they offered electricity with perpetual economic and personal use. However, the current provided would change the most humble individuals, altering daily patterns of life and with them a person's perceptions of the world and their place in it. Here, this wide-ranging idea of development dives into the psychological where development becomes the modernization of mind. Individuals, as part of this larger process, had to incorporate modern outlooks on intimate levels for the process to proceed and succeed.

International development is, by its nature, global in scope. For much of the period discussed here, industrial society, seen as the culmination of modernity, was assumed to be reaching into every society to eventually embrace the entire world. The question was exactly how that transition, fraught with political, economic, and social consequences, would be managed. It is in this global dialogue about development that U.S. formulations have to be placed. In the twentieth century there were other strong and appealing options to bring modernity to heel. Fascism and communism were just two of the most powerful and appealing of these. While self-consciously opposed to liberalism, these systems shared many basic assumptions about development. Observers at the time and scholars since have noted how, in the twentieth century, the universalizing ideologies of the left, right, and center had affection for high technology and the thoroughgoing transformation its application would bring to the people it touched.[10] Foundational to the United States accepting a new and intensified mission of development was the presence of countervailing development models. For Americans, the existence of such models was a potentially dire threat to world order. These systems, even if they shared a taste for large dams, electricity, the reshaping of individual psychology, or a barrage of other modern techniques, were necessarily fraught with social and political dangers. As politics could never be divorced from development, if these other ideologies with their own ambitions to remake the globe prevailed, the benefits of modern life could be lost. Indeed, they might even become tools of oppression and destruction. These global questions always lurk in the background of the story of how America attempted to mold the contours of world development. What is more, the challenge of other models served as justification for intense U.S. efforts to promote its own vision of modernity and in so doing aided the extension of its own global power and influence.

Over the course of this competition, preponderant resources and influence of the United States left indelible marks on institutions and ideas that continue to shape international development. Accordingly, the story becomes a "cis-international" history, to modify a thoughtful schema from the vibrant field of Atlantic History. Plurality inherent to international and global history requires a multiplicity of approaches. Atlanticists have profitably grappled with the interconnections of a vast region, explaining how peoples, states, commerce, and ideas have swirled together and in so doing have blurred once sacrosanct historical boundaries. However, this wider view does not remove influences emerging from specific historical and geographical points. Particular localities, nations, or regions can be discussed within a larger international framework. It acknowledges the uniqueness of the experience and influence of one site while exposing linkages to bigger structures and ideas indispensable for contextualizing that site in its historical milieu. Discussing how one segment of the international community—in this case the United States—interacts, refracts, and is itself influenced by international trends is a profitable means to interrogate the history of a larger global issue like development.[11]

While the tale is international, it cannot forsake domestic roots. Examples for how development might be performed abroad were provided legitimacy by apparent reform successes inside the United States. It is remarkable how domestic reform is regularly walled off as a separate fiefdom from international efforts seeking to foster similar changes with similar methods. This boundary is often artificial, as the two are constantly in dialogue if not directly connected. Modernization occurred at home at the same time and it was influenced by international trends and debates on the issues. For example, domestic debates about the state's role in economic and social life directly influenced the course of international activity and vice versa. Organizations and many individuals committed to development moved fluidly between the domestic and international because both spheres shared many assumptions about how to foster change.

The reality of interdependence is driven home when the role of civil society and private institutions is seen. A mosaic of foundations, voluntary groups, missionaries, advocacy groups, and universities (grouped under the catchall rubric of nongovernmental organizations—NGOs) as well as businesses was essential to the process. All brought skills and resources to programs at home and abroad that were vital to their completion. Often, the story of international development focuses on the role of government such that nonstate actors, when acknowledged, are cast as supporting players or co-conspirators. Private groups were not mere adjuncts or toadies to government action. For the United States, a long history of a comparatively weak central state with halting interest in overseas development was offset by vibrant civil society activism. Many nonstate groups remained committed when official interest waned. At certain moments, NGOs were the most attentive to the concept and cultivated the most innovative thinking.

When the U.S. government committed to a program of coordinated, permanent modernization in the years following World War II, it immediately turned to the expertise of these private groups. In growing numbers, they played indispensable roles in development projects. This is not to say that there was no disagreement or dissent between these groups and government (and among the groups themselves), but these private organizations embraced many of the principles guiding consensus development. International institutions were also part of this larger equation. Such institutions, particularly the United Nations, played an essential role in the process. They too adhered to consensus principles, in no small measure because the UN and its litter of "specialized agencies" were created and invested with a development mission at a time when the consensus held sway. The story of development in this period, even when focused on the United States, is a wide one that must include this collection of historical actors.

The continuing indispensability of development in global affairs and U.S. foreign policy warrants investigation of the history that shaped its present form. International development is a broad, diffuse idea and it defies attempts to mark a single moment of origin. What can be done is to trace its lineage to expose its composition and operation at particular historical moments. The revived importance of development in international affairs at the start of the twenty-first century makes an understanding of the modernization that predominated for much of the twentieth century vital. It was an evolution heavily influenced by ideas and groups emerging from the United States, which embraced a consensus on development. This consensus, prevailing from roughly the 1930s through the 1970s, was adopted and cultivated by private and governmental organizations to implement a mission overseas. Its legacy would have lasting impacts on how international development would be conceptualized and implemented. It is impossible to comprehend contemporary international development without comprehending the contributions of the United States.

The arc of the evolution and impact of these ideas on development and international politics can best be seen by taking a wider and longer view, a view that can be profitably centered on U.S. interaction with Asia. Focusing here does not mean these concepts were not applied elsewhere. In Latin America, Africa, Europe, and even North America, groups sought to utilize the principles in the development consensus to shape peoples and nations in their own image. Important aspects of the story told here can be seen in operation in these parts of the world. Asia, however, would see the largest and most intense application of these ideas while the consensus held sway. Several sites in Asia could also make claims to being the largest development programs in the world at crucial historical junctures.

In the 1910s and 1920s, new development ideas pairing modern applied technologies with the new social sciences began to emerge. Such methods were closely tied to the global progressive movement. International in origin, they found strong adherents within the United States. It was often nonstate groups who were in the vanguard of applying these new concepts to the problem of development. Overseas, a transition can be seen in the efforts of missionary and secular volunteers to transform a "medieval" China into a modern nation. What was lacking was an overarching model for a set of practices that were increasingly being marked by an exceptionalist American vision, yet were seen as universal in their application.

Within the New Deal—itself a hybrid of domestic and international reform ideas to meet a global crisis—development advocates found the model they sought. The Tennessee Valley Authority melded existing thinking and technologies for development into a comprehensive and politically palatable package. It also appeared at a moment when liberals sought to secure their legitimacy at home and abroad from the ideological challenges of both fascism and communism. The TVA stood as proof that large-scale multipurpose development, invested in state planning and dependent on technology that was international in its origins, could be blended with liberal political ideas claiming a singular American origin to produce rapid social and economic change. Its structure also accepted the cooperation of nongovernmental groups. Supporters soothed fears about state power and planning with what became known as the TVA creed. Their formulations served to set this liberal model of development apart from strikingly similar communist and fascist development ideas. These characteristics also justified universal claims of exportability to all parts the globe. The TVA was a grand synecdoche, standing for a wider liberal approach to economic and social development both domestically and internationally. Its example was absorbed into a reformulated international development meant to secure the pale of liberal life against totalitarian challengers with their own blueprints for modernity. Global war continued the ideological combat and offered the opportunity to refine these ideas as they were put to work fostering reconstruction and development worldwide.

As world war gave way to cold war, development ideas were mobilized as a means to secure and extend an American-dominated liberal order. The TVA remained an expression of American mastery of applied technology within a liberal political framework. Newly titled "modernization," this activity was ongoing from the end of the war. This type of development was consciously set apart from aid, however massive, to rebuild states already seen as modern, such as Germany and Japan. It became increasingly important as the United States began to counter Soviet influence in "underdeveloped" areas of the globe. Because of this, the state became increasingly involved in areas where nongovernmental groups had been the leading lights. The U.S. government therefore sought to forge cooperative links with private organizations that held considerable experience in applying these concepts. The United Nations also evolved a development mission, often through American initiatives. Harry Truman's announcement of his "Point Four" program in 1949 placed modernization in a prominent spot in the grand strategy of the American state.

South Korea became a "proving ground" for these modernization ideas. Even before the announcement of Point Four, South Korea was a test bed for the broad spectrum of modernization concepts. These efforts dramatically accelerated after the start of the Korean War. Advocates were clear that programs in South Korea were far more than recovery from war damage; they were viewed as an accelerated program of development. The United States saw to it that the UN, with its new development agencies, and a host of NGOs were inserted in the vast efforts to remake South Korea. It became the largest development effort in the world in the 1950s, but consensus ideas did not produce the rapid change they promised.

During that decade, development took on increased importance to American foreign policy and society at large as decolonization accelerated and the confrontation with the Soviet Union deepened. Although the U.S. government oscillated in its approach to international development, various private groups remained strongly committed to the project. There was a rapid expansion of nonstate activity in the 1950s that mirrored an increasing feeling that modernization was a key mission of the United States and a gauge of national success or failure in waging the Cold War. Nonstate groups became powerful advocates and saw to it that consensus ideas remained in mainstream foreign policy. Despite mounting activity, attractive communist models for national development and troubles implementing American ideas injected frustration and doubt into a critical theater of the Cold War.

The Kennedy years brought renewed emphasis and optimism on the modernization front. Modernization ideas began to drift back into American domestic life as social science methods worked out overseas were deployed to deal with nagging issues of race and poverty. Abroad, apparent success in South Korea led Americans to believe that a modern, anticommunist nation could be built in South Vietnam. Modernization was enlisted in counterinsurgency efforts. Lyndon Johnson put great stock in a TVA-style program to help quell conflict in the riparian nations in Southeast Asia while assuring the international community of the positive aspects of American involvement. This, and postwar planning for the development of South Vietnam, were prominent components of U.S. efforts to justify its presence in the region. All were based on the tenets of the consensus on development. However, war exposed limits to the approach, strained relations with NGOs, and soured opinions toward the type of large-scale technological programs the United States advocated.

The unpopular war in Vietnam helped to discredit many of the development ideas intimately connected to it. Frustrations with development were coupled with an increasingly vocal environmental movement that questioned whether the massive technological programs, so favored in the postwar period, best met the needs of people in poorer areas. Voices across the political spectrum and the globe questioned many of the assumptions behind mainstream development. Frustrations with development raised questions as to whether the massive technological programs, so favored in the postwar period, best met the needs of people in poorer areas. Part of this shift was a growing distrust of the state to be the primary agent to promote development. Out of this "crisis of development" a new concept emerged that emphasized environmental needs and a focus on poverty, preparing the ground for talk of "sustainable development." The official U.S. foreign aid program was radically changed in response to the searing experience of Vietnam. However, other international institutions, especially the World Bank, would be consciously pushed forward by the United States and other wealthy nations. The multilateral development approach claimed by the Bank was seen to hold fewer political costs. After the tumult of the period the Bank emerged as the central institution in a chastened international development community.

By the 1970s, the consensus on modernization that had been cultivated by the United States had been shattered. Statist programs, planning, and the large-scale transformation that had characterized modernization's heyday were viewed with a jaundiced eye. In fact, the concept of modernization fell out of fashion, because of its close associations with Cold War thinking, ethnocentrism, and cultural imperialism.[12] With the end of the Cold War, foreign aid declined in importance. Development, in general, was fractured and lacked a clear rationale and set of approaches to guide its implementation. Its decline provides a coda to modernization's mission in the twentieth century. Still, it is hard to provide a tidy conclusion for a set of ideas that had such powerful sway on international affairs. With the attacks of September 11, 2001, and the "War on Terror" that followed, development aid was shoved back into the spotlight. Many ideas and institutions that had lain dormant in international affairs insinuated their way back into American strategy and the agenda of the international community. "Nation-building" in Afghanistan and Iraq, along with a hope that development would stifle the appeal of extremist ideologies and the movements they stirred, again gave development a new mission to mold the world in an American image.

Considering the breadth of this study, it makes no claim to be an exhaustive history of international development or even U.S. overseas aid activity during the period discussed. Programs and thinking were diverse, and Americans were involved in all parts of the globe with the aim of bringing a version of modernity to people they considered less developed. My research focuses on how many Americans conceptualized what needed to be done to reform various societies at different historical moments. I write with full knowledge that there remains considerable work for historians in defining how the vast and varied modernization programs of the twentieth century actually operated. Connected to this, there is much discussion here of how Americans perceived various societies as "backwards" and requiring aid. This should not be taken as a statement of what conditions actually were in all situations. American observers were prone to statements colored by their own bias, racism, ignorance, enthusiasm, and cynicism. The goal here is to describe what U.S. perceptions motivated and then shaped actual modernization policy and activity. Although outside of the scope of the study, people within the countries receiving U.S. aid were not passive recipients of these ideas. In various forms, they negotiated, collaborated with, or resisted these schemes—all actions that actively shaped outcomes.[13]

Ideas matter. It is a bland truism to note that they motivate and legitimate action. One goal of this work is to open the way for a deeper discussion of the nexus of interaction between ideas and deeds that development demands. Instrumental to liberal modernization was thinking, global in its scope and focused on planning, growth, and change that was drawn into and Americanized by the New Deal. It is indeed striking how often the reputation of the reform movement and the flagship TVA were utilized to make one approach to international development comprehensible to various constituencies worldwide. Equally telling are the globetrotting careers of numerous advocates who found modernization a compelling mission in the postwar period. However, the goal is neither to supply a traditional intellectual history of modernization nor to track the international career of the TVA or a catalog of individuals who projected many of these ideas into the world. It is to look at how a broader liberal vision of development emerged and was utilized by the United States to confront threats internationally. The recurring stories of individuals and the influence of various models are used to demonstrate the continuity of concepts in the liberal development consensus over time and space. This study happily acknowledges that there are more facets to the extensive historical theme of development. There are numerous other perspectives that might be heard. This study is humbly offered as one element in a wider discussion of the profoundly diverse global history of development.

If the scope is vast, the terms are also tricky. While usage of the word "modernization" goes back to the eighteenth century, its contemporary meanings are a relatively recent phenomenon. Not listed in the massive

Encyclopedia of the Social Sciences that appeared in 1933, the term only made an appearance in the revised edition of the encyclopedia in 1968.[14] Closely related to development, what constituted modernization in the twentieth century is more easily defined. It was regularly seen as an attempt to achieve modernity, which is what is "up-to-date" at a specific time. Typically, it was Western forms that defined what was seen as current, and those forms were contrasted against "traditional" ideas and structures within a society.[15] It put great stock in science and its application, but important parts of a modern society were not just technology but the outlooks of its members. Modernity required certain institutions, technologies, and infrastructure and, just as important, that individuals accept an elaborate division of labor, considerable personal mobility, impersonality in daily interactions, and a forward-looking worldview, as opposed to "traditional" outlooks of passivity or fatalism.[16] Admittedly, these perceptions were closely tied to the application of technology and a type of society shaped by technological imperatives. Nevertheless, in important respects, modernization was a social process. In the words of one prominent member of the school of modernization theory, Alex Inkeles, "men are not born modern but are made so by their life experience."[17] Modernity, simply put, was in your head. In the period discussed, modernization was widely approached as a historical question. Traditional societies were viewed as backwards and separated by time from the exemplars of modernity in Western Europe and the United States. However, with outside aid they could traverse this historical gap to embrace modern relationships, institutions, and outlooks through a process of modernization.

Development is a more amorphous concept and has no single agreed upon definition. However, it does imply a "far-reaching, continuous, and positively evaluated process of social, economic and political change which involves the totality of human experience."[18] Development is closely bound up with the larger idea of social change and progress implicit in modern societies. It may be seen as a broader concept than modernization, indeed, one in which modernization is subsumed. At its base, it implies a process to guide progress (or simply change)—a "development" leading to a set of new occurrences or relationships. Nevertheless, in this study, I use "modernization" and "development" as those in the post–World War II period did, as nearly synonymous terms. Each term was then used to describe a process assumed to be broad and transformative on many levels. It was only in the 1960s and 1970s, as modernization came under increasing attack from numerous quarters, that the terms were regularly treated as different, if interrelated, concepts. The outside aid used to foster this development was also diverse. It came from various institutional and state (and even individual) sources but also lay under various monikers. Particularly as aid became more "official" (meaning dominated by state institutions) after World War II, various branches emerged. Categories of capital, technical assistance, educational, food, military, and other kinds of foreign aid were defined. While not ignoring these important distinctions, this study treats aid aimed at promoting change within a society as developmental in content and goal.

The diversity of development aid and the institutions invested in it ensured that the ideas emerging out of the consensus had effects across U.S. and international society. This study puts a basic theme of international life into a wider historical frame. Modernization has both a longer history and a continuing legacy. A historical view emphasizing the evolution of the process and practice of development reveals how important elements are products of historical moments during the twentieth century. Much activity was never entirely the province of the state, long operating on numerous levels and influenced by a host of actors—from NGOs to international organizations. Understanding that multiple actors traditionally have been responsible for executing development programs complicates the narrative. Such plurality also explains the concept's endurance on the international scene. It helps explain how the concept of development has been retooled to fit a new world situation. Understanding how development was brought to bear in the international arena at different historical moments by the United States allows indispensable insight into the history of a powerful international theme and provides critical perspective on how it relates to the world today.

Chapter 1

THE RISE OF AN AMERICAN STYLE

OF DEVELOPMENT, 1914–1937

We [the United States] are doing this for your own good.
—*Victor Heiser, 1936*

THE IDEAS AND PRACTICES that would comprise modernization were extant well before the term earned its common currency in the years following World War II. New approaches were emerging from the social sciences and the institutions that were their incubators that would transform how reformers conceptualized the needs of societies they saw demanding their intervention. These attitudes were a departure from what had come before, but that is not to say they did not have a history. No matter how new the methods, the impulse to development had a long heritage in international life and in an American self-concept that embraced a mission to serve as an example for the world. In the United States, the new development was connected historically to projects to "reconstruct" societies at home and abroad to respond to the modern world. This legacy set the stage for the changes that would course into development activity in the years following World War I. Much of the initiative for these changes came from nongovernmental groups, and their largest and most visible testing grounds would be China. Americans, as part of a community of international progressives, increasingly saw the need for large-scale programs moved by the social sciences and utilizing imposing technologies to promote widespread social and political change. As the world sank into crisis during the 1930s, they had a set of concepts buttressing a liberal approach to development; all they required was something that embodied their agenda in a single example.

ROOTS OF MODERNIZATION

The development concepts that predominated in the mid-twentieth century can find roots in European thought contending with the difficulties of industrialization and demographic shifts in the early nineteenth century. Henri Saint-Simon and his disciples are considered crucial to the formulation of a doctrine of development. Seeing the disorder and waste of early European industrialization, the Saint-Simonians did not ask whether advancement was necessary or possible but whether it could have been achieved more rapidly and effectively than under the prevailing laissez-faire system. The most prominent member of the Saint-Simonians, Auguste Comte, believed that order must be brought to the disjointed industrial progress of his time. Development, for Comte, was the basis by which order could be infused into progress. However, development required the intervention of those freed from material labor. He envisioned an elite of capitalists and technologists who could act as "trustees" for society (and eventually comprise a new ruling class) who, through their knowledge, could effectively channel economic and social change for the benefit of society at large. Comte believed, "It is only when we have determined what belongs to the elite of humanity that we can regulate our intervention in the development of more or less backwards peoples, by reason of the necessary universality of the fundamental evolution, with due application of the characteristic circumstances of each case."[1] Comte certainly cannot be credited with the creation of the idea of development. Nevertheless, the positivism and the concept of trusteeship he and other Saint-Simonians championed informed much. In their formula development become a force invested with agency. The present could be modified into something entirely new by the actions of "those entrusted with the future of society."[2]

The tutelary nature of what Comte discussed meshed with an important segment of American republicanism. Even before the revolution, technology was perceived as a defining element of colonial life in Great Britain's North American colonies. There was great pride among the colonials in their cultivation of "useful knowledge" in the technical arts.[3] It was after the revolution, however, that the useful art of technology came to the fore in theorizing about the social, political, and economic health of the new republic. Threatened by the ever-present lure of luxury that deadened civic virtue and could cause the decline of the fragile nation, leaders looked to expansion, trade, and industry as means to keep the people, prone to indolence, diligent and industrious.[4] Tench Coxe, a Philadelphia merchant, explained in 1787 that manufactures, dependent on technology and integrated in a republican political system, would forestall decline by cultivating frugality and industry. While he envisioned the factory as a school for republicans, Coxe's contemporary, Benjamin Rush, saw the school itself as a means for instilling the values to transform raw students into "republican machines." John Kasson has described an early alliance between technology and republican ideals where the former served as means of achieving the promise of republican society, and republicanism a means for controlling and containing the dangers of the mechanical world.[5]

This theme reappeared through American history. Persons had to be tutored not only in the technologies themselves but also in the social and cultural values that encased them. In part, this education was necessary because danger always lurked in technology. Ralph Waldo Emerson saw a threat from technology that was no longer driven by society but instead drove it. Although he often lauded particular technologies, he was a critic of the tendency to equate technical accomplishments with progress. Emerson saw an important place for mechanical advancement in achieving a better life, although this was a qualified assertion. Technology also had a tendency to inspire materialism and other morally questionable behavior. The employment of technology required a firm commitment to republican ethics. While there was great confidence in technology as a means to fulfill the promise of the republic, there were always concerns that this powerful force in human affairs could get out of control or fall into the wrong hands.[6]

As industrialization picked up pace in the second half of the nineteenth century, technology assumed a new position in the republic. For a polity nearly destroyed in a fratricidal civil war, mastery of technology became an important means to reestablish a national sense of purpose and accomplishment. It was in this period that technologists, particularly engineers, became great symbols of America's capability to wield technology to effectively solve social and political problems.[7] They were particularly popular with those seeking reform in contrast to calls for revolutionary change. These efforts might now be called "development" but at the time they were often referred to as "reconstruction."

RECONSTRUCTION AS DEVELOPMENT

Reconstruction, as a label for reform, is often linked to a specific era in the American mind. The "Reconstruction" marks the period following the country's civil war, roughly 1865 to 1877. A remarkable period of change and upheaval, it included attempts to integrate African Americans, only recently freed from slavery, into the political system. Dramatic social and political reforms were coupled with attempts by Reconstruction governments to promote economic development. Such development was undertaken to repair the damage of war as well as to move away from the old slave system that influenced all aspects of society. Modern technology, in the form of railroads, was the great hope for regional growth. It would bring economic growth and with it feed transformational social and political change. In this all-embracing formula, sketches of nation-building projects attempted later by the United States have been perceived. However, these ambitions largely failed. The reaction that followed left the region mired in segregation and poverty well into the twentieth century.[8]

After its abrupt conclusion in 1877, the much-maligned Reconstruction was largely forgotten as a model of social transformation, and the term "reconstruction" was given new meanings in an international conversation on progressive reform. By the early years of the twentieth century it was used to describe diverse efforts to effect change within societies through reform based on "scientific" and "rational" methods. This broader type of reconstruction demanded considerable social change and was closely tied to Progressive Era reform, which itself was part of an interconnected international movement of social politics. Within it progressives were preoccupied with the impact of modern industrial life on societies globally. Indeed, the pragmatic philosophy that underlay the urge for tempered change has been seen as premised on reconciling society to the modern world.[9]

Generally, progressives internationally saw the application of reform ideas, guided by the new and increasingly influential social sciences, as the efficient way to reconstruct inefficient social, political, and economic relationships into systems that ran on modern lines. In the 1920s, one advocate in the United States noted:

> [In] the American mind that word still retains some of the flavor given it by the events following the Civil War, and in one sense it may not seem inaccurate to caution, "Beware of reconstruction!" . . . If then, this is to be reconstruction in the true sense, it must be founded not upon passion but reason . . . it must "look to the sciences for its view of the facts and to the happiness of men on earth for its ideal."[10]

Walter Lippmann shared such views in his earlier summation of the reformist spirit, *Drift and Mastery*. It was an early statement in a lifetime dialogue on the impact of modern forces on society globally. Lippmann believed "mastery" of these forces was best achieved through the embrace of science and the rationality it demanded. However, science could not operate in a social vacuum, as "democracy in politics is the twin-brother of scientific thinking. They had to come together." Science and its products could not be divorced from their social surroundings. This not only meant politics, where liberal democracy nourished science and science fed democracy, but also the impact of science at a personal level. A scientific bearing within individuals was necessary for the benefits of a technological and rational society to effectively take hold around them. Cultivation of this "scientific spirit" within a political framework amenable to it was a crucial part of any larger enterprise to reshape societies for the demands of modern life.[11]

The daunting task of rebuilding a Europe savaged by World War I shows the developmental nature of what was labeled reconstruction. It retained its reformist content even as the process contended with immediate war relief. In Britain and France, advocates of reconstruction agitated for revised industrial, social, and imperial relationships as much as they sought to repair the damage of war. The term was also employed to describe the necessity of carving out from the Austro-Hungarian Empire a collection of new and viable smaller states in Central Europe on the basis of modern principles.[12] Countries beyond Europe were seen to require a more intense reconstruction. As early as 1910, Western commentators lauded Japan's attempts to reconstruct the "backwards" society of newly annexed Korea into a modern colonial dependency. During the interwar years, the U.S. military occupation of Haiti was extolled as an opportunity for the "pragmatic" employment of modern ideas and technology to reconstruct that country. Elsewhere in the Caribbean, various reforms sponsored by its American trustee during the Depression to "reorganize Puerto Rico on a large scale" were also packaged under the reconstruction label.[13]

This talk of reconstruction lay among hopes about modern industrial society's ability to deliver global progress. In the United States this faith was exhibited in a series of expositions in the late nineteenth century. One of the most influential was the Chicago World's Columbian Exposition of 1893. Burnham designed it to be a living *"illustrated encyclopedia of civilization"* to instruct visitors "to formulate the Modern" (emphasis original). Science and its application were accepted as the basis of civilization as defined at Chicago. The effects would be lasting, and commentators have since seen the continuing influence of the fair on urban planning, ethnology, and architecture, as well as reformers. Chicago and the other expositions like it were part of a period where Americans felt technical and scientific accomplishments could produce a sort of paradise on earth. Edward Bellamy's *Looking Backward* shared this vision. While the fiction of Bellamy betrayed anxieties about the state of republican values in the United States, it was also an unmistakable expression of the faith in technology to achieve a better world.[14]

The late nineteenth century also witnessed a transformation of religion in the United States. Within American Protestantism there was an embrace of the "social gospel" and its strong desire to attack social ills both at home and abroad. Such a view had a succinct expression in the Reverend Josiah Strong. His tremendously popular 1885 book, *Our Country*, had a profound influence on the direction of American Christian activism. Strong's belief was that, among the "Anglo-Saxon" peoples, the United

States had been ordained by God to lead. With the world headed toward a *"final competition of the races, for which the Anglo-Saxon is being schooled,"* the United States found itself with the divine task of Christianizing and civilizing the world or facing the Lord's wrath (emphasis original). The United States was therefore impelled to engage the world with the goal of "extinction of the inferior races." This was not to be annihilation but the alteration of these peoples through America's "vitality and civilization." Christianity leavened the mix, which would "dispossess the many weaker races, assimilate others, and mold the remainder, until . . . it has Anglo-Saxonized mankind." The international mission Strong defined for the United States would underlie much evangelical activity in the coming decades and was a precursor of elements of Progressive Era reform in the United States itself.[15]

Numerous contemporaries in Western Europe agreed with Strong's belief in the superiority of Western civilization. Validation of cultural chauvinism often lay in the capacity of Westerners to create and apply technology. Nineteenth-century European and American accomplishments in science and industry which included the railroad, modern medicine, the telegraph and the Maxim gun provided the means to extend their authority over much of the globe as well as the justification. Yet, these technological accomplishments were not the sum of the yardstick by which Westerners measured others. A crucial part of the perception of the "backwardness" was the way these societies and cultures were viewed. A perceived lack of thrift, discipline, and promptness as well as traditional beliefs, indolence, and superstition prevented people in places such as Africa, India, and China from mastering modern technology.[16]

This perception regularly manifested itself in a belief, held by many Westerners at the time, that these peoples were little more than children. Their inability to internalize the behaviors necessary for modern technologies to be effectively utilized made them appear to be lost in a state of arrested development. Although race was clearly part of the equation, this prejudice cannot be reduced to a racial schema. Many Americans and Europeans believed that Africans, Indians, and Chinese could be lifted out of their historical circumstance of immature "backwardness." There was a belief in many quarters that if "traditional" customs, practices, and institutions could be removed, underdeveloped people could be taught to utilize the products of the modern world. Obviously only the most technologically advanced people could be expected to lead these backward peoples out of their historical condition. Americans believed that with their demonstrable accomplishments in science and technology, they should lead others to a similar state of advanced development. This belief was coupled with the expanding missionary activity of the later nineteenth century. By the early years of the twentieth century, the transfer of and education in technology was an inseparable part of American missionary enterprise.[17]

War with Spain in 1898 brought American military forces to the Philippines and abruptly brought a mission to reconstruct that society. The reasons the United States embarked upon a colonial experiment have been long and heatedly debated. How the United States justified that project is much more easily discerned. Members of the Philippine Commission, a group of men deputized by the U.S. government in 1900 to outline the policies to be implemented in the new possession, were in agreement on the lack of Filipino ability. President William McKinley articulated a common belief that they "were unfit for self-government," and later asserted, "We hold the Philippines for the benefit of the Filipinos."[18]

But it was not only the Filipinos that were responsible for the backward state of the islands in the eyes of the Americans. The previous imperial overlords were responsible for leaving the archipelago underdeveloped. The Americans believed that their technology, provided through a benevolent trusteeship, would redeem the Philippines from centuries of Spanish misrule. Americans pointed to the technical shortcomings of the Spanish Empire—their failure to fully exploit the resources of the islands, the lack of public works, crumbling bridges, poor roads, and public health conditions described as "mediaeval"—as proof that their trusteeship was a necessity.[19]

The vision for the American colony in the Philippines did have some differences from those of the Europeans and Japanese. It was conceptualized as a grand and progressive public works project. The American's plans were always placed in a "tutelage" framework rather than the "peace, order, and justice" mantras of British and French imperialists. The tutorial was publicized as an attempt to prepare the Filipinos for eventual self-rule, not as a means to perform maintenance on an empire. The Philippines were to get schooling in politics as well as the creation of a new, modern society that would lead to a well-ordered democracy with commercial and social relationships opening it to a wider world while lashing it to the United States.[20]

The early years of American rule were marked by a series of programs designed to fulfill this goal. Many infrastructural improvements (particularly roads) were connected to the military efforts against Filipino resistance; however, the overall program was one of "social engineering."[21] Best exemplifying the developmental mind-set of the colonial authorities was W. Cameron Forbes. A Boston businessman, Forbes was governor-general of the islands from 1909 to 1913. Forbes rather naively felt that the United States was set apart from past colonial masters because it was concerned with the welfare of the people.[22] That concern was to be expressed by the grand programs he planned for the islands under American tutelage. He enticed Burnham, still riding his fame from the Chicago Exposition, to create an urban plan for Manila. A "reformation" of the "sloth-ridden city" would turn it into a commercial hub and model for modern urban life in easy view of the rest of Asia.[23] Forbes also entertained the idea of having Burnham design an entirely new capital at Baguio—a replacement for the old, unsanitary, crowded, and premodern Manila.[24]

RECONSTRUCTING THE PHILIPPINES

While neither of these plans ever took the form Forbes hoped, other projects did take shape. As a man of the "machine age," fascinated by the mechanical and efficient, Forbes saw infrastructure was a pivotal part of the colonial government's program. Equally significant was the belief that road construction would serve as an "educator" of the Filipinos. Members of the Philippine Commission noted in 1900, "People without roads are necessarily savage, because society is impossible; and just to the extent that roads are lacking or defective, real progress is retarded and prosperity hindered."[25] Forbes himself would rate his tenure as governor-general by technological accomplishments. The modernized roads, bridges made of reinforced concrete, reconstructed harbors, electricity, and fresh water brought to the Philippines by their American trustees were, in many eyes, the best measures of his regime's success.[26] As he left his post, Forbes summarized his approach:

> I have made material prosperity my slogan while governing these islands. I have worked for material development. I have done it on the principle that a chain is no stronger than its weakest link, and our weakest point was the backwardness of our community from a material point of view, due to uneconomical and unscientific methods, lack of adequate means of transportation, lack of capital, lack of education on the part of the people, lack of incentive for labor, lack of physical strength on the part of the laboring and directing classes the result of poor nutrition and hygene. I have set myself to seek out the fundamental reasons for this backwardness and remedy. I have not done this because I believed material development was the whole thing, but because it was the thing most needed here.[27]

For these wider technical changes to take root fully, Filipino society had to be changed. Education was linked directly to the larger project of "nation building" in the Philippines. Again, the military was responsible for the initial efforts. The U.S. Army was the first to organize schools during the Philippine-American War, largely as a means to pacify the Filipinos and demonstrate American benevolence. Over time, civil authorities assumed responsibility for education, which became increasingly focused on a sort of technical education similar to that advocated by Booker T. Washington and offered to African Americans at places like the Tuskegee Institute. Americans thought that industrial and agricultural education on these lines was "revolutionary" as it would instill a new set of outlooks on a previously passive Filipino population long mired in tradition and superstition.[28]

The implementation of up-to-date public health procedures was also a priority for the American authorities. Health programs were regularly couched as a paternalistic good for the Filipinos. Backward customs had to be removed and new principles ingrained into Philippine life. These changes appeared obvious to Americans and prompted surprise at Filipino noncompliance or resistance to certain schemes. Victor Heiser, Commissioner of Public Health from 1905 to 1913, believed the islands' inhabitants simply did not understand that "we [the United States] are doing this for your own good."[29]

Empire in the Philippines was not a solo effort by the U.S. government. Various private groups contributed to the reconstruction of the islands in America's image. There was a strong voluntary ethos in education. Volunteerism mixed with a sense of mission permeated the "Thomasites," the hundreds of men and women who formed the backbone of the American public school system in its early years.[30] Missionaries were also quick to take up the educational mission with both Protestant and Catholic groups establishing schools around the archipelago. Even the American Medical Association joined the cause, helping to form the Philippine Islands Medical Association to support efforts in public health and as part of a larger effort to increase the skills and professionalism of Filipino doctors.[31]

The nation building done by the United States after the seizure of the Philippines was not immutable. Historians have noted an important shift after the election of Woodrow Wilson in 1912. The Democrats, never as keen on the imperial mission as the Republicans, quickly replaced Forbes. Common consensus associates the end of the era of "social engineering" begun after the initial American conquest with the appointment of Francis Burton Harrison as governor-general.[32] After Harrison assumed the post in 1913, there was a rapid "Filipinization" of the government, bureaucracy, and educational system. This did not mean an end to American colonial rule, which endured until 1946, but the emphasis shifted. Economic development of the islands remained a goal but was tempered by the slow progress toward political independence. The broad, intense transformation of the Philippines sought in the first fifteen years of American occupation was no longer the focus of U.S. policy on the islands.[33]

The literal construction of an American empire in the Philippines provides the outlines of the developmental ideas and practices that would become so important to modernization later in the century.[34] The central place of technology as a means and a justification for American engagement is readily apparent. Equally important is the plural nature of development work. The participation of private groups was a necessary part of the larger program of the U.S. government. This would not change in coming decades. The expertise of private groups, from missionaries to professionals, in implementing programs that could modernize societies would remain a vital resource for the U.S. government to fulfill strategic goals.

However, the early years of the United States' Philippine adventure were missing important elements that would play a crucial role in later modernization efforts. Key among these were large philanthropic foundations and social theories emerging from the rapidly maturing social sciences. The first third of the twentieth century saw the creation of a multitude of foundations from the industrial fortunes amassed during the nineteenth century. The Rockefeller family produced the Rockefeller Foundation (1913), the General Education Board (1903), the International Health Board (1913), and the Laura Spellman Rockefeller Memorial (1918).[35] They were joined by Andrew Carnegie, who endowed the Carnegie Foundation for the Advancement of Teaching (1905), the Carnegie Endowment for International Peace (1910), and the largest foundation of its time, the Carnegie Corporation of New York (1911).[36] Outside these philanthropic fiefdoms were organizations such as the Russell Sage Foundation (1907), the Commonwealth Fund (1918), and the Social Science Research Council (1923). Many foundations would appear in the coming decades, but these prominent institutions would do much to shape the terrain of this influential sector of American life in ways that can be clearly felt in the present. But, in their constitution, the foundations cannot not easily be divorced from the past, linked as they are to the established liberal capitalist order as well as to strains of evangelical Protestantism (especially in the case of the Rockefeller family). Nevertheless, in important ways, they were a departure from what came before. The most influential and well-endowed institutions were strongly affected by thought emerging from the rapidly expanding social sciences. These concepts had already worked themselves into international affairs in the United States, showing their increased mainstream credibility as an effective means to attack social ills.[37]

International in conception, progressive reform in practice was not a purely domestic effort, sequestered within the borders of the United

States. Recently, scholars have emphasized the interconnected nature of reform thinking in the United States and Europe in the decades preceding the Great Depression. As a set of practices, progressive reforms with emphasis on technocratic change and social control became an American export to many parts of the globe. Programs similar to the public health and education programs established in urban America as well as in the South and West were extended to Latin America, Africa, Asia, and even parts of Europe from the 1910s through the 1940s. These ideas were welcomed by parts of the government as well as by various established private groups. No set of organizations moved more quickly to put these ideas to work in reform efforts than the foundations. Their financial resources and independence gave them considerable latitude of action and they were instrumental in bringing social science ideas to bear on social, economic, and political issues. Indeed, they created a feedback loop by helping to sire or support many of the institutes and departments whose theories they could then draw upon for their own reform projects.[38]

Victor Heiser's career demonstrates the international scope of reform work. Pushed out of his job by the arrival of Harrison's Philippines administration, he found a new position with a recently formed foundation that gave him the opportunity to put his public health ideas into "worldwide service." In July 1914, Heiser set sail for New York to join a new private institution that would become a locus for modernization activity, the Rockefeller Foundation.[39]

In the midst of the work of the growing foundations, activity by the U.S. government—particularly projects executed by the U.S. military—to foster what would be called development continued. Countries in Latin America and the Caribbean received American tutorials in civilization. Haiti, under the trusteeship of the U.S. Navy from 1915 to 1930, was subjected to wide-ranging reforms that attempted to alter its political institutions, schools, public health practices, and infrastructure. Although most of these projects were closely related to the military's demands, they were seen as broadly transformative to society.[40] The U.S. Navy found an ally in its efforts in the Rockefeller Foundation. As part of the Foundation's larger international public health efforts, it provided funds for a medical school and fellowships to Haitian physicians to study in Europe, Canada, and the United States. Over time, however, the United States tired of its mission. Even Forbes, sent by Herbert Hoover in 1930 to review American policy, advised the government to abandon direct attempts to modernize Haiti, assuming the process would be measured in generations.[41]

Attempts by the American state to cultivate a world hospitable to its commercial and political interests continued in the interwar period, but in a much less formalized manner. In general, the Republican administrations of the 1920s preferred the dollar and informal relationships as the instruments of progress. Herbert Hoover, who had a well-earned reputation for relief work at home and abroad, avoided connecting his work to more progressive visions of "reconstruction." In his later memoirs Hoover stressed the voluntary nature of the post–World War I efforts and did not suggest that there were any long-term developmental implications. Throughout his public life Hoover shared a faith in the power of science and technology to produce prosperity. As president, Hoover's foreign policy in Latin America did attempt to cultivate modern institutions, relationships, and outlooks through economic growth and technology transfer. However, these efforts were decidedly bilateral and informal, in line with Republican commitments to laissez-faire liberalism. In addition, there were no nagging strategic or security imperatives, comparable to those of the 1930s or the Cold War, defining these piecemeal efforts. Revealingly, there never was a permanent official program or bureaucracy entirely devoted to foreign aid to promote development.[42]

Nonstate Groups in the Lead: The Case of China

If the U.S. government's activities were episodic and hesitant, the work of private groups was more focused. Asia was a particular target of American interest during this period, and no country received more attention than China. Activity there in the first three decades of the twentieth century demonstrates how new concepts were changing the scope and ambitions of development. Nongovernmental organizations rather than the U.S. government drove these changes. They would meld ideas emerging from an international discourse of how to reform societies on modern lines to the demands of one of the world's perpetual crisis centers. China was not the only place where such ideas were put into practice; however, it would be one of the most high-profile and intensive areas of activity. Importantly, ideas forged in China would carry over into the postwar period.

For Americans, in particular, the allure of reforming China was almost irresistible. The perceived inertia of Chinese society was often attributed to political despotism and firmly rooted customs. The desire to bring change was connected to hopes to tap the "China Market" and reap commercial gain. Beyond the promise of trade was a mission of redemption. As one veteran of the late nineteenth and early twentieth centuries' missionary work recalled, "China was the goal, the lodestar, the great magnet that drew us in those days." Toward the end of the nineteenth century China, recovering from the horrendous effects of the Taiping Rebellion, buffeted by demographic shifts, and preyed upon by imperial powers, appeared prostrate. To many Westerners, the problems lay in China's inability to come to grips with the modern world. China was trapped by an ancient political system, a backwards economy, and alien customs, all of which served to prevent it from employing modern ideas to pull it out of its malaise. China's enduring crisis offered a unique opportunity for Americans to demonstrate how their ideas of modern civilization could raise up "backwards" peoples.[43]

Missionaries were increasingly joined by private, secular groups. In the 1920s and 1930s, the U.S. government would support educational and economic programs to advance China's development, but they would not conducted on the same scale as post–World War II activities. Instead, American missionaries, voluntary groups, and foundations invested in a series of long-term programs aimed at altering large tracts of Chinese life, particularly in rural sectors. These programs of "rural reconstruction" sought to integrate modern technologies while transforming social structures in Chinese life. In so doing they would gradually adopt new methods of reform appearing on the international scene and graft them onto a long-standing mission.

A significant segment of all overseas American activity, missionaries were particularly busy in China. In part, this was due to a qualitative shift in missionary activity in the early twentieth century. The aftershocks of World War I spurred a strong liberal ecumenical movement within American Protestantism (parts of which drew the participation and financial lubrication of John D. Rockefeller, Jr.) that reshaped approaches in its overseas missions in a rapidly changing world. Evangelists increasingly supported the performance of good works for those they desired to convert—part of a belief that "to get at the soul, treat the body." Early "treatment" expressed itself through medical and educational programs, but by the early twentieth century there were growing efforts to demonstrate the general benefits of Western science and technology.[44] In this emphasis and the need to alter social structures that came with it, missionaries stood on common ground with their secular counterparts in the international reform community.

American-sponsored reform accelerated after the collapse of the ailing Qing dynasty in 1911. This rising interest was fueled by a perception that China had entered a stage of acute crisis and desperately needed outside help to escape. The troubles China faced were a challenge but also a supreme opportunity for missionaries who sought to mark it with Western ideas of progress. Dwight Edwards, a prominent American Protestant missionary who would spend the next four decades working in relief and development in China, wrote in 1911 that the nation had to adapt itself to modern conditions to realize its full potential.[45] This feeling only grew after World War I, when missionary and secular groups reoriented their existing programs to promote a long-term reform in China. Among the

Protestant missionary community there grew a feeling that a vast "medieval civilization" was finally "awakening" to the modern example of the West.[46] A number of institutes and universities were either founded or turned to the task. Similar endeavors were supported by American universities, the most active of which were land-grant institutions like the Pennsylvania State University, which had a history of agricultural outreach and extension work in the United States itself.[47]

The North China Famine of 1920–21 was a seminal moment for many working to reform China. As many as 20 million persons were slung into destitution. In response to this massive crisis, the diverse Chinese and international groups combating the famine formed the Peking Union International Famine Relief Commission (PUIFRC) to coordinate otherwise disparate efforts. Member institutions were predominantly missionary or religious groups, although secular organizations like businesses, universities (including Yale in China and the Peking Union Medical College), and the Red Cross made significant contributions. While the commission was international in composition, Americans contributed over half its funds and supplied a majority of the staff (317 out of a total of 537). Perhaps half a million people died in North China in 1920–21. According to PUIFRC leaders, their relief efforts were successful particularly when compared with a famine during 1877–78 in the same region, when as many as 5 million perished.[48]

For many of the Americans involved in the relief efforts, food, or the lack of it, became a defining element of Chinese history. Commentators noted that between 108 BC and AD 1911 there had been 1,828 famines, "one nearly every year." However, American observers were increasingly convinced that the chronic state of famine in China was not the result of natural disasters. The real problem, they maintained, involved the structure of Chinese society. They saw the disrupted state of Chinese politics in the 1910s and 1920s, the parasitic armies maintained by warlords, the fragmentation of government authority, the decline of public granaries, and heavy taxation all contributing to privation. But, beneath these political problems, Americans discerned deeper troubles in the very structure of Chinese life. Rapid population growth was a nagging concern as it strained China's already meager resources. This problem was linked in American thinking to the practice of "ancestor worship" which was understood to make the Chinese favor male children. Early marriage, concubinage, and other customs were also viewed as troublesome because they supposedly elevated the birth rate. Americans also worried about Chinese practices that they deemed wasteful, such as lavish spending on festivals and ceremonies. Foot binding was also seen as an ally of famine, as it lowered women's productivity while they worked in the fields.[49]

Mass starvation was a reflection of underdevelopment. Edwards encapsulated the new thinking of Westerners working on the issue. Although famine workers had the benefits of modern technology and the scientific method, he chose an anecdote from Mencius to illustrate his point. When a ruler blamed bad harvests for the suffering of his people, a sage pointed out that the king had failed to provide necessities for his people and chidingly told him, "don't blame the crops, oh king."[50] Groups increasingly saw their aid as part of a mosaic as "famine forces us to examine our social and economic system to determine . . . the causes of such general suffering." An attack on poverty had to be mounted with a palette of relief programs to strip away layers of problems, to make China compatible with the lessons imparted by the West's experience of industrialization.[51]

Edwards and others foreshadowed much thinking that is now commonplace on the economics of famine. They comprehended that mass starvation is the product of structural problems in a country's economic, social, and political life not a result of natural disasters. Such an understanding propelled aid work outward. Infrastructure, particularly dikes, roads, and railroads, was required. This was not only necessary to speed relief in a crisis but also to improve the overall lot of rural people. Education in forestry and agriculture as well as vocational training could also provide for overall community improvement, assuring that they created and maintained their own capacity to face times of trouble (Edwards and others did worry that mild prosperity might unleash the problem of overpopulation). If famine was the product of a tangle of "backward" structures within a society, the only solution appeared to be to strip them away with modernity. Famine prevention had become development.[52]

As Americans became more convinced that China's problems were products of its society and culture, they began to promote a new and extensive agenda of reform activities. What was required to tackle the problem of starvation, seen to be so intertwined with Chinese culture, was a varied program that could address immediate problems linked to natural disasters as well as provide economic improvement, improved agricultural techniques, infrastructural improvements, and broad educational changes. These activities were conceived of as a means to buttress China's economy and a way of fundamentally altering how the Chinese lived.[53]

The permanent institution that emerged out of this ferment was the China International Famine Relief Commission (CIFRC). To explain its origins, Edwards borrowed Topsy's comment from *Uncle Tom's Cabin*, "I wasn't born, I just growed." But the CIFRC was not conceived accidentally. From its founding, the CIFRC had a mission transcending the mere distribution of food. Ending famine required a "permanent improvement in the economic condition of China," and any hope of effecting a "real and permanent improvement of the country is through an adequate national program." Under different conditions, the CIFRC acknowledged, this was a task better left to the Chinese government. However, the political turmoil of interwar China convinced the CIFRC of its own indispensability as a trustee; it argued that it was "the only organization in China under international control which is designed . . . to carry out comprehensive conservancy projects on a national basis." In the eyes of CIFRC members, only a sweeping transformation of Chinese life could prevent famine. In the early 1920s, the CIFRC undertook a series of programs to catalyze this national transformation.[54]

An international community of reform influenced these efforts. Americans in China were very comfortable drawing on ideas out in the world to attack problems they saw in the Asian countryside. The lack of easily available credit was a nagging problem in Chinese agriculture that limited its expansion in good times and made bad times worse. The CIFRC offered a solution pioneered by a European agricultural reformer. A Rhineland village mayor, Fredrich Wilhelm Raffeisen, had begun rural credit cooperatives for peasants in Germany during the 1860s. A variant of existing rural associations, these were started at the village level by an initial loan and were then supported by the ongoing contributions of its members. This provided access to a self-sustaining font of credit on reasonable terms, and members had a stake in the continued operation of the system. The idea quickly spread to England, France, Italy, Ireland, and Denmark. Raffeisen's template also crossed the Atlantic, where it was regularly copied by American rural reformers from the late nineteenth century onward.[55]

Faced with what it perceived as a similar problem in China, the CIFRC imported Raffeisen's concept. This shows how developmentalist projects in Asia were dependent on international progressive trends. Before they implemented their program, the CIFRC sponsored a sociological study of 240 villages carried out by students from nine different universities in North China. Armed with this data, the CIFRC established its first credit cooperatives in early 1924.[56] The concept took hold quickly and spread rapidly in the CIFRC's area of operation in North China. From an initial class of eight cooperative societies with 256 members in 1924, the CIFRC's program expanded to 952 with 23,754 members by 1933. Of course, such figures do not seem terribly significant when compared to the sheer size of the agricultural sector. However, the steady expansion of the program attracted attention and helped to spur other efforts that eventually had a much broader impact on Chinese rural life. By the mid-1930s, the Chinese government and banks had joined in supporting the cooperative credit movement, leading the CIFRC to turn supervision of its programs over to the Nationalist regime.[57]

But the cooperative societies were more than a mechanism for badly needed credit. They also quickly became centers for fostering changes in all sorts of cultural practices. The CIFRC came to see a cooperative society not as a simple lender but as "a social agency, and as such its greatest services are to be rendered . . . in pioneering new fields."[58] The societies not only hosted demonstrations of scientific agricultural techniques by the new agricultural institutes and colleges (most of which were established or supported by Western largess) but also distributed agricultural technology. These technologies—including seed, cropping methods, and equipment—were seen to require social change for their efficient employment. Accordingly, the cooperatives served as a mechanism to modify the structure of rural society to provide the rational and "scientific" outlook necessary to employ Western technology effectively. Beyond mere technology transfer, societies sponsored education programs, and some went as far as to seek changes in marriage and funeral customs to make rural life more hospitable to modern practices.[59]

For the CIFRC, the social change needed to make China modern went hand-in-hand with physical changes to the landscape. Engineering projects comprised a large segment of the CIFRC's work. By the early 1930s, Edwards saw them as an expression of emergent techniques. Ambitions were growing. Among aid groups there was an attraction to large-scale resource development. As a means to control flooding and contain famine, the Red Cross became interested in the development of the Huai River Basin. Damming a river that flooded regularly and channeling its waters to irrigation meant agriculture and life generally in the region could be transformed. Plans for the Huai were extensive, with boosters hoping it might underwrite major change for China as a whole. Such grandiose ambitions were increasingly shared with many around the world, where nature was conceptualized as a motor for technical progress. A 1911 initiative supported by the Chinese government and foreign backers broke down during World War I and political turmoil. Still, the dream of using a river to foster development lingered in the minds of many.[60]

One of those was the CIFRC's chief engineer, Oliver J. Todd. Born, raised, and educated in Michigan, Todd believed infrastructure would insure against famine by contributing directly to the uplift of China's economy, culture, and society. Modern construction projects and the physical benefits that improved lives would revitalize and enrich the "centuries old" tradition of civil engineering in China. Todd did not believe that the Chinese lacked the innate capacity to control nature with technology. On the contrary, he was convinced that the social and political situation had stifled this national potential and caused it to lag behind the West in the critical field of applied technology. He believed that "China needs help modernizing . . . she needs engineers. No other group produced by modern civilization can help her more." A transfer of knowledge would allow China to recover its lost abilities and close the gap hindering interaction with the Western world.[61]

Todd and the CIFRC were never alone in attempts to transform Chinese society. Even as its programs were at their height in the 1930s, a number of other American-dominated groups were endeavoring to bring modern practices to the Chinese. Westerners and Chinese increasingly spoke of the necessity of reconstruction for China as the basis of shepherding that nation, beset by political turmoil, to the comfort of stable modernity. As one British commentator in the 1930s put it, "reconstruction" there was "not merely the repair of war damage but the general building up of China on modern economic lines." During that decade, U.S. nongovernmental groups took comments like these literally, sponsoring programs to produce a profoundly transformative "rural reconstruction" in the Chinese countryside.[62]

Interest in agriculture was especially strong among Protestant missionaries, particularly among those affiliated with the University of Nanking. Its agricultural college undertook several projects in areas such as rural reform and cotton improvement. The college also counted well-known researcher Lossing Buck among its faculty. Buck carried out extensive studies on the Chinese farm economy, and completed his opus, *Land Utilization in China*, in 1937. A massive, multi-volume study, the work reflected Buck's determination to apply Western social science to China's agrarian problems. He believed that after critical data were collected and analyzed, a selection of technocrats could use social science techniques to solve the problem. Buck's approach was consistent with the views of the organization that sponsored his study, the Rockefeller Foundation, which was gearing up for its own massive intervention in China.[63]

The foundation's new program in China coincided with a broader change in American perceptions of that country. In 1931, Pearl Buck, who was then married to Lossing Buck, published *The Good Earth*. The novel quickly became a best seller, surprising its author, who won the Pulitzer Prize and saw the book transformed into a Hollywood film. Buck's characters resonated with the American public, perceptibly influencing their view of China over the next several decades. The 1930s also saw an increasing acceptance of the Nationalist (Guomindang or GMD) government. Its successful 1926 "Northern Expedition" put much of eastern China under the GMD's control. Although many American missionaries and government officials initially were wary about the intentions of the GMD, concerns eventually abated. This was due to the efforts of the leader of the GMD, Generalissimo Chiang Kai-shek, and his wife, Soong Meiling, both of whom actively courted Western opinion. One of their most dramatic steps was the conversion of Chiang to his wife's Methodist beliefs in 1927. Crucially, Chiang's conversion to Christianity brought him the support of media mogul Henry Luce. Born in Qingdao to Christian missionaries, Luce had a lasting interest in Chinese affairs. He threw the resources of his empire behind the Generalissimo, whose conversion to Christianity undoubtedly helped convince the mogul that he was the right man to lead China to a modern, Americanized future. *Time* and *Life* magazines were unfailingly laudatory of the Generalissimo and his regime. This positive and simplified coverage of a complex and often confusing Chinese political and social landscape made all types of American engagement in China more attractive and sustainable.[64]

Chiang's regime had its own agenda for the foreign development aid facilitated by this sort of coverage. Sun Yat-sen, the party's founder, had seen development as foundational to national unity and power. His 1922, *The International Development of China,* proposed a massive plan of industrial development to be achieved with international aid. It has been cited as one of the earliest cohesive statements by a nationalist leader on the need for national development.[65] His dreams left the GMD predisposed to development. As it exerted more control, the government sought to "reconstruct" China into a modern society. They took a page from Sun with an ambitious agenda to rebuild cities on modern lines, dam rivers, and electrify the country, all to shake China's "stagnant race" (in Sun's words) into action. This would be managed by Chinese technocrats steeped in "scientific" approaches and aided by the international community.[66]

One source of technical assistance the Guomindang leaned on was the League of Nations. During the 1930s, the League sent several missions to offer advice on various topics ranging from agricultural reform to intellectual cooperation. The advisers on these missions reveal the changes coming to the concept of development. The programs were carried out with respect for the sovereignty of non-Western states, a characteristic that would shape postwar development programs. Nevertheless, the experts sent by the League were steeped in many of the time's prevailing assumptions. They were certain that the "undeveloped, ill-educated, and poverty ridden masses in less fortunate countries" had outlooks that were "resigned and apathetic" that left them "not yet able to stand by themselves under the strenuous conditions of the modern world." Modern technology and intellectual trends were seen as the forces that were reshaping the globe and were the means to shake less developed peoples from their "backwards" state. Revealingly, perspectives of some technocrats were themselves shaped by ideologies that were transforming international affairs in the period. English technicians saw their work in a liberal colonial framework. Other reforms offered by European advisers were inspired by Social Democratic ideas. An Italian working for the League tried to export a vision of Fascist modernity. He used Mussolini's ambitious Agro Pontino as a template for the programs he suggested for the Chinese. The League's varied operations in China do preview the role that international institutions would play on the issue following World War II. But they also offer an overture for the ideological differences and conflict that would mark the application of development over the coming decades.[67]

Rockefeller's program matured in this changing climate. From its inception, the foundation embraced China as a key arena for its philanthropic efforts. In comparison to the rational and scientific worldviews of the West, foundation officers thought "traditional" Chinese outlooks were a false framework for understanding the world. Seeing a serious lack of "the scientific spirit" so necessary to support modern society, Rockefeller pushed programs that would instill such perceptions in Chinese culture. This bred an assumption that any effort to modernize China demanded a change in psychology. Chief among the means of achieving this was the Peking Union Medical College (PUMC) that opened, after years of planning, in 1921. The PUMC was intended to be apolitical, dedicated to the promotion of improvements "not only in medical science but in mental development and spiritual culture." Western science would eventually filter out into important sectors of Chinese life, inspiring the rational, scientific outlook Americans believed vital to the construction of a modern society.[68]

The PUMC fell short of these lofty goals. Although it endured (and remains a respected medical institution in China), there were serious reservations about the approach it represented in the decade following its founding. Officers believed that the college's failure to make a serious impact on Chinese life sprang from its focus on research as opposed to the social application of scientific knowledge. This view on the part of the Foundation staff was shaped by an emerging consensus within the philanthropic community about the role of social science in future reform efforts. Some of this change was influenced by the particular experiences of Rockefeller and other private groups working to contain the "rural crisis" in the American South during the 1910s and 1920s. However, it largely reflected the attraction of the pronounced positivistic posture within the social science disciplines after World War I. With this focus, social sciences claimed that their empirical, scientific approaches allowed them to offer solutions to social problems.[69]

The social science turn came gradually at Rockefeller, but its early arc did bring indirect support to groups seeking to influence China's modernization. It was part of a growing emphasis on social science approaches to understand and solve problems implicit in modern global life. It also revealed the roles of other private organizations in organizing the research and action that framed a new approach to development. Foundation funding primed much activity in the NGO arena. There were a few direct grants by the foundation to Chinese universities for social science research between 1928 and 1932—grants that were welcomed as the Chinese government and academy were embracing social science to further national development. However, much of the Rockefeller money given to the social sciences in Asia flowed through the Institute of Pacific Relations (IPR). Rockefeller provided nearly $1 million to the IPR for various projects between 1928 and 1933, about a quarter of which was devoted to research. Formed in 1925 in Honolulu, Hawaii, the IPR was comprised of national councils in countries committed to the "study of the conditions of the Pacific peoples with a view to the improvement of their mutual relations." The eleven councils provided a means of unofficial diplomatic interaction and fostered communication across the national boundaries. During this time, the IPR took an increasing interest in social science as a means to comprehend and manage the changes wrought by the "machine age" on the "traditional" cultures of the Pacific. IPR studies covered most countries in the Asia-Pacific region; however, China absorbed by far the greatest share of its funds.[70]

Raymond Fosdick, an internationalist who took the reigns of the Rockefeller Foundation and the General Education Board in 1936, was responsible for assuring that the Rockefeller Foundation became strongly invested in cultivating overseas programs utilizing social science. A progressive, his career demonstrated the deep interconnection of domestic and international reform issues. He had grappled with police reform, been part of the U.S. delegation at Versailles, and was an advocate for the League of Nations. He shared a common view that modern technology was remorselessly reshaping the globe. Powerful and inescapable, this historical trend raised pressing questions of how it could be reconciled with the individual and society. Fosdick became a leading advocate of using social science to grasp these changes and mobilize reforms. His opinions (and grants) shaped the galaxy of foundations, institutes, and universities that felt Rockefeller's influence. Fosdick's ideas were shared by the vice president of the foundation's European operations, Selskar M. Gunn, who argued for their application in Asia.[71]

During a 1931 trip through China, Gunn had become severely disheartened. The keystone of the foundation's China program, the PUMC, was out of touch with the needs of China, and other Western-sponsored efforts seemed no better. Although considerable attention and money had been devoted to a variety of programs, these disparate efforts seemed uncoordinated and generally ineffective. The new GMD regime did not inspire confidence. As Gunn put it, GMD leaders were "more like a group of youngsters running a high school society rather than the affairs of a country of 450 million people."[72]

Despite this gloomy assessment, Gunn rejected any thought that Rockefeller withdraw or retrench in China; rather, a new and better-organized effort was necessary. Instead of the hodge-podge of small and isolated projects, he argued, Rockefeller needed a more broadly conceived program to push greater change. Over the next several years, the foundation evolved a plan for a vast reconstruction of Chinese rural society. A "plastic" moment lent itself to "efforts designed to reconstruct a medieval society in terms of modern knowledge." Even with the financial troubles visited on the foundation by the Depression, the trustees were sufficiently impressed by the program's potential to allocate $1 million in 1935 to start work. China stood out in Rockefeller documents as an explicitly national program and one that absorbed a large chunk of foundation resources.[73]

Gunn's proposal was a departure from the foundation's established approach in China, and it shows the ferment in development ideas during the 1930s. Ideas that made extensively conceived programs more acceptable found their way into practice. At Rockefeller, there was a conscious embrace of the idea of planning, something increasingly popular internationally. With established measures brought to crisis by the Depression, planning had increased authority as a way of organizing reform. However, it inspired extraordinary controversy in public life. A gauge of this was the resistance to Gunn's initiative within the foundation. At the outset, members of the Rockefeller staff were cautious about emphasizing aspects of the program, feeling "it is unwise to put rural reconstruction in China explicitly under the caption of social planning. To do this has no advantage, and some manifest disadvantages." Roger Sherman Greene, a founder of the PUMC, opposed Gunn's program, urging the continuance of projects seeking "knowledge for its own sake." Continuing this course would have greater long-term impact than a social science–based program with "fundamental investigation which would be closely related to the solution of . . . problems." But Greene's methods were now seen as being behind the times, and his 1935 resignation helped clear the way for a new approach in China.[74]

Rockefeller forged ahead. It sought to coordinate the operations of the various universities, missionary groups, and Chinese programs working on various aspects of Chinese agriculture. By selecting some of the strongest existing institutions and programs, Rockefeller would use its funds to transform these institutions into the arms of its larger rural reconstruction effort. Initially, the foundation placed great hopes in joint work with the Chinese Mass Education Movement (MEM) that had been created following World War I under James C. Yen, with YMCA support. Yen had developed a village-level approach for literacy education in China and subsequently became a strong supporter of the "rural reconstruction" concept during the early 1930s. Although Gunn and others found the MEM and its founder "inspiring," they eventually discovered a significant flaw. It lacked the ability to perform social scientific research thought necessary to the operation. To remedy this deficiency, the foundation created the North China Council on Rural Reconstruction (NCCRR) in 1936 to serve as the center of its China program.[75]

For the Rockefeller officers, "reconstruction" implied more than rehabilitation of previous abilities. It spoke to the creation of new capacities across national life to deal with the imperatives brought by the global impacts of modernity—it was modernization in all but name. Consequently, the NCCRR had greater aspirations than undertaking the overhaul of agricultural techniques or rural credit. Indeed, the council aimed at nothing less than the transformation of the daily existence of millions of Chinese. Cooperative in orientation, the NCCRR knit together the activities of the Mass Education Movement with those of five Chinese universities (including the PUMC and Nanking) in a quest to modernize China. The extent of the Rockefeller vision for China's reconstruction is revealed in some of its grants under the program. Keeping with the NCCRR's declared intent to "bridge the gap between knowledge and utilization," the council developed the capacities of certain institutes and universities within China to gather and analyze data from the countryside. Chinese were to be trained to collect this information in order to coordinate the attack on the root problems that prevented modernization.[76]

At the same time, the council explored the possibilities for overhauling Chinese education at the grassroots level via the injection of modern educational training techniques. Reform was "strategic," emphasizing structural transformation while making sure that education was "thoroughly integrated with . . . comprehensive reconstruction." For the council, training was critical; reforming the teacher was at least as important as reforming the curriculum. Convinced that "the elementary school teacher plays one of the most important roles" in rural life, the NCCRR decided that education would be critical in any effort to foster social change. Accordingly, the council supported the establishment of normal schools in the countryside to educate teachers who were trained to produce students whose perceptions fit the goals of rural reconstruction as defined by the Rockefeller Foundation. These basic programs were buttressed by further grants focused on public health or adult education.[77]

Like the CIFRC, the NCCRR assumed many aspects of Chinese culture would have to be discarded. Of all of the NCCRR's reform targets, perhaps the most elaborate involved plans to overhaul the Chinese language. Convinced that both spoken and written Chinese were incapable of conveying scientific and technical information, the Council considered how it might develop a new vernacular grammar that would allow mass audiences to grasp essential modern ideas. Without significant changes, the language itself would remain a barrier to a larger development program that desired the "superimposition on a mediaeval community of training utilizing scientific knowledge four hundred years in advance." Such language reform, the Council reasoned, should be based on an understanding of how the "unsophisticated Chinese" thought. By using normal and village schools established by the MEM as bases of study, a new "folk rhetoric" could be devised as a "tool for education and propaganda" to serve the larger goal of modernization. This particular objective was tied to other Chinese language reform efforts promoting Basic English as an alternative in order to cultivate international exchange and impart a scientific outlook.[78]

The ambitions of the CIFRC and the Rockefeller Foundation highlight the ferment in international development during the interwar years. American NGOs were not alone, as many other organizations and governments were coming to similar conclusions. Their ideas were not dissimilar to those that had gained currency in the French and British empires following World War I. In order to increase economic productivity and safeguard their respective imperial systems from unrest, colonial authorities attempted to reconfigure their African subjects into their vision of "industrial man."[79] Reshaping individuals to fit modern life demanded changes in their outlooks and daily life. The development of the "new man" was something preoccupying contemporary communist and fascist regimes as much as liberals. As these new methods were embraced, the conceptualization and content of "reconstruction" changed. Executors of programs were increasingly comfortable with planning in the development process. All assumed that modern industrial technologies would be part of the modernization equation. The extent of development shifted as projects were increasingly conceived as large-scale, embracing wide regions and large populations. For all the new ideas, a single incarnation of what they were attempting eluded liberal advocates. Like many others during the 1930s, members of the CIFRC and Rockefeller sought something that both inspired and symbolized the style of development that they were helping to refine.

SEARCHING FOR A MODEL

Todd kept abreast of the changes internationally, and was soon drawn to the Tennessee Valley Authority. So impressed by its potential, he made a trip to the South in 1935 to see it firsthand. Inspired by its attempts at "revamping the whole life of this broad region," Todd had found ideal representation of the type of program he and the CIFRC sought. The TVA was a living example of how to undertake modernization on a large scale, reinforcing many of Todd's beliefs about the transformative powers of planning, social science, education, technology, and engineering. The immediate appeal of the TVA to Todd and so many others was that it utilized existing concepts that assumed social and economic change to be two sides of the same developmental coin.[80]

Hopes that these new ideas might find expression in China were dashed by the same forces propelling development into a new importance in international life and U.S. foreign policy. Returning to China, Todd joined reformers clustered around a new journal titled *democracy*. He told its editor, Edgar Snow, that "Roosevelt democracy" was the best method to reform China and urged the publication to emphasize the potential of the New Deal.[81] Unfortunately, Todd and his fellow editorialists had little time to spread this reformist gospel. The 1937 outbreak of war between China and Japan crushed *democracy* and dispersed its staff. The conflict unraveled development programs as well. Hostilities forced the CIFRC to regress to relief as the commission succored war victims. The crisis soon overwhelmed the commission, and by 1938 it had been rendered impotent. The NCCRR, also swept into the chaos, shelved its ambitions and Rockefeller was forced to provide emergency aid to keep its various organs in existence.[82]

Japanese aggression in China was part of a deteriorating world situation. Primed by new ideologies, a swelling tide of aggressive forces opposed to liberalism challenged the existing world order. The appeal of these ideologies was heightened because they also promised to harness the forces of modernity to provide better standards of living. In response, internationalists and liberals renewed their focus on development. It was in the crisis years of the Depression that an evolving variant of development was loaded with a strategic import to secure the pale of liberal life against such challengers. While the imperatives driving a commitment to development were new, many principles and practices had been hammered out in the interwar period. Development had become amenable to extensive projects that provided massive technologies and assumed the process would bring significant social alterations. Many saw natural systems, from rivers to crops, as items to be pressed into the service of these modern transformations. Increasingly, important players were gravitating to the power of social science to guide reform as well as the contentious concept of planning. Among a constellation of missionary, business, and voluntary groups there was a latent inclination to work with governments to implement their visions. These formed a basis of the modernization concepts that would be used to reshape the postwar world and create a set of institutions and ideas that resonate down to the present. Yet, in the upheaval of the 1930s, the outlines of a model of how these ideas might be applied worldwide were only just being discerned. For many partisans, the best means would be found not in the Chinese countryside but in the American South.

Chapter 2

THE ONLY ROAD FOR MANKIND

"MODERNISATION" TO MEET THE CHALLENGE
OF TOTALITARIANISM, 1933–1944

The immortal contribution of the TVA to Liberalism,
not only in America, but all over the world, is the blueprint it has drawn, and that it is now transforming into
a living reality, of the road which Liberals believe is
the only road mankind should travel.
—*Odette Keun, 1937*

The economic millennium . . . will not be brought
about by hoping for it.
—*Eugene Staley, 1939*

"SPINELESS," essayist Odette Keun called her fellow liberals in the face
of ideological challengers to their legitimacy.[1] Keun was among commentators during the 1930s who shouted for liberals to take heed of the dual
menace of fascism and communism. Of French birth and Dutch parent-
age, Keun had been raised in shifting settings and traveled extensively.
Part of an international collection of liberals heavily invested in domestic
and global politics, she was alarmed by the threat posed by "totalitarian"
ideologies. More important, she feared liberals did not fathom the reality
that their ideological foes had to be confronted and contained on a variety
of levels. She used terms with which many of her ideological kin would
have agreed. Keun sketched liberal society as one based on private property and initiative with the "resourceful" intervention of government. In
their ideal form, liberal societies protected all individuals against exces-
sive control by either business or government while maintaining rights of
conscience, thought, and expression.[2] At a moment when these core values were embattled, liberals had to show the capacity of this social, political, and economic system to carry societies to higher standards of living,
just as their opponents appeared to have done.

This had to take place in the midst of a global economic crisis that had
left the credibility of liberalism in tatters. Liberals were compelled to base

their appeal on improving conditions by harnessing powerful catalysts of modernity—science and technology. However, communist and fascist opponents displayed considerable prowess with those same forces. At the time, many saw communism and fascism as the best types of political and social organization to control these forces. Internationally, there was a swelling acceptance of the government intervention or planning popular under communist and fascist regimes. But these carried the deep marks of statism, something that challenged foundational elements of liberalism itself: individual rights and private property. As this liberal reconstruction of societies—increasingly referred to as "modernisation" by the early 1940s—was given a new role in global affairs, the international debates over means to this modern end were always present. Liberals had to find methods that claimed to reconcile a jumble of concerns. Regardless, as the decade wore on the demand for development became urgent. Liberals had to demonstrate they were masters of modernization—at home and abroad—if their system was to survive.

In 1937, Keun offered an answer to this problem. Her proof did not come from typical organs of international affairs, nor was it found in New York, London, Geneva, or some other cosmopolitan locus. Rather, Keun was inspired by the environs of Knoxville, Tennessee. After seeing a developmental "experiment" in the South, Keun marked the Tennessee Valley Authority (TVA) as a rallying point for liberals. It was a specific program that served to demonstrate how a broader program of liberal development could be achieved domestically and internationally. The TVA was not entirely new; it was an amalgam of many ideas and assumptions worked out by various constituencies internationally over preceding decades. Yet, it was a unique variant of development and incredibly significant in an ideologically charged period. Claiming the best elements of planning that combined both mechanical technologies and social control, the TVA proposed an acceptable solution to the dangers of statism within an attractive package of participatory, liberal democracy.

Keun's intervention is interesting, at the very least for the brio and prescience of some of its arguments, but also for its connection to decisive shifts in U.S. geopolitics. The TVA and development programs like it offered a means to parry the influence of fascist and communist models of development. The remedies for the liberal dilemma suggested by Keun and grasped by others demonstrate how larger concepts and practices of development, which could claim liberal politics and be draped with claims of exceptional American origins, became established means to achieve strategic aims. Her commentary was part of a broader mobilization of evolving liberal ideas about development into a new global mission for the United States. It was inspired by the imperative to articulate and deploy an

Americanized liberal brand of development to woo those around the world yearning for what George F. Kennan in 1932 dubbed the "romance of economic development."[3]

This need would endure well beyond the 1930s. There is agreement now that the Cold War was a global competition between liberal capitalism and state communism. Such a struggle can easily be recounted in part through those efforts to offer peoples around the world economic and social development in a manner representative of each side's ideology.[4] However, this type of developmental antagonism hardly began with the bipolar struggle of the Cold War. Liberal development, symbolized by the TVA, already had established a strategic significance during the 1930s. World crisis transformed the American vision of what development should accomplish and how it should be achieved. By virtue of its resources and ideas, the United States assumed it was required to lead efforts, newly labeled "modernisation," with unambiguously global ambitions. Through this period, into the Cold War and beyond, when threatened by movements or ideologies, liberals claimed that their system was the best means to deliver the promise of development.

OTHER ROADS TO MODERNITY: LIBERALISM EMBATTLED

The Depression smashed liberal pieties. It closed a decade of liberal internationalist ascendance. After World War I, a menagerie of new parliamentary states appeared in East and Central Europe, Japan enjoyed a liberal interlude, and the international economy was shaped by a capitalism dominated by laissez-faire principles. So the speed with which the global capitalist economy unraveled, and the inability of liberal governments to contain the aftershocks, raised sudden and acute questions. Edmund Wilson felt the ideological nadir in 1931: "What we have lost . . . not merely our way in the economic labyrinth but our conviction of the value of what we are doing."[5] Reinhold Niebuhr, at the emergency's trough, noted that the inability of a "senile" system to deal with the difficulties besetting a modern, integrated, and mechanized world demonstrated that "western society is obviously in the process of disintegration." In 1933, Harold Laski saw a globe despoiled, breeding "a temper of feverish haste" where "the spirit that denies has triumphed over the spirit which affirms." Noting this was reminiscent of other revolutionary moments in history, he appreciated the temptations of other systems. He felt "the only answer capitalism can make to the challenge of communism is . . . proof that material benefits it can secure are definitively greater than those of an alternative system."[6]

Liberals believed technological wonders of an interconnected world economy—air travel, mass communication, and industrial production—ushered in by science and engineering and their promise for general prosperity were being squandered by outmoded politics. For one of the most devout, Raymond Fosdick, traditional liberalism seemed devoid of the means to contain the hazards of industrial society that was, by its nature, globally interdependent. This failure left "the world . . . very sick."[7] Free market capitalism, extolled only years before as the surest means to progress, was questioned by a chorus of voices "on all sides of the political frontier." Laissez-faire policies quickly came to be seen as wrongheaded and inefficient—a damning perception among more technologically minded progressives.[8] For others liberal capitalism's exploitative and wasteful characteristics were simply aggravated by the crisis. Governance of modernity seemed beyond the capacity of liberalism. This view did more than challenge specific policies or particular governments. It struck at the basic, systemic ideas behind liberal democracy and capitalism as a means to organize societies.[9] In a true test of its ability, universal liberalism appeared to have universally failed.

Liberals were thrown onto the defensive internationally, embattled on one side by a crisis that had exposed the failures of capitalism and on the other by ideologies that claimed to master the intricacies of modern life and offered a route to the future. They seemed to truly understand development, adopting approaches that reverberated around an unsettled globe. It was the era of the Autobahn, the Agro Pontino, and the Five Year Plan—state-sponsored development to implant prosperity. Liberal societies had to contend with a spectrum of active and appealing ideological challengers with convincing claims to have social, political, and economic systems better attuned to modernity. Critiques of liberal life ran deep. Excesses of capitalism were attacked, as was "parliamentarism" and even a basic building block of liberal belief, the individual. Fascist and communist approaches had a dramatic impact on the world scene, an appeal enhanced by the capitalist implosion. Both were based on utopian visions of the future and promised results with social and economic regiments that were often discussed in opposition—and, more ominously, as successors—to a tired, bankrupt liberalism.[10]

Even in the United States liberalism was not insulated from the appeal of its challengers. Fears of novelist Sinclair Lewis that Americans could be lured to embrace autocracy were not pure fiction.[11] The accomplishments of fascism were on display and lauded in the heartland of the United States itself, as evidenced for example by "A Century of Progress," a World Fair held in Chicago during 1933. It was one of a species of international fairs showcasing faith in progress brought by science even as exhibitions trumpeted political differences and, occasionally, reticence toward technology in the wrong hands. Chicago repeated the era's received wisdom that modern technology reshaped the landscape as well as its human inhabitants in a profound and far-reaching manner. Science and technology created a web of new ideas and structures surrounding the individual, which "affects his environment, changes his whole habit of thought and living." Transformation was all-encompassing, demanding that "individuals, groups, entire races of men fall into step with . . . the march of science and industry." Lewis Mumford repeated such conventional wisdom in his opus *Technics and Civilization* the following year. Machine society demanded a "reorientation" of human life but could only promise "well or ill as the social groups that exploit it promise well or ill."[12]

As might be expected, the fair showcased industrial accomplishment in the United States even as the Depression scraped bottom. Nevertheless, some of the strongest praise for international technical accomplishment was reserved for Italy, where Mussolini's regime retained the early positive impression it had made on American public opinion.[13] Listed first in the international section, Italy was described as "vibrant with the heroic deeds of Fascism speaks more resoundingly, more intelligently and more forcefully . . . than . . . any foreign nation participating." Benchmarks of modernity—engineering, physics, aviation, astronomy, and medicine—in the Italian example convincingly conveyed "the message Fascism has for the world."[14] The world could be made to believe that not only were the trains being made to run on time, but broader change was being brought by a regime with a new ideology that could cultivate modernity in seemingly inhospitable terrain. Mussolini's government brought new roadways as well as the massive reclamation program to clear the Pontine Marshes south of Rome for agriculture and planned communities. An assault on malaria, a disease long seen as a drag on social and economic growth, was continued (with help from a somewhat conflicted Rockefeller Foundation) as part of a campaign to create a fascist modernity. While historians have exploded much of the cant exported by the regime, at the time fascism was seen to provide a model by which a poorer nation could be redeemed.[15]

Those looking for other examples of a smooth road to the future could also find elements to admire in Nazi Germany. Drunk on a militant nationalism worshiping a mythic Germanic past, the Nazi regime was nevertheless infatuated with modernity. While private property and markets were not abolished, the government became the prime mover in the economic sphere. A multitude of government-supported programs in science and industry brought technical advances in such areas as chemicals, metals, rocketry, and aeronautics. Construction of the Autobahn heralded a concrete effort to motorize German life, signaling the arrival of a new, advanced, and prosperous society. All was done with an urge for autarky to create an economic unit secure from the unsettled international market-place and militarily self-sufficient. Through these and other policies the Nazis sought to remold society. Their vision of modernity was tied to a brutal Social Darwinism that saw races grappling for survival and pro-jected a grim racial worldview into policies at home and abroad. How-ever, this struggle also required the transformation of the Germans them-selves. Educational, cultural, and industrial policies were aimed at creating a fascist new man, modern in outlook and primed for the strug-gles the Nazis sought. While the gruesome nature of Hitler's racialist poli-cies quickly became apparent, scholars now also question whether his economic program produced a sustainable recovery in the mid-1930s. Nevertheless, many at the time saw an enticing model for political and economic life in the German example.[16]

Its mirror opposite was the imposing visage of the Soviet Union. Stalin's industrialization in the 1930s riveted global audiences.[17] And this indus-trialization was modernization in step with a communist melody. State planning was the indispensable tool by which socialism would be etched into the Soviet empire. In theory, central control would eliminate the waste, inefficiency, and inequity embedded in capitalism, allowing social-ist modernity to take hold. Stalinism was the development of a new civili-zation intent on the construction of gargantuan steel mills and entire cities and explicitly focused on altering the most intimate of individual activi-ties. Where and how a person worked, spent leisure time, or was educated had to change to fit the socialist version of modernity. Their very percep-tions would have to be transformed as an integral part of the moderniza-tion process.[18]

National in scope, the impression was global. The communist goal of converting a "backwards" society into the exemplar of socialist moder-nity was done in direct ideological competition with liberal capitalism. Stalin's steel city of Magnitagorsk and the Dneprostroi hydroelectric pro-gram demonstrated to many that state planning had quickly mastered the "brute force" technologies of industrial society. Because of its ostensible success, the Soviet Union could offer proof that it was the true inheritor of the Enlightenment. Carrying the baggage of a persistent global crisis, capitalism could legitimately be cast as a drag on progress. From the early 1930s, liberals and internationalists were aware of the appeal of the Soviet planning model. There was plentiful Soviet propaganda about the techno-logical wonders springing up in its empire. Added to this were the atten-tions of a swath of activists, commentators, and scholars who detailed the wonders of Russian industrialization. It all seemed to prove that com-munism, not the liberal West, had successfully harnessed the forces of science and technology to forge a universally applicable model of development that would lead humanity to a better world.[19]

Searching for Answers to a Liberal Dilemma

With the rise of these competing development visions, a new migratory pattern for reformers took shape. Progressives, grimly aware of the limitations of liberal capitalism, flocked to the USSR to see this new society rise and borrow ideas they could apply at home.[20] One of the more radical was Stuart Chase, an advocate of a "third road" away from the precipice of economic collapse to which laissez-faire capitalism had driven the nation. Chase was part of the global journey to find an example of how a planned society might look. He called for an American turn to central planning based on expert knowledge to do away with the excesses and inefficiency of the capitalism system. His 1932 book, *A New Deal*, lacked a tangible example of what such a drastic shift might entail, but it discerned stirrings in its oft-quoted closing:

> The groups are actually beginning to form. As yet they are scattered and amorphous; here a body of engineers, there a body of economic planners. Watch them . . . If occasion arises, join them. They are part of what H. G. Wells calls the Open Conspiracy. Why should the Russians have all the fun of remaking a world?[21]

Ironically, while investigating the Soviet example he found in full form what he imagined at home. It was "spiritually refreshing" to behold the Tennessee Valley Authority in its early stages. Chase hoped it might segue to a "Great Transition" to planning. Although linked to earlier reform ideas, the TVA marked a new turn from unvarnished and destructive competition to an effort "schooled in science" for the common good. Its dams and power plants were imposing but were only the "bony skeleton." It was in the "flesh and blood" where real change was taking place. TVA-sponsored programs were revamping local life with new crops, agricultural practices, electric power, and education. Most of all, this sprang from a special type of "planning based on consent." He told readers of *The Nation* that the TVA was "the New Deal's best asset," an invaluable commodity that would have a career elsewhere.[22]

Other progressives dipping into international reform currents for inspiration also greeted the TVA with excitement, Julian Huxley among them. English by birth and a biologist by training, he had fashioned himself into a popular science writer and commentator on current events. Experienced on the topic of development, having reviewed conditions in British colonial Africa, he was among an international cohort transfixed by the possibilities of social and economic planning as means to deal with pathologies exposed by the Depression. Like numerous others, he initially turned to the Soviet Union. A visit to Russia in 1931 revealed the Soviet Five Year Plan and its "new spirit, the spirit of science introduced into politics and industry" that "heralds the birth of a new kind of society, a society which is coherently planned."[23]

Although the USSR remained in "a transition between a mediaeval past and communist future . . . between a chaos and a plan," Huxley could already deduce a change in "spirit." Huxley described how an egalitarian ethos worked its way into daily interactions among Russians of all classes. He also lingered on the physical changes that could easily be seen in the Russian people. The vogue of "physical culture" that was an outgrowth of this new approach had produced robust, happy people by Huxley's measure. There was even the possibility that a "new attitude toward the human body . . . more like the Greek ideal" would be conceived in the USSR. Indeed, he worried that Russian physiques would soon "outstrip" the unathletic British.[24] Huxley's interest in how the new society evolving in Russia appeared to transform people was not entirely fetishism. Like other reformers, he assumed the technologies and ideologies behind planning would drift into the everyday living standards as well as into the psychology (and perhaps physiques) of individuals.

Returning to a Britain facing an unremitting depression, Huxley felt a solution could only be found in "wholesale planning." Rampant individualism had stripped away common aims, making liberalism appear directionless when measured against the disciplined faces of fascism and communism. Russia was only a partial answer. Huxley wrestled with his estimation that some curtailment of individual liberty was inevitable if such planning programs were implemented. He believed that coercion could coexist with real enthusiasm for a project among the people if the larger goal reached beyond "individual profit."[25]

Still, Huxley knew that the types of programs they desired had not been tried on a large scale. Accordingly, he immediately registered the appearance of "Roosevelt's gigantic experiment . . . remolding industry and life in general, within the planned region of the Tennessee Valley."[26] The TVA embodied the type of reform that melded economic growth with social change and a flexible style of planning for which Huxley and others had yearned. Eager to see hopes made real, Huxley beat a path to Tennessee in 1935. He was thrilled to witness an integrated "experiment in applied social science" blended with the claims of "grass roots" democracy. While he recognized it was controversial, the TVA seemed to have answered hard questions of individual liberty bound up with development. The American South provided needed proof that broadly conceived development based on planning could effectively be implemented in a liberal, democratic society.[27]

More important, Huxley saw the "experiment" as an American take on development that was potentially international in application. Programs in the South were undoubtedly similar in intent and even execution to the vast programs in the Soviet Union as well as fascist Italy and Germany. However, he believed the intimate involvement of state power in these programs was unattractive. "Indirect" powers and the cooperative, demonstrative approach exemplified by the Americans offered another option. But the TVA fulfilled something larger, "science and vision . . . combined in a way and on a scale new in human history . . . the large-scale application of the experimental method in social affairs." Huxley, like others, was coming to see it as a fulfillment of a global demand for large-scale transformation based on rational state planning drawn from a specific American example.[28]

The commentary of Chase, Huxley, and others regarding the TVA betrays the struggle between models of socioeconomic development in the period. Liberals were grasping for a means that would demonstrate that planned economic and social development was possible without autocratic methods. What would make the TVA so influential globally that it would become nearly synonymous with liberal development itself was a claim it could reconcile destabilizing forces within a framework of liberal politics.

THE TVA AS LIBERAL DEVELOPMENT

The TVA has rightly been called "the granddaddy of all regional development projects." Proposed in 1933, it promised a new model through social and regional planning. However, the TVA was not new in terms of its means to the end of development. In fact, part of its almost immediate popularity was the TVA's blending of existing elements of existing development thinking into one comprehensive package. It counted itself part of a heritage of ambitions to use water resources to help modernize the "backwards" American South. The immediate impetus for it came from various plans for the Wilson Dam at Muscle Shoals, Alabama, to be a mechanism for economic improvement. The dam, originally planned for World War I, had been completed too late to play a part in the conflict. Industrialist Henry Ford considered buying it in the early 1920s and making it the commercial keystone of a "new Eden of our Mississippi Valley." After this private scheme miscarried, progressives pushed the federal government to put the dam's electric power to public use, only to be fought to a standstill by private utilities.[29]

Franklin Roosevelt broke this logjam. After a personal visit to Muscle Shoals, Roosevelt proposed a sweeping plan in 1933 as part of his "First New Deal." Although inspired by earlier ideas put forward by Senator George Norris, FDR's plan reached far beyond Muscle Shoals. It would create a regional program to build more dams for flood control and power generation, distribute that hydroelectric power, produce fertilizer, support agricultural programs, promote public health, further education, combat soil erosion and deforestation, and dig an inland waterway on the Tennessee River. Essentially, it was a massive, integrated program for regional modernization. It all was necessary because, in Roosevelt's continuing estimation (affirmed by the National Emergency Council), the South was "the nation's No. 1 economic problem." Such a burden demanded government intervention. All was to be overseen by a government-sponsored public corporation, the Tennessee Valley Authority.[30]

It was a development project par excellence, utilizing elements long employed in America's own "nation building." A significant element of the New Deal project was harnessing the natural resources of the region for its development goals. The environment would provide many of the resources instrumental to the process. Rivers were particularly attractive. They appeared as vast, untapped sources of potential energy that could serve modernization. Such thinking helped fuel expansion in the late nineteenth-century American West. Vast water projects, made possible by the imposition of advanced technology, were essential to settlement and commerce as well as the extension of political authority and a capitalist order. Damming rivers became a popular developmental pastime during the twentieth century, with perhaps 45,000 large dams erected worldwide. Such projects were touted as "multipurpose"—conceived as having numerous impacts beyond a specific technological program. For example, damming a river would provide for flood control while assuring its waters could be mined for the "White Coal" of electric power and diverted for irrigation. Commodities culled from the river fed large-scale or commercial farming, industrial development, or urban growth. Supporters regularly spoke of the positive effects of such "resource exploitation" as means to stoke larger programs of economic and social development. From the start the staff knew they were attempting something big. They comfortably stated, "The TVA is . . . a *regional development agency*"[31] (emphasis original).

A focus of the TVA's mission was to turn the ornery Tennessee River from an unpredictable force into a docile servant of regional development. The river's regular flooding was to be ended by a collection of thirty dams. The Tennessee would then offer hydroelectric power, irrigation, and navigable waterways. Yet, such ambitions were not exclusive to American engineers and managers. International colleagues also saw these resources

Figure 2.1. The Heavenly City: The Norris Dam, a centerpiece of the TVA's extensive program of regional development in the American South. Courtesy of Franklin D. Roosevelt Presidential Library, Hyde Park, New York.

as the means to provide for other programs for long-term development. Long before the TVA, various countries constructed dams to promote visions of progress cutting across their economies and societies. Contemporary Soviet hydraulic programs shared affinities for technology applied on a massive scale. Germany's engineers had considerable skill in harnessing water for human ends, and this bred a sense of superiority toward American counterparts viewed as less adept.[32] Modification of nature did not end at the water's edge. It would be continued by agricultural reforms. Establishing modern farming brought new seeds, fertilizers, and machinery to the fields as well as a commitment to extensive and, very often, corporate agriculture. Attacks on the local disease ecology were one crucial element, because a healthy population was a productive one. To this end, malaria eradication was a key part of the TVA's work. Such demands made on nature were not unique to the TVA; these sorts of efforts had long-standing international constituencies. Nevertheless, the TVA's draft-

MIGHTY DAMS SPRANG UP WHERE THERE HAD FORMERLY BEEN FOREST

Figure 2.2. A communist model: In the 1930s, the illustrated periodical *The USSR in Construction* was one way the Soviets publicized how their vision of modernity—in line with many international assumptions—could successfully produce massive technological edifices by harnessing and transforming nature in the service of development. This picture shows how that model displaced a forest and harnessed a river with a symbol of successful modernization, a large dam. From *The USSR in Construction*.

ing of nature into its service is a reminder of how wholesale environmental transformation was central to twentieth-century development efforts.

In order to make the Tennessee Valley "exhibit A of the new America," retrograde social attitudes would have to be altered along with the landscape. Above all, the region required a "new education . . . to prepare it for the change." Within the evolving modernization framework during the interwar years, multipurpose programs had to promote social change. Educational reforms would cascade new ideas into rural life. Along with its grand technologies, the TVA had programs meant to change the attitudes of the people of the region (declared by some to be one hundred years behind the rest of the country). In a region where the popular media casually referred to existing social and economic relationships as "feudal," a strong dose of social change had to go hand in hand with the technologies brought by the TVA. Important members of its administration would regularly emphasize the social aspect of development as part of the mix: "the multi-purpose character of TVA program—the significance of this aspect of TVA in terms of developing multi-purpose people." In the valley itself there was some apprehension with the onslaught of such a massive experiment. But reticence was outweighed by hope that the plan would bring needed economic opportunity.[33]

The initial administrative momentum for the TVA was the product of its first chairman, Arthur E. Morgan, and demonstrates its attachment to a longer legacy of American reform. He saw the TVA as a harbinger of "the new social and economic order we are striving for." The TVA stirred a nineteenth-century utopian streak in Morgan. As a young man he was awestruck by the "White City" of the 1893 Chicago Columbian Exhibition and Edward Bellamy's *Looking Backward*. Morgan became a leading hydraulic engineer and an active member of the progressive education movement. A believer in education as a means to approach human perfection, Morgan was also influenced by eugenics, and talk of "elimination" of the unfit can be found in his writing. The moralism underlying Morgan's views was unpopular at Antioch College, where he became president in 1921, but his writings on education brought him to the attention of Franklin Roosevelt, who appointed him to head the TVA board in 1933.[34]

Roosevelt's support allowed Morgan to bring his moral vision for an "integrated social and economic order" to the valley. This was daunting in its scope, but not removed from what others had advocated. Morgan stretched beyond many of his contemporaries in his reckoning of the means by which the program was to be implemented. To achieve the changes the New Deal promised, there was a need for "actual changes in deep-seated habits, social, economic and personal" through "conscious deliberate effort." To this end, he proposed an ethical code for TVA employees that included demands for no "intemperance, lax sexuality, gambling, and . . . habit forming drugs." It was a sign of his determination to use the program to create new social relationships. Morgan's vision provides a link between earlier perceptions of technology as a means to the uplift of societies and individuals and the new strands of reform that were coalescing.[35]

Morgan's vision aside, the "unified" program of the TVA necessarily drove it into many aspects of life. Agriculture, industry, electric power, flood control, river navigation, public health, housing, malaria control, education, urban planning, and a host of other smaller issues lay on its agenda. Among these, electricity has become a basic way the TVA is remembered. The provision of electricity has been a major part of the story of the TVA. The authority's dams and hydroelectric power plants became its most recognizable emblems. Historians have dwelled on the "power fight" between the TVA and private electric companies and how the authority generated demand for its electrical current by marketing cheaper electric appliances to the residents of the valley.[36] Like other development efforts of the time, while technology was an important element in and of itself, its potential to foster social change within the wider development program was seen as an important part of its mission.

Across the nation, progressives had long fought public utilities in order to put affordable electricity into the hands of people so they could use it to improve their homes, their enterprises, and themselves. Public power advocates firmly believed that cheap power and appliances brought into the home would bring "social modernization" through electricity. Advocating a rational housework movement they asserted that electric power allowed the operation of appliances that could free women of tedious work at home. At the same time, affordable current spurred decentralized manufacturing that might allow women, who now had more time, to enter the workforce and earn money, transforming social relationships at a basic level, the family.[37]

While the TVA's power program was hardly designed to emancipate women, it displays how one technological element was believed to produce social change. It was not solely a question of getting energy to the people in the valley, but instructing them on how to use it, as in many areas electricity use had been limited by high utility rates and unyielding poverty. The TVA's program to provide affordable electric power and appliances to poorer communities operated under the assumption that providing these new technologies would modernize economic and social relationships. The TVA and various local institutions in the valley provided a range of vocational and educational courses on how to best employ new electric appliances in business and day-to-day life. It even designed large refrigerators that communities could share. The assumption

Figure 2.3. Electrical Modernization: A community refrigerator of the type the TVA sought to distribute and train people to use. It was one example of how modern technologies instrumental to the development process were assumed to work their way into societies to transform individual lives on intimate levels. Courtesy of Franklin D. Roosevelt Presidential Library, Hyde Park, New York.

was that poorer people did not fully understand how to employ these modern devices and had to be instructed on their use. But this was itself a part of the extensive transformation such modernization sought. The assumption was that through the instruction and use of modern technologies the outlooks of people would be altered.[38] Americans at the time would hardly have seen this as drastic as the type of change that was assumed to be needed in places like China. Nevertheless, the emphasis on electrical modernization does display how the provision and use of technologies was directly tied to social and psychological change in the agendas of those sponsoring development projects.

The transformational aspect of this evolving style of development reached out to embrace entire communities. The most visible attempt by the TVA was the model town of Norris, Tennessee, in the shadow of a dam sharing its name. The new planned community provided TVA employees with modern homes with electricity and modern appliances—a dramatic improvement over most housing available in the valley. Norris had progressive schools and its own library. In the TVA's calculus, towns like Norris were the logical outgrowth of modern development. As science and technology continued a rapid advance, the modern life they supported would transform behavior by changing where and, most important, how people worked, lived, and were educated. It was best to channel these changes with the forces of modern, rational community planning that would prevent haphazard growth and the dangers of decay. In its concern about housing and community development the TVA was not alone; it was gospel to New Dealers and many international progressive reformers. Community planning, like other elements, was part of a package, displaying how comprehensive change to communities and individuals marched in step with the imposition of large regional plans.[39]

Education was part of this vision. It was a way of improving and modernizing the people of the valley. Schooling for children was indispensable, but there was also a need to reach adults. The TVA, to enrich the labor pool, supported vocational training and adult education. This reached beyond improving workers' capacities. Poorly educated and informed people would not be able to comprehend the intricacies of this approach and, therefore, would be less inclined to support it. There was a belief at high levels in the TVA administration that:

> [T]he citizen, whether he be farm owner or tenant, industrial or building trades worker, merchant, banker, school teacher, manufacturer, or what not, has a vital part to play in understanding and solving our national problems. If he does not understand and appreciate the need for an integrated and well-directed effort toward their solution, he will fail to do his part, either as an individual or as part of a

larger group in whatever daily livelihood or activity he or they may be engaged. This understanding cannot be assumed; it must be the result of the individual's assimilation of a reaction to the facts of modern living and modern problems.[40]

Accordingly, the TVA established a "General Education" component to "increase the employees' store of knowledge" and "develop powers of observation and critical judgment of one's own activities in relation to the well being of society" and "stimulate and develop a desire for further study." Education programs were built on assumptions that would be staples of postwar modernization theory. People assumed to have passive or fatalistic worldviews would be given new skills and perceptions to orient them toward the future and realign them with larger communities and national issues.[41]

A library service for TVA employees and surrounding communities was created whose buildings and bookmobiles provided reading material while serving as an integrated component with other areas of the TVA's job-training and adult education programs. By 1937, it was circulating 218,000 books annually to over 6,700 members in the valley. Another part of these efforts was a recreation program, which sponsored everything from athletic events to dances to community theater. The goal was to foster community social activity, not simply for the people's enjoyment but to build their "health, character, and citizenship." Capping these programs was visual education, using film and other media to educate and train valley residents. Movies reached some 167,000 people during 1937 alone. As Earle Draper, the man responsible for constructing the town, noted, the TVA would carry communities seen as backwards into a modern future. Norris was just "one phase of that vast system of regional planning in the Tennessee Valley which is destined to bridge a social and economic gap of almost a hundred years."[42]

However, the town, like much of the TVA, did not always live up to such grand expectations. As construction concluded and workers moved on, the town, with its higher rents, eventually became a commuter suburb.[43] Norris would also become one of the most visible symbols of the TVA's inability to reconcile reformist rhetoric with the dim realities of American racial prejudice. Promotion of social change did not mean challenging racism. It emerged as an all white community, as TVA officials had no desire to challenge the local segregationist regime. Acceptance of racial exclusion reflected the TVA's larger failure to treat African Americans equitably in terms of hiring, pay, and housing—chronic problems that did not escape the criticism of national civil rights groups.[44] The training program segregated its classes by race. Recreational programs required that blacks use different areas of public parks or even excluded them from certain parks altogether. Even the library program discrimi-

nated, creating a separate, smaller library for blacks in Knoxville. Supporters, however, found it easy to turn a blind eye to the taint of segregation worn by the TVA.[45]

They could also overlook other less savory aspects of the TVA. Hydraulic development meant flooding sections of the valley to create reservoirs
to feed power generators and slake the thirsts of agriculture. Such activity
also had pronounced negative consequences on many individuals, often
the least powerful. Over 125,000 people were displaced by the TVA's
construction projects—dams being the biggest culprit. Resistance, including rare outbreaks of violence, was sometimes the grassroots response to
the forced resettlement and other brands of dislocation brought by extensive development projects. Boosters evaded the issue but it reveals that,
early on, the TVA provided hints of unintended consequences that would
haunt similar attempts at modernization.[46]

The raw scale of what TVA was attempting required far-reaching collaboration. Its efforts drew on an existing thicket of institutional resources that lay mostly outside the state. Liberal planning advocates like
Wesley Claire Mitchell, Charles E. Merriam, Frederic Delano, and Beardsley Ruml in the preceding decades had overseen the creation of institutional sinew indispensable to the New Deal. Their handiwork produced
a range of influential institutions including the Social Science Research
Council, Columbia University, the University of Chicago, the Rockefeller
Foundation, and the National Bureau of Economic Research. These, in
turn, had broken ground on numerous economic and social planning issues. These individuals and the institutions they cultivated were vital to a
"make over" of liberalism from a classical nineteenth-century ideology to
a system interfacing with the demands of modern, urban-industrial society. Their ideas and programs were the product of a complex amalgam
of government, business, voluntary groups, social science research, and
philanthropic activity. Their own research quickly diffused into international trends in social reform. All collaborated to square economic growth
with its social consequences while highlighting the relationship between
public-policy specialists and the government.[47]

For the social science community the TVA had a siren's call. Many
believed it was impossible to discuss it "without realizing the tremendous
social implications it carries." It was an outstanding example of the evolving integrated approach to development that utilized social sciences.
Every breed of social scientist was needed to do the surveys and analysis
that would define what needed to be done in the valley—from education
to resettlement. A collaborative outlook prevailed, where social scientists
consciously integrated themselves with an assortment of politicians, bureaucrats, agriculturalists, and engineers arrayed in different institutions
and involved in the wider program. It was an attitude the TVA actively
cultivated, as collaboration offered tangible rewards. Early on, the Rocke-

feller Foundation and SSRC swiftly reoriented regional social science research to support a project seen as imperative. Howard Odum, a University of North Carolina sociologist who saw issues through a regional prism, found the pull of cooperation with the TVA irresistible. He mobilized and expanded social science research for the program with the express goal of making the "materials already gathered and bearing on emergency problems which will arise in the early stages of the Government's Tennessee Valley Project."[48]

It was both a continuation of the tradition of nongovernmental activism and a preview of post–World War II development methods. The TVA required the assistance of local government, business, and what would now be called civil society organizations. This was particularly true in more socially oriented areas of its program. It required the help of local universities, public health organizations, foundations, and local governments, often working together, to execute complex educational or disease eradication programs—as was the case in the TVA's far-reaching malaria control efforts.[49] During the Cold War a similar collaboration would prevail overseas between state and nonstate actors.

The social planning and collaborative aspects of the TVA are a reminder that its overall program was much more than the provision of new industrial technologies. Development in the valley was strikingly similar to peer programs abroad. It was a total project, vast in its scope, where social and cultural changes were integral. The dams and electric power plants it built were central elements of its program, but the modern social changes they were to foster were equally important. The project would reach deeply and intimately into peoples' lives and transform how and where they lived, worked, and how they saw the world. These assumptions would carry over into the postwar rush of development. But because the style of development the TVA epitomized was invasive, it was politically controversial. After all, the Germans and Russians used planning to lay down imposing infrastructural projects and employed their own brands of social engineering. Because the TVA was always situated in an international dialogue on development, it became increasingly important to enunciate those political aspects that set it apart.

Although many of the reforms supported by planning advocates owed much to international trends, they were promoted as exceptionally American variants. Unique American political traditions and particularly their history were highlighted to draw distinctions. The TVA's emphasis on public-private cooperation in planning performed by the United States could be consciously set apart from statist counterparts in fascist Italy, Nazi Germany, the Soviet Union, and imperial Japan. This has often obscured the international elements that fed into the TVA but that very masking was precisely what supporters were trying to do.[50]

Making this distinction became increasingly important as the TVA was but one model in the vogue of state-centered economic and social planning during the years straddling World War II. During the 1930s, planning gained a growing following. Walter Lippmann apprehensively noted that "collectivism" had become the "dominant dogma of the age":

> Throughout the world, in the name of progress, men who call themselves communists, socialists, fascists, nationalists, progressives and even liberals, are unanimous in holding that government with its instruments of coercion must, by commanding the people how they should live, direct the course of civilization and fix the shape of things to come. They believe in "the overhead planning and control of economic activity" . . . . No other approach to the regulation of human affairs is seriously considered.[51]

James Burnham agreed, seeing the urge to collectivism in all its guises as reflective of the arrival of "managerial society." Sociologist Karl Mannheim asserted there was "no longer any choice between planning and laissez-faire, but only between good planning and bad." Yet planning in many countries was often less about planning per se (at least in the comprehensive, rational manner described by its advocates) than about who held vital levers controlling social and economic life. Despite a grab bag of meanings attached to the term, planning partisans held a common faith in the power and ability of the central government to direct people and resources to produce greater prosperity. In the liberal West, it often was seen as a counterpoint to the inadequacies of the free enterprise system laid bare by the Depression and later by war. Planning, for numerous reasons, clung to a reputation as the best mechanism to promote all forms of development.[52]

Power was at the core of planning. This assured it would be dogged by controversy (which has not entirely dissipated today). Planning combined the raw power of technology with the imposing authority of the state, a brew some found noxious. Its embrace by the New Deal was ominous for its varied and vocal ranks of opponents. Programs like the TVA could potentially destabilize a host of local political and economic relationships while concentrating power in the hands of the central government. A more activist state caused obvious discomfort among businesses. Utility companies were goaded by the specter of government-financed competition and regulation. But antagonism was not limited to industry. Numerous poles of opinion saw it as a malignancy introduced into the American body politic. Culturally, certain Southern Agrarians were uncomfortable with what they saw as alien methods it brought to their region. The social engineering at the TVA's core deeply worried others. Many saw a toxic import that brought the worst of opposing systems into American life. It was reflexively denounced as "socialistic" and, as the term became one of derision, "totalitarian." Traditional American anti-statism motivated other critics. All saw the TVA as an early symptom of metastasizing centralized planning and feared that if it found a host in the Tennessee Valley, it would soon spread throughout the nation.[53]

Although the Depression opened doors to reform experiments that might otherwise never have been attempted, domestic opposition to those policies had critiques with traction. Supporters of the New Deal had to negotiate and define its position within American political traditions while explaining that it was an innovative approach to development standing apart from other options at work in the world. This was particularly true of the TVA, a program that took cues from planning and development concepts that were international in scope. To deflect attacks, these global links had to be obscured—the TVA had to be domesticated. Advocates had to demonstrate it could produce economic growth and social change while remaining securely grounded in the best of American political life. The basis of this response was "grass roots" democracy, a popular cry across the New Deal. Domestic debates threatening the very existence of the TVA forced an articulation of political elements that so engaged international progressives like Huxley and Chase.[54]

It fell to one of its early leaders, David Lilienthal, to knit existing threads into a "TVA creed." For all of its imposing physical accomplishments, much of the TVA's appeal was a product of the rhetorical talents of Lilienthal. Son of an Indiana shopkeeper, Lilienthal was no stranger to reform. Student of Felix Frankfurter at the Harvard Law School, after obtaining his degree Lilienthal cut his teeth in Chicago with progressive labor lawyer Donald Richberg. His work on public utilities questions brought him attention and eventually an appointment to Wisconsin's Public Service Commission in 1931. Throughout, Lilienthal remained loyal to his Brandeisian background—skeptical of distant, central authority but accepting an activist government as a positive force. Such a view fit the early posture of the Roosevelt administration and was a reason he was made one of the triad of directors of the newly created TVA in 1933.[55]

Admirers described Lilienthal as a "wonder boy." One indisputable talent thirty-three-year-old Lilienthal had was the ability to motivate supporters. Lilienthal's activities made the organization a powerful symbol of the New Deal and the benefits brought by large-scale technological programs and scientific planning. Although Lilienthal and Morgan both shared great faith in the ability of the TVA to modernize the valley, the relationship between the two men quickly became adversarial. In a complicated series of events, Morgan leveled unsubstantiated charges about Lilienthal's conduct that eventually brought a 1938 hearing adjudicated by FDR himself. Morgan's failure to answer the president's direct ques-

Figure 2.4. "Wonder boy" with power. David Lilienthal at the TVA's Wilson Dam power station, 1933. David Lilienthal Papers. Public Policy Papers Division. Department of Rare Books and Special Collections. Princeton University Library.

tions brought his dismissal. While Morgan's views tied the TVA to older strands of reform, Lilienthal crafted the enduring terms by which the TVA gained much of its reputation as the best example of how liberal development could be implemented worldwide.[56]

Lilienthal cribbed elements from Morgan's vision for the TVA and shibboleths of New Deal reform. However, it was not a case of borrowing concepts wholesale. As the United States was a large and diverse country, its central government was bound to suffer from a "lack of knowledge of local conditions." In view of this, bureaucracies centered in Washington had the potential, over the long term, to be a threat to democracy. However, the answer was not to limit the authority of the government, but to change the way its powers were exercised. A decentralized administration of federal functions could overcome the dangers of a top-heavy and over-centralized bureaucracy. Lilienthal saw the TVA as the boldest and best example of this decentralization. As a matter of course, he claimed its operations reached far down into the "grass roots," allowing decisions to be made in the field as well as utilizing local people and institutions in its programs. While smaller community bodies were franchised, Lilienthal's idea of localism often meant the participation of established institutions like state and local government or regional universities. Nevertheless, decentralization provided administrative agility within the TVA unthinkable in a centralized bureaucracy; technology and expertise could quickly and easily be dispersed for use by ordinary people. Lilienthal was clear that "cookie cutter" copies of the TVA could not simply be transferred anywhere they might be needed. The point lay in the basic grass-roots concepts behind the institution. These ideas, because of their decentralized and inclusive nature, had potential to be applied in a variety of places and situations.[57]

Lilienthal's thesis fell onto prepared ground, in part because he was using common tropes. But it was also due to the fact that it acknowledged tensions about harnessing what has been called the "juggernaut" of modern industrial society. Its power to transform—for good or ill—human life was already well appreciated. Lilienthal offered assurances that riding the juggernaut was possible, even beneficial. The United States appeared to have shown, through the TVA, a concrete example of the integrated, large-scale, planned development many had long imagined could safely be encased in liberal politics. This made the TVA an exceptional creation, a vision of development that could have emerged only in the United States. Nevertheless, his thinking was flexible; the template for development arrived at in the American South had the potential for universal application.[58]

Nationally, progressives welcomed the TVA (the "Heavenly City," as some called it) as a single statement of how favored reform ideas could actively be applied. Liberal arbiters like Max Lerner, Charles Beard, Felix Frankfurter, as well as Eleanor and Franklin Roosevelt, found the grass-roots concept of development compelling. The president's opinion was such that, during one of the TVA's administrative feuds where Lilienthal's job was threatened, FDR stated that failure to reappoint Lilienthal would be an act against the principles for which his presidency stood.[59]

The ready-made appeal of the TVA was a product of larger shifts in liberalism. The search for conviction was a continual part of the crisis for liberals. The imperatives of industrial society brought rolling changes to liberalism, but the Depression demanded reformers stand at the forge and recast the intellectual bases of their worldview.[60] Even liberal titan John Dewey, who preferred to keep his distance from both the New Deal and communism, was impelled to reconstruct an ideology dismissed as a "mealy-mouthed . . . milk and water doctrine." Massaging the heart of his faith, Dewey asserted that liberalism could be a radical doctrine for human development rather than a tattered cloak for laissez-faire capitalism. Though a more socialized economic life (a recurring theme for Dewey), liberalism could provide the means for all individuals to develop their full potential. No academic enterprise, his intervention was an explicit attempt to craft a "fighting faith" to show that liberalism remained relevant to global debates on the shape of modernity. Overlooking liberalism—which many appeared ready to do—could "narrow the issue for the future to a struggle between Fascism and Communism" and bring "catastrophe."[61]

WAGING "MODERNISATION" WORLDWIDE

Dewey's comment acknowledged an unforgiving reality: domestic debates were inextricably bound to the international fate of liberal ideas. Internationalists who had invested heavily in the construction of a liberal order in the 1920s were dumbstruck by the potent stew of chauvinistic nationalism, economic exclusion, and bleak racism stirred by the Depression. This compelled internationalists of all stripes to reformulate their own views and programs to fit within an altered world. A spectrum of liberals in the United States and abroad was waking to the new realities brought to international life by the rise of authoritarian regimes. As the expansionist policies of Japan, Italy, and Germany strained the international system, the statism, police powers, and cults of personality credited to these regimes came to be seen as diametrically opposed to the core values of the United States. The ideologies were no longer a critique or a diplomatic nuisance but an existential threat to liberalism.[62]

Symptomatic of this shift were efforts begun in 1936 by the Council on Foreign Relations, an epicenter of liberal internationalism, to study the origins and operation of what were initially termed "dictator states." Included in this taxonomy were fascist Germany and Italy, as well as the USSR.[63] It was assumed this new and rapidly spreading form of political and social organization was an established fact in the global body politic. Opinion makers saw fascist and communist states linked by a common set of political, economic, and social structures leading to disturbingly similar behavior domestically, despite some different international interests.[64]

A new term for these states gained currency: "totalitarian." Initially used by Italian fascists in the 1920s to describe their political and social worldview, the term found quick, if vague, application to describe the ideologies challenging liberalism in the 1930s. By the end of the decade the major foundations, unsettled by the totalitarians, were shepherding public opinion toward global engagement.[65] Rockefeller, as part of this effort, began research programs to grasp "the fundamental challenge which they represent."[66] Motivating these actions was an assumption that all societies carried a latent bacillus for totalitarianism that was easily made virulent by the forces of modernity. This was not alien (indeed, it was foundational) to similar outlooks during the Cold War.[67] Economic and social development over the preceding century had produced democratic, liberal, and individualist revolutions at some points and authoritarian regimes. These trends needed to be mapped by the social sciences so that they could be understood and confronted. Such a view coupled with a belief that development, impregnated with liberal concepts, could inoculate societies, assuring the disease need never arise.[68]

The fear of total state power abroad ran parallel to fears of the concentration of government power at home. Both assumed a corrosive impact on American life. On the international front in the later 1930s, political scientist Harold Lasswell effectively articulated an idea that illiberal fragmentation brought conditions where martial elites gained control of the levers of power, skewing societies. The argument was eventually extended to a fear that such devolution abroad might force the United States itself to adopt the domestic regimentation of its opponents to combat their influence.[69] During World War I, Woodrow Wilson and others had expressed similar fears that degenerative effects of German militarism and Bolshevism globally could alter American society domestically. Their answer had been an attempt to refashion international affairs to assure U.S. national security.[70] Elements of this formulation were in the calculations of the 1930s. However, the totalitarians were considered unique to human history and, because they appeared when modern societies were in crisis, were likely to remain a persistent concern in international politics. If these ideas were allowed to advance unchecked abroad, an unnatural "garrison state" would result at home. This formulation worked into the marrow of American geopolitical thinking in the late 1930s and endured through the Cold War.[71]

Facing totalitarianism was more than an intellectual exercise. Historians have traced the critical shift in how liberals internationally recognized the threat from the newly defined "totalitarian" states in the late 1930s.[72] A commitment to international development was part of the new U.S. globalism that sought to contain dangerous forces loose in the world. In the mid-1930s, liberals internationally saw nationalistic economic policies as corroding the structure of international life. For increasing numbers of American elites the peril was not abstract. The breakdown of international trade, exchange, and agreements negatively affected the United States itself. Internationalists from Henry Wallace to the members of the Institute of Pacific Relations argued that a fractured world economy offered little hope for prosperity through revived and integrated international trade. It was a formulation that eventually won over significant sectors of opinion. By 1936, Roosevelt was repeating such formulations, asserting "a dark modern world faces wars between conflicting economic and political fanaticisms," because "without . . . liberal international trade, war is a natural sequence."[73] Totalitarian states, organized around an unholy trinity of unalloyed statism, venomous nationalism, and stern autarky, came to play the villains in this formulation. Before the outbreak of hostilities in Europe, internationalists were articulating a need to take concerted action to promote and protect an integrated international economy dominated by liberal principles. It was Eugene Staley, a Tufts University economist with ties to the Council on Foreign Relations, who best projected American fears and the strategic need for international development in the critical years between 1937 and 1941.

Staley's liberal internationalism was at his core. His 1923 undergraduate essay on Allied war debts, written at Hastings College in Nebraska, won a prize from the Carnegie Endowment for International Peace. His admiration for Beatrice and Sidney Webb and the influence of John Dewey suffused his doctoral work at the University of Chicago, where Staley sought to find a way to employ his discipline as a means to solve social problems.[74] As the global situation darkened during the 1930s, Staley engaged a cross-section of international issues, proffering analysis echoing current debates over globalization. He agreed with contemporaries who believed technology was dramatically altering all aspects of life as it bound the world tightly together.[75] One of his mantras was that integration demanded the free flow of raw materials, capital, people, and knowledge. Those who impaired the normal flows of raw materials, capital, and

Figure 2.5. Working for the Millennium: Economist Eugene Staley at Tufts University, ca. 1943. Courtesy of Digital Collections and Archives, Tufts University, Medford, Massachusetts.

the other lifeblood of the international economy were standing in the way of progress and social welfare for all. Like debris blocking a rushing river, localist and nationalist economic policies disrupted the natural flow of the global economy. In the end, economic nationalists were fighting the forces of history. But they were more than inconvenient; they were potentially mortal for liberal societies. If such vices entrenched themselves in international life, the fragmentation already wrought by the Depression would become permanent.[76]

Other dangers loomed. Staley joined other prominent internationalists involved in the peace movement in calls for greater international cooperation. But events were accelerating, rushing the world into what Staley feared would be an "era of totalitarian war." A trend toward the establishment of "power economy," where the ultimate goal was the expansion of military might, was eroding commitment to the "welfare economy" focused on raising living standards for the population as a whole. International politics and trade were being skewed by aggressive policies, incited by economic crisis but increasingly becoming naked quests for national power. While nationalistic policies of the United States and others were a problem, the search for autarky by totalitarian states was cause for alarm. In the arenas of international trade and economic development, the threat to the United States of such "national localism" was acute. Aggressive foreign policies and barriers thrown up by nationalistic economic programs emerging from polities corrupted by totalitarian ideologies had global impacts. This opinion was integral to a new geopolitical view that saw the maintenance of a global system hospitable to American values as imperative to long-term security. As it had for so many other liberals, the shadow of the "garrison state" had darkened Staley's gaze. Failure to bend the world to liberal principles would eventually force the United States down the road to regimented social and political life in order to survive in an ideologically inhospitable world.[77]

With the stakes so high, history needed a push. With nations increasingly caught up in nationalistic "war fever," misdirecting resources to military spending instead of global trade and the general welfare assumed to flow from it, international cooperation had to be renewed. However, this commitment required the cultivation of agreements and institutions as well as new capacities to guide growth. Capital and raw materials were spread unevenly across the globe, and the requirement that they move freely and easily could not be guaranteed in the darkening world of the 1930s. This movement was vital if a peaceful, healthy international economy was to be maintained. Cooperation of this sort had the added benefit of constructing a foundation for collective security against totalitarian aggression.[78]

Staley's proposal to solve this problem was a comprehensive program of international development in a form recognizable today. It presupposed systematic intervention in poorer areas of the globe to guide economic and social change. Through various means, technical knowledge would be injected into poorer areas of the globe to smooth the way for freer movement of raw materials and commerce, assuring the stability of an open, liberal world order. Planning, made safe for free society, would make such expansion possible. Staley believed any effort necessarily required cooperation across a set of institutions.[79] Internationally, it was the task of governments as well as voluntary and international groups, including the League of Nations (which sponsored some technical aid missions to China and elsewhere), to increase the capacities of the peoples of poorer, often colonial, nations. Discussing his ideas, Staley chose not to dwell on the contradictions emerging from colonial development. Like many predisposed to development, his attention was drawn to China, assailed by colonial powers but nominally independent and a major international flashpoint. It became his example of how international development might be conducted. If China received technical assistance on liberal terms that fit its perceived needs, the country could eventually become a productive member of a liberal international economy.[80]

Education in the technical arts would eventually unite a rank of modern, technologically minded persons with the capital that would foster growth. Staley shared a view common internationally, that development was one interconnected process, linking the economic and the social. "Bringing roads and schools and technical institutes and machinery to China and India and Borneo" would create a "self-reliant generation . . . equipped with modern tools for meeting their own needs and for exchanging with other peoples." There was a further reason to act. If liberal forces did not lead such development, these areas of the globe would fall under the sway of "nationalistic imperialisms." Following these false prophets to the future would bring revolution and war that would not only harm peoples in the underdeveloped nations but, perhaps more important, continue dislocation within the international economy. According to Staley, the United States had to be the engine of history and drive the process. The "economic millennium," Staley scolded, "will not be brought about by hoping for it." American leadership was an acknowledgment of its considerable economic and technical resources. It also reflected a bleak understanding that if the United States did not assume the role, someone else—whose goals were deemed less savory—would do it. By default, global leadership and specifically command of world development lay in the hands of the United States.[81]

As international affairs became more contentious after the outbreak of war in Europe, non-interventionists spoke of securing the United States by fortifying the Western Hemisphere. Interventionist liberals undermined these arguments by defining the sphere necessary for the defense of the United States as global rather than regional. One of the most effective voices was Staley's. He energetically joined the acrimonious debates through newspapers, radio, and a host of public lectures in the years before the U.S. entry to the war. He drubbed a leading anti-interventionist, Charles Lindbergh, as a confused dupe of Hitler's divide-and-conquer strategy.[82] In an influential article in *Foreign Affairs*, Staley unraveled the limited, defensive formulations advocated by the likes of Charles Beard and Jerome Frank.[83] Dissenters could not see the "world was round." Secure continents were now "myths," as new technologies, particularly aircraft, made hemispheric defense obsolete. Blindness to totalitarian (which by the beginning of the 1940s effectively meant German) success voided assurances that the economic, political, and social systems of the United States could survive in one corner of the globe. Physical realities of geography could not be altered, but "human meanings" given to those elements could "change." Technologies rendering distance moot and forcing interdependence among nations at the same time sired the distortions of totalitarianism, creating a situation that demanded the United States take the reigns of global leadership to secure itself. It was one element of a foreign policy accord bridging left and right, solidifying support for intervention, even among those who had no great affection for Roosevelt or the New Deal. In fact, this general strategic formulation with its imperative of U.S. global leadership found its way into Henry Luce's famous 1941 essay, "The American Century."[84]

What is important is that a historically specific variant of international development that took its cues and justification from the experience of the United States had a clear strategic rationale within a new American globalism. Its aim was to assure and extend the sphere of liberal life against ideological challengers whose social and economic organization was corrosive to liberalism. Even with its international and private components, the role of the United States in pushing the whole program forward was seen as indispensable. Staley's views matured in the international discussion in which the subfield of development economics was rising. They were a remarkably cohesive expression of ideas that would predominate postwar. Indeed, Staley has been credited for loading "international development" with its current meaning.[85] These formulations easily flowed into global reconstruction activity during World War II. Staley stated the global importance of international development to contain a totalitarian threat, but did not initially explain the specifics of implementation. However, that was a question other liberals were in the process of solving.

It is here that Odette Keun returns. Keun was a proud internationalist, claiming to have always been a liberal. This was an exaggeration, as an earlier commitment to socialism had not survived a 1922 trip to the Soviet Union. An intimate of H. G. Wells, she was a fixture in his influential circle. That sphere included Huxley, who described Keun as "no nymphette, but the most articulate . . . explosive female that ever was." Her wide-ranging travels were the basis of a number of books on world events in the 1920s and 1930s. They also made her sensitive to the crisis brought about by the Depression. As early as 1935, she saw the threat of fascist Germany to global order and called for preparations to resist.[86]

Keun's 1937 *A Foreigner Looks at the TVA* outlined methods for resistance. With the Tennessee Valley already a global attraction, Keun retraced Huxley's steps, spending several months in 1936 in the region. For Keun, the global situation was already a crisis, as liberalism was challenged from within by the forces of discontent and without by fascism and communism. In an assessment with which many would have agreed, Keun described a liberalism on the defensive across the globe in the mid-1930s. Routed in Russia, Germany, Italy, Hungary, and Spain, and with the Depression lingering, liberalism's Western European and American bastions were not secure. Readers who thought Keun's tone exaggerated or shrill were dismissed as gambling on luck to ride out the world crisis. She brusquely rejected such complacency, saying, "You will not have it. You will get a concentration camp instead." Keun decried her own tribe as "so dilatory, so indecisive, so theoretical and rhetorical that we never do anything *in time*" (emphasis original). Liberals had to stand up—to sit back and debate was to invite "extermination." She pleaded that they awaken to the opportunity emerging in the American South. The comprehensive program of development the TVA offered was an effective weapon for the denuded liberal arsenal. It provided hope that liberals might "band . . . together and begin fighting . . . before it is too late for us."[87]

Keun was one who saw development as not just one element of liberal society but a means to directly grapple with liberalism's totalitarian challengers. She articulated the belief that the TVA and the larger style of development it epitomized could be more than a means to restore the global legitimacy of liberalism; it could contain the appeal of totalitarian ideologies. Specifically, what the TVA promised was "*a model*" of "a middle-road technique, applicable throughout the land . . . it may destroy those evils and infamies of exploitation . . . which render capitalism unendurable"[88] (emphasis original). Its comprehensive approach to social and economic planning for development made it the best single representation of how this could be done. Grim truths of poverty and racism visible in the South did not dissuade Keun (and others) that the program offered proof that liberal, democratic societies could translate their ideas into resolute, organized action. The TVA was much more than a successful regional project, it was "the most authentically glorious feat of modern America." Keun felt it was proof that the United States, for all its failings, alone had shown that it could "put in harmony" the forces of industrial life in a democratic manner. In a world besotted by destructive ideological "myths," the "maturity" displayed by the Americans' social organization set them on the path to assume "world authority" to lead "Occidental civilization." Keun thought only the Americans could assume such authority, and with the world darkening, she hoped they would soon grasp it.[89] Accordingly, it was the best example to summarize how modernity could be achieved by liberal means on a global scale. In Keun's opinion:

> The immortal contribution of the TVA to Liberalism, not only in America, but all over the world, is the blueprint it has drawn, and that it is now transforming into a living reality, of the road which Liberals believe is the only road mankind should travel.[90]

The sheer depth of Keun's hosannas may not have been shared by all internationalists, yet her excitement reveals the essentials of the TVA's already wide appeal. A reform program had shown that a liberal state could muster the forces to control the divisive components of the modern world. It was the United States that had hit upon a unique variant which showed that liberalism could carry forward the larger process of social and economic development, and that ability was inextricably linked to a struggle with totalitarian ideologies. Her writings, outspoken and idiosyncratic as they could be, summarize much of the liberal idea of development.

The experiment in the valley did more than inspire discussion; it brought action. Various groups, particularly NGOs already invested in developmental missions, gravitated to the TVA concept. It came to be seen as the exemplar of the same basic ideas they had been evolving. The program already had the attention of the Rockefeller Foundation. For the foundation's personnel, the TVA appeared as a tailor-made example of the sort of multipurpose development based on applied social science and technology they had come to advocate in the early 1930s. Efforts in the South, like those the foundation had embarked upon overseas, sought to reach down into the social life of the region and bring the social changes necessary for modern, progressive outlooks to take root.[91] Lilienthal's grassroots philosophy provided a convincing argument that broadly conceived programs could easily be tailored to fit a variety of people's needs and were therefore transferable to regions very different from the Tennessee Valley. By the later 1930s, many adherents were campaigning for the creation of other TVA-style authorities across the United States.[92] Partisans at the Rockefeller Foundation took that faith a step further, seeing it as a template for economic and social development they could actively export across the globe.

In China, the TVA became an example of how liberal development could be extended. Enthusiastic officers with the Rockefeller Foundation compared their own China program with the ongoing New Deal project. Differences between programs in these two parts of the world were believed to be of "degree and not kind" and a distinct similarity was seen in "principles, objectives, and obstacles." Rockefeller staff served as brokers, passing along information from the TVA to Chinese officials work-ing on rural development.[93] Attention has been given to the TVA's role during the Cold War as a major developmental tourist destination. How-ever, this trend began in the 1930s as part of the larger shift in develop-ment thinking. It was not only the likes of Huxley and Keun, but also a selection of officials, thinkers, and technicians from around the world—including China and India—who visited. Rockefeller eagerly participated, sponsoring trips to Knoxville by numerous foreigners. Many Chinese had their firsthand views of the New Deal program paid for by American sponsors. By serving as a travel bureau, Rockefeller was part of a growing trend. In 1937 alone, the TVA claimed to have entertained more than 600 foreign visitors in addition to over 110,000 American tourists. For those Chinese who saw the region, the TVA became one of the best examples of what rural reconstruction and planning could achieve in their country.[94]

This was not intended to be a purely one-way exchange of ideas. High-level officials at the foundation thought China provided "the social sci-ences with something which has heretofore been lacking, namely, a 'labo-ratory' where experiments can be carried on under controlled condi-tions." Rockefeller staff hoped that ongoing "experiments" within the Depression-wracked United States could provide materials to be tested in their Asian lab while, at the same time, experience gained from moderniz-ing China could be fed back into reform in the United States. They be-lieved the social science community would be inspired by the foundation's Asian program. Eventually, strategies would be picked up by American institutions to solve problems in the South and elsewhere.[95]

As it turned out, Rockefeller did not have much time to conduct experi-ments in its "laboratory." The Sino-Japanese and world wars that fol-lowed blotted out the opportunity. By 1944, Rockefeller officials were impatiently awaiting the war's conclusion to restart their programs. They even considered tapping one of the early directors of the TVA, H. A. Mor-gan (a Lilienthal ally), to direct a revived postwar version of the rural reconstruction effort.[96] As was the case with other internationalists, for Rockefeller staff the start of World War II modified but did not end com-mitment to a liberal vision of world development.

With development finding a strategic rationale, the U.S. government began to actively implement programs internationally. During the critical years from 1937 to 1940, Americans, with Franklin Roosevelt in the van, revised their vision of the international order and the role of the United States within it. Roosevelt's attempts to bolster the British and French militarily to resist Germany are well known. Yet, a new geopolitics to secure the pale of liberal life required more than weapons. There were other, "softer" policies. Increasingly, the United States turned to cultural and economic diplomacy as a way to contain the influence of fascism, particularly German influence in Latin America. The clear outlines of how development should operate as part of an ideological confrontation were already being drawn. Americans rapidly came to the conclusion that they had to actively guide economic development to assure stability in the region. As early as 1938, a range of official State Department cultural and economic programs, built on the experiences of various American non-governmental groups, appeared for this purpose. These would eventually include the flamboyant Nelson Rockefeller, well aware of the experiments of the foundation sharing his name and influenced by Beardsley Ruml's personal faith in the ability of the social sciences to solve social problems. At the request of Roosevelt, they drafted an influential 1938 report that made technical assistance an important part of U.S. economic intervention in the region. An outgrowth of Rockefeller's activism was the Institute of Inter-American Affairs, and its range of technical assistance, agricultural, and cultural programs that are rightly seen as forebears to Cold War government aid programs.[97]

The start of the European war in 1939 appeared to some internationalists as an opportunity to imagine a world reshaped on liberal terms. However, these dreams had to contend with the reality of those ideologies already inscribing their own "new orders" on the globe. In this continued debate over the shape of the world, the TVA enhanced its reputation as a proven means to effect liberalism's promise. Huxley took a whirlwind tour of the United States during the fall and winter of 1939–40 to size up American attitudes toward a postwar settlement. His status was such that it seemed he could get the ear of just about everyone involved in international affairs. Walter Lippmann, officers at the Rockefeller Foundation, and the Roosevelts, among many others, entertained Huxley. The TVA was a popular topic in conversations about creating a world based on rising prosperity to justify Allied war aims and liberal aspirations generally.[98] Huxley heard many Americans assume their country would play an outsized role in any settlement and the worldwide reconstruction that would follow. Their visions were not restricted to areas in conflict, as the globe had to be covered by any successful development schema. Among the groups considering the world to come was the World Peace Foundation, which gathered prominent academics and activists in early 1940. They saw development of "backward" areas as one of the "economic essentials of durable peace." South America, Africa, and Asia were all marked for large-scale development on the TVA model. China, for one, was to receive a "T.V.A. for the Yangtze Valley." All would secure a revitalized liberal world order after the war.[99]

Hopes for an early peace were soon dashed, but thinking about global development ground on. As was often the case, Staley systematically explored what others only sketched. If the peoples of the globe were to achieve the "freedom from want" promised among Roosevelt's "Four Freedoms," much more was required. Staley knew the issue of postwar stability and prosperity went beyond repair of war damage. The establishment of an integrated global economy based on liberal principles was a necessity. "Mixed" economies where cooperative planning principles blended with capitalist markets served as the means to greater global productivity. Accordingly, the imperative of reconstruction brought opportunity. The need to deal with underdevelopment remained a staple of discussion on the economic basis of peace. Staley, who joined the wartime United Nations Relief and Rehabilitation Administration (UNRRA), asserted recovery would easily segue into a larger effort to develop the world economy in a refashioned liberal international order.[100]

Capital investment and informal exchange were not enough to stimulate this conversion. As Staley outlined before the war, comprehensive technical assistance was foundational to an effective global process. Wealthy nations had to serve as catalysts by providing the necessary development aid, but there was also need for devoted international institutions such as a "United Nations Development Authority." He pointed to Sun Yat-Sen's *The International Development of China* as a template. Indeed, the postwar development of what he hoped would be non-communist China remained one of Staley's leading examples of how and why a continued commitment to international development was necessary. Fears in the West that emerging nations would eventually become technologically adept competitors were misplaced. A rising economic tide brought by development would lift all boats, and his evidence was drawn from recent domestic experience. Quoting FDR, Staley recounted the argument that New Deal aid to the American South had not brought a competitor to the industrialized North but a set of fresh markets. Staley posited that with a positive program of development, the same would occur worldwide.[101]

By 1944, Staley used the term "development" in the expansive manner that would come to be accepted during the Cold War and beyond:

> What is economic development? It is a combination of methods by which the capacity of a people to produce (and hence to consume) may be increased. It means introduction of better techniques; installing more and better capital equipment; raising the general level of education and the particular skill of labour and management; and expanding internal and external commerce in a manner to take better opportunities for specialization. Economic development is a broader term than "industrialization."[102]

Importantly, Staley and others began to treat the term "modernisation" as synonymous with this process. The term was not new in and of itself, but applying it to these activities helped distinguish them from the older and ever more ambiguous rubric of "reconstruction." During the war, reconstruction had become increasingly confused with "recovery"—the reclamation of previously existing capacity. The new label of "modernisation" was a unified banner for maturing development approaches with a predilection for large-scale development programs and tempered planning. Along with other liberal advocates of development, Staley embraced the TVA as proof that this liberal transformation was possible.[103]

These hopes, while vague on certain details, departed from previous official U.S. approaches to development. It was not the informal, nongovernmental, and bilateral attempts to spread "civilization" that had reigned in the years after World War I. Rather, the new vision of liberal development Staley and others articulated made a prominent place for planning. It assumed the U.S. government would permanently be insinuated into the process. Even with this increased state role, nongovernmental and international bodies remained instrumental to what was seen as a global mission. Again, Staley acknowledged that modernization was a political and social process as much as an economic and technological one. He subscribed to existing assumptions that it would necessarily rearrange social and cultural relationships in the societies on the receiving end. More to the point, the liberal "modernisation" Staley had identified was perpetual and universal. In the framework he helped craft could be found the basic structure organizing U.S. development policies during the Cold War.

Lurking behind the imperative to modernize were the fears etched into the liberal mind by the tumult of the 1930s. Failure to embrace an international modernization mission would have profound consequences. Staley's worldview assumed all societies were on the path to modernity but had varying ways to complete the journey. Without aid and guidance, developing nations would make their own choices about how they would modernize. Before the war ended, Staley worried they might succumb to persistent temptations of "exclusive nationalism." Most vexing was that this path remained marked by the Soviet Union, a demonstration that national development could be achieved divorced from the wider international economy. Added to this, aggressive demagogues might once again marshal disaffection brought by recurring economic misery and social dislocation. The "ultimate totalitarian dictatorship" and war would result. Modernization based on "voluntary, democratic co-operation" offered an escape from a repetition of the recent past.[104]

Staley's wartime assertions were core beliefs he would carry into a long academic and policy career. They were not singular. Numerous others came to see development as a spine to support liberalism's legitimacy. Liberal internationalists, however, were starkly aware that their ideological competitors had their own appealing modernization programs. As they looked for the means to implement their vision, eyes fell upon evolving methods and institutions emerging from contemporary cycles of reform. From these the TVA emerged as a liberal champion. In a period where modernization models were always part of an international dialogue, the TVA could distinguish itself from other development approaches with a claim that its large-scale, socially transformative, planning-based development was securely encased in liberal politics. World War II was an opportune moment to implant in global affairs the liberal developmental ideas that germinated in the hothouse of the 1930s. The ease with which these ideas flowed through global war into Cold War strategies was a reflection of the fact that modernization was already a weapon to combat ideological threats to liberalism.

Chapter 3

A GOSPEL OF LIBERALISM

POINT FOUR AND MODERNIZATION AS NATIONAL POLICY, 1943–1952

> In President Truman's Point Four program it [international development] has been given a sharp focus. While neither the problem nor the basic methods to deal with it are new, Point Four is both bold and new.
> —*Raymond Fosdick, 1950*

ON JANUARY 20, 1949, Harry Truman, reveling in his surprising reelection, delivered his inaugural address. The speech was shaped by the "momentous" challenge of the Soviet Union, and its rhetoric was stern. He described a confrontation between the freedom and liberty promised to the individual by American democracy and the tyranny of arbitrary rule by the "false philosophy" of communism. Truman's rhetoric was laden with assumptions of the superiority of liberalism as an ideology. America's promise was not only human dignity, the ability to govern oneself, and religious freedom but the right to "material well-being" allowing the individual "to achieve a decent and satisfying life." In other words, the United States and the social organization it advocated provided the best hope for the world to enjoy the fruits of the modern world.[1]

The pretender of communism threatened to undo the stability the world needed to achieve this millennium. To confront this challenge, Truman laid out a four-point plan. He promised to continue support of the United Nations, lauded the European Recovery Program (ERP) as a success, and threw his weight behind the nascent North Atlantic and Rio de Janeiro pacts. But the climax was presented in the speech's fourth point—as its architects planned:[2]

Fourth, we must embark on a bold new program for making the benefits of our scientific advances and industrial progress available for the improvement and growth of underdeveloped areas. More than half the people of the world are living in conditions approaching misery. Their food is inadequate. They are victims of disease. Their economic life is primitive and stagnant. Their poverty is a handicap and a threat both to them and to more prosperous areas. For the first time in history, humanity possesses the knowledge and skill to relieve the suffering of these people. The United States is pre-eminent among nations in the development of industrial and scientific techniques. The material resources which we can afford to use for assistance of other peoples are limited. But our imponderable resources in technical knowledge are constantly growing and are inexhaustible. I believe that we should make available to peace-loving peoples the benefits of our store of technical knowledge in order to help them realize their aspirations for a better life. And, in cooperation with other nations, we should foster capital investment in areas needing development. Our aim should be to help the free peoples of the world, through their own efforts, to produce more food, more clothing, more materials for housing, and more mechanical power to lighten their burdens. We invite other countries to pool their technological resources in this undertaking. . . This should be a cooperative enterprise in which all nations work together through the United Nations and its specialized agencies whenever practicable. It must be a worldwide effort for the achievement of peace, plenty, and freedom. With the cooperation of business, private capital, agriculture, and labor in this country, this program can greatly increase the industrial activity in other nations and can raise substantially their standards of living. Such new economic developments must be devised and controlled to the benefit of the peoples of the areas in which they are established. Guarantees to the investor must be balanced by guarantees in the interest of the people whose resources and whose labor go into these developments. The old imperialism—exploitation for foreign profit—has no place in our plans. What we envisage is a program of development based on the concepts of democratic fair-dealing. All countries, including our own, will greatly benefit from a constructive program for the better use of the world's human and natural resources. Experience shows that our commerce with other countries expands as they progress industrially and economically. Greater production is the key to prosperity and peace. And the key to greater production is a wider and more vigorous application of modern scientific and technical knowledge.[3]

Truman's speech was not, as some suggest, the origin of development aid. The president's own words reflect existing and widespread assumptions about the content and possibility of development. It was an attempt to confront the problem of an emerging postcolonial world with these development concepts within a Cold War context. During the 1940s, the

United States took the lead in constructing a worldwide liberal order in opposition to the threat posed by communism. "Order-building" necessitated the establishment of institutions like NATO and an "archipelago" of overseas American military bases. However, the creation of liberal hegemony that relied upon the "permeation of values and understanding throughout the global system" also rested on development aid and the institutions that could provide it.[4] Modernization was a preexisting means to assist this "permeation" and to establish the stability required for a functioning international system on liberal lines. It also served to contain communism with its own enticing brand of modernization. As the United States expanded its responsibilities during and after World War II, development became a basic means to meet and secure global commitments.

Truman and his advisers were hardly creating modernization out of whole cloth. Rather, they were stitching together a patchwork of existing ideas to produce a useable policy. What is telling is that the scope of his modernization mission was no departure from thinking in the 1930s. Those who had long pleaded for global development to tamp down ideologies corrosive to liberalism were gratified. However innovative the "Bold New Program" might be, it was ancestry that reassured supporters. Development methods already credentialed from earlier attempts to come to grips with totalitarianism would inform and justify the creation of a permanent aid bureaucracy. Equally important was the mobilization of groups already committed to the process. A range of private, governmental, and international efforts growing out of the Depression and war assured this official brand of liberal modernization could draw on methods with considerable cachet. The U.S. government was tapping an emerging consensus that saw technologically primed development as a means to promote politically acceptable social and economic change in a divided globe. This was best done through a tempered form of state planning with room for the input and expertise of nongovernmental groups as well as a battery of new international institutions. However, they would be increasingly drawn into programs sponsored by the U.S. government. Their knowledge, experience, and techniques were seen as indispensable means to implement these projects. It was not a beginning but an acknowledgment that development had a prominent and permanent position in the global strategy of the American state.

Earlier programs were the inspiration for the policies seen as necessary to make the "new nations" (as postcolonial states would be called) economically and socially viable in the face of communist allure. It was Asia, with its raw materials, large population, and strategic importance where the application of these concepts became crucial. Development based on technological aid would provide stability but keep the important regions of East and Southeast Asia in the anti-communist camp, allowing global, particularly European, reconstruction to pick up pace, guaranteeing the pale of liberal life. The United States' own experience with development would be held up as proof that economic and social development was possible within a particularly American framework. Specifically, the reputation of the TVA would continue to be broadcast to demonstrate the validity of larger liberal development concepts for the world at large.

IDEOLOGICAL ARGUMENT CONTINUES:
MODERNIZATION AND WORLD WAR II

World War II is an often-overlooked moment where elements important to postwar modernization were sorted out. It was also a continuation of the 1930s' ideological argument over the best means to promote development. A struggle without precedent in human history brought a rush of technologies that were hardly dreamt of before the war. The imprint of these technologies was impossible to miss. Jet aircraft appeared, revolutionizing warfare and further shrinking distances. The use of radar transformed combat. The rigorous application of the new insecticide DDT slashed the occurrence of insect-borne disease, and the antibiotic penicillin cut mortality rates from infection that had decimated armies in the past. Looming above all was the atomic bomb. It sat squarely at the intersection of basic science and applied technology. Collaboration among scientists, engineers, and managers produced a weapon of almost unimaginable and decisive power.[5]

Of equal import to solving the daunting theoretical questions, the Manhattan Project had successfully figured out how to put an atom bomb into production. Nuclear weaponry required an entirely original industrial process. Magnets essential for this process consumed enormous amounts of electricity. An entirely new plant had to be constructed at Oak Ridge, Tennessee, for this express purpose. The site was chosen because it could draw upon the vast electricity generation capacity installed in the region in the preceding decade by the TVA. Weapons development of the Manhattan Project fed directly into the economic development projects of the New Deal (and was the reason Lilienthal was made chair of the Atomic Energy Commission). This forced marriage was only a fragment of wartime service performed by the TVA. Historians have seen this era as transformative in the life of the authority, a period of increased industrial focus that helped accelerate a shift away from the initial goals of social and economic reform. However, the ability of TVA infrastructure to bolster the rapid expansion of war-related production was another reason supporters billed the program as a success.[6]

As much as the weaponry it produced as one of the "arsenals of the United Nations," the TVA itself was potent propaganda, an authoritative, living symbol of how a liberal world could be constructed postwar. Foreign visits increased as the U.S. government stepped in to sponsor tours as part of wartime information programs. A collage of individuals ranging from Jean-Paul Sartre to Lord Halifax shuttled to the valley. As the war's end could be seen, TVA staff rightly anticipated increased global interest and a swell of visitors. Whatever changes war brought the TVA organizationally, it granted a huge opportunity to extend the reach of development ideas the United States advocated. Deferred desires for development found an outlet as eyes turned to rebuilding—and improving—the postwar world.[7]

Lilienthal embraced the moment. As the war deepened, like other liberal internationalists he turned to the question of postwar development. From his post as chairman of the TVA he mused in 1942:

> There seems to be a definite sequence in history in the change from primitive or non-industrial conditions to more highly developed modern industrial conditions. Whether all of those steps have to be taken and all the intervening mistakes made is open to question. . . Don't we have enough control over our destinies to short-cut those wasted steps?[8]

Toward the end of the struggle, Lilienthal answered his question with *TVA: Democracy on the March*, published in 1944. It was an evolution of ideas articulated in the 1930s, only now they were extended worldwide. As a tool for the massive task of global reconstruction, Lilienthal claimed the TVA spoke in "a tongue that is universal, a language of *things close to the lives of people*" (emphasis original). This appeal was not based on material development alone. The TVA idea promised all peoples the possibility of "grass roots" democratic participation in a "public development corporation." Such methods assured a just framework to provide technical assistance for development. Lilienthal also saw the TVA to be a response to decolonialization. In his view, the TVA had always been set against a sort of colonialism (which he defined as the exploitation of hinterlands by a center) prevailing within the United States. Successful programs in the Tennessee Valley provided a rising tide of economic development that lifted all, exposing and rendering moot unequal policies that kept the South and West subordinate to the Northeast. From the South it was a short leap to the rest of the world. Lilienthal claimed the TVA could provide an example of inclusive development that would allow people local control while supporting the growth of an interconnected world economy. By using this example from "our own backyard . . . we can best prove our aims for the wide world."[9]

His book has been rightly called a masterpiece of American rhetoric and the chief expression of the organizational ideas—and myths—around the TVA.[10] It was a concise statement of how the United States could help the globe modernize. More important, it appealed to audiences at home and abroad. In fact, by 1945 the Office of War Information (OWI) distributed over 140,000 copies of the book internationally in numerous languages, including English, French, German, and Chinese. The OWI's interest in Lilienthal was a function of continuing ideological battles. Debates over who had the best version of the future did not conclude with the beginning of World War II. German propaganda had done an effective job promoting its economic system in occupied Europe while disparaging the United States as a land of economic extremes. Countering this "intellectual blackout," the OWI continued the ideological argument over development originating in the 1930s. It had to convince those, already distrustful of liberalism, that the United States could offer prosperity and stability. The growing appeal of the Soviet Union was one of the campaign's targets. Economic and now military success validated the assumption that only a totalitarian state could manage the large-scale, planned programs so many equated with development. Smashed societies appeared malleable and likely to embrace radically new approaches. There was a pressing need to demonstrate that the United States offered its own peerless approach for promoting economic and social change. Lilienthal's book fit the bill perfectly and appeared at just the right time.[11]

As the OWI pushed U.S. development ideas, there was a strong pull from those around the globe seeking inspiration. The TVA aroused such interest that a prominent OWI staffer, the historian and sinologist John King Fairbank, sought out Lilienthal for radio broadcasts to the Far East. The OWI even considered sending Lilienthal to China on a speaking tour to energize reconstruction efforts. Fairbank was a partisan of the TVA idea in his own right. He and his wife Wilma personally distributed various publications on the TVA during cultural exchange programs in China. In fact, as copies of Lilienthal's book found their way to China, American advisers there soon found the Chinese quoting the "principles" of *Democracy on the March* to them. Undoubtedly, the book influenced the Nationalist regime's postwar reconstruction plans, which included a "Yangtze Valley Authority."[12]

Even as his book worked its way into the far corners of the globe, Lilienthal wrestled with the realities of modern technology exposed by war. Miracles of science they may have been, but these came with searing lessons of the juggernaut's destructive nature. In the winter of 1944–45, as an already bloody conflict reached a frenzied pitch of violence, Lilienthal preempted fears it might be unredeemable. It was readily apparent what happened when dangerous ideologies wielded modern technologies.

Figure 3.1. An arsenal of ideas too. This cartoon demonstrates one of the ways the TVA served Allied propaganda efforts. Its reputation was also drafted by propagandists to demonstrate the Allies had sound development ideas for the postwar world. Courtesy of National Archives, Washington, DC.

He resisted simple views and clung to his pervasive optimism, asserting that technology was a neutral force as "the machine is neither good nor evil in itself. It is good only when man uses it for good. It is evil only if he puts it to evil purposes."[13] War only reinforced his view that restraints were needed to create a "technology shaped and directed by belief in people, a belief in the ethical and moral responsibility of technology." The TVA proved that humanity had such power. He believed this lesson vital to "those underdeveloped regions that even now are laying plans for changes through technology on a scale and intensity heretofore unknown." Those abroad, witness to this unique "American experiment," could only be impressed by its mastery of technology to promote prosperity.[14]

Lilienthal accepted the link between domestic and international development. Excesses of the moment aside, he predicted an "era of creation" (remarkably, he suggested it would run until about 1975). At home this "American Development Program" would offer compounding prosperity. Flowing across all economic and social sectors, this unparalleled effort would be done in accordance with American traditions. It would be voluntary at its core, requiring the cooperation of all manner of individuals and organizations—public and private—governmental and nongovernmental. This participatory approach would guarantee success, and if inspiration were needed, Lilienthal thought all that was necessary was to again gaze on his TVA, one "kind of American development." But he drove home the fact that the overriding lesson was not purely the "physical and economic results" but the "*method*" of development that required the "*participation of the people and the people's institutions*"[15] (emphasis original). It was "democracy intimately nurtured by socially-minded science and engineering" and was universally applicable as a model for global development.[16] He continued to contrast the American style of development and the liberalism in which it was rooted against other alternatives as the best way for humanity to achieve a better world.

Julian Huxley shared hopes for the TVA idea. During wartime Huxley continually referenced the TVA as the great example of how development planning on the international scene could be responsive to local needs.[17] He agreed that nongovernmental groups played an important role in the process. Not only could they cooperate with the actual implementation of projects under a planning regime, but input from organizations like the Institute of Pacific Relations or the British National Institute of Social and Economic Research could avert bureaucratic rigidity. Huxley had an eye on how planning methods could be employed in the underdeveloped areas of the world, particularly Britain's overseas colonies. Here, planning ideas were decidedly not anti-colonial. While Huxley thought the colonies should be perceived as being held in "trust or guardianship" rather than as possessions, he nevertheless believed that raising standards of living for colonial peoples could best be done within an imperial framework. His vision centered on large, "Regional Development Authorities" like the TVA. Contortions were necessary to avoid the implications of the TVA creed. Since development could take democratic or totalitarian courses, Huxley admitted that there was a need to see that effort in the colonies "squares with democratic principles." This did not mean "immediate political democracy with its . . . votes and elected representatives," merely a paternalistic trusteeship where development was done "primarily for the benefit of the native peoples" and not with an emphasis on the interests of the colonial power or big business.[18]

Although Huxley's thoughts about development planning in the colonies sported numerous contradictions, excitement about the TVA's potential on the international scene was clear. It remained a "symbol of a new possibility for the democratic countries—the possibility of obtaining the efficiency of a coordinated plan without authoritarian regimentation," making its appearance of "first-class importance in the evolution of human society."[19] Huxley carried his enthusiasm for the TVA to the UN as the first director-general of the United Nations Educational, Scientific, and Cultural Organization (UNESCO).

Internationally, the TVA idea moved the influential. Harold Laski assured Lilienthal the living example of the TVA was seen as a "grand example of the proper relation of man and machines." Before the end of the war, the International Labour Office commissioned a major study on the lessons of the TVA for international programs, concluding it would be an excellent tool to provide technical assistance to war-damaged regions. The tirelessly progressive vice president of the United States, Henry A. Wallace, was blunt. For the world to effectively confront the task of reconstruction, he stated, "there must be an international bank and an international TVA."[20]

Distinctions that liberals struggled to draw between development approaches had a noticeable impact. As the war lurched to conclusion, there was growing interest in Europe for the TVA to serve postwar rehabilitation. War-weary Norwegians saw the democratic ethos of the "revolutionary" TVA in direct contrast to a "dictatorial" Soviet style of development. It was the "first concerted effort by a capitalistic country to solve important social and economic problems by a large scale plan and along the lines of democratic ideals . . . TVA concerns the entire United States, and—this is no exaggeration—the entire world." Other Europeans backed a "DVA" for the Danube Valley after the war, although the proposal was attacked by an eloquent foe of planning, F. A. Hayek. Even areas largely untouched by the conflict found the emblem of liberal development attractive. Boosters in Wales turned to the TVA as a means to promote economic growth. Swedes sought Lilienthal's advice on natural resource development in their remote north. Staff in Knoxville began providing advice for a "JVA" on the Jordan River as early as 1942. Indian scientists toured the region shortly after the conflict, continuing a long-standing interest. Advocates of a TVA for New Zealand found Lilienthal's "grass roots" principles to be the central part of its appeal. With such varied and sustained interest there could be little doubt that to many abroad, the TVA had indeed become easy shorthand for liberal economic and social development based on broad transformations guided by social science and planning.[21]

Accolades for the TVA came in the midst of general applause for technology's role in the American war effort. Stuart Chase wrote in 1945 that Thorstein Veblen would have cracked a "sardonic smile" in response to this situation as "his technicians and scientists have come roaring into their own as the acknowledged and undisputed arbiters of human destiny."[22] But the understanding that utilizing technology had political and social repercussions caused considerable anxiety in the mid-1940s. At war's end, Vannevar Bush, leader of the Office of Scientific Research and Development, sounded an alarm to safeguard the United States' continued international preeminence. Bush inspired considerable discussion inside and outside the government and reinforced the vital place of technology in American society, both domestically and in its international affairs. Belief in the importance of American science and technology for national security expanded beyond military innovation. Emblematic was a 1947 report by the National Planning Association (NPA), asserting "our technology is now one of our most precious national resources . . . it has helped put us, and it will help keep us, in a position of world leadership." It was the best means to aid "the masses of mankind . . . reaching for higher living standards." The need to actively offer these resources internationally touched a reality of the emerging Cold War learned in the 1930s. Any country offering technological aid to promote its vision of modernity bought influence, for "with their technology will go a strong imprint of their own economic and political structure."[23]

FROM RECONSTRUCTION TO MODERNIZATION: DEVELOPMENT IN A CHANGING WORLD

As these discussions were occurring in Washington, international programs to further economic and social development were well under way. At the forefront was the United Nations Relief and Rehabilitation Administration (UNRRA), which had been operating in China through the war years. Dean Acheson, who was present at UNRRA's conception in Atlantic City, New Jersey, in 1943, recalled that "rehabilitation" was hastily added to the body's title. At the time, members of the wartime United Nations alliance were beginning to see that postwar aid might be more than relief. In practice, rehabilitation could be indistinct. It could be repair of war damage or thorough reconstruction of societies whose real problems were rooted in underdevelopment. One of the first actions of its staff was to attempt to clarify the meaning of the words used to describe UNRRA's work. It was a sign the organization shared in the confusion brought by shifting meanings in developmental terminology. "Rehabilitation" and "relief" with their promises of immediate succor were distinguished from "reconstruction," which retained its long-held (albeit increasingly fuzzy) meaning of restructuring societies to meet modern demands. However, they were not mutually exclusive. Rehabilitation was also a moment to lay deeper foundations for a larger and longer process to produce what some, like Eugene Staley, were beginning to label "modernisation."[24]

The Americans dominating its staff undoubtedly influenced the organization's outlook. There were also direct connections to the New Deal. UNRRA's head, Herbert Lehman, New York State's governor during the Depression, had strong connections to other New Dealers, and early candidates for important posts were high-level members of the TVA. UNRRA's developmental aspects were popular with many around the globe. However, the organization's mandate, laid down in the midst of World War II, only ran until 1947. As that date approached, numerous governments as well as international and U.S. NGOs urged UNRRA be maintained indefinitely, with its emphasis turned to development. The U.S. government's interest, however, had waned. UNRRA's initial popularity among the American public quickly ebbed after the war. It was compared unfavorably to parallel efforts headed by Herbert Hoover (reprising a similar role he played after World War I), and Truman grew frustrated with Lehman's management.[25] Critics in Congress saw continuance as an open-ended, expensive commitment. They had a point: the United States contributed nearly 70 percent of its $3 billion budget. As the Cold War took form, there were accusations that the emerging Soviet Bloc was misusing funds. Discontent was not confined to communists, however; there were suspicions Britain was using UNRRA as a till for proxies in Greece and elsewhere. These accusations only made it more politically unpalatable and the United States refused renewal. By the summer of 1947, UNRRA had concluded its operations in Europe, and its programs in Asia followed before the end of the year.[26]

Considering the shattered state of the world after a war and the early Cold War rivalries it had to negotiate, UNRRA's tangible accomplishments were impressive. Into the 1960s, UNRRA was seen by many as a defining moment in post–World War II aid efforts. While modernization had not been an explicit goal of UNRRA at its inception, in operation it was seen as a logical outgrowth of the agricultural, public health, and industrial reconstruction the organization had performed. By the end of UNRRA's mandate, modernization had become an inextricable part of the organization's activities in underdeveloped parts of Asia—and by extension the new United Nations which had subsumed it following the war. Its example tutored those who continued to work in the expanding field of international development. It not only justified conceptually that development could be performed on a global scale but was instructive on the practical elements of development. UNRRA drove home existing beliefs that technical assistance was not merely desirable but "an indispensable element" of any large program to remake societies.[27]

In UNRRA's place the United States wanted to emphasize bilateral aid relationships. Of course, such an approach also allowed more direct U.S. control over how the funds were used. However, this shift did not mean the United States abandoned the United Nations as a means to help foster the modernization of the world. After UNRRA dissolved, the United States took pains to assure that the UN family of organizations had a set of institutional resources to promote modernization. In fact, the United States took a leading role in grafting a developmental mission onto the United Nations Organization from its conception. As with UNRRA, much of this was connected to the needs of postwar reconstruction. However, the creation of various bodies within and connected to the UN system were outgrowths of the wider goals of the UN's founders. At its founding in 1945 there were great hopes that the body would be the central means to promote world stability and prevent conflict.

Its creation and the establishment of its institutional capacities were a reflection of the broad importance and acceptance of many liberal development ideas internationally. The UN also serves to illuminate many examples and ideas that would serve as the core of a consensus on development that would reign during the postwar years. Efforts to promote harmony through the UN were a multifaceted application of liberal internationalist ideas. The founders of the UN realized that conflict was as much social and cultural as political and economic: as "wars begin in the minds of men, it is in the minds of men that the defenses of peace must be constructed."[28] Nevertheless, economic issues were a cornerstone, particularly in light of the hard lessons of the 1930s and 1940s. Worldwide depression was seen as the catalyst for the militant nationalism that sparked World War II. A belief that economic growth fostered political and social stability was etched into the UN Charter. Chapter IX, Article 55(a) called upon all members of the body to pledge their support for the "creation of conditions of stability and well-being which are necessary for peaceful and friendly relations among nations . . . the United Nations shall promote . . . higher standards of living . . . economic and social progress and development." Initially, the Economic and Social Council (ECO-SOC) was nominated as the "principal organ" through which the UN would promote economic growth worldwide. Weak powers granted to ECOSOC and institutional overlap with other UN institutions worked against these ambitions. Nevertheless, it would evolve into a clearing-house of development ideas and its regional committees would serve as platforms from which numerous modernization programs would be launched.[29]

The "specialized agencies" would come closer to fulfilling this vision. Leading the way were the World Health Organization (WHO), the Food and Agriculture Organization (FAO), and UNESCO. All were active glob-ally, providing technical assistance from the end of World War II onward. They helped to fill the void left by UNRRA following its dissolution. The FAO, a wartime creation, assumed responsibility for technical assistance programs in nine countries in Asia, Europe, and Africa when UNRRA expired. Programs in China show the spread of its activities. By the late 1940s, FAO technicians were managing a massive rinderpest control pro-gram for livestock, flood control on the Pearl River, irrigation projects near Canton, surveys in North China, and a collection of extension pro-grams to modernize agricultural practices. These continued until the FAO withdrew from the mainland before the communist advance in 1948. The WHO also found some of its early missions defined by UNRRA's legacy. It would inherit UNRRA's malaria control programs, which were seen as a vital component of agricultural rehabilitation programs.

Endemic to many parts of the world, malaria lowered human produc-tivity that, in turn, brought poor agricultural yields. This made the dis-ease, and the mosquitoes that carried it, a barrier to modernization. Here, the transformation of the environment as a critical element to the postwar modernization process reemerges. It was not only malaria but also a col-lection of infectious diseases that had to be removed or controlled. Funda-mental alteration of disease ecology was another way natural systems had to be transformed to serve development. The excitement over DDT fol-lowing its introduction as an insecticide in the 1940s was a function of this perception. Lavished on the countryside of numerous countries, DDT's express purpose was often the annihilation of malaria's hosts as an overture to rural development programs.[30]

At its creation in 1948, the WHO took the reigns of anti-malaria ef-forts. It was not the first body to undertake such public health programs to control infectious disease. The interwar period saw numerous govern-ments and the Rockefeller Foundation commit themselves to disease erad-ication programs. Malaria was a prime target, with Italy being a locus of activity. Mussolini's Fascist government, with Rockefeller's support, made impressive gains, particularly in Italy's Pontine marshes, opening up to habitation and cultivation areas that had once been hives of disease.

Following World War II, the Pontine was recalled by UNRRA and the WHO. However, they turned to the United States—specifically the TVA—for a more politically correct model. A basic part of the TVA's own program was an extensive and successful malaria control campaign. It was also untainted by dealings with dictatorship. Because of this it was a reputable source of technical and material support for UNRRA's and the WHO's anti-malaria campaigns. Into the 1950s, health officials from the UN looked to the TVA for inspiration for global malaria eradication and larger public health schemes linked to economic and social development. For these sorts of operations, one leading health official mused that "a world TVA would . . . be a fantastic thought."[31]

UNESCO also invested in development. Its early attentions were on "Fundamental Education"—the extension of popular and universal schooling for all the peoples of the world. Within this project lay the assumption that there was "interdependence between economic and social development and education." This connection was acute in poorer and less developed areas where basic education would serve the establishment of modern societies.[32] To demonstrate this link, UNESCO fell back on the TVA. It demonstrated that "economic progress . . . is greatly advanced by a broad programme of fundamental education." By pioneering new methods of extension and education it had become "probably the best example . . . of what can be accomplished by bringing scientific knowledge and technical assistance to areas which are . . . underdeveloped." UNESCO's Director-General, Julian Huxley, continued to be "astounded" by the progress these methods brought to the South. This American example was "of great value to the world," in no small measure because it "showed what can be done by a democracy" in areas essential to development.[33]

Also counted among the specialized agencies was the International Bank for Reconstruction and Development (IBRD—later known as the World Bank). It was given a developmental mission "almost by accident" at formation. Even so, the conception of its role was pregnant with assumptions articulated by Staley and others in the 1930s that global stability could be secured by prosperity based in economic growth.[34] The bank's initial concept came from a U.S. Treasury official, Harry Dexter White, in 1942. His initial proposal was focused on the "stupendous task of world-wide economic reconstruction." However, the bank and attached "stabilization fund" (eventually the International Monetary Fund) were also assurance to the global public that a UN victory would not return a flawed prewar economic system. They were signs the United States would remain engaged with the "war torn and impoverished" to "help them in the long and difficult task of economic reconstruction." A conduit for capital and technical expertise, the Bank's mission presupposed that reconstruction would go beyond repair to *increase* world production, including areas lying well outside the theaters of war.[35] In its early years, the Bank provided only limited funds to Europe and underachieved even in that restricted role. Only in the 1950s did the IBRD reorient toward the developing world. However, the broad mandate given the Bank at inception allowed it to evolve into one of the most important actors on the international development stage.[36]

As the UN grew into its developmental mission, the proliferation of councils, commissions, programs, and specialized agencies demanded coordination. This was due, in no small part, to the fact that there was demand for their services. Numerous countries were already turning to the UN as a means to get the technical aid they felt they needed for reconstruction and development. As early as 1948, Asian countries were petitioning the Economic Commission for Asia and the Far East (ECAFE) for help in gathering technical assistance from the Supreme Command of the Allied Powers (SCAP) in American-occupied Japan. There were requests from ECAFE to SCAP for the release of Japanese technicians to parts of their empire that had only recently seen them depart.[37] The desire of underdeveloped nations for technical assistance for development also led to new institutional arrangements within the UN. In response to calls for aid and the increasing activities of the specialized agencies in technical assistance, the UN established the Technical Assistance Program in 1948.[38] While the program was popular with poorer states, the United States was a prime mover. Although its budget was relatively small, the new program was also seen as a mechanism to complement and integrate the work of the international organization's assortment of development bodies.[39]

The Gospel of Liberal Modernization

When the UN discussed how modernization might actually be achieved, the TVA and the liberal development it stood for led the conversation. In 1948, Arthur "Tex" Goldschmidt, an old hand from New Deal efforts in the South, corralled the TVA to participate in a major scientific conference on development at the UN.[40] The TVA staff did not have to search far for examples. They turned to a place that Lilienthal had told Henry Wallace was already a "symbol" of TVA's economic and social development prowess—Alabama.[41]

Decatur, Alabama, specifically, served as a reading from the TVA's "gospel" of economic progress. In fact, citizens of Decatur were flown up to the UN's temporary headquarters on the TVA's own airplane. They described the transformation of their poor community through the out-

side intervention of the TVA, with the all-important consent and participation of the locals themselves. "The Decatur Story" was the centerpiece
of the U.S. presentation to the conference, but there was still a "field trip"
for delegates from forty-two countries around the TVA itself.[42] The TVA
offered more than just a development model for the programs of the in-
fant United Nations. It helped shape the institutional contours of the new
body. At the request of Dean Acheson, in 1946 the TVA detached members of its own Regional Studies and Engineering staff to serve with the
UN on administrative issues. One specialist, Howard K. Menhinick,
served as the director of the Headquarters Planning Staff, responsible for
selecting a permanent home for the UN in the United States.[43]

Obviously, these efforts did not turn the fledgling United Nations into
a TVA extension service. What they do demonstrate is how existing development concepts were coursing through international society and the construction of an American-dominated liberal order. That the TVA appeared
so easily and often in the context of so many basic discussions regarding
modernization demonstrates the importance of the liberal development
ideas it represented to the overall conception of how modernity could best
be cultivated in a changing world.

Such prominence also exhibits another aspect of the TVA's role in U.S.
foreign affairs. By highlighting the TVA and the economic advance of
the South, the U.S. government distanced itself from its colonial legacy.
Demonstrating capacity to raise standards of living did not have to touch
on politically inconvenient examples of imperial adventures in Puerto
Rico, the Philippines, or Haiti. What is striking is how rarely these experiences were invoked by American officials as modernization took on increasing importance in global politics. Placing emphasis on domestic success had a further benefit. Again and again, American officials would tell
emerging nations that development aid was being offered by a nation that
had confronted its own underdevelopment and overcome it.

There was a great gap between what developed and underdeveloped
nations required. The differences were apparent as American officials confronted the numerous global issues surrounding relief, recovery, and development across the globe in the years after World War II. Flush with
the success of the New Deal, American planners advocated ideas rooted
in what has become known as "productionism" to repair and enhance
economies in Europe. Here collaboration among government, business,
and labor leaders would assure that harmful disputes and competition
over the fruits of industrial production would be curtailed. Contentious
issues were to be solved by supposedly impartial forces of engineering,
and scientific management, as well as state and regional planning. What
once had been political concerns could now be dealt with as technical
problems. The result would be increased productivity that would provide

economic benefits for all, easing social divisions. Such ideas were fundamental to the ERP. Their apparent success was supremely gratifying to
Americans. But there was an early understanding that while many parts
of the globe could use benefits similar to those produced by the Marshall
Plan, its reproduction was simply not possible outside industrialized
areas. Western Europe, despite the destruction visited upon it, retained a
deep technological and human infrastructure upon which to rebuild. The
skeletons of factories, power grids, and transportation networks all remained. Even more important, large numbers of well-trained and experienced technicians, engineers, managers, and bureaucrats were available.
Psychologically, these individuals already held the outlooks and had
crafted the institutions that made their societies modern. What the Europeans needed were the funds and organization to put them back to work.[44]

In essence, the perception reigned that Europe—and Japan—were already modern in decisive qualities. Many non-industrialized societies simply were not and would require a more thoroughgoing transformation.
This meant ideas and policy were very different when conversations
turned to strategically vital areas, particularly Asia. Programs which presumed massive technological as well as social change, like the TVA, were
prescribed, rather than replays of the Marshall Plan or the occupation
of Japan. Although Germany and Japan received enormous amounts of
American aid, they were not considered to be in the same category. They
were not to be modernized, at least in the same manner as places like
South Korea, China, or Iran might demand. Such assumptions cut across
official and unofficial worlds that were adopting new terms for processes
finding an important role in an international environment dominated by
the Cold War.

A moment where these views were apparent was a 1947 conference on
the "economic and social reconstruction of the Far East" at Stratford,
England, convened by the Institute for Pacific Relations. As it gathered
eminences to participate, the IPR was taking a critical look at its own
place in a radically new international situation where East-West relations
were "being drastically altered." This was also transforming institutional
arrangements, challenging the place of NGOs like the IPR with an "increasingly official world" populated by state institutions. Nevertheless,
like many other nongovernmental groups, IPR staff felt they held some
"notable advantages."[45] One advantageous element was the IPR's ability
to attract important constituencies to its meetings. Stratford included
members of the IPR and a selection of officials from the Dutch, British,
U.S., South Korean, Canadian, Indian, and Chinese Nationalist governments as well as various private groups (including the Rockefeller Foundation). Luminaries included Arnold Toynbee, John King Fairbank,
Wilma Fairbank, Lossing Buck, and Owen Lattimore.[46]

Their discussions were complicated by terminology in transition. Delegates, like most involved in policy, knew the keyword "reconstruction" no longer exclusively meant the recovery from war damage. H. Belshaw defined the term as it was commonly used at the time:

> In the narrower and more precise sense, the term is used to connote the rebuilding of material equipment and reestablishment of the economic and political organizations that have been destroyed or damaged by war; but since the world has changed greatly in the meantime, and with it the requirements of the separate countries, it is not desirable that reconstruction should aim at re-establishing the same economic pattern as existed before the war. Rather, it should be concerned (as an intermediate goal) with restoring both economic potential and living standards to the levels which previously existed. . . Reconstruction, as we have just regarded it, extends beyond the period of relief and rehabilitation, but should normally be completed in most countries in five to ten years. *We shall use the term more loosely, however, as covering also the continuing process of economic progress and development, and it is with this long-run objective, covering at least several decades, that we shall mainly be concerned.* It would be more accurate, therefore, to use the phrase "economic, social, and political development or progress" than the term "reconstruction"; but the latter is easier to handle, and there is some advantage in preferring a term in common use, even at the expense of somewhat straining its content.[47] (emphasis original)

Belshaw's comments indicate that reconstruction was indeed conceptually strained when it came to the postwar world. Increasingly, discussants turned to a term being loaded with developmental meanings—modernization.

Proceedings at Stratford showed the general agreement that development could be a valve to defuse root causes of political and social instability. However, there was skepticism about "superimposing an industrialized structure upon an unreformed agrarian economy." To participants it was misguided to measure the development of "the ancient civilizations of the Orient by the yardstick of European or American development." Solutions acceptable in Europe could not have the same impact. Modernization in Asia had to be seen in context with the "traditional inertia" of its peasant societies. Western education and technology were viewed as a means to break Asians out of their perceived torpor, but both faced the cultural barriers of "conformity and subordination to the social will." Even the need to modernize the vocabularies and writing systems of Asian languages, viewed as a hurdle to economic and social change, was discussed.[48] The consensus was that while Asia (and by extension other poorer nations) urgently required extensive change brought by Western expertise, it was best applied in manners that allowed underdeveloped societies to better absorb the aid.[49]

Influential members of the U.S. State Department shared much in these assumptions. Increasing difficulties inspired a reassessment of U.S. policy in the Far East in early 1948. Tenacious focus on the recovery of Japan was a concern, as was the decline of the GMD regime. With the possibility of China being a development beacon rapidly receding and the rest of the region buffeted by crises, there was need for a comprehensive plan for the development of Asia. The ERP demonstrated such regional planning was possible and heightened hopes the United States would implement a similar program for Asia. Mostly its example made it harder to justify inaction while "the Orient falls apart."

To hold it together, members of the State Department suggested an Asiatic Recovery Program (ARP). Its title was about all it borrowed from the European program. It was steeped in established modernization assumptions. The critical need was to install greater economic capacity than existed prewar. It was understood that such an expansion would require the creation of new institutions and social capacities to overcome the "tenacious ancient ways" within most Asian nations. For the Americans it was "inescapable . . . that whereas the ERP implies recovery to something like pre-war status, ARP implies new industrialization and development on an impressive scale." Many Western innovations would require alteration to fit local circumstances as "the grosser foibles of caucasian institutions are probably more transparent to the mongoloid-malay-indo-polynesian world than to the less critical bulk of the western world." Dollars alone could not be relied upon. The United States would have to promote deep technological and institutional change that would, by their nature, alter societies. This was viewed as a long-term and expanding program that would evolve over decades.[50]

Through 1948, the Far Eastern bureaus of the State Department considered remedies for a swelling communist threat. The discussions would draw in figures of growing importance in American strategy, including Paul Nitze and Henry Labouisse (a Marshall Plan staffer and later head of the ICA). The assumption was that communism had "systematically shifted its attention to Asia" because of the success of the Marshall Plan. However, the European emphasis of American foreign policy had created increasing complaints on the part of Asian nations that concern with Europe was overshadowing their own reconstruction. Proposals were put forward for the United States to funnel aid through the Economic Cooperation Administration (ECA) or a similar body for a "Far Eastern Recovery Program."[51]

In the fall of 1948, Nitze summarized thinking that U.S. economic policy had a "definiteness and comprehensive purpose in Europe which seems to be lacking in the Far East." The need was to find a means to stitch together disparate efforts in a diverse region. Modernization was the means, but it faced considerable obstacles. In part, this was due to the fact that the nations in Pacific Asia did not share common religious, political, and cultural traditions. They were deficient in modern technical capabilities. Chronic instability only accentuated such problems. Nitze agreed with many contemporaries who saw the qualitative differences in efforts in poorer countries, stating a "Marshall Plan approach . . . would not necessarily apply in the Far East." A comprehensive program was needed to coordinate U.S. economic aid programs in the Far East. The ECA was considered a prime candidate to play such a role. However, implementation of such broadly conceived ambitions was beyond the capacity of a single government entity. Nitze urged the participation of UN, private, nongovernmental, and "quasi-governmental" agencies in any operation to improve the economic life of the region.[52]

These suggestions were greeted positively as insightful statements on U.S. political and strategic posture in Asia. Emphasis on a program that centered on economic and social development would go far in combating the impression in Asia that communism was the best means for "overthrowing the old order and achieving social and economic progress." It would avoid a negatively conceived policy that was disposed to merely "pointing out the evils of communism." An affirmative program required modernization to fulfill "aspirations of the Asiatic masses." It would be best built upon a "substantial program of technical training . . . as well as . . . economic assistance." It was imperative because Asia lacked "trained personnel and knowledge in the field of government administration as well as in that of engineering and production techniques." But providing the modern skills and outlooks that came with this training would have outsized impacts and come at a "modest cost . . . [with] greater benefit than large programs of capital imports."[53] Propaganda would accompany these efforts to persuade Asians that U.S. aims were constructive and free of "imperialistic aspirations." All of this was cast as collaborative, done with the cooperation of NGOs and the United Nations.[54]

These early thoughts demonstrate that liberal modernization assumptions were well rooted in international politics in the years just after World War II. Perceiving societies as backwards, the solutions U.S. planners put forward were regimes of technical assistance that would bring social and political change. All was done to combat a totalitarian threat. The ARP idea, while never implemented as such, shows how American planners already saw modernization as a strategic mechanism. Their thinking was already steeped in widely accepted assumptions about how development should be implanted. It was from this milieu that a global technical assistance plan took root in the Truman White House. Development ideas already in operation in various institutions and sites around the globe rose to the fore as a means to contend with the political and social problems of the "backwards" and "traditional" societies in Asia. In this formulation, it was not just American wealth that was a weapon, but also the richness of America's technical and scientific capabilities that could promote modernization. Enmeshed in an American liberal outlook, modernization promised a desperately needed counterpoint to communist influence.

BOLD BUT NOT SO NEW: POINT FOUR AND MODERNIZATION AS OFFICIAL POLICY

Such discussions were part of the varied official and nongovernmental ferment on modernization that paved the way for Truman's "Bold New Program." The immediate political origins of Point Four are credited to Benjamin Hardy, a former press officer with Nelson Rockefeller and the IIAA during 1944–46. He had been impressed with the impact of technical assistance programs sponsored by the IIAA on areas of Latin America.[55] After moving to the State Department, Hardy, like so many others, was inspired by the success of the Marshall Plan. It raised hopes that the United States could regain the initiative worldwide in the deepening Cold War. In the fall of 1948, Hardy composed a report, the "Use of U.S. Technological Resources as a Weapon in the Struggle with International Communism," based on this premise.[56]

Hardy felt that American foreign policy was too easily tarred as anticommunist and unconstructive—essentially negative. A broader aid program was needed to silence this critique while building on the momentum of the Marshall Plan. An "excellent instrument" to fulfill this plan lay in "America's immense technological resources," and its "affirmative use" placed strength against comparative Soviet weakness. An extended program of technical aid "would show the common peoples of other countries how the application of techniques and procedures that have proved themselves in this country can directly benefit them." Hardy agreed with colleagues: the Marshall Plan formula could not work everywhere. Nevertheless, the United States had the perfect method for modernizing poorer nations—the "TVA concept." Its reputation could convince the world such liberal modernization could be implemented in wide portions of the globe. With its methods to achieve the "definite promise of a better life," Hardy's proposition departed from existing development thinking only in scale.[57]

When his plan bogged down in the State Department bureaucracy, Hardy went directly to George Elsey, a close Truman adviser. Elsey was instantly taken with the concept. He had been seeking a central idea for his boss's inaugural address, and Hardy's idea "was exactly what I had been searching for." Other White House advisers gravitated to the proposal, and with the inaugural looming, Truman included the plan in his address. Political considerations lay in the foreground, with the president's technical assistance program clearly defined as a program to help people help themselves—remembering the dismissal of earlier calls by Henry Wallace for global aid as mere "Milk for Hottentots." Qualifications aside, Truman invested because he thought it bore a strong resemblance to TVA efforts to develop parts of the South.[58] Still, State Department officials were leery of the poorly defined proposal. The late date of the idea's appearance and the speed with which it emerged as a policy statement left many out of the loop. Dean Acheson claimed his introduction to the plan came at the inaugural (although prominent Truman staff disputed this). Emphasis on the surprise of Point Four has fed a belief that the program was a radical departure from established policy.[59]

In fact, the genealogy of Point Four was widely discussed at the time. A week after his speech, Truman said it had been percolating in his mind since the start of the Marshall Plan and aid to Greece and Turkey.[60] Whether the president's claim was entirely true is open to question, but those directly involved in the sponsorship of technical assistance at the time saw its origins. In February 1949, the State Department placed Point Four in context with existing programs such as the IIAA, ECA, and those of the UN. Paul Hoffman later claimed the ECA initiated discussions for a larger technical assistance program. Arbiters at the Council on Foreign Relations saw diverse and deeper historical links. They discussed the "phenomenon of the year" as just "a catalyst that led to the coalescing of many ideas, projects, and drives." In essence, they thought there was "nothing really new" about the program since many of "our fathers were engaged in private point fours for a long while."[61]

The significance of the 1949 inaugural is not that it created postwar development as such but enshrined it as a permanent part of the official foreign policy apparatus of the U.S. government. A permanent bureaucracy then served as a center point for the integration of existing private and government development activities. Diverse thinking on modernization had been given a policy shorthand in "Point Four." When it came to convincing domestic and international publics that Point Four was worth supporting, its links to domestic reform were pushed to the fore. The successful development of America's own South during the Depression was regularly trotted out to explain not only what the U.S. government was attempting but how it was going to do it. Pitching "Point Four" to the public, Truman was quite comfortable equating his new foreign assistance program with the TVA, noting:

> We [the United States] are somewhat famous for . . . technical knowl-
> edge. What I propose to do is to present to the peoples of the world
> that know-how . . . That is what Point Four means . . . I see immense
> undeveloped rivers and valleys all over the world that would make
> TVA's . . . All it needs . . . is somebody who knows the technical
> approach to their development.[62]

Truman's reference to the TVA was hardly accidental, reflecting think-ing among his own advisers who saw it as an international model of how to promote development. It was not simply the material gain the TVA had delivered that made it appealing as a synonym for the global development being proposed. The "grass roots" concepts of the modernization spon-sored by the TVA were understood as inclusive and democratic, and were assumed to be transferable to the rest of the world. Bathing Point Four in the glowing reputation of the New Deal development program was a way to make the content, extent, and goals of the project legible to domestic and international audiences.[63]

Truman did not have to carry the comparison far. In the months follow-ing Truman's speech a chorus of support struck up, with the loudest voices coming from liberals who saw Point Four as an extension of the New Deal to the world. For some, the embrace of modernization was a way to come to terms with Truman's leadership as much as it was about finding the best Cold War policies.[64]

Many saw it as one of the brightest lights lingering from 1930s reforms. Journalist John Gunther, an early visitor to the TVA, believed that it "proves that the idea of unified development works" and applications were "almost boundless . . . its horizon could be illimitable." This was hardly surprising for "the greatest single American invention of this cen-tury, the biggest contribution the United States has yet made to society in the modern world."[65] Historian Henry Steele Commager also embraced the authority, describing it in breathless prose as "probably the greatest peacetime achievement of twentieth-century America." What it had ac-complished was "a triumph [proponents] had scarcely dared to anticipate . . . It was politics, but in the Aristotelian sense of the word . . . a shining example of William James's moral equivalent of war."[66]

Preexisting excitement regarding the TVA idea easily attached to Point Four. The framework it offered included means to effectively transfer America's strongest asset, its technological capacity, while promising to contain the negative effects of technology and planning with democracy. *The New Republic,* devoted to the TVA cause domestically, joined the chorus in support of international technical assistance following Truman's speech. As "nearly all countries are backward, from the American standard of mass production," the large and complicated technologies common in the United States could not simply be transferred wholesale. There was a need to provide technology on a smaller scale, tailored to the needs of these less developed countries. Point Four acknowledged this reality and could offer methods based on the TVA as the authority represented the finest "American 'know-how' available for export." The international appeal of *TVA: Democracy on the March* had helped it "become our best-known, most highly appreciated institution." Because of this acceptance and its adaptability, TVA-style development could be a global "foundation on which to base all phases of an enriched and growing economy."[67]

Arthur Schlesinger, Jr., in his 1949 call to arms, *The Vital Center*, stressed the importance of the TVA, and the liberal development it represented, in confronting communism. He believed that the TVA demonstrated how the state could effectively engage in economic programs without it becoming overcentralized and a "total planner." These lessons assumed more importance in a world experiencing a "social revolution." The postwar wave of decolonization had given the USSR considerable status with former colonial peoples because of its stands for racial equality and against imperialism. However, the democratic and inclusive model of the TVA allowed the United States to deploy its greatest asset, "technological dynamism," against the "political dynamism" of the Soviets. Schlesinger felt:

> No other people in the world approach the Americans in mastery of the new magic of science and technology. Our engineers can transform arid plains or poverty-stricken river valleys into wonderlands of vegetation and power . . . The Tennessee Valley Authority is a weapon which, if properly employed, might outbid all the social ruthlessness of the Communists for the support of the peoples of Asia.[68]

Walter Lippmann echoed Schlesinger, believing that TVA-inspired programs highlighted the vital difference between U.S. and communist development styles. The Soviet model promised rapid economic growth but with the penalty of authoritarian regimentation. Lippmann thought the U.S. model, illustrated by a 1949 UN survey mission report for the development of the Middle East led by Lilienthal's successor at the TVA, Gordon Clapp, showed that modernization could be reconciled with popular government.[69]

Liberal excitement with Point Four was matched by conservative skepticism. The "collectivist and statist" orientation of foreign aid was as dangerous to American political health as was the New Deal. Conservative journalist Henry Hazlitt denounced foreign aid as a harbinger of socialism in American life and equated it with the visions of Earle Browder. Hazlitt was no fringe figure: he wrote for *Newsweek* and other mainstream magazines. Views that Point Four was collectivist echoed criticism of state policies from the 1930s. This posturing aside, Hazlitt saw the extensive nature of the development represented. Echoing the perspectives of other conservatives, he thought that once the United States embarked upon a global mission to improve the lot of "economically backward people everywhere," commitments became "endless and bottomless." Stewart Alsop figured it might become an important pillar of American foreign policy or, just as easily, this "fuzzy idea . . . will peter out into nothing and be forgotten." Dissent also came from those who saw the project as open-ended and worried that an ill-defined program would squander public funds. Views like these, dissenting from the growing consensus, would continue to reverberate in sectors of public debate. They are a reminder that even as modernization ideas rose to ascendancy in policy, forceful critiques were always present.[70]

Views forged in the development competition of the 1930s were repeated. To supporters of the newly articulated U.S. foreign aid programs, principles borrowed from Lilienthal's TVA underlined the differences between the development concepts favored by the rival Cold War encampments. Using the TVA as a guide, America's new aid programs could claim inclusiveness. This made any American undertaking necessarily more flexible, alert, competitive, and, by extension, effective than its totalitarian competitors. It also reassured American liberals, reminded by war against Nazi Germany of the hazards of state planning and centralized authority, that a potentially totalitarian concept was not being exported.[71]

American Cold War grand strategy in the late 1940s privileged economic power to contain the USSR. Modernization became one node of an approach to shore up resistance to a Soviet threat that, in George F. Kennan's estimation, was largely psychological but nevertheless real. Kennan's views were freighted with many assumptions from the 1930s. Ideological struggle with communism was only a "complication to the disease" afflicting the West as a whole. Reining in the "runaway horse of technology" and reconciling the "roles of the state and of individual initiative" to display "that a free society can govern without tyrannizing" was the larger historical background against which the emerging Cold War would be fought. These questions were global in their import, although he fretted that the West had not found a way to "speak to the backward and poverty-stricken peoples of the world . . . and arouse their awareness of what they stand to lose by selling their birthrights of newly won independence to the forces of modern totalitarianism." Kennan nursed doubts about the overall importance of the developing world to the struggle. Preferring a focus on industrialized nations, during 1948 he rebutted calls for economic aid to poorer peoples who were, politically, no more than "volatile children."[72] Nonetheless, he toed aspects of the administration line on the eve of Point Four's announcement in 1949. To a War College audience, he explained the need to aid all nations in efforts to develop and deliver contributions to world "civilization."[73] Regardless of the ambivalence of the architect of containment, Point Four with New Deal bona fides was equated in many circles with foreign assistance and modernization, which were becoming vital cogs in an emerging Cold War strategy.[74]

The significance of development to decolonizing nations was starkly presented to Americans. Newly independent India's prime minister, Jawaharlal Nehru, paid an official visit to the United States in late 1949. During his national tour the TVA was one of the anticipated stops. Nehru was fascinated, seeing a means to achieve the modern India he desired. It is no surprise he was given a tour. At the time, State Department officials assumed the TVA would be high on any foreign dignitary's agenda—"it's the first thing we think of," one diplomat admitted.[75] Nehru could also articulate why having an appealing model of development was strategically important. At one of the receptions during his trip, Nehru explained the complication of the desire in the "new nations" for development. He told his hosts the nature of global ideological struggle assured that Marxism and capitalism could not coexist. One would have to disappear. Victory would come to the system providing the greatest benefits to the peoples of the world.[76]

Nongovernmental Mobilization

Nehru voiced exactly what Americans feared and his speech helps explain why modernization took on increasing international significance in the late 1940s. With the stakes so high there was concern among interested groups that the job could be done and done well. Staff at the most influential nongovernmental group on the issue, the Rockefeller Foundation, expressed common concerns with the U.S. government commitment to global development. The foundation's reaction to Truman's program provides a window on the nuanced, if imperfect, views held by Americans already engaged in development at the time. Although gratified by Point Four, it was hardly a revelation as Rockefeller was dealing with realities of postwar development well before Truman spoke. In 1946, the foundation concluded that "one of the most important problems in the world today concerns the relationship between people who enjoy the benefits of modern civilization and those who do not."[77] Joseph Willits, head of the foundation's totalitarianism project in the 1930s, felt strongly that "this country should be focused much more directly on the problems of the less industrialized (I try to dodge the word backward, or colonial, or even undeveloped) areas."[78] Attacking the problem required making available modern knowledge and technology in education, health, and agriculture. Questions about how this should be implemented forced the foundation's Division of Social Sciences to wrestle with how to increase social science capacity in areas beyond Europe and North America. Creating a cadre of skilled technicians and social scientists was seen as vital to nations facing the pressures of independence. Training individuals to take up these roles would pay further dividends as they became catalysts for a broader transformation within their societies. Here Rockefeller utilized ideas accepted by Lilienthal and others that involvement with technology itself would aid in the psychological transformation needed to make people modern.[79]

Staff members were not blind to problems. Discussions to this effect were wide-ranging and thoughtful even as they betrayed biases and touches of elite paternalism. There was an appreciation that aspects of social science education in service of development might be received as political in character or simply as propaganda for "capitalist democracy."[80] Others questioned whether programs could give people in underdeveloped nations what they desired. Rockefeller and the United States would have to make judgments on what "will be useful in improving the well being of mankind . . . decisions in terms of a coherent program for advancing basic knowledge . . . this forces us . . . to the uncomfortable position of having to decide that the kind of assistance people would like is not the kind which will be sufficiently effective." Even so, they recognized that this reflected back on domestic shortcomings. They saw an American Achilles heel in the deficit of "real understanding of the peoples and what goes on among them."[81]

Modernization was believed to be irresistible and universal. Nevertheless, it was influenced by the politics surrounding the time, making intervention imperative to assure the right process prevailed. They saw the lines of Cold War division. Poorer peoples were now left two variants of Western development—Soviet and American/European. It was hard to deny that the Soviet version was "very attractive" and in certain conditions was "bound to win out." Philip Mosley felt that expanding aid to regions outside Europe was as logical as it was necessary. But the United States had to act soon as Asia was transitioning from a passive "contemplative" to a modern "active" state and in "this transition the American form of activism is in competition . . . with the Soviet form of activism."[82]

With the U.S. government increasingly involved in this type of "activism," Willits felt the "rich storehouse of lessons" from Rockefeller international work could tutor it. A shrinking globe meant that underdeveloped nations would not be permitted to "evolve their own societies as they might choose." The cultural, economic, and political "penetration" already in gear would stay in motion. The U.S. government was joining this process laden with a "maximum sense of our own power, our own interest, our own goodness and our own knowledge." Yet, brazen confidence on such a complex subject bordered on hubris. Rockefeller staff was aware the United States had "very little knowledge of the parties of the second part. Our conceit and our desire for speed gives us very little readiness to study these matters before acting," leading to "extravagance . . . [and] injury to the peoples and cultures we are trying to serve." Arrogance and shortsightedness would backfire and "help Russia in her campaign to win the minds and loyalties of these people . . . if we mess our advances up badly enough, we may become . . . the most hated country in the world.'"

Humility as much as confidence was the lesson imparted by the long experiences of private organizations. As a full understanding of the already detailed past of overseas development activity showed:

> Over the last fifty years various private (as well as public) agencies have had a lot of experience in trying to help backward peoples to help themselves. Foundations, missionary groups, business, and public agencies started out with naïve ideas as to the way of working. Souls to save, money to burn, areas to exploit—these were prominent motivations. All the mistakes in the book were made. But the best of these ventures learned and developed sound standards. Now we are likely through the government to repeat the mistakes that have been made by others, instead of systematically using their experience.[83]

Despite reservations, Raymond Fosdick, Rockefeller's recently retired president, was excited by Truman's ambitious plan, as it embodied much of what he had been advocating throughout his long career. Fosdick felt in "President Truman's Point Four program it [international development] has been given a sharp focus. While neither the problem nor the basic methods to deal with it are new, Point Four is both bold and new." This support would eventually draw him into an advisory role to the government and make him a development advocate. One person to whom he would turn for aid in efforts to cultivate public opinion was Gordon Clapp, fresh from surveys in the Middle East. The presence of the current chairman of the TVA would help clarify what the U.S. was attempting overseas.[84]

One reason Fosdick chose Clapp was his role as chairman of the UN sponsored Economic Survey Mission to the Middle East. This plan was meant to give concrete footings to a comprehensive regional development plan aimed at soothing chronic tensions in the region. Clapp's participation lent the operation greater attention in the United States but it also illustrates the understanding that modernization would be a multi-actor process.[85] Clapp was active in international development beyond the UN mission. His experience with the TVA in the 1930s and 1940s as Lilienthal's subordinate molded him into a supporter of international development. He believed that the lessons learned in Tennessee Valley could be applied elsewhere as "experience gained there is a valuable demonstration that would illuminate future policies concerning the development of resources in other regions."[86]

Like the others who were attracted to international development to fulfill America's goals in the early Cold War, Clapp believed that the process could not be the province of a single actor. Returning from the Middle East, Clapp met with private organizations whose interests overlapped with the development program. These included business interests, with oil companies predominating, but voluntary groups were the focus. The Red Cross, CARE, and the Near East Foundation were represented, as were religious organizations such as the American Friends Service Committee, the Catholic Welfare Conference, and the Church World Service. Clapp had learned from the grassroots efforts of the TVA that "one of the most important sources of human energy and direction in the Tennessee Valley development has been the work of voluntary groups, civic groups, private agencies, and local public agencies."[87] The mobilization of NGOs was a significant part of the government's aid efforts. By the end of the 1940s, the American state had considerable experience in rebuilding and modernization activity. It was well aware that such programs were enhanced by, if not dependent on, NGO expertise. Following the announcement of Point Four, one of the first items on the Truman administration's agenda was a concerted effort to franchise these groups.

In March 1949, Dean Acheson called for the collaboration of voluntary groups.[88] Mining the resources of civil society was vital, as they could provide the trained personnel necessary to execute Point Four projects.[89] Concurrent with the evolution of the legislation and institutional establishment of the Point Four program was a program to establish what, exactly, was the full extent of NGO activity around the world. David Lloyd, a Truman assistant, charted operations and outcomes of programs sponsored by voluntary groups. His data show a diversity of projects that girdled the world, involving thousands of individuals. The groups ranged from philanthropies like the Near East Foundation, to the private operations of the International Rescue Committee; as well as the religiously affiliated Unitarian Universalist Service Committee, the YMCA, YWCA, National Catholic Welfare Conference, and the American Friends Service Committee. What they did was nearly as varied, providing relief, and refugee resettlement as well as education, job training, agricultural training, public health assistance, and even large public works such as the construction of power plants and water works.[90]

Preexisting engagement of NGOs was built into the organization born to implement the Point Four idea, the Technical Cooperation Administration (TCA). The organization would describe itself as merely an extension of a long American tradition of sharing technical knowledge. As much of this history had been made by private groups, systematic cooperation with voluntary groups was viewed as an integral part of the TCA's mission. By 1952, it had issued over seventy different contracts with religious, private, and university groups to carry out technical assistance projects.[91]

Attention to voluntary groups was a function of the types of development activities entering the Point Four portfolio. In many corners of the globe Point Four did not attempt to recreate the massive scale of the TVA. Rather, it carried out discrete rural engineering projects, agricultural extension work, and health programs. These were heirs to progressive extension and reform projects that recently served the interwar efforts of NGOs and had been integrated into the TVA's own regional development, applied in the postwar programs of UNRRA, and mobilized for the Cold War operations of the ECA.[92] In the eyes of supporters, these projects did not have to be large to have an outsized impact. A continuing assumption in the development community was that relatively limited technical programs could nevertheless catalyze remarkable social and economic change. Over time, these types of programs would allow poorer countries to absorb greater quantities of aid and eventually a stream of commercial investment. If, as was stated in the 1950s, "the goal of development is a healthy, happy and free people," it had to penetrate all aspects of life. Success at home and abroad in creating cheerful, modern people required the aggregation of smaller programs that collectively altered the industries, farms, schools, medical care, and outlooks in their local communities. There was an acceptance that this interconnected process demanded coordination at national or regional levels. Planning served this end, and proof that the swirl of different efforts could be coordinated was programs like the TVA. Accordingly, smaller technical projects could comfortably serve as modules of what have been termed vast "high modernist" state projects demanding wide and deep transformation. This is another reason that discrete technical assistance projects comprising Point Four were so often and so readily related to the TVA, now comfortably established as the emblem of the larger process of liberal international development.[93]

This approach required building on existing government-NGO relationships. Cooperation with the government was already supported by important NGOs. Many sought government involvement in their work. Most organizations had learned from wartime experience that cooperation with the government had tangible benefits. Inspired in part by Hoover's humanitarian work during World War I, the president's War Relief Control Board was created early in World War II to provide legitimacy, coordination, and government resources (such as transportation and diplomatic heft) to the loose gaggle of private groups involved in relief and reconstruction. After the war, immense reconstruction commitments and the growing importance of development led established NGOs to clamor for maintenance of this mutualistic relationship. They worried that "wildcat" groups with agendas based on "dubious social planning" might fill the void. They called for a government body to ride herd on the community to prevent a "free for all" in foreign aid. The Advisory Committee on Voluntary Foreign Aid emerged in 1946. The committee and its successors were one mechanism the state used to corral the abilities of the private aid community.[94]

Point Four appeared as voluntary groups themselves were concluding that development would be a fixture of the postwar world. Some organizations focused on relief made a turn to modernization. In the late 1940s, Cooperative American Remittances to Europe (CARE) concluded that its eponymous relief packages were increasingly less necessary. It briefly considered disbanding entirely, but instead decided to stake its own territory in the burgeoning field of development assistance.[95] Other institutions, like the Phelps-Stokes Fund, hardly broke stride, continuing the same style of agricultural training and demonstration projects they had before the conflict.[96] Nevertheless, Phelps-Stokes and related groups felt the sands shifting. As a member of the Christian Agricultural Missions asserted in 1950:

> One becomes very conscious of the radically changed and changing environment in which the Christian missionary enterprise is being carried on. These changes are probably most striking in Asia, with China now under Communist domination. Korea, the Philippines, and Burma have achieved independence of sorts. Japan was never more open to missionary activities, and plans for the expansion of a rural program begun in the thirties, but stopped by the war, are now making rapid strides . . . A new factor in the world situation, that will in time influence the underdeveloped countries in which most missionary work is being carried on, is the program of the certain United Nations organizations . . . All these organizations have been deeply interested in the work which Christian missions have been doing over the past century and a half.[97]

Religious groups also saw their work linked to growing government involvement in development. Frank Laubach, a leading member of the National Council of Churches, was a strong supporter of the concept from its inception. Several years after the inaugural, Laubach informed Truman how he continued to "burn with passion for Point Four." He was not alone and promised that "Catholics as well as the Protestants are going now to push their own Point Four along with the government program." He would later laud Truman for providing the tools to spare India and Southeast Asia from communism with a program that placed "the world on a new higher level of ethical responsibility." Laubach's reaction to Point Four bordered on the ecstatic, but the promise of increased Christian activity was not exaggerated. In 1952, there were 18,000 American missionaries working in various parts of the globe, a 20 percent increase over 1950 alone.[98]

By and large, nongovernmental groups focused on development went along with the transformation brought by intensified governmental (and international) action. There were differences regarding both methods and goals, but a majority willingly accommodated. Members of the Cooperative League of America believed existing private religious organizations were well placed to serve the larger government program. As contractors for the TCA, they could begin work immediately in all corners of the globe.[99] Foundations, voluntary agencies, and missionaries had long seen their international role as one of uplift, with a sense of their place in stretching the promise of the United States to the rest of the world. Only now their efforts reforming the world were franchised as a major element of the Cold War foreign policy of their government. As Nelson Rockefeller noted, new government agencies were merely "following up on the pioneering work done by voluntary groups."[100]

Appealing to numerous constituencies, Point Four remained a powerful presence into the 1950s. It became strongly associated not merely with the administration but with Truman personally, who brought up the idea at every opportunity.[101] In spite of the president's fondness for the program and the excitement it inspired, Point Four ran into problems in execution. After its initial announcement, it faced the obvious difficulty of building an institution out of what was really only a concept. Into the summer of 1949 there was a discussion of what exactly would comprise the Point Four program and where it would operate. There was concern about how this global program would interact with the existing crowd of aid programs, particularly the ECA. Questions of what sort of status the program would hold within the State Department, and even whether the department was the right place to house it, were the first iterations of a continuing debate.

Despite all the interest and discussion, it took until July 1949 for the administration to introduce a bill to Congress asking for $45 million necessary to make Point Four an institutional reality. In Congress, with language that recalled bruising debates over the New Deal during the 1930s, opponents rallied against the program. Senator Robert A. Taft scoffed at Point Four's New Deal roots, dismissing it as a wasteful global WPA (Works Progress Administration). Uncomfortable with the statist elements of Point Four, Republicans sponsored a counterproposal in the House of Representatives. It emphasized private investment as the catalyst for growth, laying the groundwork for a persistent "trade versus aid" debate that saddles U.S. foreign aid to this day.[102]

Resistance only galvanized supporters. Voluntary and missionary groups excited by the prospect of a global government program came to the aid of the legislation.[103] Representative Jacob Javits, a Republican, threw his support behind the legislation, and hit the issue's crux:

> The Communists are going into the underdeveloped areas and telling people that their only hope for improvement is to adopt their communist doctrine and philosophy. What we must do if we are to meet that challenge successfully is to go into the same area and say "We will show you, with technical skill, how to deliver for yourselves the very goods which the communists only promise."[104]

Eventually a compromise bill with bipartisan support emerged, although House Republicans slashed the proposed budget. Following heated debate, the relatively paltry $35 million "Act for International Development" passed the Senate in June 1950.[105] Still, this was enough to satisfy supporters that their ideas had found a place in policy, as there was a pervasive belief that the modernization of "backward" societies could be catalyzed by relatively small amounts of technology, expertise, or capital. Most of all, the law, by creating the TCA and ensconcing it in the State Department, produced a permanent bureaucracy devoted to providing development aid worldwide.

Point Four never quite escaped the controversies stirred at its creation. Difficulties faced by the program have led some to write off Point Four and what it stood for, seeing it as a victim of the crises in the early 1950s.[106] There is something to this view. Military aid came to dominate attention following the rapid (and disturbing) collapse of the U.S.-trained South Korean Army in 1950 as the Americans scrambled to shore up client states. Yet, military concerns did not displace modernization concepts that surrounded Point Four. By the early 1950s, development aid was integrated into security questions, but hardly disappeared. This frustrated labor, farm, missionary, and voluntary interests, who agitated for economic aid. Voluntary groups were particularly uncomfortable with the switch, fearing escalation of the Cold War, rather than a tight focus on modernization. This left a residue of frustration obscuring the larger trajectory of the modernization ideas Point Four represented.[107]

Even as military issues grew in importance, development remained a prominent theme. Two high-level statements commissioned by Truman in 1950, the "Gray Report" and a report by the International Development Advisory Board—dominated by its charismatic chair, Nelson Rockefeller—display how development held U.S. foreign policy in a caducean embrace.[108] Determined to put "Point Four on the March," Rockefeller's statement (not unlike the Gray Report) called for centralized coordination of all forms of U.S. aid. Operating in the development world there, it was to get its programs "down to earth" using a number of means, including "joint commissions," to provide technical aid to improve agriculture, industry, and education in these societies. Among the goals was the coordination of NGOs as well as private investors. Both reports restated the essence of liberal development. Turmoil at the start of the Korean War meant Rockefeller and Gray reports would be limited in their impact. What they do expose is how maturing modernization ideas had become a basic currency in discussions on American foreign policy.[109]

Government aid programs were eventually reformed, perhaps not in the manner some proponents of development would have liked. In August 1951, Truman grouped existing military and economic aid under one body, the Mutual Security Agency (MSA).[110] The ECA, TCA, and other embryonic programs were scotched and responsibilities transferred to the new agency. Although technical assistance and other forms of development aid had lost their bureaucratic singularity, the ideas behind them did not cease to move policy. The MSA saw its technical assistance programs in places like the Middle East and Southeast Asia as important means to stabilize these important regions. For a time, MSA development assistance programs remained branded under the Point Four label.[111] Averell Harriman, the first director of the MSA, believed:

> In the area United States economic and technical assistance are needed to assure the stability which United States interests require by strengthening the ability of the governments concerned to render basic services to their people, by assisting in the repair of war devastation and arresting economic deterioration, and by helping to lay a basis for economic advance and improvement. Economic assistance is also required in most of these countries and in close support of United States military assistance.[112]

Supporters of mutual security and its developmental contents borrowed a quote from Eisenhower about the Cold War to make their case: "Remember that this conflict—spiritually, industrially, militarily—is all tied together. And let us not try to separate the parts because they relate one to the other."[113]

The bewildering shift of terminology and bureaucracies surrounding American foreign aid has led to confusion about the fate of Point Four and the style of modernization it promised. Even Truman's advisers were sometimes puzzled by what they meant when they spoke or wrote of "Point Four." There was a feeling that those two simple words had come to mean all technical assistance offered by the West. That, in fact, was what Truman desired. Point Four, as a rubric, was not limited to any one agency or individual nation. It encompassed all sorts of aid doled out by government agencies, the United Nations, or voluntary groups. In essence, Point Four became another label for technologically laden liberal development. Jonathan Bingham, a TCA veteran and lobbyist for foreign aid throughout the 1950s, believed the term was "here to stay" as a synonym for the larger process of using a spectrum of development aid to raise living standards. Well into the 1960s, Point Four remained a synonym for larger processes to achieve modernization.[114]

NEW IMPERATIVES, OLD FORMULATIONS: MODERNIZATION AND THE COLD WAR

By the early 1950s, Point Four and the development it labeled was in the foreground of the struggle for influence in what would soon be labeled the "Third World." For the United States, foreign aid and the social and economic development it was to synthesize were crucial in containing the Soviet threat in strategic areas of the globe. However, many of the assumptions driving the application of liberal development were formulations arrived at during the 1930s. Proof lay in the voices that continued to resonate. Eugene Staley articulated the place and importance of modernization in securing a liberal order against a totalitarian threat in the new world of the Cold War. Staley continued to haunt the Council on Foreign Relations as the body discussed a topic increasingly important to its members. There he instructed names that would become better known in the modernization fraternity—Rostow, Lerner, and Black. Someone who had articulated its importance back in the 1930s modulated these voices on the emerging topic of modernization. In this sense, the rise of modernization theory should be seen not as a new beginning but as an intellectual reflection and extension of ideas already in play in public life and foreign policy.[115]

In fact, Staley's 1954 book, *The Future of Underdeveloped Countries*, which framed much early Cold War understanding of the issue, displayed the continuity of ideas born in the crisis of Depression and war. Stating assumptions common among his peers, Staley assumed mechanical technology and the "social technologies" transferred through development left deep imprints on any society they touched. Therein lay the problem—there was the clear and present danger to the West in the competing and attractive model in Soviet communism. Staley was under no illusion that communist interest in underdeveloped nations was a cloak to enhance communist power at the center (i.e., Moscow) as part of a long-term global strategy to undermine the global system of liberal capitalism. Staley reiterated the belief that totalitarian communism was not revolutionary in and of itself. Those committed to the ideology were attempting to capture an ongoing revolution of rising expectations around the globe and turn it to their own ends. World war had changed international conditions, but the enemy remained the same. Staley did not want his readers to forget the United States had to take the responsibility to halt any movement that "assumes the proportions of a world menace." Fascism was such a peril but this "totalitarianism of the right" had been duly crushed. A "totalitarianism of the left" which "at this moment in history [is] by far the most powerful and virulent menace to free institutions and the most aggressive threat to . . . free nations" remained. Staley marked the Soviet Union as merely the latest variant of an ongoing totalitarian challenge to liberalism.[116]

In this ongoing ideological combat, the question of whose development model would dominate was not tangential. Staley revealed the very stakes of the Cold War itself:

> Under which of the two competing systems of life are the underdeveloped areas to be modernized, that of Communism or that of democracy? The issue is terribly important for the future of mankind. For at some point the areas now underdeveloped are likely to hold the balance of power between the two.[117]

Before Walt Rostow, Staley articulated a germ theory of modernization. The West, with the United States at its head, again had to control the totalitarian bacillus, and the "disease of society" it could spread in the poorer areas of the globe. Staley also outlined non-communist stages of development, based on liberal, democratic principles. Touching all areas of society, the predictable phases proceeded from (1) rising levels of production and income that would then (2) lead to "progress in democratic self-governance" which would in turn (3) provide for "democratic social relations" with "opportunities for self-development and respect for individual personality" collectively assuring (4) "less vulnerability to Communism and other totalitarianisms."[118]

Staley summarizes the arguments and motivations of anti-communist liberals supporting development aid. His book was so successful it warranted a revised edition that carried its conclusions into the 1960s. But if Staley understood the Cold War threat was merely a new version of an old enemy, he also knew that the developmental methods he was advocating were not entirely new either. Like many others, Staley was mustering existing concepts and setting them to task in an altered world situation. He understood that the principles and institutions at work in the 1950s were linked to the past. The concepts to which Staley turned were evolving, but they were based on formulations from the 1930s when liberals turned to development programs to contain totalitarian influence. Staley, in agreement with many contemporaries, saw the TVA as a way to demonstrate liberalism's developmental heft. He was convinced it did not need the dark political elements contained in totalitarian systems and was certain "we can have a T.V.A. . . . without nationalizing all the enterprises along Main Street."[119]

The geopolitics of global commitment and the specter of totalitarianism evident in the 1930s remained in Staley's articulation of the means and ends of U.S. Cold War modernization policy. While Staley cannot speak for the whole sprawling development community of the time, his views were mainstream and widely shared. His was a call to take up arms against a dangerous ideology, and the weapon of choice was, again, development. The question of which form of development would prevail internationally would frame basic elements of the Cold War. To secure its vision of a liberal postwar world order, the United States was under great pressure to show that its particular variant of development could produce progress internationally in competition with an attractive communist model. The need to demonstrate the vitality of liberalism globally in the face of ideological challengers had diffused from the 1930s into the Cold War of the 1940s. Along the way, terms and institutional relationships adjusted to new realities, but basic imperatives remained constant. New aid programs with global writs fell back on the reputations of programs like the TVA to show there were successful liberal instruments for promoting economic growth along with acceptable political and social change. They required the expertise of nongovernmental groups with long experience and the new capacities of evolving international institutions be bound to global strategy. A concoction of ideas emerging in depression and war set the foundations of a postwar consensus for the promotion of liberal modernization. All these elements would indispensable in the world's largest development program in the 1950s, the high-stakes effort to build a modern, viable, and anti-communist state in South Korea.

Chapter 4

"THE PROVING GROUND"

MODERNIZATION AND U.S. POLICY IN
NORTHEAST ASIA, 1945–1960

We have the proof and here is the proving ground.
—*Paul Hoffman, Seoul, 1948*

NEWSPAPER EDITORS gathered at Stanford University on June 24, 1950, to hear R. Allen Griffin speak on Asian affairs and U.S. policy. One of their own, the editor and publisher of the *Monterey Peninsula Herald*, drew a crowd more for his recent travels than membership in a guild. Griffin had led a high-level U.S. government survey mission across Asia. It was part of an attempt to resuscitate U.S. policy in Asia in the wake of communist victory in China. Reflecting those strategic realities, Griffin's activities also show how rapidly modernization ideas permeated U.S. foreign policy discourse and action. His was one of several expeditions advocating development as the means for the United States to regain leverage in a strategically vital part of the globe. Griffin's experience as deputy chief of the ECA mission to China was why he was given the assignment. Weaving through Vietnam, Malaya, Burma, Thailand, and finally Indonesia, the mission returned to Washington via Paris in May. Along the way its members witnessed a series of crises at critical moments. Every situation in this vital part of the world was seen through the lens of development. Generally sanguine, Griffin believed aid to foster modernization "could accomplish wonders in the area." His talk reflected the American preoccupation with Southeast Asia, but Griffin's comments were dated by the time he finished speaking. His concluding remarks were punctuated by news that South Korea had been invaded.[1]

War in Korea abruptly overshadowed American plans elsewhere. As a site of open conflict with communism, all aspects of American involvement took on oversized significance. Massive efforts to build a stable, non-communist state became a marquee event to demonstrate American developmental skills. What has often been overlooked is the fact that the South had been a developmental ward of the United States before the North Korean invasion of 1950. Many modernization ideas were actively employed in Northeast Asia from the concluding years of World War II. Nevertheless, in the years immediately after World War II, China was the biggest theater of action and was set to be a leading example of liberal modernization. It was logical: China's underdevelopment was a shared global assumption and the movement to alter this condition was long-standing. During the 1930s and early 1940s, Eugene Staley and others had speculated about and worked toward the modernization of China as a significant part of the defense and extension of a liberal order. Added to that, many institutions with considerable influence on the course of modernization were well rooted in China with lineages going back to the interwar period and beyond. Their existing concepts and programming were integrated into emerging U.S. government and international aid efforts that began to coalesce after the war. These approaches would become refugees from communist victory on the mainland. However, they found a new mission in the hasty U.S. occupation of the southern end of the Korean peninsula. There a series of authorities approached a society, which they viewed as having been left underdeveloped by history and a crude Japanese colonial overlord, as a modernization problem.

After the "loss" of China to communism, which denied the United States its preferred Asian stage to dramatize its brand of liberal development, southern Korea became vital. Although there was ambivalence in the U.S. commitment to the South into the late 1940s, the demands of the Cold War assured that Americans kept at their development efforts. Rather than being the curtain for these activities, the Korean War was an overture for a dramatic and big-budget act. The development of the Republic of Korea, an economic, political, and social entity that had never existed before as such, became the world's largest single development program through the 1950s. Direct confrontation with communism demanded that the United States prove the authority of its development model to an international audience. These efforts must be seen as part of both the ideological conflict of the Cold War as well as the evolution of a consensus on liberal international development. American efforts were grounded in its assumptions. Its aid to promote development assumed the state would have a central role, found planning indispensable, sought profound transformation of society, and saw cooperation with international and voluntary groups as vital. Programs accepted the now long-standing assumptions that the development they attempted was to bring extensive change across all sectors of economic, social, and cultural life. The sheer size and global profile of efforts in South Korea made it the most important example of the American style of modernization at a critical juncture in the Cold War. Ambiguity would be the outcome. By the end of the 1950s, intensive activity by a constellation of institutions commit-

ted to all-encompassing liberal development produced frustratingly limited results. But the Americans found they could walk away. The stakes of
the ideological struggle at the core of the Cold War made modernization
strategically indispensable.

CHINA AS POSTWAR MODERNIZATION LOADSTAR

Asian development was an issue even before the end of World War II.
How pivotal parts of the region would recover and progress had political
and strategic resonance to American and international planners. China
remained the loadstar. As was often the case, UNRRA led the way. In its
Sisyphean task of undoing the damage done by humanity's greatest war, it
zeroed in on the Middle Kingdom as a lynchpin for regional development.
China received the greatest share of UNRRA's funds. The money was
largely American in origin; of the $670 million UNRRA provided China,
the United States contributed $474 million. Long amenable to interna-
tional support for development, the Guomindang welcomed such aid.
Party founder Sun Yat-sen had long urged international development. By
1945, the party, chastened by civil and global war, struggled to grasp
Sun's vision. Nevertheless, there remained excitement for major development programs. There was considerable excitement within the regime
for the much-discussed "Yangtze Valley Authority" struck from the
TVA mold. These ideas and UNRRA's activities were seen by the
GMD as a means to lay the foundation for long-term economic growth
and development.[2]
    UNRRA officials had no fundamental disagreement with their hosts.
China at the end of World War II appeared doubly handicapped. It was
staggered by war damage and inefficient "traditional" economic and social practices. Returning China to the status quo ante bellum was not an
option. Accordingly, UNRRA constructed a program in which recovery
from the destruction of war also fed long-term programs to modernize
much of Chinese life. Looking for the means to stir economic advance in
a society seen as "backwards," they turned to "promising" reconstruction
ideas from the 1930s. For its global efforts UNRRA mobilized more than
3,000 technical personnel, including about 850 Americans. Of those as-
signed to China, many were selected for earlier experience with the
NCCRR and the CIFRC. Given the continuity in personnel, there was
clear continuity of ideas. The most prominent CIFRC alumnus to return was Oliver J. Todd, who immediately set to work on the immense program to repair the shattered Yangtze River dikes. Here lay a
prime opportunity to use engineering altruistically, by making the proj-

ect serve as a vehicle for training Chinese technicians and workers in modern techniques.[3]

Time was not on UNRRA's side. The UN agency's mandate expired in 1947 and the United States held to the schedule and let the program lapse. This move, however, did not signal a decline in American interest or support for foreign aid and reform programs. Instead, the abandonment of UNRRA was part of a shift by the United States that, while continuing multilateral aid, placed more emphasis on official bilateral programs.[4] The major mechanism was the Economic Cooperation Administration (ECA). Originally the administrator of Marshall Plan aid to Western Europe, the ECA's mandate was expanded in 1948 to include economic and technical aid for much of the globe. Like UNRRA before it, much of the ECA's effort (outside Western Europe) was expended in China. In confronting the chaos of a country recovering from vast war damage while sinking into large-scale civil war, the ECA also turned to predecessors for inspiration.[5]

Unlike UNRRA, the ECA was a Cold War creation and cast to different specifications. The ECA demonstrated a signature of modernization programs—close cooperation with nonstate actors. Despite its different imperatives the ECA knew its programs would be similar in content to the programs NGOs had initiated during the 1930s and the UN in the 1940s. They were well aware these nonstate actors had left a wealth of ideas and experienced staff for them to draw upon. China was an early example of a relationship replicated at numerous other moments in the Cold War where American and international NGOs actively sought collaborative relationships with U.S. government aid programs. ECA staff welcomed such overtures. They believed earlier reform projects had not failed so much as they had been overwhelmed, and sought to expand the resuscitation that had begun under UNRRA. In 1948, Harlan Cleveland moved as head of UNRRA's China Office to directorship of the ECA's China Program. Cleveland believed that focus on rural issues was vital for economic recovery as well as gathering the support of the peasantry, without which the GMD's struggle against the communists was doomed.[6]

The primary means by which the ECA hoped to apply these prewar concepts was the Joint Commission on Rural Reconstruction (JCRR). James Yen, a veteran of reform efforts in the 1930s, worked the many connections he had fostered in the United States. A demonstration of his networking skills, as well as the stock Americans put in the program, was Yen's ability to get an audience with Harry Truman. Yen explained to the president that the JCRR should be seen as an expanded version of agricultural development work done by the TVA. The comparison to the gold standard of the TVA helped the cause, and the Joint Commission was established at the end of 1948. Despite the high-level support it received, the JCRR faced the same daunting task as had all its predecessors—"reconstructing" Chinese agriculture into a modern form—only now it also had the added burden of stemming a rising communist tide.[7]

The JCRR did more than borrow the title of "rural reconstruction" from its predecessors. In its early declarations it was explicit that its goal was to "stimulate and revitalize enterprises of the Rural Reconstruction Movement" of the 1930s. Much of the cast for the program was familiar, as were its inspirations. Yen dutifully took a position as one of the Chinese commissioners. Chang Fu-liang, another 1930s rural reconstruction hand (and recently returned from a Rockefeller-sponsored trip to North America to investigate agricultural cooperatives and make a second visit to the TVA), also enlisted. His American alter ego, John Earl Baker, had served CIFRC and UNRRA. O. J. Todd also traded in his UNRRA stripes to join the JCRR. These enlistments guaranteed the JCRR drew on interwar ideas that had worked their way to the core of liberal development. Since 80 percent of the Chinese population tilled the soil, agricultural reform remained the pivot on which the modernization of the country would turn. The JCRR relied on established ways of thinking about China's problems and proposed familiar solutions. Even after the efforts of the 1930s, the Chinese farmer still was assumed to know "nothing of scientific farming." Therefore, the JCRR proposed furnishing everything from chemical fertilizer to modern methods of seed selection. With perpetual credit problems still rampant, the JCRR fell back on the established idea of rural credit cooperatives.[8]

Above all else, the reformist legacy bequeathed the JCRR optimism in the face of China's vast problems. If anything, the situation in the late 1940s was worse than ten years previously. War damage was extensive. Crop yields remained low, threatening stability in a nation with a growing population. The GMD regime was demoralized, corrupt, and seemed incapable of confronting massive social and economic problems. Its support from many sectors of Chinese society was ebbing. Undaunted, the JCRR was as determined as its predecessors to "apply Western scientific and economic resources to Asian needs . . . to benefit the great majority of ordinary folk." It continued what some have termed the "low modernism" of agricultural reforms. Indeed, early on, the JCRR was marked as a "pioneer" organization whose synthesis of grassroots development ideas had global application. Like the Point Four organizations whose formation it influenced, despite its smaller scale it was seen as part of a larger pattern of liberal transformation. With this emphasis it could be tied to the reputation of the TVA and an emerging consensus on modernization. Its reputation would be trafficked through the 1960s to demonstrate the accomplishments of American sponsored development.[9]

Difficult realities, which had derailed the grandiose plans of the CIFRC and the NCCRR, also conspired against the JCRR. After launching just a few programs in central and southern China in late 1948, the JCRR was pushed from the mainland by the communists' swift advance. Defeat of the GMD did not spell the end of the JCRR. In fact, it provided fresh fields in which to test its methods. By 1950, the commission was deeply invested in agricultural improvement on Taiwan and would be given considerable credit for Taiwan's "graduation" from the school of American modernization in the 1960s.[10]

Such an accomplishment might have seemed impossible in 1949. Communist victory in China, while not unforeseen, threw the general U.S. posture in Asia into disarray. The bruising political criticism brought by the "loss" of China added complexity as the Truman administration rethought basic assumptions of U.S. policy toward a strategically indispensable region. Acheson, probing for options and for political cover, called upon close friend (and UNRRA veteran) Phillip Jessup to form a commission to review policy that included Raymond Fosdick, the recently retired president of the Rockefeller Foundation. They were to explore every option to contain "the spread of totalitarian communism in Asia" before Jessup took a trip to view the situation firsthand.[11]

The commission's goals reveal the growing importance of modernization in the Cold War. It framed how they saw the issues in Asia, and Point Four provided a policy through which to execute their assumptions. Fosdick, for one, admitted to being "deeply interested" in the possibilities of Point Four "because it relates to the work and technique of the Rockefeller Foundation." For Fosdick, embracing Point Four allowed the implementation of liberal internationalist principles. Fosdick's high-level input on a range of issues exposed linkages of many prewar ideas about technology and development—long tended by Rockefeller—to an evolving U.S. Cold War strategy toward emerging areas of the globe. He believed Point Four and the general trend of technical assistance it represented should "be the cornerstone of our work in Southeast Asia." However, it had to be linked to other existing efforts, and Fosdick was a particular devotee of the JCRR. Like many contemporaries, Fosdick knew the stakes. A member of his staff, Cora DuBois, spoke his mind: "Technology is a device, not a goal. It can be used by both the U.S. and USSR for different ends." In direct competition with other attractive systems, the United States had to be certain its ideas marked the way to the future. Such a goal required providing skills, along with "a sense of democratic obligations" coexisting "within a political framework consistent with the principles guiding U.S. foreign policy."[12]

Before Jessup's sortie, Fosdick urged him to explore these questions. It was imperative "to act and soon." Fosdick shared a general American fear that insecure economies and unstable political regimes were susceptible to communist propaganda and subversion. For others involved in these discussions, development programs offered positive policies on the ground as U.S. strategy reconciled to Nationalist China's fall and grappled with questions of regional integration. Acheson heard these voices and thought American technical aid could provide the "missing component" to secure Asia from the lure of communism.[13]

Armed with this advice, Jessup journeyed across much of Asia. From December 1949 through March 1950, his mission called on Japan, Korea, Taiwan, Vietnam, Indonesia, Singapore, Thailand, Burma, Afghanistan, Ceylon, Pakistan, and India, with a final stop in Paris. Like Griffin's later tour, Jessup's globe-trotting exposed him to a region seemingly ready to boil over. Korea, Indochina, Malaya, and Burma all had what he characterized as "hot" wars raging. To extend the necessary aid they nominated the JCRR, which had impressed Jessup firsthand during his visit to Taiwan. There was also the option of deploying Japanese technical personnel around the Pacific Basin. It was dryly noted that former parts of Japan's empire and "Co-prosperity Sphere" were unlikely to be amenable to the idea.[14]

China still loomed large as an example of how aid might be extended. One influential voice was Harlan Cleveland, who provided an early post mortem on "reconstruction" activities in China. Cleveland took from his experiences in the 1940s that the immediate need of societies in Asia was political stability. Without it the fundamental need of Asian societies—economic development—could not be met. Cleveland had learned the hard way from UNRRA and the ECA that instability kept modernization projects from bearing fruit.[15]

There were deeper questions to address. If the "basic need" in Asia was development, policy should be structured to displace the "utter poverty" of the region with new economic and social capacity. Cleveland dismissed suggestions that a replay of the Marshall Plan was the answer. Expressing a view shared by many colleagues, Cleveland saw the ERP as an endeavor to reassemble "with some improvements" the mature, modern economies of Europe. Reconstruction in Asia was not a question of recapturing lost or damaged capabilities. It was the remaking of societies and economies according to a new pattern. The hard lessons learned by UNRRA and the ECA demonstrated the need for programs combining managerial and technical expertise to inspire broad transformation. Unfortunately, the potential of China as proving ground had been squelched by the communist victory. But the ideas used by the ECA, based in broader liberal development concepts, presupposed universal application. Accordingly, they could be transferred to other countries facing similar problems. Cleveland noted hopefully that elements had already migrated to South Korea.[16]

THE NEW PROVING GROUND: SOUTH KOREA

Cleveland foreshadowed the shift in emphasis toward Korea. To be sure, he could not foresee the Korean War and the vast commitment that followed. But he did see vital development methods rooting in a country that was taking on increased importance in the Cold War. However, U.S. modernization activities in South Korea did not begin in 1949. The question of "reconstructing" Korea was in play before the conclusion of World War II and had always been influenced by ideas from the emerging liberal consensus on development. During the war, Korea had not captured Allied and, in particular, American attention. Still, there was determination to sever Japan from an empire that had been an engine for expansionism.[17] Important officials, including Franklin Roosevelt, believed colonies like Korea would require guidance—"trusteeship"—out of their colonial past. This paternalistic policy assumed areas like Korea needed outside tutelage for a set period before they would be eligible for independence. The 1943 Cairo Conference codified this view, declaring Korea would be freed from Japanese rule but only granted full independence "in due course."[18]

As in China, UNRRA was among the first Western organizations to actually research and report on Korea's potential postwar problems. Its investigators understood Korea had been partially industrialized. However, this was a development that had occurred on the whims of colonial rulers, leaving it an appendage of Japan's imperial system. Accordingly, the peninsula did not even have to be a battleground to feel the effects of total war. Perhaps more profound would be the effects of peace. Allied views were clear: Japan's empire had been a site of war-making capacity and a motivation for military adventurism—peacemaking demanded dismemberment. Yet, UNRRA saw the penalties for removing Korea from an economic system the Japanese had dominated. Koreans were excluded from critical technical and administrative positions throughout the economy, meaning the society was largely denied expertise. This history meant that modernization sponsored by outsiders was the only route to escape its enforced underdevelopment. Therefore, help from foreign experts appeared as the best means to establish a functional post-imperial economy.[19]

UNRRA's comment on Korea set down a pattern others followed. A colonial legacy was the reason modernization fostered by outside agents was necessary. This conceptualization would be repeated with regularity by other international and U.S. development agencies. Need was justified on the basis of an underdevelopment argument that would be rehashed many times. Technological backwardness brought by Japan's misguided rule would serve as the primary justification—as opposed to the deep effects of the division of the peninsula or World War II—for the numerous development programs that followed. UNRRA's initial report, however, assumed a unified Korea. The UN body itself would have only a limited engagement with actual postwar aid to Korea. UNRRA's latitude of action was curtailed in the Soviet zone of control in the North. This and the organization's vast commitments elsewhere meant a full-scale program would not be undertaken in either the Soviet or the American occupation zones. UNRRA contributed just under $1 million to relief and reconstruction, divided between what were becoming two hostile encampments.[20]

On the southern end of the peninsula, this aid was an addendum to the labors of a U.S. occupation. The U.S. Army unexpectedly became the South's trustee in August 1945. As the war drew to a close, the Americans grew increasingly suspicious of Soviet intentions in East Asia. After the Russian invasion of Manchuria and the atomic attacks on Hiroshima and Nagasaki impelled Japan to sue for peace, the Americans and Soviets entered hasty negotiations on spheres of influence. The night of August 10–11, 1945, a group of State Department officials, including Dean Rusk, chose the 38th parallel as the dividing line. The Soviets agreed—their troops were already in the North. The unexpected timing forced the American high command to scramble to find forces to insert into the South. The U.S. 24th Army Corps, under General John R. Hodge, was hastily inserted into Korea to stake out an American zone of occupation. It became the basis of the U.S. Army Military Government in Korea (inelegantly abbreviated USAMGIK).[21]

Like much of the rest of Asia, Korea had to endure a new cycle of turmoil as war concluded. A flood of as many as 2.3 million Koreans who left the peninsula during Japan's rule returned in the two years following the war. The war's end also spelled the end of colonial rule and the institutions that had dominated the country for over a generation. The U.S. Army oversaw a rapid removal of the hundreds of thousands of Japanese, many of whom had key roles in imperial administration. The dislocation caused by such massive shifts affected aspects of everyday life. To Americans, the upheaval caused by the Japanese departure starkly revealed shortcomings they had inscribed on Korean society.[22]

Although the overall goals of the Japanese Empire had become questionable to Americans in 1945, as a project, the empire had long been considered a modern one. Annexation of Korea in 1910 was for some in the West proof of Japan's rise into the ranks of the "civilizers."[23] Indeed, the Japanese colonial state was seen to have the hallmarks of what was considered effective, modern governance. It could project its authority at all levels of Korean society through a powerful police force, a large bureaucracy, and a comprehensive school system. While the Japanese Empire had been modern in structure, it had nevertheless maintained a population of premodern Koreans. American observers articulated a proto-dependency theory to explain its impact. Japan annexed "a backward and decadent Oriental monarchy." Colonial rule assured that "little . . . survived in Korea of the ancient native governmental tradition—antiquated as it was—upon which it would be possible to develop a truly national state organization." Japanese colonial practices and institutions had become the norm for Koreans; nevertheless, "something of the corrupt medieval monarchy of old Korea, flavored with a dash of the Chinese war lord tradition, still survives." While directly threatened by "Soviet ideology," the Americans understood that as self-appointed trustees for Korea, they would contend with the legacy of Japanese rule for some time to come.[24]

This was true in social as well as economic and political spheres. When considering plans for Korean recovery, Army planners—betraying a fondness for blunt generalizations and strained comparisons—cautioned:

> Koreans have been called the "Irish of the Orient," being sociable, fond of fun and drinking, of talking and fighting—they differ from the Irish by being afflicted with what appears to be a deeply rooted inferiority complex, doubtless engendered from the systematic and prolonged humiliation at the hands of the Japanese. The results— evident in political life—are extreme sensitivity ("face"), instability verging on irresponsibility, proneness to mob psychology, and occasional bursts of unreasoning anti-foreign feeling . . . Since the problem of liquidating the results of Japanese domination impinges on the fields of public education, propaganda, jurisprudence, and public administration among many others . . . it must be borne in mind if one is to understand the baffling paradoxes which are likely to be encountered at every step.[25]

In the eyes of the newly arrived American authorities, Japanese imperial rule had stunted the Koreans, leaving them *underdeveloped* and simply incapable of governing and administering a modern, independent state. Although Japan had—at times ruthlessly—industrialized Korea and carved modern institutions into the country, the populace differed little from other "backwards" societies.[26] To be sure, Americans were articulating what others had already asserted. Korea was in a different class. The reformist policies guiding the Marshall Plan or the occupation of Japan did not fit. Korean society was believed to lack the skills and forward-looking psychology held in these "advanced" societies. Accordingly, the thoroughgoing modernization of the sort embodied by the TVA was what was needed. Koreans were like other underdeveloped peoples, requiring American intervention to lead them to the best sort of productive and prosperous modernity—that is, one based on liberal ideas.

AMBIVALENT ENTERPRISE: MODERNIZING SOUTHERN KOREA

Any modernization campaign in southern Korea lay in the shadow of the Soviet model of progress. Because of this, it was an early template in the struggle between competing visions of modernity that characterized the Cold War. Truman was aware of this from an early stage. He had sent a friend, Edwin Pauly, to Korea as U.S. special representative in June 1946 to get a reading on the situation. Sincerely worried about communist gains in what he considered a crucial Asian ideological battleground, Pauly advocated a program of technical assistance to stem this rising influence. As a counterpoint to Soviet activities in the North, such modernization efforts would insure a healthy Korean economy and a vital propaganda success. Pauly's comments were part of a grudging U.S. commitment to the economic development of southern Korea. In the State Department, advocates for aid to the South saw the importance of propping up a region long connected to the Japanese economy. It had to be coaxed to stability to ensure a market for Japanese exports, but also to provide raw materials, particularly rice, necessary for Japan's economic health. An advocate of this strategy was Arthur Bunce, economic adviser to General Hodge. Bunce believed that the United States would be well advised to maintain its support so southern Korea could become "an example of democratic, social and economic progress in the Far East." In July 1946 Truman articulated his general support for such efforts because the president agreed Korea was already "an ideological battleground upon which our entire success in Asia may depend."[27]

The ambivalent agent of that process, the U.S. Army, was leery about expending resources in Korea. However, with withdrawal inconceivable in the face of a communist challenge, in 1947 USAMGIK proposed a five-year "rehabilitation" plan for South Korea. It was contrasted to the Army's existing program, which was described, simplistically, as geared to the prevention of "disease and unrest." The rehabilitation program was centered around a comprehensive attack on the transportation, public works, electricity production, education, industrial, and agricultural problems South Korea faced. In many respects, the plan continued the focus on areas preoccupying the Army since 1945. The major claim was that a comprehensive development plan would actually be cheaper ($496 million over five years) than maintaining the current program ($587 million).[28] Supporters of such a tack were disappointed. The Army program was not popular for budgetary and political reasons. A Korea aid bill proposed in 1947 disappeared into Congress. Still, the Army was given $113 million to continue its basic reconstruction programs—enough for operations to stagger on.[29]

General Albert C. Wedemeyer best expressed the oscillation in U.S. policy during 1947–49. As part of a larger investigation of the East Asian situation, he toured Korea in 1947. Wedemeyer's instructions made the Soviet threat explicit, noting, "the USSR has been properly described as an immense amoeba-like organism which surrounds and digests any object incapable of offering sufficient resistance."[30] Despite these fears his report to the president weighed in against any sort of "experiment in industrialization without resources" as "the establishment of a self-sustaining economy in South Korea is not feasible." Wedemeyer saw the effects of division, the collapse of the economy created by Japanese rule, and the dearth of trained technical and managerial personnel. The repatriation of the Japanese population of Korea had exposed an "almost fatal deficiency" in the South Korean economy. The sustained and massive aid required would be prohibitive, and "an investment in rehabilitation and industrialization, which would permit South Korea to subsist on its own industrial output . . . could be justified only by political and strategic consideration of the highest order." A bleak prognosis to be sure, yet the United States could not disengage for exactly that reason—strategic costs were of a high order. Immediate cessation of assistance assured total economic collapse, while withdrawal of U.S. forces would virtually assure a Soviet satellite embracing the whole peninsula. This move had an international aspect as well. The resulting loss of "moral prestige" would give the communist ideas further momentum in Asia. To Wedemeyer, there was no strong prospect for financial return or even an entirely self-sufficient economy. Yet, his suggestions betrayed the contradictions in U.S. policy. South Korea was a bad risk, but programs to cultivate social and cultural improvement were the only way to stabilize this strategically important "backward" society. He approved of USAMGIK's work of "social betterment" through education, as this counteracted the legacy of Japanese imperial rule and underdevelopment.[31]

The "social betterment" Wedemeyer discussed had been a component of the occupation from an early stage. Although much emphasis was placed on programs to resettle refugees, control disease, curtail hunger, and limit unrest, the Army's work over the course of the occupation, whether packaged under "rehabilitation" or the "prevention of disease and unrest," was predicated on making profound changes in Korean social and economic life.[32] Even though the goal of USAMGIK was not explicitly the creation of a self-sustaining modern economy, to effectively improve these sectors of society, deeper changes to institutions and the Korean people were required. The "backwards" attitudes had to be replaced by progressive, scientific, and modern outlooks. Transforming these views would have multiple impacts on society, making it hospitable to modern institutions and technologies. Basic ideas cultivated by programs in interwar China and, indeed, that were operating concurrently in China through UNRRA, the ECA, and the JCRR would be part of the Army's projects and its successors.

The colonial educational system, while a modern institution, was seen as one example of Japan's misrule. It was an imposing, if grossly unequal, system. Primary schooling, which was obligatory, was provided to large numbers of Koreans at the height of the colonial period. At the end of Japan's rule in 1945, 45 percent of Korean children were in primary schools. Schools were staffed with trained (mostly Japanese) teachers, and students were provided textbooks at government expense. While these numbers are impressive in a general sense, the rate at which Japanese students were enrolled was three times that of Koreans. After 1919, all instruction was in Japanese and students were even banned from speaking Korean to one another. While vocational training was available, few Koreans were allowed entry to professional schools, let alone universities. Education in the applied sciences, particularly engineering, was not encouraged. Only five out of every one hundred Koreans passed beyond the primary grades. Largely, schooling was to provide a baseline of skills to make Koreans capable of obtaining jobs in industry and agriculture—and to create loyal subjects.[33]

Japan's deliberate denial of access to knowledge of science and technology that gave people the ability to operate the institutions of modern society, as well as the scientific, forward looking, progressive, and rational outlooks necessary for complex and diversified modern society, was at the root of Korea's problems. If 1930s China was stuck in a "mediaeval" past, Korea was trapped by a colonial history. It was another sign for Americans (and others internationally) that Koreans were developmentally arrested in many respects, and this "backwardness" could only be undone by outside aid. This aid would foster a type of development that was extensive and intrusive. Technology had to be offered, schoolhouses had to be built, but equally important the psychology of the public had to be changed. It was a living example of the assumptions that drove the advancing international consensus on modernization.

To unravel this history, the school system was given an American makeover. Control devolved from central and provisional authorities to local and community levels. By 1948, over 2.3 million children were enrolled in primary schools, up from a high of 1.5 million under colonial rule. Between 1945 and 1947, the military government equipped nearly four hundred new school buildings. It also undertook a broad program to revise textbooks into the Korean language and distribute them free nationwide. Even more important was what the reequipped schools taught. There was a significant expansion in vocational and secondary education. Education in accounting, economics, business law, and other administrative vocations accelerated to meet the need for the managerial expertise deemed essential to modern life. Vocational education focused on the dominant sector of the economy—agriculture. Local school boards and the comprehensive high school, common in the United States itself, were put into place. School curriculum was radically changed as Confucian classics were discarded. Lessons on liberal democracy found their way into the texts but even more important was an emphasis on scientific principles and modern outlooks for the students. Education was not limited to the schoolhouse. Under the direction of the military government, a national Boy Scout program was instituted, putting emphasis on anticommunism mixed with community development. It was extraordinarily popular, and at its height one of every two young males in the South was thought to be a member.[34]

The establishment of an educational system as a part of a modern, rational society demanded reform of the Korean language itself. Attempts by the colonial authorities to enthrone Japanese as the sole language was a linguistic incarceration of Korean. This meant the language had not evolved and did not include specialized technical terminology, particularly in the sciences and mathematics. This legacy struck two blows. Without such terms the South Koreans were unable to gain a complete education or to master modern technologies. They would be unable to interact with others internationally on crucial technical subjects. Prominent nongovernmental groups were drawn into language reform. In line with the thinking that had motivated language reforms in the NCCRR, the Rockefeller Foundation explored a project to produce an up-to-date Korean dictionary. These discussions were part of a series of proposals to modernize the language that came from Korean and international scholars. Some thought that text should be presented left to right on the page, or that the Latin alphabet should be adopted. Eventually, the more radical proposals were overruled. But the idea that language also had to change to promote modernization gives an impression of how broad its reach could be.[35]

Private groups also played an important part in a push to have Korean students study in the United States. The goal was to produce trained Korean students who could return and institute modern methods into various professions and society at large. During the occupation, several American universities invited Korean students to study, although high hopes for these sorts of exchanges were hampered by a lack of funds.[36] Several foundations stepped into the breach. One was the Rockefeller Foundation, which provided support for a cohort of Korean doctors to study at leading universities in the United States in the late 1940s. These early exchanges were an overture to a larger reorientation of Korean higher education. With the occupation, the United States would assume the role as destination of choice. Between 1953 and 1979, 85 percent of Koreans studying abroad did so in the United States.[37]

Despite some impressive numbers, the education programs of USAMGIK were not unqualified successes. Hastily conceived and executed projects suffered from lack of resources. Others were hamstrung by a shortage of trained personnel or were simply incompetently run by their American or Korean administrators. Critics of U.S. educational reforms have rightly called them ethnocentric. Many American advisers were ignorant of Korean culture—something the USAMGIK candidly admitted at the time.[38] Deficiencies such as these would continue to hamper the effectiveness of American operations beyond the military occupation. Regardless, the American military government's education served the larger strategic goal of providing stability. Educational reform touched the lives of millions of people, influencing what they learned and how they communcated.[39]

Although education was important, agriculture riveted U.S. attention. From the beginning the occupation authorities knew that over three-quarters of the South Korean population was dependent on the farm economy. The breakup of the Japanese Empire meant that long-standing markets for Korean produce were in jeopardy and Korea could not obtain the vital seed it needed for its own agricultural requirements. How much this largely rural area was enmeshed in a regional economy was driven home by a food crisis in Northeastern Asia that persisted into early 1946. It also drove home that agricultural reforms common to development programs like the JCRR and the TVA could and should be demonstrated in Korea.[40]

The colonial period had seen the creation of a highly productive and export-oriented agricultural sector in southern Korea. It was a "granary" providing rice and cotton to the rest of Japan's empire (in fact, Korean rice cultivation was more productive per acre than the United States in the 1930s). USAMGIK determined that southern Korea could feed itself along with other parts of East Asia, particularly Japan. In effect, Korea was being asked to reprise a colonial role. To restart and enhance agricultural production, USAMGIK turned to the dependable process of agricultural extension. The Americans used infrastructure left by the Japanese, who had an extension service that permeated the countryside. All they needed was a new cadre of technicians. The mission given these agricul-

Figure 4.1. Reorientation: New textbooks, provided by UNKRA, are distributed to South Korean school children in the 1950s. Education was an important part of an extensive approach to modernization that required the cultivation of modern outlooks and abilities in a population. Courtesy of National Archives, Washington, DC.

turalists was not achieving self-sufficiency but to again make southern Korea an exporter of foodstuffs.[41]

Very often, ambitions to improve agricultural production dwelled on a humble topic—fertilizer. Normal planting, let alone high-yield modern farming that export demanded, made it the "lifeblood" of Korean agriculture. Chemicals produced in the North were now no longer available to southern farmers. In 1944–45, each planted acre received an average of 41.3 pounds, but during the occupation usage dropped to 18.3 pounds. Health concerns about organic "night-soil" were overruled, as agricultural advisers worried that prohibiting use of human waste would mean "ruin." The shortages brought by the upheaval of the conclusion of World War II forced USAMGIK to import hundreds of thousands of tons of fertilizer in an attempt to stabilize agricultural production.[42]

Food production was bound up by an unlikely live wire—electric power. Massive fertilizer imports replaced the chemicals produced in the North or in the now devastated chemical plants of Japan. There was significant fertilizer production in the South, but these factories were dependent upon electric power from the North. Access to electric power was a particular and chronic headache for the Americans from the early days of the military occupation well into the 1960s. It was a reminder that the American effort in South Korea was not a rehabilitation of a prostrate nation, but the construction of a new economic and social entity. Electric power generation was a priority during the massive industrialization undertaken by the colonial government during the 1930s. Through the war, the Japanese added capacity until the peninsula was producing around 5.7 billion kilowatt-hours (KWH) annually, the vast majority being produced in the North. After division in 1945, the generation capacity in the South was calculated at a dreary 80 million KWH. The North continued to furnish current to the South, but that came with financial (the Soviets made the Americans pay for the service) and strategic costs. The latter became apparent on May 14, 1948, when the North shut off all electricity. American authorities, despite North Korean claims about compensation, considered it a naked attempt to discredit the new government in the South. Whatever the motives, effects were deep and immediate as factories closed, workers idled, power rationing was instituted, and people scrambled to get kerosene and candles.[43]

The power crisis displayed the utter dependence of the newborn Republic of Korea on American aid. As a short-term measure, the U.S. Navy brought in power barges (one aptly named *Impedance*). The depth of the crisis meant they rode their moorings well into the 1950s. Power's impact on agriculture had a direct influence on attempts to cultivate Korean economic stability. Without a secure source of electricity, domestic production of its "lifeblood"—fertilizer—was hobbled.[44] It continued to hound the Army's successors in their respective quests to produce a modern South Korea. The economic problems the Army faced in education, agriculture, and industry are only part of the story of South Korea in the period, which is one of political struggle and, at times, open revolt. However, the Army's development program shows that fundamental questions, many stemming from the division of the peninsula and the end of Japanese colonial rule, would frame much of the modernization activity in the coming decade.

The power crisis also dimmed the lights on USAMGIK. For the Army, uncomfortable with its role in Korea, the creation of the Republic of Korea in May 1948 allowed it out of its commitment. Even on the positive end of the balance sheet, only "a start" had been made in energizing foreign trade and "some improvement" in industrial production. The negative side of the ledger was depressing. Financial and economic stability remained to be achieved. No comprehensive system of technical training had been put into operation. Fundamental land and labor reforms had yet to be completed. Most of all, an overall modernization program had failed to gain momentum. Even before the appearance of the ROK, members of USAMGIK felt the United States had "done little more than hold its own in South Korea . . . and has left almost untouched the basic problems of raising the economy to the respectable level."[45]

The challenge of creating a viable economic and political entity in the South was far from over for the Americans. After some discussion, the ECA was given the job of continuing the modernization of South Korea. It was part of yet another U.S. policy shift. Acheson, long a patron of modernizing South Korea, had become Secretary of State and a clearly defined position emerged in NSC 8/2 stating the "United States must continue to give political support, and economic, technical, military, and other assistance to the Republic of Korea." Particular timing, however, had a great deal to do with a cresting Asian crisis. With a Chinese communist victory looming, the markets and raw materials of the mainland would likely be closed to Japanese trade. A similar threat lay in Southeast Asia, where growing unrest and a crop of insurgencies threatened critical materials for the economies of Japan and Europe, and even access to desperately needed rice supplies. South Korea, with its legacy as a rice exporter and market for Japanese exports, found intensified strategic importance.[46]

The ECA's footprint was a sign of its importance. The U.S. Embassy in Seoul grew into one of the largest with some 2,000 staff, in part because it housed the largest ECA mission in the world. In line with much thinking around modernization in the late 1940s, what ECA staff intended for this "much simpler economy" was "a far cry" from the Marshall Plan. Paul Hoffman himself felt the stakes were high in Korea. With China deteriorating rapidly, the United States was unlikely to get a chance there to give the "world a demonstration of what western economic ideas had to offer." However, South Korea could be the pedestal to display the potential of American-led modernization. Speaking to ECA staff at the Banto Hotel in Seoul in 1948, Hoffman confidently asserted that "we have the proof and here is the proving ground."[47]

Hoffman envisioned a wide-ranging three-year development plan with a total outlay of $350 million. He argued, "Continuation of a mere relief program would necessarily result in the progressive pauperization of the people of South Korea." Despite his advocacy, there were many in Washington who worried the United States was adopting a permanent ward. A wary Congress killed the first bill to fund the ECA program. It would pass a revised bill that gave only $100 million of the $150 million requested. These cuts were significant, but strategic imperatives again prevented the abandonment of Korean modernization. The basic goals of the ECA remained stability and creation of durable foundations for a Korean economy that was a solvent trading partner in the world economy. However, even with the ends of the program reconceptualized, implementation did not drift far from predecessors.[48]

Hoffman made clear the ECA was a sequel to the Army's efforts. There was a great deal of staff continuity, particularly at higher levels. Bunce became the mission's chief. John Muccio, American ambassador to the new ROK, explained that economic emphasis would fall on those subjects that had preoccupied USAMGIK—particularly agriculture and energy. The perception of South Korea, its people, and their needs also remained constant. The ECA's early analyses read as if lifted from predecessors' reports. Justifications for American intervention remained constant. Koreans themselves still lacked the crucial technical skills to build and operate a modern economy because of Japan's corrupting rule. History had not changed, accordingly, neither had the need for American development.[49]

The ECA achieved some results. Exports and agricultural production crawled upward. There was a continued investment in educational reform and facilities. However, much of these improvements, even those in agricultural production, were reliant on commodities provided through American aid (e.g., fertilizer).[50] But the ECA could not easily undo the structural problems created by the collapse of empire and arbitrary division. Electricity remained a chronic problem. Shortage of current affected numerous aspects of Korean life and even the activities of the ECA mission itself. The situation was such that in the early 1950s, the mission asked its staff to curtail personal electricity use, as electric lights burning at all hours looked rather bad when power to the rest of Seoul remained rationed.[51] Staff was unaware of the greatest factor working against them, time. Within less than a year and a half, the mission itself was evicted.

A Vast Opportunity: War and Modernization

The shock of the North Korean attack on the South in June 1950 reordered U.S. priorities in Asia. As DPRK troops closed in on Seoul, the ECA mission, with the rest of the U.S. embassy, fled to Japan. Ambitions to create a modern South Korean state seemed moot as the remnants of the South Korean Army, with the battered American troops committed to its aid, struggled to hold Pusan on the southeastern tip of the peninsula.[52]

American officials tried to put the crisis into context. Comments show that modernization already framed how Americans saw events in poorer areas of the globe. Perhaps most stark was Warren F. Austin, U.S. representative to the United Nations, who explained the North Korean success in a modernization idiom. As part of a carefully planned act of aggression, he asserted, North Korea's communist allies had provided technical assistance to execute an invasion. This exposed the malevolence of modern technology in communist hands, guilty as they were of "using technical training for destructive purposes." Austin shared an opinion that Korea was a communist probe to exploit weakness produced by poverty and unrest—things best combated with modernization. He also articulated some common American condescension toward people in poorer countries when he said development aid could be an inoculation against aggression because "people who barely know how to use a wheel in peacetime cannot be expected to use a machine when attacked."[53]

Modernization did not stay in the realm of rhetoric for long. As the military tide began to turn in favor of the United Nations during the late summer of 1950, demand for a new Korean development policy appeared. A view emerged in Washington that the United States should make full use of international organizations for relief and development. In July, the Security Council requested that ECOSOC and the specialized agencies provide aid to the UN military command and the Korean people. Particularly active were the International Refugee Organization (IRO), the WHO, and the FAO. Seeing these activities, by the late summer of 1950, the State Department was discussing the merits of a UN-sponsored "recovery force" whose duties would clearly cross the line into modernization.[54]

Although wary of the UN, Dean Acheson saw the benefits of internationalizing efforts in Korea. Burden sharing was an obvious benefit, but it would help draw global attention to the possibilities of development conducted under an American aegis. In September, he asked the General Assembly to create a UN body to oversee a thorough development of Korea. Acheson stated:

A vast opportunity awaits us to bring, by such means as the United Nations has been developing, new hope to millions whose most urgent needs are for food, for land and for human dignity . . . The place to begin, I submit to the Assembly, is Korea . . . Here, focusing on one place of extreme need, the United Nations and the specialized agencies can demonstrate to the world what they have learned.[55]

This "reconstruction" organization assumed Korean "economic and social problems . . . will involve many questions and issues that go beyond the immediate job of providing relief."[56]

Pains were taken to assure that the chief was an American whose experience was in line with prevailing ideas about development. Discussing the issue with Acheson, Truman felt Gordon Clapp, chairman of the TVA and fresh from leading the UN survey mission in the Middle East, was the best choice. The interest in Clapp reveals the firm connection between large-scale modernization and the TVA in policy formation. When faced with a foreign policy problem seen as essentially developmental, the president and his chief advisers turned to it to provide a framework of response. An explicit TVA in Korea did not have to be established to show the influence modernization ideas had on perceptions at the highest levels of government. After some deliberation, Truman and his advisers decided that Clapp was too important in his domestic position. Instead, J. Donald Kingsley was nominated. Although lacking the same institutional cachet, he had served with the IRO and was known within an international aid community. While not the first choice he was, nevertheless, steeped in the assumptions of a congealing international consensus on a liberal approach to development.[57]

The General Assembly established the United Nations Korean Reconstruction Agency (UNKRA) by a nearly unanimous vote on December 1, 1950. From the start, the United States dominated the organization, providing over half its initial $200 million budget. UNKRA was born at the military high tide of the U.S.-led UN coalition. The UN forces gained the initiative with a dramatic series of victories against the North Koreans in the fall, followed a daring amphibious assault at Inchon. As UNKRA's organizational details were being finalized in Washington and New York, the UN force retook Seoul, crossed the 38th parallel, and marched on toward the Yalu River. Such success led to enthusiastic assumptions that UNKRA would oversee the modernization of a unified peninsula when the fighting ended. Before UNKRA had even been granted a formal mandate, three hundred thousand Chinese "volunteers" struck UN forces in late November. This stunning blow handed the United States and its allies a series of disastrous defeats that by February 1951 bundled them back beneath the 38th parallel and drove them out of Seoul.[58]

Battlefield reversals highlighted UNKRA's awkward position in Korea. The ECA had returned to the peninsula after the victories of the fall (and would continue operating in Korea until April 1951). Staff members were uneasy with the new UN agency. There were complaints that it was simply being "shoehorned" into Korea with little thought to repercussions. Even more constricting to UNKRA were military demands. The military UN Command (UNC) jealously guarded its control of relief aid.[59] This caused frustration, but Kingsley understood UNKRA could not implement any plans while the fighting raged, blandly stating in May 1951 that it was best "not to have the agency begin operations at the present time." Nevertheless, UNKRA did begin to formulate a critical element of the development calculus, long-term planning. UNKRA coordinated actions of assorted UN agencies, including the WHO, UNESCO, and the FAO as well as some American organizations.[60]

Despite these moves, UNKRA was subject to considerable international criticism for moving too slowly. There was displeasure in the ROK with an organization that was seen to have rigid views of Korea and its future. Some observers thought UNKRA was dithering. Others believed it employed too many international civil servants with a "colonial" outlook. There was some basis to the criticism. UNKRA's 243-person staff included some seventy-three Americans, sixty-one Britons, and the rest were European or Canadian. The UN, like many government aid programs, had to draw on those with experience—NGO veterans. Many had comfortably worked in colonial settings. Added to this, there was a perception within the Western military and aid community that the organization was saddled with second-rate personnel. Robert Nathan sniffed that the UN lacked "many, if any, world beaters."[61]

New Plans, Established Ideas: The Modernization Community at Work in South Korea

Criticism from these quarters stung, but it was the Eisenhower administration that truly undercut UNKRA. After winning the White House in 1952, Eisenhower dispatched Henry J. Tasca on a six-week survey of South Korea. Tasca's visit produced a plan to strengthen the Korean economy, appearing in mid-1953. In a number of important respects, Tasca's conclusions did not depart from the accepted paradigm of South Korea's needs. The long-term goal of American involvement had not changed from the days of the ECA or the Army. The end was not simply the relief but the construction of a stable, modern economy that would quickly turn Korea into a "self-supporting nation." Like his predecessors, Tasca also laid blame for shortcomings within Korean society squarely at the feet of the Japanese. Tasca did see that war had radically changed the situation, placing massive new burdens on a frail economy. Fighting had smashed many gains made during 1945–50, and estimates of damage in the South ran to $1 billion. The massive expansion of the South Korean military during the conflict was an unsustainable proposition for a state with slim resources. Chronic problems of the prewar period had been enhanced. Tasca grimly noted the battleship USS *Missouri* alone produced more electric power than all of South Korea.[62]

Despite structural concerns, Tasca saw many of the issues confronting South Korea as easily solved with the application of technology and expertise. New technologies would establish fresh fields of production on the "virgin ground" of Korea with high returns. In his view there were numerous and simple "for want of a nail problems" in the Korean economy. Removal of these bottlenecks in transportation, industry, and agriculture meant wider growth would begin relatively easily. One of the basic impediments remained the shortage of technical skills in the population at large. The report noted that there was a shortfall of at least a half million technicians and professionals indispensable to a modern economy. However, this gap could be bypassed in the short run. While the training of technically minded Koreans had to continue at a "maximum speed," in the interim, technicians could be imported from abroad. Accordingly, "[n]o development of new technical or managerial research is needed in Korea. The vast reservoir of knowledge available in Western civilization need only be tapped. And Koreans, like the Japanese a hundred years ago, have the will and ability to do so, and are not inhibited by irrational traditions and institutions." The technical assistance of these Western experts, inserted at all levels of government and industry, would "generate a cumulative process of imitation," thus unlocking the latent "human productivity reserves" in Korean society. With these resources, an economic base could be established to prevent the privation, disease, and misery that left openings for communism. With economic threats contained, as standards of living improved, so would the "psychological resistance" of the South Korean population to communist propaganda. Stability was important in a client, but South Korea had deeper global resonance. The ROK was a prime spot to demonstrate the efficacy of the American modernization model. Events had drawn attention to its fate. Perhaps more important was South Korea's need to be viewed as the same as other countries in the "early phases of . . . modernization."[63]

In Washington, Tasca's report was greeted as "an excellent statement on the Korean economic problem and . . . a basis for . . . an expanded program of economic assistance." There was a belief that the four- to five-year program laid out in the report was a viable course of action and would not cost the United States more than $1 billion in total economic aid. This did not mean that the Americans had forgotten their own recent experiences. The National Security Council (NSC) acknowledged, "Experience in Korea of four years of military government, a year of ECA, and several more of active war, has demonstrated that bottlenecks of supply, inexperienced staff and Korean institutional and political conditions may place a limitation on the speed with which a program can be carried out." This memory, however, was checked by the desire to reap Cold War propaganda gains by rapidly developing South Korea.[64]

Tasca's optimistic recommendations occupied a particular place in the Eisenhower administration's overall aid policy. A posture of "trade not aid" initially favored private investment over government allocations to prompt economic growth in poorer countries. There was a turn away from the Truman administration stance that international bodies could be supporting mechanisms. This was tied to a view in Washington that various UN programs had been compromised by Soviet activity. This made bilateral aid politically appealing. However, there were no illusions that free trade ideas could guide modernization in South Korea. The Republicans, in fact, would oversee a massive expansion of bilateral American aid. Eisenhower accepted this reality, because he believed that for the want of "a few million bucks" the United States had been drawn into a war in Korea. The president nurtured a view that aid was "the cheapest insurance in the world" against a similar crisis.[65]

Even with the growing bias against using the UN as an important platform for modernization projects, Tasca felt that UNKRA should not be "phased out of the Korean picture." The war was still seen as a collective UN action, and liquidating the reconstruction agency would require that the United States assume all of its commitments. Abandoning UNKRA might suggest the United States was willing to cooperate with other nations only in war but not in peace. It might also set a precedent where the United States might have to bear all the responsibilities for reconstruction in a future crisis. Tasca's recommendations removed any pretense of UNKRA being the central aid mechanism; it soldiered on as one part of a "single integrated program of economic assistance to Korea." The "integrated" development structure that was suggested included expanded NGO operations. Although not a focus of Tasca's report, the work of voluntary organizations was recognized as a means to provide immediate relief, funds, and technical experts to the combined effort.[66] UNKRA and the voluntary groups remained resources for the American Foreign Operations Administration and the Mutual Security Agency. Overall, the Republicans made explicit U.S. primacy in the modernization mission.

Kingsley grew frustrated and resigned, stating bitterly that "never had so many worked so hard for so long to accomplish so little." A clear signal of the direction of American policy was his replacement, U.S. Army General John B. Coulter. Not only did the selection of a military man soothe some of the civil-military tensions, but Coulter also adhered to the administration's new tack on Korean reconstruction. Most of his rationales were expressed in a Cold War idiom. Coulter believed failure in Korea would hand a "ready-made" propaganda victory to the "diabolical schemers" in the Kremlin.[67]

Despite the delays imposed by war and demotion by the Eisenhower administration, UNKRA still had considerable influence on efforts. Ironically, the long-term planning it sponsored during the war years was defining for postwar modernization goals. Even so, UNKRA, like so many official aid bodies, had to turn to nonstate actors to execute important technical details. Much of the actual research and planning was done by a U.S. consulting firm, Robert R. Nathan Associates. Nathan himself was

Figure 4.2. Calling the modernization tune: U.S. Ambassador to the UN, Henry Cabot Lodge, Jr., hands over a portion of the United States' 1954 contribution to UNKRA to Secretary-General Dag Hammarskjöld. The United States contributed the bulk of UNKRA's funds. Despite reservations of the new Eisenhower administration toward multilateral aid efforts, Americans wielded considerable influence over the organization's operations. The American nominated by the Republican administration to head the organization, General John Coulter, is at right. Courtesy of National Archives, Washington, DC.

a veteran New Dealer and a founding member of Americans for Democratic Action. He, like many other activists in the 1940s, had turned his attentions to the world and sought international work. Nathan's input assured UNKRA's 1954 report was saturated with assumptions about modernization springing from this reformist past.

The work of his consultant group produced a massive 1954 report, totaling nearly five hundred pages and a fine representative of a genre of twentieth-century development planning documents. Although UNKRA had commissioned the report before the end of the war (and the issuance of the Tasca Report), its recommendations reflected policy changes, meaning they were not explicitly aimed at implementation by the UN organization. Rather, it was a general report on South Korean conditions and needs, reflecting a consensus view on what needed to be done. Based on prevailing assumptions about the ability of planning to shape development, the "Nathan Report" was the touchstone for all development activities in South Korea, referenced (and criticized) into the 1960s. Nevertheless, the thinking behind its conclusions was far from new. Assumptions guiding its analysis were remarkably similar to those held by the UNRRA, the U.S. Army, and the ECA. Nathan, in his early visits, noted the impact of Japanese rule, and this "tough history . . . hardly provided a foundation for a prosperous, well-knit, knowledgeable and vigorous government and economy." Korea was a "classic example" of a "dearth of and need for brains." Nathan was enthusiastic about a big job whose "importance was of the first order of magnitude," yet it would be a "rough, tough, huge assignment." What set Nathan's conclusions apart from predecessors was a predicted finish line. The report envisioned a "self-supporting" South Korea by 1958–59 if its dictates were followed.[68]

Nathan knew modernizing Korea involved more than just the creation of a healthy economy. It had global import in displaying the value and possibilities of large-scale liberal modernization.

> To the free world, Korean reconstruction affords an opportunity to constructively participate in a great endeavour—an endeavour to build a progressive and dynamic economy in a part of the world where millions are unable to eke out a bare subsistence, where competing systems of government and economics threaten freedom and peace. They have an opportunity to help in a practical demonstration of the immeasurable benefits of a free economy and a democratic way of life. The stakes are so high as to dwarf the sums and sacrifices required.[69]

While war damage was the immediate challenge, the fundamental goal was modernizing South Korea. In discussions that could have been cribbed from the Army and ECA, the Nathan report asserted that, in a manner similar to other underdeveloped countries, aspects of Korean culture stood in the way of modern, industrial society and, to insure growth, a new progressive attitude and scientific outlook had to be instilled in the population. Japanese rule, modern in many characteristics, through its exclusionary and discriminatory practices had allowed Koreans to participate in a technological economy without being modernized themselves. Because of this,

> The Koreans retain many basic institutions and attitudes from the pre-Japanese age. With limited opportunity to participate in the management of their economy, Koreans bear the scars of living for more than a generation in low estate in the Japanese empire [sic]. At the same time they benefited from Japanese induced technological development, however distorted to Japanese ends. Disorganization

and destruction since liberation have left their mark on the Korean people ... These developments further aggravate the already difficult task of paralleling political independence with economic independence. Thus, the Korean people bring to the task of reconstruction a varied background that will influence at every turn the design and pattern of the future economy. Then transformation of Korea into a self-sustaining, independent economy will require a concentrated effort in developing new abilities in overcoming the harmful effects of war suffering and in adapting ancient traditions to new requirements.[70]

There was a belief that "certain traditional attitudes will require some adaptation to the needs of a modern democratic economy." Since Korean culture was still prone to "disparaging the practical arts and commercial activities" and "the co-ordination of technical or practical training and general education is a relatively new and underdeveloped educational principle," the United States and UN would have to impose reforms in these areas to support the larger development effort. While these reforms to education were taking shape, foreign technicians would have to pick up the slack, and $41 million was being set aside to bring experts to Korea. There was rhetoric that the "historic opportunity" to harness the potential of development fell to the government of Korea. However, Nathan demanded that planners "recognize ... that the handicaps of the Korean people are a product of their cruel history." This view fed an assumption that, in the short term at least, modernization would be managed by outsiders.[71]

Much in the Nathan group's plans for the Korean economy rested squarely on research performed by the UN's specialized agencies. Their studies were the basis of many conclusions that would guide development in the ROK through the 1950s.[72] The report emphasized the need for integrated planning coordinating all development efforts. Focus would be on making exports the basis of the economy. Growth in overseas trade would support postwar recovery and the long-term health of the ROK's economy. With mainland China obviously unacceptable, Nathan saw Japan as "Korea's most logical trading partner." Euphemistically, they noted the change in circumstances between the colony and colonizer, assuring trade "could now be conducted under vastly different conditions than in the past."[73]

Similar to its predecessors and collaborators, Nathan and his associates believed agriculture held the "central role in the Korean economy." The program for rural Korea was very similar to those undertaken by USAMGIK and the ECA. It was more than repair of infrastructure in the countryside. Like other efforts in Asia, the Americans sought improvements in the access to farm tools, farm credit, and technical assistance. Farm extension work and agricultural education to train thousands of Koreans in "modern" techniques was stepped up. The agricultural environment was to be altered. There were plans to change the types of crops grown and the very food Koreans ate. Rice production was kept high. Other high-yield crops, particularly potatoes, millet, and soybeans, were planted to replace expensive food imports and free rice production for international markets, particularly Japan. The politics of food in the ROK is an example of how economic development can quickly force itself into the most personal aspects of individual life. A basic part of Korean life was changed to fit into a modern, agricultural economy. This had to be taught. Even culinary arts had to be revised. Recipes from other parts of the globe were gathered by aid agencies to show Koreans how to use these staples in their kitchens.[74]

The linchpin remained fertilizer. The Nathan group estimated that fertilizer imports would be $288 million over the course of its five-year plan and all other agriculture projects, $196 million. The central place of fertilizer in the central sector of the Korean economy made its increased production crucial. However, fertilizer production greedily consumed electricity at a time when generation capacity was stunted. Electricity production inched up to 655 million KWH in 1949—but these gains had been crushed by war. Nathan predicted that to meet agriculture's needs, a domestic chemical industry alone would need 300 million KWH annually. When requirements for the rest of the chemical industry, mining, agriculture, and public use were added, there would be a daunting demand for 1.9 billion KWH in South Korea by 1958. The creation of new power generation and distribution sources was, therefore, "a major determinant of the pace" of South Korea's development.[75]

From the Nathan group's perspective, changes to South Korean society would lead to economic improvements. These reforms were a critical buttress to the general economic development effort. Some programs were direct responses to the privations of war, with the construction of modern housing and urban facilities to replace those destroyed in the war being a priority. But wider investments in public welfare that included health and education were seen to "permit them [the Korean people] to participate more effectively in the creation of a progressive democratic economy in Korea."[76]

A UNESCO survey served as a template for the Nathan group's conclusions on the educational needs of Korea. Repair of war damage was obviously the most pressing concern. Nearly a quarter of all the 42,000 classrooms existing at all levels before the war had been destroyed or damaged in the conflict, and 36,000 new primary and secondary school rooms were needed for population growth. But education demands went beyond infrastructure. Education on a modern standard was a critical need so "the people can effectively participate in the economic and political life of the country." However, reform faced hurdles from the legacy of the Japanese system aimed at creating obedient subjects; moreover, "certain traditions deeply rooted in the Korean life also need to be adapted to present-day needs."[77]

A considerable amount of UNKRA's funds devoted to this area simply went to the repair and construction of school buildings. Connected to this construction plan was UNKRA's establishment of a number of engineering and vocational training programs and schools to begin to produce the technical personnel so coveted by development planners. Activity in mass education was not simply confined to construction of buildings and institutions. A number of Western (largely American) educators were brought over in the 1950s to train local teachers. This was another case of foreign expertise filling in what were perceived as critical gaps in Korean capabilities. They contributed to the larger ambition of UNKRA's education program to provide Korean teachers and community leaders training in subjects that would allow them to carry knowledge to their people. This would inspire a grassroots "desire for technological and social advance" to feed economic development.[78]

The keyword was "reorientation." In its postcolonial condition, South Korea remained in the "grip of history"—hobbled by the heritage of Japanese colonial rule and the effects of war. Korean education had to continue to move away from its Japanese foundations toward what was seen as more modern, international, scientific, and egalitarian. This shift would not be just curricular, but ideological. There would be an ongoing campaign to establish local school boards modeled on those in the United States, as it showed that education was moving away from being something imposed from the top down to something that was responsive to the population. Another important part of this catalog of changes included a renewed effort to establish fellowships and other programs funded by a number of governmental and nongovernmental sources designed to provide for the overseas education of Koreans, largely in the United States, in technical subjects. Funds from UNKRA, the U.S. government, and NGOs supported the retraining of Korean agriculturists, technicians, and educators in the West that was billed as "modern." It continued the trend, started during the occupation, of tying Korea to American educational institutions.[79]

Language reform of the type already initiated by USAMGIK was outlined as one of the serious educational tasks facing Korean reconstruction. The Korean tongue remained a victim of Japanese underdevelopment. Efforts continued to create a new vocabulary of technical terms and a new standard dictionary of the Korean language. Language reform was connected to the provision of new textbooks to the schools. UNKRA and the U.S. government had to supply schools and other education programs with approximately 30 million new books per year as well as other materials, such as laboratory equipment. The provision of these items was not to replace those that had been destroyed by the war. Rather, revised textbooks and classroom materials were designed to assure that the "scientific" values planners were trying to cultivate were instilled in the students. This requirement spun the education needs of development back on industrial plans. To fulfill the demand for textbooks, the agency oversaw the construction of both a paper mill and a printing factory and even geared forestry programs to paper production.[80]

Not all the reforms endured. Local school boards, an important part of American hopes, were abolished when the South Korean government centralized education administration in the 1960s. Taken as a whole, many scholars have noted that goals to use education as a means to produce the "human capital" to support modernization had mixed results. The accumulation of an educated population did not necessarily increase the pace of development. However, some assert education did have a modernizing impact on the Korean population, instilling in many people the view that they were part of a new national social and political environment and encouraging a progressive, future-oriented outlook. But perhaps its most important role was the power it gave the government to impose its modernization policies and authority on the population as a whole.[81]

With the resources lavished upon it, South Korea became a hive of development activity, one that was observed from all corners of the globe. The National Planning Association spoke for many in the United States when it declared that in South Korea, "we have involved ourselves, under the guise of a 'reconstruction' effort, in a fairly unique experiment in rapid development policy." The United States and the UN were not attempting to undo the damage of war, but "to make for the first time a going concern out of an economy . . . bisected from its northern half less than a decade ago, [something] never before accomplished." Korea presented a unique case in some respects; however, most of its problems were those of underdeveloped areas in general. A modernization program carried out with dispatch was necessary. The "urgency of the contest between communist and Western modes of development" required that the United States move quickly to develop South Korea. South Korea was seen as an "experiment" for Western—particularly American—development ideas to demonstrate that they could cope with the massive forces of change that had been unleashed in the underdeveloped parts of the globe.[82]

Vast goals required that the United States turn to bodies they had long planned to utilize in such a situation. South Korea saw the massive participation of NGOs within a broader U.S. government strategy. It should be clearly stated that they were not simply conduits for government and international organizations. Although they largely agreed with the means and ends that made up the modernization of South Korea, NGOs brought their own agendas to the table. They also were an instrumental element in conveying modernization ideas down to the village level. The commitment of these NGOs assured that many average Koreans were directly touched by the larger strategic plans that demanded the modernization of their country.

UNKRA, along with the U.S. aid agencies, saw voluntary groups as a means to reach the population at large. They gave block grants in the millions of dollars to missionary and nongovernmental groups to perform what were broadly termed "community development" projects. These were diverse and often locally specific, ranging from agricultural to education to health programs.[83] To further streamline these activities, the U.S. government also forged agreements with the South Korean government to allow materials for voluntary programs to enter the country duty-free.[84] The U.S. government not only provided financial assistance to these NGOs but also sought to bring them into line with the larger aims of the development effort. By 1958, the Korean Association of Voluntary Agencies (KAVA), a blanket organization for NGOs, had brought fifty-two bodies under its aegis, including stalwarts such as CARE, Catholic Relief Services, and even the Boy Scouts (it did not include universities or foundations active there). The overall aim of this coordination of voluntary groups was to prevent duplication of effort and to organize and deploy the expertise of these groups in the larger project of creating a viable South Korea.[85]

High-level American and UN officials appreciated the role that these groups played. William E. Warne, the Economic Coordinator for the UNC in Korea, was well aware that the $2.5 billion invested by all the groups involved in South Korean development up to 1958 gave the effort considerable importance. Voluntary agencies contributed over $69 million of their own funds in 1958 alone, a sum larger than the entire U.S. government technical assistance program for Latin America. By 1960, at least eighty-three voluntary groups from ten countries (sixty-two of which were American) were working in the South. In the seven years following the end of the war, they would serve as an important mechanism for delivering relief. These bodies dispersed over $121 million in food, clothing, medicine, and other emergency supplies (much of which was supplied under the U.S. government's Public Law 480 which made American agricultural goods available as overseas aid) directly to the population.[86]

Even more important was the activity of NGOs in long-term operations. They took the lead in community development that brought education, health, housing, and agricultural programs down to the village level. These community-based efforts were trumpeted as an expression of a grassroots approach that was centered on cultivating a self-help ethos. Programs included aid for schools, agricultural support, and animal husbandry. Community development attempted larger projects as well. The Save the Children Foundation (whose chief in Korea was a veteran of UNRRA) provided significant aid for local infrastructure improvements, offering supplies and technical assistance in the construction of flood control and irrigation systems in various parts of South Korea. The foundation saw its activities as a model for other international development efforts, an assumption manifest in its publication entitled *Korea—Proving Ground for Self-Help*. Warne saw that government and voluntary programs ran parallel. Emphasis on community development that trained Koreans to run local institutions as part of a modern economy was an invaluable contribution to building "a stable, enduring society geared to the demands of the modern world."[87]

Voluntary groups were willing allies with government and international aid organizations. However, members saw their own programs as more flexible and having greater freedom to experiment and therefore better able to implement community development. Their domestic history was taken as a sign they could "spearhead" social change in Korea. They had long served as "watchdogs" or the "social conscience" in nations in North America and Europe, assuring that governments carried out or altered their responsibilities. They assumed they were playing similar roles in South Korea and elsewhere. There was an acknowledgment that tensions between official and voluntary agency staff went beyond policy and into social, political, and religious differences. However, they found common ground in their frustrations with the "ancient tendencies" of Korean society, perceived as barriers to the shared effort to build a modern society.[88]

"DOWN THE RATHOLE": MODERNIZATION AND ITS LIMITS IN SOUTH KOREA

The frustrations experienced during the 1950s would have been familiar to the members of the Army command in the 1940s. In 1958, with UN-KRA's mandate expiring and the end of the Nathan Report's five-year

Figure 4.3. An employee of Bechtel Corporation oversees South Koreans welding at an all-important power station, ca. 1956. Private organizations were instrumental in executing modernization plans. Courtesy of National Archives, Washington, DC.

plan approaching, the International Cooperation Agency (ICA) took stock. While they congratulated themselves on repairing the majority of the war damage in the South, they frankly admitted that the timelines in the Tasca and Nathan reports were overly optimistic and funds had been underestimated by hundreds of millions of dollars. Exports were not growing as quickly as hoped and a dearth of electricity hamstrung development efforts in the South. There was real cause for concern. "Spotty" summed up growth in 1955. In 1956, there "were no dramatic changes in the economic situation." The picture was not without its bright spots as gains were shown in manufacturing and mining and there was a feeling that the immediate relief phase of the program, necessitated by the havoc wrought by the Korean War, had been successfully completed. However, inflation continued at crushing rates (50 percent during 1956 alone), the trade gap remained high, and agriculture—still seen as the ROK's principal sector—struggled. Even in 1957–58, when fragile signs of improvement appeared, it was credited to direct U.S. aid rather than Korean initiative.[89]

With these concerns came increasing criticism singling out the Koreans for the continuing problems. The ICA's 1958 review replayed much of what had been said since the occupation. Confucian culture, the policies of the Japanese colonial authorities, lack of technical and managerial skills in the population, and even the communists (said to have kidnapped 30,000 technicians in 1950–51) were blamed for the stagnation. There was disappointment with the amount of cooperation shown by Koreans. It fed a belief that "the skills and knowledge of the ROK officials and population were not equal to this Herculean task." Officials thought the problem often was "unrealistic" economic thinking in the ROK, particularly the "belief . . . Korean economic problems can be solved by dollars alone." Notable among the frustrated were American technical personnel who saw Korean incompetence as the source of failure. The application of modernization ideas was rarely faulted. An example was electric power. By 1955, trouble in the sector was attributed to a lack of "managerial and technical efficiency" among Koreans. American observers were certain the power system produced enough current but was paralyzed by mismanagement, inefficiency, poor maintenance, and outright corruption on the part of the Koreans. Poor conditions at one plant administered by Koreans, where basic procedures were being ignored, were chalked up to either "stupidity or sabotage."[90]

These problems dimmed hopes. Needs seemed insatiable. What successes there had been appeared entirely dependent on large amounts of American aid, technology, and expertise. Economic aid peaked in 1957, when the ROK received $382 million in economic assistance. Although this sum declined in the following years, through 1960 the country received well over $200 million annually. By comparison, the entirety of

U.S. economic aid to Western Europe in 1959 was $259 million (Taiwan and Turkey rated, respectively, $226 and $246 million). This was only economic aid. When military aid and the expense of maintaining the American garrison were included, the annual bill for the U.S. commitment to South Korea came close to $1 billion. Despite all this, at the end of the decade there was no sign the ROK could be weaned.[91]

To U.S. observers, part of the problem was the government of the ROK. The Rhee regime, and the nationalism to which it appealed, stood in the way of the best means to solve persistent economic dilemmas. A mantra among Americans was that the exports to shore up South Korea's balance of trade and stimulate growth would come with the revival of a close trade relationship with Japan. However, they were frustrated by the "emotional overtones" seen in Korean relations with Japan. Despite U.S. prodding, the ROK government limited diplomatic and commercial connections and was slow to come to agreement on basic trade issues, which, in American minds, made long-term recovery much more difficult. The ROK even made it difficult for UNKRA to procure materials from Japan. Such actions flew in the face of long-standing American policy "to secure two dollars of benefit—one for Japan and one for Korea—from every dollar expended."[92]

Rhee was a focal point of recalcitrance. An ardent nationalist, Rhee understood the constraints—and opportunities—of South Korea's Cold War relationship with the United States. While the ROK was dependent on U.S. financial and military support for survival, the Koreans also knew their importance to the Americans. South Korea's place in the Northeast Asian economy, its military significance, and its psychological importance in the confrontation with communism allowed Rhee latitude to maneuver. Containment prioritized maintenance of a strong regime over liberal reforms in the ROK. Yet the United States found there were limits to its leverage on Rhee. He was able to resist elements of the American-dominated East Asian system he thought neocolonial. He also managed to turn the flood of aid money into grease for his political machine. Rhee's political power was cemented, in part, by budding industries in South Korea, which turned to Rhee's government for contracts and capital. Receiving these, the commercial class then provided kickbacks and political support to Rhee's party. This "triple alliance" of the South Korean state, Korean capitalists, and the United States was a defining feature of the ROK's political economy in the 1950s. Ironically, it may have hampered economic development.[93]

However, the authoritarian apparatus Rhee constructed with the help of American aid could not last. There was increasing criticism at home and abroad of the excesses of the president's one-party (and, in some respects, one-man) rule. At the end of the 1950s, Rhee's critical patronage machine began to sputter as aid funds declined. It may be one reason Rhee was without many allies when he attempted to steal the March 1960 election. Blatant bribery, violence, and fraud led to nationwide demonstrations. Sprawling protests in Seoul on April 19 were fired on by security forces, killing 186 people and wounding 1,600. Troops had to be called in to restore order. While the United States released some Korean troops from the joint military command to restore order, it did not unequivocally support Rhee. By this time public and military opinion were running against him. In the face of continued unrest and under pressure from the United States, Rhee resigned on April 29, fleeing into Hawaiian exile.[94]

Rhee's departure brought relief in Washington. There was hope that "moderate elements" had provided the opening for redress of grievances that had long simmered. Rhee's replacement was an intelligent and earnest democrat, Chang Myon, initially popular with American authorities. A fresh democratic start did not guarantee stability. The National Assembly quickly descended into factionalism. Chang's own party fractured into two camps and his government lost the faith of the military and much of the public. To American eyes, the democratic regime appeared disorganized and unable to implement policies to accomplish desperately needed modernization.[95]

A sign of how ideas about modernization had diffused from advocates and intellectuals into policymaking was how problems in South Korea were perceived and discussed. Troubles were read by State Department officials through modernization lenses. In August 1960, Assistant Secretary of State for Far Eastern Affairs, J. Graham Parsons, asserted:

[T]he fundamental problems of Korea are social as much as economic and political. The rate of social change in Korea has been so great as to confuse both leaders and people as to the basic values and goals of their national existence . . . So far there has not been a leader or group in Korea with the imagination, vision, and energy to give the nation the definite and believable national ideals, goals, and programs which are essential to give meaning to this democratic framework, to end the Korean spiritual and social confusion, to ameliorate the deep discontent and even spiritual hunger which underlies so many of Korea's problems, and to give the country a sense of unity, direction, and destiny. Social progress of this sort is, of course, a precondition of the economic and technical progress which is essential to the national welfare. Until adequate native leadership emerges, it is incumbent upon us to do what we can to encourage the development of the Republic of Korea in the face of social inertia and ignorance until it can ultimately go it alone in as a self-sustaining member of the Free World. We must offer the sort of guidance, inspiration,

and support which will avert the ever-present danger of social disintegration, widespread revolution, or subversion, and will bring Korea
to the stage labeled by Rostow the "take-off point." If we cannot do
this ourselves, our Communist competitors will be given an opportunity to try it their way.[96]

The language borrowed heavily from Walt Rostow, whose writing had
considerable influence by the late 1950s, but the general formulations
sounded familiar. It is another sign that the modernization theorists in
vogue at the time were gilding a set of ideas about development that already had considerable resonance in a world shaped by ideological combat. Parson's comments summarized the long-held views that social concerns were at the roots of South Korea's difficulty in modernizing. The
ever-present threat of the communist development model was a reminder
of the penalties if the United States did not play the role of patron. Facing
these realities created a desire for a strong leader who could compel the
ROK to grasp its modern "destiny."

Parson's memo reflected the perceptions held by many Americans that
the lack of capacity among Koreans was a main barrier to modernization.
Such a view had been a key part of the justification for U.S. modernization
plans from 1945 onward. Korean underdevelopment was a product of
corrupt Japanese rule and required the presence of an American trustee
to guide the republic to modernity. This role necessitated the implementation of the sort of liberal development defined before World War II and
codified into policy in various U.S. and international institutions in the
second half of the 1940s.

This perception also provided a means to help explain away the failures
of the development ideas the United States and other bodies had imported
into Korea. The continued economic, social, and political turmoil of the
long-suffering Koreans could be attributed to their underdevelopment,
which, in turn, could be blamed on Japan's misguided colonial enterprise.
This emphasis mostly ignored the hasty division of the peninsula in 1945
or the politics of the Cold War. In American eyes, it was a lack of technical
knowledge, unscientific outlooks, "social inertia," and the outright "stupidity" of the Koreans themselves that kept their country from being reconstructed in the image they desired. "Emotional" attitudes of the Koreans toward Japan were products of colonialism. But such reactions
prevented the Koreans from embracing what was thought to be their logical role as a source of raw materials and market for Japan in the new East
Asian regional economy. Accordingly, blame for many of the Republic of
Korea's enduring problems was placed on the Koreans themselves and
not on the developmental model of the United States.

Torpor in the ROK had grave import for the larger Cold War. After the Korean War, the Soviet Bloc increased its aid to developing nations. It was a declaration of "economic war" and Americans quickly found themselves on the defensive. Reaction in Washington was anxious. A moribund South Korean economy chafed American policymakers for a host of reasons. Unending aid to a struggling proxy was enough of a burden, but it also damaged the credibility of U.S. claims to have the best development model. It was not uncommon to hear the ROK referred to with keen aggravation in Washington as a "basketcase" or "rathole." Confronting the mounting Soviet offensive in the developing world was seen as a vital interest. However, the largest modernization program in the world was foundering, making attempts to contain communist influence that much harder. The challenges to American models in the "Third World" were multiplying. The most immediate was North Korea, which was undergoing its own massive reconstruction with the aid of a family of communist states. This "fraternal socialism" in the late 1950s appeared to be the better way forward than that of its liberal American rival, struggling to make progress below the 38th parallel.[97]

Persuading peoples that their aspirations were best achieved by following the route to modernity paved by the United States was the basic goal of its foreign aid program. Dramatic events had moved an initial postwar American development focus on China to the fragmentary state of South Korea. By the end of the 1950s, it had become the prime example offered to the international community of the American model of modernization. However, there were unsettling signs that many in the "Third World" were unconvinced. It was undoubtedly a blow to American prestige, but a more tangible cost was the growth of Soviet influence. Allure generated by the apparent success of the Soviet Union's own planned economy weighed on Americans. Soviet activities were only aided by a set of perceptions that cultivated reticence within the developing world. The ROK was counted among Taiwan, Israel, and Japan—important U.S. clients that were viewed with suspicion by an increasingly vocal post–Bandung Conference Third World. They also knew lethargic progress in South Korea despite massive infusions of assistance, and tarnished promises to nationalist leaders eagerly seeking aid for swift modernization. Attention given the mammoth U.S. efforts in the ROK meant stagnation was all the more visible. Americans increasingly saw underperformance in South Korea and elsewhere, as much as Soviet success, lending credibility to claims that communism was "the wave of the future" in Asia and, possibly, worldwide.[98]

A prediction in the late 1950s that South Korea would soon be considered a development success would have met derision in American officialdom. Persistent troubles faced in developing a modern, non-communist South Korea were emblematic of larger problems faced by the United States in the Third World in the 1950s. The preexisting international development concepts the United States had grafted onto its foreign policy seemed to be foundering and with them a critical means to wage the Cold War. The persistent troubles encountered by liberal modernization in practice called into question basic assumptions about American society and its ability to mold the world in its image. Eisenhower would bear many of the burdens raised by these perceptions. Toward the end of an administration whose modernization policies had fluctuated dramatically, the president was afflicted by the intractable problem of South Korea. He lamented how it was "discouraging to try to help various countries achieve stability and then find that the countries which received the most assistance became the most unstable."[99]

Chapter 5

"THE GREAT AMERICAN MISSION"

MODERNIZATION AND THE UNITED STATES IN
THE WORLD, 1952–1960

Technical assistance to the peoples of the world is the
great American mission of our time.
—*International Development Advisory Board, 1953*

THE SUBJECT OF INTERNATIONAL AFFAIRS was not unfamiliar to American movie audiences in the 1950 and early 1960s. A number of films delved into the contemporary Cold War conflicts between the United States and USSR. Among these was the lighthearted *Romanoff and Juliet,* which opened at a deadlocked late-night session of the United Nations. A crucial vote before the general assembly, expected to be an even split between blocs, is suddenly upset when the tiny principality of Concordia, headed by an indomitable Peter Ustinov, abstains from the roll call. Understanding the significance of this action, Ustinov gathers his delegation for a hasty departure from New York, saying, "Let's get out of here before the Americans can offer us aid."[1]

Ustinov's quip would have brought a chuckle from more than a few Americans. Many in the public understood that foreign aid had become an important part of the U.S. foreign policy arsenal. But the comment also reveals the understanding that development aid was foundational to the struggle for ideological influence with the Soviet Union. The 1950s saw a considerable expansion of interest in modernization as a way for the United States to fulfill its mission in the world. It is a sign of how deeply modernization insinuated itself into American views of the world and of itself. However, the U.S. government in the 1950s departed from the policies instituted during the Truman years. The Eisenhower administration did not share the deep enthusiasm that Truman and his supporters had held for a modernization comfortable with large-scale state planning. The conservative flank of the Republican Party, with a rich tradition of hostility toward the New Deal, took aim at the foreign aid programs drawing on its legacy. With overseas programs derided as "giveaways," comparison with the New Deal was a further strike. Back in the White House for the first time since 1932, the Republicans rushed to implement policies advocating freer trade as the means to global prosperity as opposed to foreign aid with a bias toward planning. There was a comparable backing away from multilateral institutions, particularly the UN.

However, the administration's oscillation on development would miss the full scope of modernization activity in a crucial period of the Cold War. The key point is that modernization was an *American* mission—one that appealed to a wide selection of individuals and institutions across society. Guiding and containing the "revolution of rising expectations" in the "new nations" of the Third World was believed to be a fundamental part of international affairs. The government primed important parts of activity, but significant parts remained outside the state. Interest in modernization united peoples and organizations of differing classes and even creeds. Missionaries, private charities, universities, foundations, businesses, and international organizations refocused or redoubled activities in the 1950s. Their varied work demonstrated that nonstate actors still had considerable influence on the process. Americans came to view overseas engagement in development assistance as a long-term, indispensable part of their place in the world and a reflection on American society. As the Republican administration shifted views on global development, many NGOs remained adherents to a larger international consensus on liberal development. In fact, private advocates were forced to better articulate many existing ideas to change government posture. Elements of the school of modernization theory emerged from their academic settings as part of a battle over policies seen as essential to the successful prosecution of the Cold War.

Vocal supporters agreed with many outside the United States that the primacy of the state and planning was foundational to successful modernization. This was not surprising when many in the West had made their peace with the "mixed economy." While a new world situation accelerated the tempo of modernization activity, the overall American approach was not conceptually new. Domestically and internationally these modernization efforts were seen to be departures of scale but not necessarily of kind from the work of the proceeding generation. Continuity between previous efforts by missionaries and other private groups, the New Deal, and the assumptions about development needs was not overlooked. Connected to this was the affirmation of the powerful social aspects of modernization. With the growing prominence of modernization in international affairs, social scientists placed renewed attention on the impacts of modernization on social and political life, down to its psychological impacts on the individual. Even as a spectrum of new institutions and scholarship emerged, basic assumptions maintained strong links to pre–Cold War thinking.

Nevertheless the Cold War tightly knit the institutional and intellectual elements together. There was a widely shared assumption that states of the Third World were universally on track to modernity, it was only a question of what engine would pull them to it. A communist "aid offensive" in the mid-1950s shook Western confidence that their ideas would prevail in this argument. There were renewed efforts by the United States to retain its position as leader and steer the progress of underdeveloped nations to fit within a liberal order. At the end of the 1950s, these demands, along with the agitation of various nongovernmental agents, swung the Eisenhower administration away from its free market posture and hostility to state planning to a consensus approach to modernization.

No Consensus: "Trade not Aid"

In the first years of the Eisenhower administration it looked as if some important ideas foundational to American development aid—particularly emphasis on state initiative—would be abandoned. After leaving office, Truman recounted bitterly that the Republicans were "now abolishing or renaming every good set-up I left in the government. Point IV is the outstanding one; if they can sabotage that, they will have accomplished their purpose."[2] The former president's comments were premature. The Republicans did not plan to entirely banish modernization from America's foreign policy repertoire. However, the first years of Eisenhower's rule did see a conspicuous shift in government priorities.

Much came down to a catchphrase, "trade not aid." The president centered his initial foray into foreign aid around the recommendations of the Randall Commission. Its report, composed in 1953, made the priority in foreign economic policy free trade. The Randall Commission set the tone during the first two years of Eisenhower's presidency. Private investment was pushed forward as the primary means to spur international development. This colored approaches to foreign aid, turning focus away from the tempered statist and multilateral approaches that characterized the Truman years. Multilateral aid was to be continued, but it was no longer to be a priority. There would also be an increased emphasis on military aid and military pacts as a primary means to contain the communist threat.[3]

One opening act of the Eisenhower presidency was the appointment of a new aid administrator, Harold Stassen. Although emphasizing his hopes for an expansion of American private investment overseas, Stassen acknowledged the Point Four idea, calling the overall program "sound." In an interview in the *New York Times* with former MSA chief Averril Harriman, he supported the basic modernization concepts marked by the

amorphous Point Four label. Stassen, like his predecessors, felt it necessary to build new capacities and outlooks in less developed societies. He
repeated conventional wisdom regarding the differences between recipients of American aid, as "it is one thing to set out in Europe to restore
what once was . . . It is another thing to build in Asia what never was and
under the handicap of scant technical know how."[4]

Still, aid officials had reason to fear being "Stassenated." There was a
strong distaste for foreign aid among important Republican constituencies. The party in power looked upon programs created with an affinity
for planning with a jaundiced eye. There came a rush of bureaucratic
reforms as the Republicans shaped the government to their policies. The
institutional heir to Point Four, the TCA, was consigned to history in
1953. It was replaced by the Foreign Operations Administration (FOA),
a body independent of the State Department that assumed the responsibilities of the MSA, TCA, IIAA, and even some of those belonging to
UNKRA.[5] Independence would be short-lived, as FOA was slung back
into the State Department and rechristened the International Cooperation
Agency (ICA) in 1955. This back and forth was one reflection of the vari-
able views of aid during the Eisenhower years. Despite all this bureaucratic shuffling, however, many of those involved in these programs clung
to the Point Four label as a generalized label for liberal modernization
efforts. Indeed, throughout the 1950s many Americans continued to refer
to a spectrum of modernization activities as "Point Four" programs.[6]
Nevertheless, even if these principles remained, across the official world
staff changed, budgets were cut, and priorities were realigned.

Reorganization also meant a decline in the UN's importance as a collaborator with U.S. aid efforts. The Eisenhower administration quickly grew
uneasy with multilateral development and its connection to the Cold War
competition with the USSR. The first probes in a Soviet "aid offensive"
after 1953 brought increased activity in the UN's specialized agencies,
raising eyebrows in Washington. There was agreement at high levels in
the State Department that these actions within the UN were cynical, intended to gain propaganda points and cause mischief in the developing
nations. Nevertheless, this activity enflamed lingering suspicions of the
organization. These were well highlighted by the response to a proposal
for a Special United Nations Fund for Economic Development
(SUNFED). The initiative had enthusiastic friends in the developing nations as it promised another source of capital for underdeveloped nations.
However, constituencies within the Eisenhower administration stood opposed to it. Under-Secretary of State Herbert Hoover, Jr., dismissed it as
a "token." Publicly, the Americans' refusal to contribute was blamed on
the Soviets. They argued that until funds were freed up by world disarma-
ment, there could be no significant monies for the special fund.[7]

Such a strained argument brought frustration with Republican priori-
ies from the NGO community. The Eisenhower emphasis on free trade
and suspicion of planning was not shared by many in the United States
and internationally. Among voluntary groups there were calls for immediate action on SUNFED. Walter Reuther, president of the CIO, called the
lack of support "utterly unrealistic," considering the United States' massive economic resources.[8] Unsurprisingly, there was frustration internationally over American intransigence. While there were concerns within
the administration and Congress that SUNFED might require a dispro-
portionate level of funding from the United States, there was serious concern that the program would provide communist states with yet another
UN stage to strut their agendas. The backing away from UNKRA in South
Korea was part of this trend. Into the mid-1950s, the U.S. government,
suspicious of the burdens and Soviet intentions in multilateral aid programs, kept its distance from international aid organizations.

THE INTERNATIONAL REACH OF THE MODERNIZATION CONSENSUS

Even as the United Nations played a less important role in U.S. development efforts, it took on an enhanced important role in explaining the
process of modernization. The institutional capacity bestowed during the
1940s provided the UN with the means. UN agencies produced a series
of studies explaining modernization, fulfilling the organization's role as
a center for modernization activity. These UN studies also demonstrate
that many ideas regarding development were based on long-standing approaches that were being restated for a changed postwar world.

The UN set an international group of experts to study the question.
Their 1951 recommendations were broad and centered on state action,
showing that assumptions about the process were shared across borders.
Local governments were instructed to increase capital formation and build
domestic institutions that could develop infrastructural, industrial, agricultural, medical, and human capacities. Population growth, too, had to be
controlled as it could complicate development. The experts urged comprehensive, preferably decentralized, planning. In an outline for action, the
international community was urged to give favorable terms of trade and
to allocate capital of up to $1 billion to support economic development.
However, modernization was more than a matter of pulling the right financial levers. It was "impossible without painful readjustments." Poorer
countries needed technology but, in many places, social organization and
individual psychology created an obstacle to the absorption of modern
techniques. The experts saw huge gaps between the advanced West and
poorer areas exemplified by the Middle East, where "agricultural tech-

niques are no better today than they were in the times of the Pharoahs [*sic*]." Western nations, accustomed to regularly embracing new scientific advances, could better utilize technology. Without technical assistance and educational aid, underdeveloped peoples would not adopt the same habits and gain a progressive "scientific attitude" that would further development. The basic assumption was "economic progress will not occur unless the atmosphere is favourable to it. The people of a country must desire progress, and their social, economic, legal and political institutions must be favourable to it." Americans were not alone in their assumptions that modernization required that much of society be transformed.[9]

UNESCO continued its work on development, initiating a series of studies and conferences in the early 1950s on modernization techniques and their cultural and social impact. American voluntary groups were an important source of information because they had operated in "every corner of the globe for a half century before the phrase 'technical assistance' became current." The UN studies of the early 1950s are a reminder that those in public policy internationally were generally not constructing new methodologies of modernization but expanding existing ideas. Existing international development experience had a critical relevance as its conceptual foundations were not different from that needed for a Cold War world. Americans queried for the UNESCO survey felt that the "*development of a spirit of self-help and initiative*" was crucial (emphasis original). It was not just the cultivation of skills, techniques, and technology, but a change in perception that marked success. Achieving this clearly meant that "development goals are inextricably related to broader social purposes." Obviously, social impacts of any program had to be considered from the very beginning of any effort. Because "virtually no technical assistance can in fact be provided that does not touch some economic, political or social nerve end."[10]

Perhaps the most durable study to come out of this international ferment was *Cultural Patterns and Technical Change* published as a guide for all the varied groups contending with modernization. Edited by anthropological superstar Margaret Mead, it was premised on the question, "*how can technical change be introduced with such regard for the culture pattern that human values are preserved?*" (emphasis original). It was a question of social stability in the face of new relationships brought by new forms of industry, agriculture, political organization, health care, or education. These new structures would change personal psychologies and, potentially, threaten the mental stability of individuals. Modernization, therefore, was not solely an economic question but also a critical mental health issue. As Mead herself noted, "of what use to introduce a tractor which made the yield greater . . . if in so doing the whole distinguishing fabric of life which had characterized a society would be ripped to shreds?" The contributors understood that technological change and attempts to control it were not new. However, the international community had the responsibility to "deal scientifically with the concomitant effects of such change" to discover the most beneficial manner for it to proceed.[11]

Mead's book endured. It went through numerous printings, remaining an important text in the development community into the 1970s. Mead's work and the other projects of the newly formed "specialized agencies" demonstrate the influence of the UN on expanding modernization efforts globally. It also proves that many understood that the transformation they sought was powerful and potentially dangerous. It would change societies and economies in dramatic ways, and that change necessarily reached down to individuals.

Assumptions that modernization would reach down to these most personal levels demanded models that acknowledged such views. The growing popularity of the TVA concept reflected this demand. The concepts it represented had not altered since the 1930s. It continued to highlight claims that there was a tried and true means to approach the problem of modernization while reconciling ominous politics and technologies with individual and popular needs. For the United States, it continued to provide a modernization model that could claim origins setting it apart from communist competitors.

If the TVA's reputation grew after the war, so too did that of its biggest booster. Lilienthal also became a global presence. A stint heading the Atomic Energy Commission between 1946 and 1950 only raised his profile. Social arbiters at the *New Yorker* feted him in their columns during the 1950s and early 1960s. *House Beautiful* even ran a photo spread on his Norris, Tennessee, home in 1947.[12] Sliding into private life, he cut a truce with corporate America, extolling the role of regulated big business, and even coined the term "multinational corporation."[13] Surprising some, in 1955 he joined this for-profit world, helping to found a consulting firm, Development and Resources (D&R). The company sought to make a profit by putting to work U.S. "government development experience" accentuated with "private business and financial talents" promoting modernization around the world. The company advised Colombia, Puerto Rico, Iran, and eventually South Vietnam (among many others) on modernization programs. Drawing much of its staff from Knoxville, this emphasis was natural for what was "virtually a T.V.A. alumni association."[14] Executives trumpeted that Lilienthal formed D&R to "carry on . . . the development philosophies which had evolved in his TVA experience." But any lingering New Deal emphasis on the public good had been subordinated to a corporate outlook where staff saw themselves as "businessmen who mean to make a profit at what we're doing."[15]

Figure 5.1. Worldwide high-wire act: Lilienthal, then head of the international consulting firm Development and Resources Corporation, crosses the Dez Canyon in Iran with John Blumberg, March 1961. David Lilienthal Papers. Public Policy Papers Division. Department of Rare Books and Special Collections. Princeton University Library.

Despite this change there was strong continuity in the conceptualization of development. Lilienthal continued to offer the TVA as the best single example of a liberal approach to global development. Release of the "creative energies of men" remained the goal of the process. Technology and management had to be combined in a way that provided material gain for the people subject to a development effort. Yet, the critical accomplishment was not the transformation of people's physical surroundings or their material well-being but the alteration of their basic outlook. The modernization campaign gave people a host of new skills, but it also changed their basic psychology. Lilienthal saw a dramatic payoff:

> If a great dam or new system or roads inspires people in a country with a feeling that this is theirs, and that it provides an opportunity, a leverage by which they and their young people can look to the future with hopefulness in specific ways, then that great dam as an inspiration will produce more than electricity and irrigation, the road network more than transport. It will produce a change in spirit, a release of energies and self-confidence which are the indispensable factors in the future of that country.[16]

Lilienthal pointed to the transformation of Tennessee by bringing the river to heel, making electricity widely available, and by upgrading industry as well as education. Decisive all, but the leading contribution was not in the physical sense but the changes it made to people's minds. What made the Tennessee Valley unrecognizable from its pre-1933 days was that its 7.5 million inhabitants were able to find the "self-reliance, independence and creativity" inside themselves through their collective work with the programs of the TVA.[17]

Development and Resources assumed the story would be similar overseas. Early projects in Iran and Colombia reinforced Lilienthal's assumptions. If a foreign program was based on the experience of the TVA, such a program held promise to transform the natural environment and the people who inhabited it. In this way, a modernization program imposed by outside authorities could have a radical impact on a target society. Technology provided through a program in which the locals were *"given a chance to become a part of that process of change"* would uncover "latent" technical talents of a people or would provide new technological skills (emphasis original). Eventually, those people would be able to take on technical and managerial tasks. They would become an indispensable wedge to drive out backwards, ignorant, and traditional outlooks with those that were optimistic, forward looking, hopeful, and decidedly modern in society as a whole.[18] While influential, Lilienthal's thinking should be seen as one part of an existing and evolving consensus on development.

It was not merely something ex-New Dealers bandied about but a view shared by an array of international and private institutions.

The maturing World Bank grasped these ideas as it turned its attentions toward the "Third World." The ascension of Eugene Black to the presidency ended a prevailing Eurocentrism. Black felt transfer of Western technology was a vital part of this new development mission. Western development assistance, brought by technocrats whose skills and disinterested internationalist outlook put them "above politics," would soothe relations between newly independent states as well as provide for economic growth. Republican Party loyalties aside, Black found the TVA concept a useful means to implement bank policy. So did many of his subordinates. The gaze of staffers saw many areas of the globe, particularly the Middle East, riddled with opportunities to lay down TVAs. In fact, the TVA model became the basis for a diplomatic success that shaped the Bank's early reputation.[19]

In 1951, Black picked up a copy of *Collier's* magazine to discover an article by Lilienthal on the increasing tensions between India and Pakistan in Kashmir. Lilienthal, writing after a trip to India, thought the issue was "pure dynamite" but could be defused. Central to this solution was the development of the Indus River with benefits for both countries as "a unit—designed, built and operated as a unit, as is the seven-state TVA system back in the US."[20] Lilienthal had already taken the initiative. Contacting the Pakistani ambassador to the United States with his plan, Lilienthal received a favorable response.[21] Black added the weight of the World Bank that same summer. After first seeking Lilienthal's opinion, Black spoke to the Indian and Pakistani prime ministers, extending World Bank technical assistance in resolving the Indus dispute. In his letters to each leader Black took care to highlight the fact the negotiations he was suggesting had been inspired by Lilienthal.[22] The offer of the Bank's good offices and technical aid helped bring India and Pakistan to the negotiating table. To fulfill this promise Black dispatched Raymond A. Wheeler, head of the World Bank engineering staff, to facilitate the discussions.[23]

Prolonged negotiations brought a 1960 settlement. Success was also the product of Indian Prime Minister Jawaharlal Nehru's affinity for the sort of resource development the Indus represented. Lilienthal met him during his 1951 trip to the subcontinent and was impressed by someone he termed a "predominately modern man." Lilienthal was perceptive; Nehru was enamored with the power of science and technology, but still held a reverence for India's past. Most pleasing to Lilienthal was the stock Nehru put in modernization to strengthen his nation's economy and society.[24]

Nehru's ambitions had allies at home. Before and after independence, a slate of Indian technologists looked to the United States as an example.[25]

One leading engineer, Kanwar Sain, felt the United States, the "child of modern engineering," had successfully shown how to tap rivers for their cheap and renewable energy, the "life-breath of industry." But lessons were not just in the technical accomplishments. The United States provided some of the best thinking to contend with the deep social impact of science and technology.[26] After independence the Damodar Valley Corporation (DVC), directly modeled on the TVA, was among the first major development projects to be established. Programs for other Indian rivers would follow.[27] Nehru rhapsodized about the dams, calling them modern temples, asking "where can be a greater and holier place than this, which we can regard higher?"[28] The appeal of the TVA model for Indians, and Nehru in particular, was a reflection of the international preference for large technological programs in the service of national development.

While there was widespread support for the style of liberal development embodied by the TVA, it was not total. At home, conservatives were all too aware of modernization's New Deal genealogy. A flank of the Republican Party never warmed to it and the American public could be receptive to their criticism characterizing development programs as mere "giveaways." Eisenhower played to these feelings early in his tenure, deriding the TVA as "creeping socialism," and threatened to sell the whole thing off.[29] Treasury Secretary George Humphrey voiced conservative suspicions. Multilateral aid through the UN was likely to create burdens disproportionately carried by the United States. But his reticence was also ideological, based on a discomfort with the prevailing orientation of dominant development thinking. Humphrey distrusted approaches privileging the state, stating, "My great criticism of our past programs has been that we have been . . . building up governmental regimes . . . [Accordingly] we are tremendously strengthening the state as opposed to the individual and lessening the opportunity for the individual ever to compete with the state." It seemed counterproductive "in a great contest between two opposite ideologies: one based on freedom of the individual in the development of the individual initiative for his own benefit . . . the other based on the all powerful state." Aid that generally promoted the consensus approach seemed to be working against "the ideology we are spending so much money to defend."[30]

Humphrey's view might have appeared parochial when compared to the evolving international consensus on modernization that placed national economic planning at the core of development. Revisiting an issue from the 1930s, Karl Mannheim asserted democratic planning was the third and best way to freedom—between the extremes on the right and left—in a world in profound historical flux.[31] In the 1950s and 1960s, the influential figures in international economics—Gunnar Myrdal, W. Arthur Lewis, Alexander Gerschenkron, and John Kenneth Galbraith—made state planning and intervention a point of emphasis. Extending ideas that germinated in the 1930s and 1940s, all held that central governments in emerging nations had to perform certain economic and social tasks as critical sectors of civil society and economic life were too weak.[32]

Accord was part of what some declared the "end of ideology." Daniel Bell famously posited that the acceptance of the "Welfare State; the desirability of decentralized power; a system of mixed economy and of political pluralism" had exhausted utopia, emptying systems of thought of their rancorous passions. As elites in the West accommodated themselves to this mellow reality, there were still tumultuous issues loose in the rest of the world. The "rising states" were fashioning new mass ideologies of "economic development and national power." The West encouraged these goals but was concerned with how they might be achieved. Bell saw Russia and China as increasingly popular models to fulfill these desires. While he did see communism's promises of mobility and improved living standards in the midst of social change as alluring in mass society, his worry was not communism per se (he believed it a doctrine without content). Rather, the ferment raised an older question whether this economic advance would be built on democratic, voluntary principles or shackled to totalitarianism.[33] The ascendancy of "collectivist" approaches in political economy in the West made statist efforts acceptable, even attractive, in the race to court developing states plotting their course to modernity.[34] In fact, state planning was so widely acknowledged as an integral part of effective development that in the *International Encyclopedia of the Social Sciences*, appearing in the 1960s, "development" did not have its own entry; it was a subsection under "economic planning."[35]

Such views were assuredly a consensus, not absolute dogma. There were voices that broke ranks, even within development economics. Economist P. T. Bauer railed against prevailing assumptions by questioning whether state-led planning could effectively manage development. Sharing other views long held on the right, he was skeptical of the social change and engineering that many consensus partisans accepted. If there was a role for the state, it was in protecting the rights of individuals to allow them to pursue their interests. Bauer had a cogent perspective but was well aware he was dueling with the dominant trends in economics and international life.[36]

For all the critiques circulating among intellectual circles and the Eisenhower administration, the TVA and its liberal statist modernization did have a limited place in U.S. diplomacy. Even at the height of the influence of "trade not aid," a 1953 TVA-sponsored report on the Jordan River Valley became an important component of the Eisenhower administration's "Water for Peace" program. As with the Indus, cooperative devel-

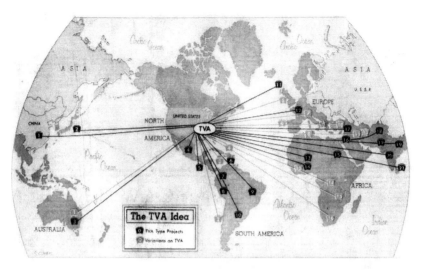

Figure 5.2. The TVA's World Offspring. An American conception of the global plans inspired by the TVA's example of development, as published in the *Milwaukee Journal*, 1958. Courtesy of *Milwaukee Journal-Sentinel*.

opment of the Jordan would serve to forge lasting peace between the riparian Syrians, Jordanians, and Israelis.[37] Still, there were limits in the early 1950s to how it would be applied. Eisenhower's "Water for Peace" initiative might have suggested U.S. interest toward an evolving TVA inspired scheme to harness the Mekong River in an increasingly tense Southeast Asia. The concept had been taken up by the Economic Commission for Asia and the Far East (ECAFE) in the early 1950s and welcomed by the riparian nations of Southeast Asia—Cambodia, Laos, South Vietnam, and Thailand. Through the UN regional commission they planned to implement the multipurpose river development scheme to serve them all.[38] The U.S. government hesitated, uncomfortable with the plan's multilateral nature, preferring its own bilateral efforts centered on a Bureau of Reclamation study to implant a TVA-style program.[39]

Hesitancy on the part of the Eisenhower administration aside, the example of the extensive, state-led development the TVA embodied was hard at work during the 1950s. It seemed every corner of the globe had programs modeled on it either being planned or under way. Supporters could see development proposals in Colombia, Iran, Ghana, and Japan draped in the program's reputation. One of the most advanced, Australia's "Snowy Mountain" scheme with extensive investments in irrigation, water control, and electricity that would reshape social and economic life across the southeast of the continent, thrilled development advocates.[40]

Figure 5.3. In the American style: Officers of Tanganyika Community Development Cooperatives visit the Loudon Dam of the TVA, ca. 1966. The TVA was a
major tourist attraction for foreign visitors and an important stop for dignitaries.
This developmental tourism was one way the United States articulated its model
of liberal development to global audiences. Courtesy of National Archives, Washington, DC.

For all their popularity, large modernization programs brought Cold
War concerns. The Aswan High Dam demonstrated these fears were not
idle. Gamal Abdel Nasser, nationalist leader of Egypt, wanted to follow
through on existing ideas to yoke the Nile River with a new dam above
an existing dam at Aswan (hence the "high"). Like other water resource
development it promised to transform the unpredictable energy of a major
river into commodities like irrigation and electricity to feed national modernization. Outside aid was sought for what was a massive and complex
undertaking. Here the project touched the live wire of the Cold War. The
United States and the West did not have a monopoly on the technologies
necessary to implement such a program. The USSR's own massive dams
were compelling evidence that communism could provide the infrastructure as well as the ideology necessary to drive modern societies. In late
1955, with the Soviet Union offering aid, the United States and Great
Britain, in conjunction with the World Bank, advanced their own plan to

fund the Aswan project. The World Bank would provide technical support and be the largest single source of outside capital—$200 million of the initial funding for the twelve-year, $1.3 billion endeavor.[41]

However, growing concern about Nasser's ambitions in the region, his plans for the Suez Canal, and his ties with the Soviet Bloc led the Americans and British to revoke their support for the Aswan project in July 1956. The USSR stepped into the breach with remarkable ease. Soviet technicians were able to fulfill the blueprints drafted by German engineers. This move, along with Nasser's East Bloc arms purchases and eventual nationalization of the canal, baited the British and French who, with the Israelis, plunged headlong into an adventure to seize the Suez. The resulting crisis had profound international repercussions but did not halt the construction of the dam. Construction began with Soviet help in 1960 and was completed with much fanfare in 1971.[42] Aswan was a stark illustration of the stakes of the Cold War modernization contest. This stoked the need to highlight the ideological content of each side's development models and shook complacent formulations guiding U.S. government policy.

ADVOCATING THE CONSENSUS AT HOME AND ABROAD

Government aid posture was already being challenged at home. Eisenhower's policies were far from the totality of American development activity in the 1950s. The state was undoubtedly the single most powerful actor when it came to modernization, but there were a collection of influential and active groups within U.S. civil society that made modernization, on various planes of action, a central part of the United States' activity internationally and an important factor in the way it understood its place in the world. Foundations, universities, and missionaries saw modernization built around large-scale technical aid and steeped in the consensus as vital to the U.S. position in the world. Lilienthal was not alone in pushing a liberal approach to foreign aid. There was considerable support from those on the left who embraced the reform effort of the 1930s. Support for Point Four-type modernization did not subside as the Democrats surrendered the White House. From his position at the Ford Foundation, Frank X. Sutton witnessed a procession of exiled New Dealers into foundation staffs in the early 1950s. This migration from the government undoubtedly had an impact on the private activity. Lobby and informational groups devoted to modernization sprang up in Washington and New York. Clearinghouses appeared to coordinate information and activity between the assortment of governmental and nongovernmental groups working on modernization overseas. New Dealers like

Chester Bowles and Robert Nathan became advocates, agitating for funds for overseas aid.[43]

New organizations joined established actors. The Rockefeller Foundation continued to be one of the most influential private institutions in international development. Under Dean Rusk, released from his post as Under Secretary of State, the philanthropy renewed its development efforts. Rusk's watch saw the creation of the Los Baños Rice Research Institute in the Philippines. Its goal was to increase the yield of various crops in order to feed growing populations in Asia and elsewhere. This was considered crucial, as population growth was seen as a major challenge to successful economic development. During the 1950s, however, the topography of the foundation world shifted and Rockefeller surrendered its primacy in international development. This was true even for Los Baños, where Rockefeller partnered with one of the newest and by far the biggest of U.S. philanthropies, the Ford Foundation.[44]

Although founded in 1936, Henry Ford's death in 1947 allowed a massive expansion of the Ford Foundation's program. By 1957, the foundation had assets of $3.31 billion, nearly five times that of the Rockefeller Foundation. Rusk described it as the "fat boy in the philanthropic canoe." Paul Hoffman, recently retired head of the ECA, was selected in 1950 as the first non-family member to head the foundation (cries of a "leftist slant" in programming soon followed). Under Hoffman, Ford invested heavily in the Cold War, supporting cultural programs in Europe that matured under the guidance of Shepherd Stone. It also directed considerable resources toward the developing world. Hoffman, after studies and discussions, including consultations with Nehru, decided to put particular emphasis on Asia. In a 1951 trip he came away with the belief that "Asia can still be saved from communism" with judiciously applied modernization. Ford promised initiatives to fill in the gaps of government programs. Hoffman's tenure lasted only two years, before disagreements with the foundation's board brought a "purge," but Ford would retain this orientation, playing a powerful role in modernization in the coming decades.[45]

The foundations continued to underwrite a growing community of development institutions and research into the process itself. The final member of the troika of large American foundations, the Carnegie Corporation of New York, picked UNRRA, ECA, and MSA veteran Harlan Cleveland, then dean of the public affairs school at Syracuse University, to lead an investigation into the place of Americans in international foreign aid. The "Carnegie Project" provides a historical snapshot of the collection of state and nonstate actors promoting modernization and the assumptions behind their work.[46]

Cleveland's experience made him a logical—even if he was not the first—choice to head such an inquiry.[47] The "Carnegie Project" articulated mainstream views of the stakes for the United States in overseas development at the time. Cleveland, who claimed to have coined the phrase, "revolution of rising expectations," was well aware that the world was being remade by the rush for national independence.[48] For these new nations the conflict between the United States and USSR was secondary to the urge for development. They were motivated by what was seen as the great idea of the age, "*the idea of constant growth*" (emphasis original). National leaders looked longingly at American and European accomplishments in science and technology as the keys to progress, which was viewed, in turn, as the basis of postcolonial success. This was part of the wider global consensus, that national economic performance was the gauge of development achievement.[49]

Like many Americans, Cleveland was aware that there was more than one route to modernity. Western Europe, while responsible for dramatic technological accomplishments, was saddled with the moldering legacy of colonialism. Even putting this history aside, the most inspiring cases of national development in the preceding generation were not Western. Before World War II, the authoritarian regimes of Japan and the Soviet Union marked massive economic gains. In the 1950s, this history was coupled with the Soviet-Chinese economic offensive in the less developed countries. This was merely a new front since overt military action, the "diversionary attack" in Korea, had been stymied by UN military action. It was simply a new spin on Lenin's maxim that "the road to Paris runs through Peking." Only now, perhaps, the revolutionary highway ran through "New Delhi, Djakarta, and Cairo."[50]

At the core of modernization was "economic progress and the nature of the political and social institutions required to get it going and keep it in hand." There was no doubt the communists could deliver on promises to build the dams, roads, or factories that were the benchmarks of progress. What unnerved Cleveland about modernization by peoples in the "East" was not whether "they *can* but how and under what auspices they *will*" (emphasis original). His considerable experience instilled in Cleveland the belief that it was less important what task a modernization project performed so long as it built institutions to administer various aspects of social life. This was not merely transplanting American institutions but doing "something of what TVA did for our own Southland," constructing new institutions based on the existing resources and skills of a particular country. But this left an indelible mark on social systems. Hence the communist strategy of courting the Third World with economic and technical aid had to be countered. Their promises of modernization to leaders in Africa and Asia tended to emphasize "not *how* the dam will be built but *that* it will be built" (emphasis original). This cloaked the fact that the communists were selling a "Forced Way" of social organization, luring the peoples of the underdeveloped world down a road to economic development whose terminus was slavery.[51]

Cleveland suggested that representatives of the United States, which included those working for government, voluntary, missionary, and business groups abroad, should develop a program that was neither strictly anti-communist nor purely humanitarian. They had to help the people of the developing countries navigate the tumult of independence, the communist threat, and the revolution of rising expectations. It was in the U.S. national interest to see these new states meet "the challenge of the 'triple revolution,' without coming under the domination of any outside power and without adopting a repressive system of internal regimentation." Again, this was not supposed to be an uncritical export of American ideas. Modern institutions had to be built in the Third World with local participation and with an eye to local needs. Nevertheless, the United States was stepping up to lead because of its particular capacity to shepherd the world forward—not to clone "our form of government" but to support "the universal idea that man is free."[52]

Cleveland had articulated the conventional wisdom and the "Carnegie Project" used it as a starting point. In explaining "overseasmanship," they started with the shifts in American interaction with the world. The postwar period had seen dramatic changes especially in the magnitude of American overseas activity. This was an extension of existing trends. The numbers of Americans drawn overseas had increased massively in the fifteen years following World War II. Tourism was one measure, with approximately 4 million Americans traveling abroad in 1960, compared to an annual average of 400,000 in the 1930s. Another was the vast overseas military deployments, meaning 1.2 million servicemen were abroad in 1957. But most significant were the 1.5 million American civilians living abroad by 1959. Of these, over 100,000 were hard at work on projects with U.S. organizations (excluding those working for the U.S. military). They were split among the government, missionary, business, educational, and voluntary groups. Much of their work was related to modernization to create a new world order.[53]

These Americans were operating in a transformed world, defined politically by nationalism and economically by industrialization. In the countries recently freed from colonial rule there were rising expectations and the desire of leaders to cultivate modern economies and industry. Logically, these societies should follow the path illustrated "most vividly by the United States." In the contemporary world, "international affairs were now internal affairs" as modernization required direct activity by Americans inside these countries to foster the deep change required by modernization. The Soviet efforts to "isolate the West from its former dependencies in Africa and Asia" forced a competition. The speed with which "operations on a global scale in military, economic, social, [and] psychological fields" expanded was due to the Soviet threat. Nevertheless, the authors asserted that American attempts to influence the course of these nations rested on values that desired a "rising standard of life and a growing measure of personal freedom" for all peoples.[54]

Despite rapid changes, many overseas activities had a long heritage. Missionaries certainly had the most impressive legacy, but the postwar world had revised their activities. Programs by Christian groups were increasingly described as "ecumenical" with the missionary "increasingly . . . a specialist who adds technical skills to his basic desire to serve" rather than a disciple. These new, modular missionaries could be more easily coupled with others. Secular groups had a wealth of experience that came not only from contending with the shocks of war and recovery but also from projects that preceded World War II. American businesses had long been operating globally and knew how to interact with peoples on the ground. They were also an important means of transmitting skills as businesses were increasingly subcontractors in major development projects worldwide. Cleveland and his contributors believed the goal of all these efforts was the construction of local institutions to support modern societies, economies, and governments. In this effort, U.S. government authorities in a foreign country were merely the hub of a diverse set of modernization efforts. The international arena presented new problems and they could not be mastered through modernization without utilizing the experience and expertise held by non-governmental groups.[55]

The forces demanding an increasing number of Americans overseas were not going to relent anytime soon. Even the newer government and private institutions focused on foreign aid work were giving the impression of setting down deep roots. This fact, and the importance of the task the United States was engaged in, required changes domestically. Central to this was education, particularly at the university level. Universities, according to the study, needed to take on a greater role in preparing Americans for their global role. There was a pressing need to expand the scope and enrollments of international and area studies to meet the personnel requirements of U.S. organizations committed to development.[56]

The calls for more activity on the part of American universities were unnecessary. The spectrum of U.S. university involvement in foreign affairs in general and development in particular was undergoing a transformation during the 1950s. While American institutions of higher education had long been supporting development activities in various parts of the world, there was a qualitative and quantitative shift in this engagement. The FOA and ICA, like their predecessors, continued to need university capacities. Repeated calls were answered by a variety of schools across the country that were soon sending their own modernization missions to diverse corners of the earth. By 1957, Turkey alone could count Georgetown University, New York University, and the University of Nebraska among those providing technical assistance under U.S. government contracts.[57]

One of the most active was Michigan State University (MSU). A land-grant college with a tradition of extension work within the United States itself, MSU was quick to capitalize on the need for technical assistance. In the early 1950s, it worked with the TCA, sending technical assistance missions to the Ryukyu Islands, Colombia, and Brazil. Its largest exertions would be as part of the Eisenhower administration's nation-building efforts in South Vietnam. There, in collaboration with Catholic charities and the International Rescue Committee, MSU assisted South Vietnam in assimilating nearly 1 million refugees fleeing the North following the 1954 Geneva Accords. However, MSU put its largest effort into building the local institutions seen as essential to the construction of stable, modern societies. In South Vietnam, a team of experts from MSU, funded by the U.S. government, trained a new civil service and national police force.[58]

Part of this institution building included the construction of elementary and higher education in various parts of the world. American foundations and universities helped build or develop a wide array of educational institutions globally. But modernization would change American education as well. Universities greedily consumed massive amounts of federal and foundation money to establish specialized "area studies" institutes to cultivate knowledge that could be applied to overseas operations and Cold War analysis. At the height of the Cold War in the 1950s and 1960s, federal research money (for all subjects) fluctuated between 12 and 26 percent of total university revenues, up from a slight 5 percent in 1946. Strategically placed grants by Ford, Carnegie, Rockefeller, and other foundations were critical to the growth of these university programs. Between 1953 and 1966, Ford alone gave $270 million to thirty-four universities for area and language studies programs.[59] Beyond the cultivation of university capacity, the large foundations supported programs that tapped academic knowledge that could be placed in the direct service of overseas development projects. In an influential 1964 report, John Gardner, president of the Carnegie Corporation, advocated strengthening ties between the governmental aid bodies and academia. One of the leading examples of such links was the Southeast Asian Development Advisory Group (SEADAG), established by the Asia Society in 1966 to transmit the expertise of academics directly to policymakers.[60]

Perhaps the most significant institution to emerge from the confluence of government, foundation, and university collaboration was the Center for International Studies (CENIS) at the Massachusetts Institute of Technology (MIT). Propaganda and "political warfare" efforts of the early Cold War supported by the university eventually brought calls for a permanent center at MIT. CENIS appeared in 1952 under the leadership of economist and academic entrepreneur Max Millikan, seeded by $850,000 from the Ford Foundation. The center's goal was not a single grand social theory but "problem-oriented" studies to inform policy. The assumption was such investigations could be done without conflict of interest arising from close contact with the government and other centers of power, because American social science had achieved a "value-free" set of methodologies. CENIS hoped to stand at the intersection of academic research on human behavior and public policy. Gathering a collection of political scientists, economists, and communications specialists under his banner, Millikan placed an institutional focus on broad structural issues in international life and the American role in promoting change. Attention quickly turned to modernization.[61]

The faculty roster at CENIS held the best and brightest of early modernization theory. Among those Millikan recruited was Daniel Lerner. Heavily influenced by the behavioralism emerging out of psychology during the first half of the twentieth century, Lerner was transfixed by the social impact of modernization. Lerner, whose 1958 book, *The Passing of Traditional Society*, achieved near-canonical status, restated an assumption carried over from the 1930s—modernization was catalyzed by technology. The most powerful catalysts were mass communication technologies, particularly newspapers and radio. These media exposed people rooted in traditional structures to new opinions, attitudes, and ideas that created a greater empathy and association with others. This exposure also gave them new desires and aspirations and carried them away from older social structures. There were dangers. Dislocation brought about by the process of modernization opened the door to the long-standing fear of "deviation . . . or deformation" of its positive ends. It was this concern with deviancy that would inform other, more directly policy-oriented studies by other CENIS faculty.[62]

Walt Rostow, a recruit who would become a close collaborator of Millikan's, fought hard to move aid policy away from "trade not aid." In fact, central parts of what would become known as the school of modernization theory should be seen as part of a debate over the shape of government development policy. Millikan and Rostow were among those in the policy community who were hostile to the early focus on trade in the Eisenhower years. Each shared the widespread belief that modernization had the potential to deform societies, so it had to be done in the right manner.

They were among those who assumed many poorer nations could not absorb investment or were not attractive markets for private capital and needed policies that were responsive to their special needs.[63] At the same time their belief shows how modernization always reflected back on the image the United States had of itself. Developing the world was a barometer of success in the Cold War, proof that the American pattern for modern life was up to the ideological struggle abroad and vigorous at home.

Opportunities for the duo to shape policy came early. By 1954, Secretary of State John Foster Dulles was concerned with Soviet initiatives in the developing world. He recruited C. D. Jackson, the president's former assistant on psychological warfare, to defuse the "Crisis of 1954" with a new "World Economic Plan." Jackson found the talent for the project outside the government. Rostow and Millikan were among those recruited for an off the record conference at the Princeton Inn in New Jersey.[64] Afterwards, Millikan and Rostow distilled the meeting's findings. Echoing formulations articulated in the 1930s, their report demanded that an ideological threat be contained. To do so, economic development was a necessity to create a world environment where "societies which directly or indirectly menace ours will not evolve." A "partnership for growth" was the framework to achieve this better world. It would provide desperately needed capital to developing countries, not just through private investment but with aid grants. However, capital was not enough. The problem was most underdeveloped nations just did not have the capacity to employ the aid. Here the question became social and political. Technical assistance was necessary to tutor peoples in modern techniques to allow them to put aid to the best use. This required "sustained participation of private as well as public authorities." The institutions of the UN family were still needed, as were private engineering firms, universities, medical associations, and management groups in the United States. Connected to this would be the development of local and regional scientific centers that would cultivate technological training in the poorer countries. Rostow and Millikan said that much of the initiative had to come from local sources. However, outside aid to prime these activities was indispensable as the "transition to sustained growth involves complex and difficult changes that go deep into society."[65]

Millikan and Rostow were reciting mantras common in international development circles. Despite the verve of their argument, conservatives like Humphrey and Under Secretary of State Herbert Hoover, Jr., parried initiatives hatched at the Princeton Inn.[66] Regardless, the Princeton meeting provided a basis for much later work by Rostow and Millikan. From their sally port at CENIS, Millikan and Rostow were able to intervene in the debate, a sign of the influence nongovernmental bodies had on the course of development thinking in the period. They repeated that holding the line against communism demanded the United States intensify efforts to bend the world to its version of modernity as communist approaches necessarily deformed the process. Technical assistance was still a fundamental part of this endeavor. But more important, the social and economic model of liberal development provided by the United States, to lead less developed peoples through the technological and social changes that delivered them to a stable modernity, was a sine qua non of Cold War success.[67]

Academics were not alone in their faith in modernization. Religious groups continued to expand their engagement with overseas development activity during the 1950s. Protestant groups urged the United States to provide sustained support for technical assistance, believing it had "prime and long-term importance in United States foreign policy," because of its "critical importance [for] increasing the social, economic and moral strength of the less developed areas." Many of these groups believed that for it to be successful, multilateralism was necessary. They pushed a recalcitrant government to cooperate with UN proposals like SUNFED. The Catholic Church, echoing its Christian brethren, asserted that technical assistance was "one of the most effective long-range means of justly distributing the world's resources of knowledge and skill to all men so that all countries and peoples may learn to use better the great natural resources with which the earth has been blessed in the Divine Providence of God."[68]

American religious groups had great enthusiasm for the uplift mission fundamental to overseas development. Church groups offered public statements about the need for foreign aid while continuing their own long-standing missionary work. By some counts over 29,000 U.S. Christian missionaries were working around the globe by the late 1950s, a significant increase from already high numbers earlier in the decade. Combined annual outlay for these bodies was $130 million by 1956. Jewish groups engaged in foreign activities added another $86 million to that total. Supporters of modernization noted with satisfaction the role missionaries played in America's private "Point Four" activities.[69]

Many religious groups, like secular voluntary organizations, were comfortable coordinating their overseas work with those of government development agencies. However, religion was not merely a means to supply staff and funds as a buttress to larger state-sponsored programs. Within the aid community there was a view that religious beliefs within underdeveloped nations could be made compatible with development. This was not only true of Christianity, where missionary drives could be turned to the objective at hand, but also of other religions whose themes could provide support for economic and social development. Taking examples from NGO and U.S. government operations in Afghanistan in the 1950s, aid officials were hopeful that Islam's traditions could be used to support modernization programs sponsored by international groups.[70] Courting "judges and mullahs" was crucial, as their influence at the local level was considerable. Verses of the Koran that blessed the improvement of social conditions were cited. There were even suggestions that certain sections of the book endorsed the status of experts. It was asserted "Mohamed said that any professional man is a friend of God; which gives encouragement to the modern specialists."[71] Similar elements were seen in Buddhism and other "more primitive" religions that could be put into the service of development.[72] This ran counter to much thinking that set modernization against "traditional" social structures. It nevertheless shows that significant groups believed social and cultural forces could and should be mobilized by outsiders for the sake of modernization.

For supporters, the potential of religious activism was proven by the activities in rural areas of the United States, particularly in the American South. There, in the early twentieth century, local churches had been instrumental in sponsoring community-based activities from education to agriculture. Intertwined with their communities, they were the best site in a small town to begin a program that might alter the social fabric of that community. This emphasis could be carried over to overseas technical work.[73]

This was particularly important as programs proliferated in the 1950s. Missionary observers could see massive multipurpose hydraulic development programs, inspired by the example of the TVA, springing up on the Litani River in Lebanon, in the Khuzestan region in Iran, in the Helmand Valley in Afghanistan, and on the Indus in South Asia. They saw their smaller programs fitting into such extensive projects promising to bring a better material life to peoples in these areas and elsewhere. American missionaries felt they could be an important cooperative element with the U.S. and local governments within these larger endeavors. With their emphasis on localism, they could work closely with people at the grassroots level to satisfy "more basic unmet needs."[74]

Religious groups had a slew of new partners emerging from other corners of American society. In 1960, the American Council of Voluntary Agencies for Foreign Service (ACVA) counted seventy-eight U.S.-based organizations committed to solely international technical assistance. This somewhat incomplete tally included religious groups, businesses, and foundations (groups providing direct relief and other types of aid were excluded). It also counted various secular voluntary organizations with a tangential commitment to modernization, including 4-H Clubs and the National Council of Women of America. The ACVA noted that while voluntary organization participation went back into the nineteenth century, the preceding decade saw a remarkable "growing interest in technical assistance and the increasing role of voluntary agencies in this field."[75]

The ACVA's survey is a reminder that while modernization could lose focus at the government level, it remained a powerful motivator within civil society. One group not listed by the ACVA, but which had long supported overseas development, was the Federation of Women's Clubs. In testimony before Congress in 1955, its members summarized the motivations of many in the nongovernmental world when they stated their belief that "enduring world peace" depended upon the success of American-led technical assistance programs.[76] ACVA itself saw that larger goal through the lens of U.S. foreign policy:

> During the 20th Century it is impossible to escape from the fact there exists a struggle for the minds and souls of men. This struggle may be conducted by words and by every means of propaganda, and it also may be conducted by deeds and by example. The voluntary sector, besides promoting peace and abiding sense of brotherhood through programs of cooperation to meet human need, performs a basic service to truth which is deeply significant to the whole future development and ultimate goals of American foreign policy.[77]

The expansion of the already significant numbers of voluntary organizations involved in development became an increasingly visible and integral part of international affairs. Emblematic was the International Voluntary Service (IVS), formed in 1953. While secular in orientation, it grew from religious roots. The American Friends Service Committee, the Mennonite Central Committee, and the Brethren Service Committee had hands in its organization and all its volunteers were initially from Protestant backgrounds.[78] While not true of all new voluntary organizations, the religious connections of groups such as IVS expose the continuity between earlier missionary efforts and burgeoning secular efforts following World War II. Like other NGOs the IVS trumpeted its cooperation with the government. The group proudly announced that it was "a mechanism for coordinating governmental and private agency efforts at village levels" by providing government efforts with a "cadre of trained [American] specialists who had demonstrated a capacity to engage in development under alien conditions." IVS quickly won a reputation as an exemplar of community development with its programs in Africa and Asia. Part of this outlook and status was forged after 1956 through rural development work under U.S. government contract in South Vietnam.[79]

While the activities of these private groups exemplify the broad consensus in American society on modernization, it is not to suggest that these groups were monolithic in their outlooks. Disagreement about priorities and goals of development programming complicated cooperation. A sign of this was the attitude of members of the American Friends Service Committee. Much of the group's overseas work was focused on technical assistance. This programming often took place in cooperation or with the financial support of the U.S. government or UN agencies. The Society of Friends believed strongly in the developmental mission and agitated for the United States to continue to play a "leading part . . . in the constructive revolution that has already begun in vast regions of the world, especially Asia." Although the Friends acknowledged the need to collaborate with the U.S. government in guiding this revolution, they did not uncritically accept elements of state policy. There was a belief in the mid-1950s that modernization aid was getting lost in the government's emphasis on military aid. In the long run, this hurt ongoing projects, and importantly, it damaged American credibility with Asians who could not reconcile the martial nature of American aid to certain governments when they were surrounded by poverty.[80] This led the Friends to call for U.S. aid to be doled out multilaterally, and crucially, to call for a distinct line between military aid and development.[81]

LOSING THE BATTLE? THE COMMUNIST CHALLENGE AND MODERNIZATION IN AMERICAN LIFE

If there was disagreement on international development, there was also anxiety. Modernization had become a crucial symbol for a wide variety of groups by the mid- to late 1950s. It became a means to understand the scale of American involvement in the world as well as a measure of that engagement's success. The persistent troubles of major recipients of aid— South Korea being only one—and the apparent momentum of the Soviet Bloc in courting developing nations called the American model into question. The frustration with the perceived failures, ineffectiveness, and the general malaise of American aid programs in the 1950s had perhaps their best expression in William Lederer and Eugene Burdick's 1958 novel, *The Ugly American*. Lederer, a former U.S. Navy officer, and Burdick, a professor of political theory, decried most U.S. development efforts in the Third World as dilettantish, disjointed, and largely ineffectual through their story of the battle to win the loyalty of the fictional Southeast Asian nation of Sarkahan. Most of the American characters look inadequate when stacked up against their fictional Soviet counterparts, well versed in the area's language and culture.[82]

While deficiencies of government policy were given a great deal of play, other institutions invested in the development mission were not spared. A fictional recruiting session at American University, which had recently founded a school of international affairs, was used to hammer at the quality of individuals drawn to the mission. Led by Hamilton Bridge Upton, a stiff diplomat, and Joe Bing, a callow government public relations man, recruiters present the foreign service as a sort of government-sponsored shopping spree. Most of those attracted, drawn by bargain merchandise at embassy commissaries, are disdained by Upton as sub-caliber "slobs." The message is simple. An area vital to U.S. strategy was entrusted to low-quality personnel in overseas service for poor reasons. Others agreed such complacent wallowing in the comforts of abundance reflected a society ill prepared for the challenges of promoting modernization.[83]

In the end, the best hope for the American cause comes from an "ugly American," Homer Atkins. An engineer, Atkins, advising fictional French, American, and Vietnamese authorities on the economic development of Indochina, is critical of the dominant focus on "big" modernization programs. "You want big industry . . . You want big T.V.A.'s scattered all over the countryside," he scolded, "that all takes skilled workmen, and mines, and lots of money, and a whole lot of people who are production minded . . . That's why I recommended . . . that you start small with little things." His advisees do not listen, yet the marginalized Atkins remains committed to technical assistance. Working with the locals directly the engineer designs a new type of pump that they can use in their rice paddies that gives hope the United States will eventually win over the Sarkahanese. Regardless of the literary merits of the work, the authors adhered to a long-standing view of why the struggle they described was decisive. Gradually, as communist influence supplanted that of the United States, the world would become inhospitable to liberal values. The choice was as stark as the 1930s—pull back to a "Fortress America" garrison state or venture into the world and guide it in a positive direction.[84]

Propelled onto the bestseller list and into the lexicon (even if it is often used incorrectly), *The Ugly American* became a focus for debate.[85] Critics of foreign aid were quick to utilize its arguments. The book's impact was such that the ICA put together a retort for its staff and the public, refuting Lederer and Burdick's assertions point by point.[86] Revealing of the significance of *The Ugly American* is the vehemence with which supporters of development assistance assailed the book. Senator J. W. Fulbright castigated the "intellectually lazy" authors for "perniciously and dangerously [suggesting] that we are engaged in a political struggle for which we have neither talent nor the will to win." The depth of this official reaction was a measure of the appreciation of the role development played in public perception of world affairs. Fulbright spent the last of his venom on a movie to be based on the novel, fearing it would be about "sex in the tropics" rather than the difficult question of international development.[87]

Fulbright could rest easy regarding eroticism. The 1963 movie version of *The Ugly American* did not dwell on exotic romance. It starred Marlon Brando as Gilbert MacWhite, the fictional U.S. ambassador to Sarkahan. Brando's role was perhaps a fulfillment of a desire to do a film on the hot topic of development; a few years earlier he had discussed doing a movie based on the UN technical assistance program's work.[88] The film, following a different plot from the novel, also was not sanguine about American development in Asia. MacWhite returns to Sarkahan only to alienate his friend and populist leader, Li Pang, with the standard U.S. line on international development. MacWhite fails to see that the Sarakahanese do not want the major U.S. development program for the country, "Freedom Road." Exacerbating the situation, the ambassador changes the road's course. Instability brought by modernization helps the Chinese, Russians, and "North Sarakahanese" dupe Pang and foment an uprising. After the assassination of his friend, MacWhite belatedly realizes his mistakes, but the ambiguous ending leaves the viewer wondering if the United States at large will learn from its foreign experiences.[89]

Brando's appearance in a film about development would not have been out of the ordinary for audiences accustomed to the likes of *Romanoff and Juliet*. Indeed, there were a significant number of films that dealt with the intimate relationships the United States was initiating in the "Third World." *The Quiet American*, an adaptation of Graham Greene's novel, appeared in 1958 with Michael Redgrave as the world-weary English journalist, Fowler. War hero Audie Murphy played Pyle, the naïve American in thrall of the modernization theory of a fictional "York Harding." Joseph Mankiewicz, the film's director, was convinced (some later said "brainwashed") by a "Vietnam Lobby" of prominent American supporters of the Diem regime to moderate the tone of Greene's scathing story. On screen, Pyle was not portrayed as an intelligence operative, but rather a concerned private citizen, to accent American altruism.[90] Moviegoers saw a modernization parable in the Rogers and Hammerstein musical *The King and I* (1956), where a Western teacher, Anna Leonowens (Deborah Kerr), alters the worldview of the King of Siam (Yul Brynner) and eventually cultivates a progressive heir.[91] In an only slightly more indirect manner, film audiences got a lesson in the power of development from Elia Kazan's 1960 picture, *Wild River*. Starring Montgomery Clift as a soft-spoken technician, it explored the transformative effects of the TVA on a small town in the American South. Clift and the ideas he brings with him break down existing social and economic injustices. The community's African Americans, locked in servitude by the town matriarch, are brought into federal service. Work with the project brings them higher standards of living in the form of equal pay and decent housing—with the unknown amenity of electricity—that brings opportunity, happiness, and a new outlook. Dislocation and tension were unavoidable for a community portrayed as static, but the ending showed that modernization provided hope while transforming relationships on intimate levels (especially for the Clift character, who finds love with Lee Remick). Kazan recognized his film's connection to the past and present when he invited Lilienthal to its premier.[92]

That there were a number of major studio films with modernization themes during the 1950s and early 1960s shows the topic resonated with the public. This gestures to the wider commitment to modernization that existed outside the American government in a wide variety of groups that continued to find development essential to America's mission in the world. The second half of the 1950s brought new worries about these Soviet and Chinese Communist efforts in the "Third World." The United States publicly decried the communist moves as political—a cloak to gain influence over less developed countries. There was attention to the ends of communist activities seeking to "recommend its type of planned and controlled economy as a model for Asian economic development."[93] There was a genuine concern that the communists were having greater success in the Third World than the United States. In Asia the Soviets were understood to be assiduously cultivating the perception that communism was the wave of the future. This fanned anxieties in Washington that the "Great American Experiment" was being overshadowed by a "Great Russian Experiment."[94]

American unease about its position as a global leader deepened when the USSR launched Sputnik, the first man-made satellite, into earth orbit in 1957. The overheated reaction in the United States included questions about whether this dramatic accomplishment gave the communists increased leverage in the Third World, as these technological "spectaculars" were psychological weapons.[95] Sputnik and its successors dealt a blow to perceptions of the United States as the global leader in science and technology that so many commentators and policy makers had leaned on since the 1930s. Congressman Henry Reuss, returning from a trip to Southeast Asia in 1957 backlit by the glow of Sputnik, fretted that an "American monopoly" on technological leadership had been broken in the face of Russian accomplishments. If communism allowed the USSR into the heavens, the rest of its social system might hold promise on earth and swing world opinion toward it, particularly across the developing world.[96]

Other routes to modernity were starting to open up. As a country that had recently "stood up" after persistent abuse by imperial powers, the People's Republic of China offered an attractive vision to other societies recently freed from colonial domination. It would be followed by Cuba and Algeria, which, after their respective revolutions, touted their own particular approaches to socialist development as the best path to prosperity and national power for "new nations." By the early 1960s, regimes across Asia, Africa, and the Americas had a varied global marketplace of development ideas to draw upon. State-led modernization outside the capitalist order had special appeal. In part, this was because the capitalism promoted by the United States was part of an international system that had tolerated colonialism. In many postcolonial states this bread a nationalist suspicion of liberal modernization.[97] The fact that major U.S. clients were having limited success did not help matters. Stagnation in South Korea while communist reconstruction in North Korea claimed impressive gains lent credibility to Mao's 1957 assertion that the "the East Wind is prevailing over the West Wind."[98]

EISENHOWER CHANGES COURSE

By 1956, the limitations of Eisenhower's foreign economic strategy in the Third World were apparent to influential voices in American society.[99] Reinhold Niebuhr appreciated the fascination of Marxism to poorer nations breaking from imperialism and with aspirations of their own. Ironically, the United States had been tarred with the legacy of European imperialism, complicating its appeals to less developed people from a perch of prosperity and technological complexity.[100] Walter Lippmann used his influential newspaper column to restate the stakes at the start of the year. He asked whether American exceptionalism in terms of its unparalleled postwar prosperity was a liability on a crucial Cold War front. Eisenhower's advisers were working within the "framework of the Thirties and Forties," endeavoring to show a capitalist economy could generate stable expansion. But they had lost sight of whether the approaches given credit for growth in the United States were replicable globally. What Lippmann described as "old, crowded, politically primitive" countries added complication with their own interests. Lippmann channeled the consensus view that "the initiative in . . . development has to be taken by the Government . . . it cannot be expected to come from private enterprise." The United States had to comprehend the developing nations had the "standing example" of "forced industrialization" to follow and communist power lay "in the visible demonstration of what the Soviet Union has achieved in forty years, of what Red China has achieved in about ten years." Asia was the main battleground against a belief the Russians had "mastered modern technology . . . and [with] a powerful government" and this model was "at present the only obviously effective way of raising quickly the power and standard of living of a backward people." Failing to mute this "temptation" and the "air of inevitability . . . that Communism is the only wave of the future" would hobble the United States in a contest from which "we cannot run away."[101]

Lippmann saw development as symbolic, a view shared in corridors of power. If, as Eisenhower's NSC believed, the core of the Cold War was psychological, "a struggle to capture symbols . . . that express man's aspirations and thereby influence political behavior," then modernization was vital to demonstrate the United States had mastered such economic and social symbols.[102] The limited success private trade was having in spurring growth in poorer areas of the globe was not just bad for the bottom line but undercut American claims to leadership. By 1956, the contradictions could not be sustained. The Soviets were forcing the Americans' hand. Dulles could not ignore that the "second round was now beginning" and foreign aid had to again become "an essential part of our foreign policy."[103]

But that essence was "unclear, at times contradictory, and . . . subject to increasing criticism" in the view of the International Development Advisory Board. This government-sponsored advisory panel was established in the wake of Point Four. Revitalized, it had become a platform for the opinions of Paul Nitze, Frank X. Sutton, Robert Dahl, and Thomas Schelling, as well as the omnipresent Millikan and Rostow. Drawing from analysis percolating outside the state, it urged greater attention to the dual challenge posed by the communist threat and the aspirations of "low income countries." The transformation of these nations was crucial. The United States had to convince such strivers, in the face of an attractive communist model, that it had the means to guide them into modern political, economic, and social life.[104]

It was a threat that received attention. Rapidly, a view took hold in the administration that Soviet Bloc aid constituted a dangerous economic and psychological threat. Total aid in the form of loans, grants, and credits may have been comparatively small (estimated at $1 billion between 1954 and early 1956) but it allowed the Soviet Union to identify itself as the force to satisfy rising expectations of poorer peoples. The USSR's own transformation to a global power gave credence to its claim for "the inherent advantages of the Communist system for achieving rapid industrial and technological development." There was conjecture the aid offensive put a dual burden on the communist bloc. Its scale left the ambitions of recipients unfulfilled, producing diplomatic tensions and forcing the USSR to struggle to fulfill promises.[105] Such speculation could not tamp real concern within the Eisenhower administration about the "boldness" and successes of Sino-Soviet attempts to court underdeveloped countries. American planners understood the competition made remarkably similar promises about what their modern technology could deliver. Some thought the emphasis on "our official bogie man" of communist aid was undesirable as it "makes us [the United States] look like pikers" to denigrate Russia and Chinese-sponsored projects that so resembled their own. In the face of a dynamic communist challenge, American aid officials asked, "We say we are not in an 'aid race' . . . then why are we running scared?"[106]

Under this pressure, the Eisenhower administration rapidly backed away from its early international economic policies. Clarence Randall, architect of "trade not aid," authored a 1957 report articulating a new aid posture. In the face of a sustained communist effort, there was recognition that the "private trade and investment climate . . . in many countries (particularly certain of those now being penetrated [by Soviet aid]) . . . is quite unsatisfactory . . . any marked increase in U.S. trade and investment must be preceded by a major change in such climate." Promoting such climate change meant expanding official governmental modernization activity worldwide.[107]

The structure of aid policy was again in play and a throng of nongovernmental groups jumped into what became a public debate. They had remained committed to a set of modernization principles and here was their chance to return them to U.S. strategy. A cohort of policy groups participated in congressional hearings, including the Brookings Institution, the National Planning Association, and the University of Chicago, among others. These organizations had never abandoned basic tenets of the liberal modernization consensus. They assumed governments were central although dependent on the assistance of NGO and international organizations. They were comfortable with state planning. The modernization offered was to profoundly transform nations economically, politically, socially, and culturally. Many important texts from the school of modernization theory were, in fact, interventions in this wide-ranging discussion to reshape a critical part of U.S. foreign policy. What is more, the discussion shows how nonstate actors helped to guide important shifts in modernization policy.

The most influential interventions emerged out of CENIS, authored by Millikan and Rostow. Earlier work by this developmental duo became the basis for intervention into congressional debates at this critical moment.[108] Testimony was recycled into an influential 1957 policy treatise, *A Proposal*. It was a restatement of many ideas that were already circulating in the development community. Fostering modernization was a way for the United States to influence these nations while developing the social and political capacities of the new nations. Devotion to the development project provided a constructive outlet for nationalism as well as a "social solvent" to break down differences between classes as well as urban and rural people in the poorer states. Most of all, focusing on modernization would have a psychological impact. It would prove to peoples that "they have it in their power to improve their own lot." This would not only instill a faith in progress but political confidence, to "demonstrate political democracy in action." The authors believed that politics did not have to be loudly broadcast, as "economic programs which are neutral with respect to the political issues which rouse men's passions nonetheless can be effective instruments of political influence."[109]

Central was the provision of large amounts of capital from government and private sources propelling countries to a "take-off" into sustained growth. Establishing these preconditions required "a great deal of technical assistance" to clear the way for capital aid to operate effectively. Millikan and Rostow repeated a standing formula that underdeveloped countries were often limited not by the availability of capital but by their absorptive capacity. Not only was technology needed but also educational and training programs to provide scientific, technical, managerial, and administrative talent to control a modern economy. Such technical assistance was the best means to restructure these societies to make them receptive to infusions of financial aid. International experts, provided by U.S. or UN agencies, were the best means to shore up deficiencies and train local talent.[110] The authors saw benefits at home as well. Transforming the world would keep American society vigorous. Their hortative introduction asserted:

> [W]e need the challenge of world development to keep us from the stagnation of smug prosperity . . . Our great opportunity lies in the fact that we have developed more successfully than any other nation the social, political, and economic techniques for realizing widespread popular desires for change without either compulsion or social disorganization. Although our techniques must be adopted to local conditions abroad if they are to be effective there, they represent an enormous potential for steering the world's newly aroused energies in constructive rather than destructive directions . . . In their largest sense the proposals in this book are designed to give fresh meaning and vitality to the historic American sense of mission.[111]

In 1958, the Carnegie Corporation funded a sabbatical for Rostow to extend his ideas. What emerged was his magnum opus, *The Stages of Economic Growth*, which was another attempt to state the importance of American leadership in modernization. Subtitled *A Non-Communist Manifesto*, the book was explicitly a Cold War tract. Often treated as a starting point for understanding modernization thinking, *Stages* was more a summary of arguments made during the policy dialogue of the 1950s. In important respects it restated many assumptions brewing since

Figure 5.4. Keeping the consensus in play. Walt Rostow straddled lines between academe, advocacy, and government in debates over the place of modernization in foreign policy during the 1950s and 1960s. Here he is at tennis, ca. 1960. Courtesy of Jim Hansen, *Look* Magazine Collection, Library of Congress, Washington, DC.

the 1930s—even the concept of stages was reminiscent of the steps to modernity laid out in Eugene Staley's earlier work.

Using the history of the industrialized West as a starting point, the book described a universal progression from traditional organization to the "takeoff" stage of sustained economic growth. Rostow accepted the truism that modern society was revolutionary. It had swept away the scarcity marking human existence throughout history. Abundance was not something limited to postwar American society. It was a global phenomenon, transforming how people lived and thought. Rostow repeated formulations made familiar by scholars like Staley and the ideological debates of the 1930s. The instability brought by modern life left peoples susceptible to opportunistic ideologies. Communism remained a "disease of the transition" preventing the healthy culmination of social evolution to high-consumption liberal societies. Rostow highlighted a new aspect, nuclear weapons. For great powers they brought paradox, constraining actions rather than enhancing ability to apply military force. This "diffusion of power" gave more latitude for action to smaller states. However, as they were transitional societies, "the ideological dimensions of the Cold War heighten a sense of choice . . . of whether the Communist method should be followed." As their evolution was crucial to the creation of a stable globe, shepherding them down the liberal, democratic path was "the single most important item on the Western agenda."[112]

Rostow and Millikan's writing was one part of the advocacy emerging from universities and other nonstate actors. This accelerated a turn back to multilateral assistance, and more important, a recommitment to elements of the development consensus. Establishment of the Development Loan Fund and broadening of mutual security programs to include more multilateral aid were signs of a shift in U.S. government policy. Part of this course correction was the administration's support of some of the basic ideas behind the SUNFED proposal. In 1957, the United States put forward a revised plan that offered "preinvestment" aid for surveys and technical assistance working in tandem with existing UN bodies. However, the United States took steps to blunt multilateralism. When the "Special Fund" finally emerged in 1959, the United States, paying some 40 percent of its budget, exerted control by reserving its directorship for an American. That chief was Paul Hoffman, late of the ECA and Ford Foundation. The United States would also put aside earlier reservations and join the Mekong project in 1957. There too, the United States reserved the chair of the program for an American.[113]

With global events and domestic advocates pushing it back toward consensus policies, the Eisenhower administration revamped its relationship with NGOs. Although long attentive to their presence, the later 1950s brought renewed government consideration to their support of strategic goals. The scale of NGO activity could hardly be ignored—their annual expenditures were estimated to be as high as $500 million by 1960.[114] While their actions in critical regions like Southeast Asia or Latin America had valuable impacts, more important was their contribution to the psychological impact of U.S. foreign aid in combating the threat of "revolutionary totalitarianism." Voluntary groups continued to offer their funds and technical talents while adding flexibility bureaucratic government programs could not match. Less tangible was the good will their actions motivated, accentuated by personal interactions and the fact that they offered the American public another avenue to engage international issues. They were a human example of one aspect of the liberal American system. Voluntary groups and missionaries demonstrated the "freedom and pluralism" and private initiative innate to American life to contrast statist Soviet programs.[115]

After attempting to craft a policy consciously differentiated from the postwar modernization consensus, Eisenhower had generally turned back to it. This was due in part to the advocacy of a swath of nonstate institutions that had struggled to keep a selection of ideas at the forefront of national and international discussion. These groups felt the accepted approach to modernization remained vital to how the United States—not just as a government but as a community of interests—maintained and extended its place in the world. The diversity of actors influencing the shape of modernization in this and other periods should be remembered. Modernization cannot be reduced solely to the official policies of the U.S. government.

Even so, advocacy by NGOs and course changes by the U.S. government did not disperse the lingering belief that communists were winning the battle in the Third World. A refrain that U.S. aid policy was rudderless was heard from a chorus of experts. In Cleveland's 1959 view, development policy resembled someone "recovering gradually from multiple sclerosis" after a "poisoning" brought by undue emphasis on security and the blows of political foes. Lilienthal put himself in the middle of this debate, calling for a fresh start in foreign aid. Paul Hoffman offered a vague yet positive spin, asserting, "We have acquired experience during the 1950s and can profit from past mistakes." Barbara Ward noted the success of communist aid in the Third World. This had served communist goals and heightened distrust of the West. Only the massive scale of Western aid tempered these gains.[116]

At the end of the 1950s, the American image of development and the reflections it cast on American society was dour. Communism appeared to be on the march in the developing world, unhindered by limp American foreign aid policy. For some this was a judgment on a modern, high-consumption American society that seemed unable to rise to the challenge. What is remarkable is how quickly the perception reversed. Many of those who had struggled to maintain elements of an international consensus on development in U.S. foreign affairs would be heartened by the arrival of John F. Kennedy and an administration steeped in modernization ideas. As established ideas were reintegrated into official pro-

grams, the perception appeared that the consensus on liberal modernization not only could work, it *did* work. By the early 1960s, Americans felt
they had domestic and international examples to prove their model. As
the United States renewed its commitment to confronting the ideological
challenge of communism in the Third World, new imperatives and old
ideas merged to help convince Americans they could win a conflict brewing in Southeast Asia.

Chapter 6

A TVA ON THE MEKONG

Modernization at War in
Southeast Asia, 1960–1973

I want to leave the footprints of America in Vietnam . . .
We're going to turn the Mekong into a Tennessee Valley.
—Lyndon Johnson, 1966

AT THE START OF THE 1960s, modernization was at the apex of its influence globally. It framed basic elements of international life.[1] The whole period was even declared the "Decade of Development." Ideas surrounding modernization had become a basic means for the United States to perceive problems in the Third World and even understand its own place in the world. After Eisenhower's wavering on modernization, John F. Kennedy returned consensus ideas to a prominent position in U.S. strategy. Faced with a mounting insurgency in Vietnam, the United States turned to prevailing methods to promote development. A foundation of the style of counterinsurgency waged in South Vietnam, modernization was also a means to justify U.S. involvement in the region to a skeptical world public. Such importance meant that many groups faithful to the postwar development consensus—universities, businesses, and voluntary groups—factored into the struggle. Relationships honed since the 1930s were put into action. A variety of recent American modernization projects inspired confidence that similar attempts would succeed in Southeast Asia. Distinguished individuals were recruited to serve the cause. Vast resources and boundless optimism were thrown into a nation-building effort. With all these assets, the consensus went to war.

The importance of modernization to efforts in Vietnam assured its fall was hard. The failure of these ideas to stem insurgency and promote stability was a body blow to the consensus on development. War posed problems that no development planning could surmount. But the conflict exposed tensions among the institutions working on development that were larger than the war itself. Collaboration was shattered by the pressures of an unpopular war. Criticism appeared in quarters invested in the reigning modernization paradigm. Government policy and institutions were reshuffled by failures abroad. The crucible of Vietnam dissolved many of the assumptions and cooperation that had guided international development. War in Southeast Asia brought only part of the troubles that modernization would face in the 1960s, but it was a powerful catalyst to rethink the means and ends of development.

RETAKING THE RIGHTFUL ESTATE: KENNEDY'S NEW FRONTIER OF MODERNIZATION

Frustration with the state of foreign policy in Eisenhower's last years became political fodder. Aiming for the White House, John F. Kennedy made the lethargy of the administration (an impression not helped by the death of Dulles and the recurrent health problems of the president himself) an issue. Persistent economic troubles in America's client states complemented the picture Kennedy drew. Soviet triumphs in the space race and the apparent momentum of its "aid offensive" accentuated criticism. A serious recession in the United States delivered further blows to the president's approval ratings. Figures at 79 percent in 1957 drooped below 50 percent by 1958.[2] Capitalizing on this, the Democrats highlighted the energy Kennedy would bring to the presidency. In the campaign, modernization was not a central issue in and of itself. But it was utilized to show Kennedy was forward-looking and grasped global trends. This brought an embrace of consensus ideas, deeply intertwined with other facets of foreign policy, to demonstrate Kennedy's assertive Cold War posture. To help him shape policy, Kennedy gathered a crowd of individuals who had struggled to keep their vision of modernization in public debate in the 1950s. Chief among them was Rostow, who carved out a niche as an important adviser, coining the slogans "Let's Get America Moving Again" and the defining "New Frontier."[3]

Reestablishing American leadership on development was a theme in Kennedy's campaign. He rebuked Republicans for allowing an "economic gap" to grow in the developing world, as dangerous as the heralded (and fictional) "missile gap."[4] This had eroded the validity of the American way of development. While critical of the Eisenhower administration, Kennedy nevertheless shared many bedrock assumptions of an ideological struggle demanding the United States recapture its position as a leader of the global "revolution of rising expectations":

> It is we, the American people, who should be marching at the head of this world-wide revolution, counseling it, helping it come to a healthy fruition. Yet we have allowed the Communists to evict us from our rightful estate . . . We have been made to appear as the

defenders of the status quo, while the Communists have portrayed themselves as the vanguard force, pointing the way to a better, brighter, and braver order of life.[5]

When the Democrats recaptured the presidency in 1960, the rites of transition in Washington demanded a slate of "task forces" for a top to bottom foreign policy review. Foreign aid's review brought together an influential posse, including consensus boosters Harlan Cleveland, Robert Nathan, and John Kenneth Galbraith, as well as the tireless Millikan and Rostow. It dismissed Republican policy as "obsolete." This opened the door for ideas from inside and outside the administration for foreign aid reforms. The biggest was the creation in 1961 of the U.S. Agency for International Development (USAID), combining existing foreign aid bureaucracies in a body independent of the state department with overall responsibility for official U.S. development aid. The new institution was committed to producing economic growth through a liberal approach to modernization. Growth would allow the achievement of whatever ends were desired, an assumption shared in much of the mainstream of the development community.[6]

Changes to the aid infrastructure went beyond reshuffling government bureaucracies. A new institution appeared during Kennedy's campaign. Initial inspiration came from Henry Reuss's 1957 trip to Asia. Worried about the erosion of American technical leadership and the damage done by the U.S. failure to support nationalist aspirations in former colonial areas, Reuss advocated a "Point Four Youth Corps" to demonstrate American benevolence. Kennedy adapted the idea for his campaign with an October 14, 1960 speech at the University of Michigan. In terms the authors of The Ugly American would have understood, Kennedy lambasted the dilettantish development efforts of the Republicans as unequal to the Soviet challenge. Kennedy promised a "peace corps" of talented and trained Americans to meet this threat. As plans for the organization gained momentum in the first months of the administration, the pattern of a well-respected voluntary group, IVS, was publicized to lend credibility to a government program based on its example. Signaling the proposal's seriousness was the presence of Millikan and Rostow, who were called in to flesh out details. The Peace Corps was one of the first items on the new president's agenda, established by executive order in March 1961.[7]

Proposals were one thing, implementation was another. Kennedy's initiative required extensive use of the relationships between the American government, NGOs, and international organizations that had come to characterize the consensus on liberal development. Sargent Shriver, the first head of the Corps, initially hoped to deploy its volunteers with UN development programs. Harlan Cleveland, a new Assistant Secretary of

State, sought and received a statement by ECOSOC on the value of voluntary aid work. The connection of the Peace Corps to the UN was an attempt by the Kennedy administration to draw attention to the program while connecting it to international development structures. UN involvement eventually disappeared, but the publicity and the popularity of the ideas behind the program brought a surge in recruitment. Although the Peace Corps tapped the same spirit motivating many private groups already involved in development, it soon dwarfed them in size. But links to venerable voluntary traditions explain why the "Point Four Youth Corps" has transcended Cold War origins and lives on to this day.[8]

Nongovernmental connections paid dividends beyond publicity. Kennedy sought the experience of various people and institutions to ballast the program. One of the first to whom the president turned was David Lilienthal (who had urged candidate Kennedy to appreciate the TVA example for aid reform), recruited to serve on the Peace Corps' National Advisory Council. Lilienthal's involvement touches upon the overlooked question of who actually trained this unique government program's first members. Nothing quite like it had existed before, meaning the corps had to turn to existing development bodies. They had the experience and reputation for local work and the capacity to immediately start teaching the inexperienced volunteers. Lilienthal's D&R reaped benefits from his connections, creating the Center for Advanced Technical Training in California's Imperial Valley to train the Peace Corps in agricultural methods. The ACVA welcomed the Corps, and members lined up to cooperate. CARE, for example, helped the new Peace Corps implement pilot programs. Government bodies also honed this cutting edge of the New Frontier. The TVA provided training in technical arts and agriculture to the first classes of volunteers.[9]

Skills instruction was only one of the tangible contributions the TVA made to an expanding development galaxy. It retained the luster gained in the 1930s as a destination for audiences curious about modernization. Training and tourism aside, the TVA actively shaped the technical resources available to the international aid community for large-scale resource projects. Its work reflected the variety of areas such development touched. The assortment of fertilizer and agricultural research programs the TVA conducted fed into the coming "Green Revolution." These programs are another reminder of how important harnessing environmental elements was to modernization. TVA-led surveys of government ministries to improve administrative capacities in places like South Korea demonstrated the importance that state and human capacity held in the modernization equation. It was also further proof that the TVA, while far from the sum of liberal development efforts, remained a means to integrate institutional as well as intellectual aspects of modernization.[10]

Figure 6.1. A usable liberal past for a liberal future: John F. Kennedy speaks at Muscle Shoals on the thirtieth anniversary of the TVA, May 18, 1963. Lilienthal is seated behind Kennedy, second from left. David Lilienthal Papers. Public Policy Papers Division. Department of Rare Books and Special Collections. Princeton University Library.

More than a tutor, the TVA legitimated the new institutions and strategies of the 1960s. According to the Brookings Institution, the United States had an "exceptional obligation" to share its expertise with developing nations and TVA was a leading "symbol and example" of how to do so.[11] USAID concurred. As the new agency gestated, it studied the TVA and came to well-tried conclusions. It was a success, with philosophy and methods "no longer experimental" but proven. As the TVA was "based on certain universal truths," its ideas applied to the ambitions of peoples in developing countries. Although it might not always be the "complete answer," its representation of the "flexibility and adaptability of our democratic tradition at its best" as a means to differentiate the liberal goals of the United States had not lost its importance.[12]

Kennedy himself linked the TVA to a reenergized aid program. After taking office he urged the TVA to reflect on "the lessons it has learned . . . [that] may be exported abroad, and applied to our great objectives of human enhancement."[13] For the thirtieth anniversary of the TVA Act in

Figure 6.2. Way station on the "New Frontier": Peace Corps volunteer training in TVA facilities, ca. 1962. Courtesy of National Archives, Atlanta, Georgia.

1963, the president was in Muscle Shoals, where he honored the TVA as a certified development success. The president dismissed dogged critics who continued to see it as creeping or any other type of socialism. Rather, the TVA remained "an answer to socialism." It showed the productive potential of coordinated private industry, popular participation, and government aid. Because of this, the valley continued to draw thousands of visitors who came for insights on how to implement development.[14] In part, the speech was Kennedy's attempt to show he was the rightful heir to FDR. But the TVA remained more than an emblem of a liberal past; it was reasserted as a means to secure a liberal future. Throughout the 1950s, the TVA retained its signal cachet for larger processes of liberal modernization with a devoted following among NGOs and the international community. Kennedy was now reaffirming its role as a touchstone for an administration committed to the policy of modernization. The *New York Times* saw the restoration, declaring, "The Kennedy Administration has re-embraced the concept on which the old Point Four program was based."[15]

As much as various bodies forged or enhanced their links to carry modernization forward internationally, links to domestic development ambitions remained apparent. Lilienthal also celebrated the thirtieth birthday of the institution whose reputation he had sculpted. Even as he spoke of its application abroad, he focused a gaze back on the United States. The country needed to "look homeward" to advance its own education and employment potential even as it sought similar gains abroad.[16] Lilienthal took his own advice—D&R was already seeking contracts for domestic work on everything from water resource management to adult education in a period where "growth liberalism" promised unlimited butter as well as guns.[17] Lilienthal was speaking as Americans "rediscovered" poverty in the midst of unprecedented prosperity. Michael Harrington's *The Other America* refocused debate on the issue. He noted how poor people in the United States, dominated by fatalism and passivity, were no different from "Asian peasants." A concept of how the poor were trapped in a "culture of poverty" itself had roots in scholarship on international issues that had blossomed in the postwar years as development had become a prominent global issue. Indeed, the concept owed much to international research like that conducted by anthropologist Oscar Lewis in Mexican and Puerto Rican communities.[18] It was another sign of the blurred boundary lines between international and domestic development. The Cold War had not changed this truth and, in certain respects, this interdependence intensified in the 1960s as the United States sought to extend development ideas to more Americans and the world.

Abroad, modernization was indispensable for Kennedy's aggressive confrontation of insurgent ideas in the Third World. The same March the Peace Corps was brought to life, Kennedy launched the Alliance for Progress to parry the threat of "Castroism" in Latin America. The Marxist shuttle to prosperity offered by Castro and his followers threatened to lure the region off the liberal path. American-sponsored development was served in place of revolution.[19] The international community was courted in these efforts to recover the United States' "rightful estate." In September 1961, Kennedy called on the United Nations to declare the 1960s the "Decade of Development."[20] Kennedy's emphasis on development as campaign and foreign policy tools shows the imprint modernization had made on American life. By utilizing the existing critique of the Eisenhower administration's foreign aid programs, Kennedy confronted an anxiety nagging the American public. Rapid establishment of the Peace Corps, the Alliance for Progress, and reform of the aid apparatus was, among other things, a signal by an activist president willing to sharpen the U.S. approach to foreign aid and wield it as a weapon.

This was reassuring to many Americans who had come to see their nation's development performance as an important barometer of its capacity for global leadership. By the mid-1960s, commentators began to look favorably on development efforts that only a few years before had inspired dismay. The "graduation" of Taiwan from the school of American developmental assistance in this period boded well.[21] Other recipients of U.S. aid following World War II, like Lebanon and Greece, became inspiring successes.[22] Opinions had changed among many of the prominent public commentators on foreign aid. Barbara Ward, an unofficial adviser to Kennedy, saw considerable improvement on the aid front by 1964. In some cases, communist development strategies were wanting and Western activity could mark successes. More important, modernization had "succeeded in the profoundest sense—at the level of human imagination and understanding."[23] One moment of this understanding and imagination came in May 1961 when three South Korean economists visiting Washington called on Walt Rostow. Flattered, he indulged their questions on his *Stages of Economic Growth* over a long lunch at the Hay-Adams Hotel. Rostow fondly remembered the "Hay-Adams Boys." To him, they were emblematic of the new outlook taking hold in South Korea. Already personally aroused by the potential of a reappraised South Korea, Rostow saw what he termed "erotic" excitement among these Koreans in the promise of modernization.[24]

It Can Be Done: South Korea as Success Story

Rostow's lunch sheds light on the remarkable reconsideration of South Korea that was part of the growth of American confidence on development. He was not alone in his views that the ROK was turning a corner.[25] William Bundy, Assistant Secretary of State for Far Eastern Affairs from 1964 to 1969, recalled the thinking of many in government during the period:

> [T]he process through which Korea passed in the next two years [after 1962] became for many American professionals . . . a touchstone and partial model for later hopes and plans in South Vietnam . . . after the intense discouragement and "rat-hole" feelings of the early 1960's [and] had come to be a substantial proof that American assistance and advice could help greatly in the constructive transformation of a developing Asian society. Given enough patience, and of course enough material support, but above all enough time for methods to sink in, and "it could be done."[26]

These perceptions had not come quickly. Eisenhower's forlorn comments on South Korea in 1960 were initially shared in the Kennedy administration. The ROK remained the prime example for a "never again" club in foreign policy circles when it came to direct U.S. involvement in land wars in Asia. Chronic weakness in the Korean economy and the failure of massive American aid to alter that condition reinforced the view. Politics was no solace either. Although the mercurial Syngman Rhee fell from power in 1960, Americans were hardly pleased with his successor. Chang Myon's government had left the democratic revolution it rode to power "unfinished." It seemed directionless, hamstrung by corruption, unstable and, most of all, unable to shake off the past to undertake coordinated economic action. As one U.S. official wrote, "endemic Oriental problems of graft, corruption and fraud" left the "the Republic of Korea . . . a sick society."[27]

Into early 1961, economic development issues were seen as the knot perpetuating troubles in Korea and also tied into other critical Asian concerns. Myon's government, like Rhee's, was "touchy" when it came to closer economic relations with Japan, something Americans saw as vital to regional stability.[28] There was no option of throwing off the Korean millstone. As a recipient of massive aid, it had profound international and regional resonance as the United States faced other emerging crises in Asia. Even as Americans felt they snuffed a possible "Korean explosion," they could not rest in a race to create the right mix to produce a "viable South Korea before it crumbles like Vietnam may." Yet, these efforts required even more "moolah." Faced with this unwelcome and expensive reality, Kennedy's advisers imagined an idealized ruling party allowing "vigorous, imaginative U.S. action in directing and supervising ROK economic development."[29]

Dreams had a chance to become reality after the disposal of the democratic regime by military coup in May 1961. Initially, Americans feared the new cabal's leader, Park Chung Hee, might be a communist.[30] Apprehension dissipated as it became clear Park and his followers would do what the Americans saw as crucial to South Korea's economic development. By the end of 1961, American ambassador Samuel Berger saw Park as the "forceful, fair, and intelligent leader" of a clique of "capable, energetic and dedicated men." Authoritarian tendencies were played down with the rationalization that "it is not realistic for us to insist on full-blown democracy and complete disappearance of military leadership." Other less than stellar qualities—the junta's unpopularity, its penchant for vote rigging, and corruption—were overlooked in exchange for stability compatible with U.S. strategic goals.[31]

It was an appeal based on a commitment to modernization, a concept important to Korean politics during the 1960s. Officially Park was "Chairman of the Supreme Council for National Reconstruction of the Republic of Korea." Seeking "reconstruction" he began a program for the "modernization of man." Although it was not the sum of his political posture, it was a pervasive theme. In fact, critics would see his government based not on a democratic mandate but its promise to promote national modernization. Park and South Korean elites hardly marched in lock step with their American patrons; they negotiated and tailored development ideas to fit their own imperatives. Nevertheless, modernization remained a central plank in Korean political and social life. Indeed, Park justified a return to the presidency in 1967 because he could not relinquish authority in the midst of his party's program to "modernize our fatherland."[32]

Under Park's rule industrial production and trade expanded. Most of all, he did what other South Korean leaders had been unable or unwilling to do—normalize trade relations with Japan. The 1965 treaty between the two countries brought no admission of guilt on Japan's part for the colonial period and a smaller reparations payment than demanded by the ROK. However, it massively increased Japanese loans and trade, further binding South Korea to the American regional system in East Asia.[33] It seemed to show that a strong hand, buttressed by the right modernization plan, could bring calm and political stability with meaningful economic growth on a model acceptable to the United States. It also demonstrated that modernization ideas that so often claimed a commitment to liberal politics to set them apart from communist competitors could be made comfortable with autocrats in U.S. policy. In the ROK, the liberal development sponsored by the United States made peace with what has been termed "developmental autocracy."[34]

Park's Korea became increasingly relevant as U.S. engagement in Vietnam mounted. In 1966, Berger drafted a secret memorandum that was circulated to those within the decision-making circles of the Johnson White House. Berger felt that "certain of the problems in the Republic of Viet Nam which appear so intractable resemble those which have over the years perplexed us in the Republic of Korea." The ROK provided a case study of how military government could navigate the problem of modernizing societies. The Park regime's strong executive leadership overcame some of the problems that had beset the democratic government. There had been less glamorous but important reforms of the bureaucracy as well as their determination to rein in student demonstrations and bring an "irresponsible and corrupt press under control." Although military governments could not be counted on over the long term, the Park regime revealed another assumption that developing countries required strong central government. Politically, "too many checks and balances on the executive can be a hindrance rather than a help."[35]

Berger shared a view that South Korea offered options for Southeast Asia. If a similar type of strong regime devoted to rigorous modernization was propped up in Saigon, the communist tide could be reversed. These assumptions were part of a trend toward what has been termed "authoritarian modernization" in U.S. foreign policy. In an era when liberal regimes in the developing world had a reputation for weakness and economic disarray in Washington, noncommunist autocratic forces provided an answer. They could maintain stability and mobilize resources to promote the modernization Americans assumed indispensable to their societies. Militaries had a particular appeal in the policy and academic communities discussing the issues. Naturally technocratic as institutions, militaries cultivated modern attitudes in the people that cycled through them. The martial option gained ground despite the fact that in practice it ran counter to much rhetoric of U.S. development aid cultivating "grass roots" democracy, liberal institutions, or even free markets. Beyond South Korea and South Vietnam, the United States threw its support behind autocratic regimes in Indonesia, Iran, and parts of Latin America that claimed a commitment to modernization.[36]

South Korea fed beliefs that events had started to run in the United States' favor in the developing world. With his influence within the government waxing, Rostow reviewed the world situation in 1965 and saw history's tide turning. Most "extremists" who had caused the U.S. political problems—a roster including Sukarno, Nasser, Castro, Nkrumah, Ben Bella, and even de Gaulle—had been humbled by domestic problems, political infighting, or other difficulties. This shift in momentum away from the "extremists" boded well. It meant the application of American military, political, and economic strength could "tip the balance" toward moderates favorable to the United States. It was a direct demonstration that "free world methods can match or outmatch communist efforts at modernizing underdeveloped countries." Such methods promised stability that leaders ("men") in underdeveloped countries interested in international cooperation could capitalize. This fixed them firmly to the international economy and compelled their behavior to fall in line with U.S. interests. Stability was best fostered when peoples moved from "abstract ideological debate" to a consensus that modernization was the primary goal of national politics.[37]

The promulgation of policies that brought transformation down to basic levels of everyday life was therefore central to world affairs. Rostow saw a great deal of "validity in the doctrine" and declared a series of development successes. He was confident that economic growth in Thailand, Malaysia, India, Pakistan, Turkey, and parts of Latin America promised stability and hushed more extreme elements. Leading the list, however, was South Korea. There, the increasing tempo of modernization was clearly linked to the growing political equilibrium of the once unsettled country. South Korea and the rest were a sign that "we [the United States] appear to be on the right political track in encouraging programs of economic development in underdeveloped countries." Following a similar pattern was the solution in other problem areas, particularly Vietnam.[38]

MODERNIZATION AT WAR IN SOUTHEAST ASIA

In Vietnam, development had been part of U.S. commitment almost from the start. Following the Griffin and Jessup missions in 1950, the United States had provided a Special Technical and Economic Mission to aid the French. After the French defeat the United States continued to provide aid to the shaky Republic of Vietnam (RVN). Aid ran the gamut. Complementing U.S. government activities were a set of nongovernmental programs, led by the likes of IVS and Michigan State University, which carried out a succession of technical assistance programs during the 1950s.[39]

As U.S. involvement in the region deepened in the early 1960s, modernization became further intertwined with the war effort in Southeast Asia. It was one part of a massive American-led exercise whose goal was nothing short than the construction of an entirely new state in southern Vietnam. As the anti-government insurgency gained momentum in South Vietnam, the United States turned to influential theories of counterinsurgency to help prop up their proxy. Counterinsurgency grew into a mantra of the Kennedy administration and found a great patron in Rostow, a man who had done so much to define modernization as theory and policy in the 1950s. Rostow's colleague, Secretary of Defense Robert McNamara, also held a firm belief in the necessity of modernization as a part of larger strategies in a postcolonial and Cold War world. In a speech to newspaper editors in Montreal in 1966, McNamara stated a maxim, "Security is development. Without development there can be no security. A developing nation that does not in fact develop simply cannot remain secure."[40]

Counterinsurgency, as employed in Vietnam, was not a pure military activity. From the very beginning U.S. planners believe that its success required coordinated development. The "strategic hamlets," the backbone of counterinsurgency plans from 1961 to 1963, were set in modernization footings. Inspired by British operations in Malaya, the goal was to secure villages and isolate the National Liberation Front (NLF—the Viet Cong) guerrillas from sources of support. The question brought the intervention of another guru of modernization thinking. In 1961, Eugene Staley was enticed from his post at the Stanford Research Institute to lead an influential survey of counterinsurgency policy in Vietnam. Staley again provides a link to the past. His dip into the world of counterinsurgency shows the continuity within the modernization concepts marching to war in Southeast Asia.

The "Staley Group" viewed armed insurgency as a problem inseparable from development. Their recommendations held the force of a "conviction that the subversive intensive warfare . . . can be brought to a successful conclusion only by the prompt application of effective military power, coupled with large-scale economic and social action reaching every part of the country." The report, greeted positively by both Rostow and Rusk (then Secretary of State), saw central economic planning as indispensable to the eventual construction of a viable nation in South Vietnam. Even so, security was the immediate priority. Rural areas were of greatest concern, and the expansion of the South Vietnamese Army in both size and its operations there was a priority. As part of this strategy to enhance government authority in the countryside, Staley pressed for the construction of fortified "agrovilles."[41] In contested areas, the population would be resettled in newly constructed villages where armed inhabitants could defend against incursions. Beyond this martial element, the overall program contained strains of the social engineering common to modernization thinking. Agrovilles would provide a moment to expose the peasants to modern forces. By breaking the peasants of their traditional ways with roads, electrification, better communication, or new agricultural techniques they would be given material gains as well as an outlook based on an idea of progress. This was likely to build increasing support for the RVN government and further isolate the rebels.[42]

Great hopes and grounding in the development consensus could not overcome painful realities. By 1963, the "strategic hamlets" had foundered. Undermining the effort was a combination of poor planning, mismanagement, corruption, NLF activity, and, most of all, resistance to the forced resettlement required by the very peasants it was supposed to benefit. A program born of the liberal development consensus proved remarkably illiberal in practice.[43]

Dramatic failure, however, did not decouple development from the overall goal of defeating the communist challenge in Vietnam. "Pacification" programs for South Vietnam quickly reemerged, finding new expression in the form of "Revolutionary Development" (RD). Proposed in 1966, the program was part of the expanding American military commitment to the RVN. The essential point was to demonstrate that the NLF did not hold the monopoly on promises of positive social change. With more than an echo of the "strategic hamlets" the RD program leaned heavily on development activity. The initial concept worked out by Johnson's special adviser, Robert Komer, saw development as fundamental to what became known as the "Other War." Winning this conflict meant reducing the Viet Cong threat while enticing rural people with schools, textbooks, public health programs, infrastructural improvements, and agricultural aid, as well as the construction of local institutions to shepherd these changes. Undeniably, the "Other War" aimed to reach deep into Vietnamese life.[44]

The importance of the RD program is shown by the attention it received from McNamara. Although by 1966 he believed, "pacification is a basic disappointment," he urged that vigorous efforts be continued as it remained "the main talisman of ultimate U.S. success or failure in Vietnam."[45] As the war deepened, RD was absorbed by the U.S. Army, re-emerging in 1967 as the CORDS (Civilian Operations and Revolutionary Development Support) program. Pacification and counterinsurgency were far from the total of U.S. development aid in Vietnam, but they were very important programs and they were dependent on modernization ideas. They were not mere military operations but programs designed to bring far-reaching social and cultural change. Successful counterinsurgency required altering people's outlooks and orientations to include more modern, progressive visions.[46] In this sense, counterinsurgency in its varied forms was a logical outgrowth of the development consensus that had evolved in the late 1940s and 1950s. In Vietnam, the two concepts were codependent.

The importance of modernization to the war effort was betrayed by the rapid expansion of aid activities. As troop levels rose, so did aid staff. Much of the rank and file who fought the "Other War" was provided by USAID. The South Vietnam mission became its largest and was heavily involved in aspects of the agrovilles and successor projects. It grew from 732 American staff in 1965 to 1,856 in 1967—out of a total USAID staff worldwide of 17,311. Added to this were 293 employees from other U.S. agencies involved in aid, plus 474 from U.S. contractors, as well as some 1,395 foreign nationals and 3,537 Vietnamese (for a total of 7,555 personnel). Aid expenditures in Vietnam ratcheted up equally quickly, to $495 million in 1967, and remained close to that level through the end of the decade.[47]

Despite its size, the U.S. government programs still relied on the inputs of voluntary groups committed to the development consensus. USAID leaned on all manner of NGO resources. Rural projects focused on community development in the early 1960s relied heavily on Catholic Relief Services' well-established logistics and distribution system in Vietnam.[48] Even more important was IVS. It had rapidly earned a reputation for idealism as well as competence. Midwestern agricultural colleges were incubators for much of its staff. Although it was officially secular, expectations were that staff would maintain a religious bearing in an organization still close to its missionary roots. Devotion to duty was apparent. Many of its volunteers made vigorous efforts to learn Vietnamese culture and language. They became the largest NGO contingent in the country, but their flexibility further enhanced their impacts, making them a critical asset to the USAID mission. A commitment that began in the late 1950s grew with the rest of the U.S. mission to 151 volunteers at the height of its commitment in 1968.[49] It was one more signal of how Vietnam had become the largest single commitment of the American aid community in terms of dollars and manpower.

Lyndon Johnson was keen on the "Other War." The president's affinity for development left him predisposed, but it had a political resonance. It bolstered claims that U.S. involvement in Southeast Asia promised a better life for the people of the region.[50] The attention the president gave to this and other programs was a function of his own faith in development. But it was also a part of the general view of development as an integral tool to achieve American foreign policy goals. As American involvement accelerated to open military action in 1964–65, modernization was given double duty: to help tamp down the insurgency and serve as an example of U.S. benevolence in Southeast Asia in the court of world public opinion.

A massive plan for the development of the Mekong River, born of and embodying the international consensus on liberal development, would eventually become the flagship exhibition. From its inception, development of the Mekong River had been influenced by some of the most influential members of the club of international, philanthropic, and private groups that had invested in modernization during the postwar period. Initial inspiration came from two Chinese engineers, Dr. Shen-Yi and P. T. Tan, who, exposed to the early international boosterism for a TVA in China, sketched a plan for the Yellow River in the 1940s. Frustrated by communist victory in China, the two men extended their plan to Southeast Asia, helping inspire a 1952 ECAFE plan. Through the UN they sought to implement a river development plan to serve the region, an idea eagerly grasped by the riparian nations of Southeast Asia—Cambodia, Laos, South Vietnam, and Thailand.[51]

As noted, the Eisenhower administration was initially hesitant about the multilateral Mekong plan, preferring its own bilateral approach. Even without direct U.S. support, the ECAFE and riparian nations pressed ahead, founding the Mekong Committee in 1957. Organizationally, the committee answered to its member nations but also to the UN and those providing funding. With shifts in the U.S. government's foreign aid policy, by late 1957 these sources came to include the U.S. government.[52] The new committee undertook studies to outline a comprehensive resource development program. The showpiece was the Mekong River Survey Mission of 1957, headed by Raymond Wheeler, seconded from his World Bank post and fresh from the Indus negotiations. Wheeler's presence displayed the seriousness of the United States and the World Bank and assured press coverage (American newspapers readily compared the Mekong plan to the benchmark TVA).[53] The mission opened the door for successor programs, which required the involvement of numerous other nonstate actors. These ranged from private companies like Nippon Electric to Shell with clear financial interests to a coterie of foundations and voluntary groups.

Chief among these was the Ford Foundation. The foundation's interest in the Mekong project was part of its commitment to international development. Ford would make its presence felt with a large socioeconomic study headed by geographer Gilbert White. The influential report saw the water management promised by the project as a powerful multipurpose tool for the development. In line with mainstream thinking was the assumption that effects would reach far beyond the banks of the river. Like the Tennessee and so many other rivers, harnessing the Mekong would control the waters and generate electricity but also contribute to a stabilization and expansion of agriculture, increase fish and forest production, promote manufacturing, and lower transport costs. The tangible product of the report was a catalog of what sort of studies needed to be done, offering legitimacy to the plans. In its wake, a truly international effort took shape, with $110 million of aid pledged in 1962–63. Aid was diverse: Canada provided aerial mapping, Israel supported irrigation planning, Japan provided engineering teams, India provided rain gauges, Iran gave petroleum products, and a cross-section of UN agencies undertook a battery of surveys. Those working on the project came from a variety of backgrounds; even so, comparisons with the TVA remained direct. Kanwar Sain, now Director of Engineering Services for the Mekong Committee, acknowledged differences, but chose to emphasize similarities. In administrative and financial details, the authority's example was useful but more important was the TVA's record in "igniting, encouraging, educating, and coordinating the efforts of the seven [U.S.] states for economic and social development." If a realistic program were adhered to in Southeast Asia, the riparian nations would reap similar gains.[54]

The White House was well aware of the program. Although predisposed to the type of broadly conceived development that the Mekong project represented, the Kennedy administration was regularly prodded about it by a set of partisans. In early 1961, Lilienthal contacted Under Secretary of State Chester Bowles, urging the administration to take a hard look at the "key river in Southeast Asia." With D&R's invested in comparable schemes in Iran and elsewhere, Lilienthal saw a similar opportunity in Southeast Asia and was confident that Bowles, a New Dealer himself, "understood the TVA idea and method" and how it was "a great political asset of the United States in parts of the world other than our own." Gilbert White convinced Bowles and Cleveland to convene a January 1962 meeting to brief staff of USAID, the Bureau of Reclamation, and the State Department to discuss the Ford Foundation study.[55]

Vice President Lyndon Johnson was subject to similar lobbying. In 1961, before a wide-ranging trip to Asia, Johnson was contacted by an old friend, "Tex" Goldschmidt (they became friends while working for the National Youth Administration in Texas during the 1930s). Like other New Dealers, Goldschmidt migrated into international development work in the 1940s. He worked with the UN in various positions, from UNESCO to ECOSOC. Throughout, Goldschmidt retained a devotion to large-scale development programs. An article of this faith was a 1963 piece for *Scientific American* that connected reforms from the 1930s to the contemporary vogue of development. Goldschmidt made the connection with domestic reform explicit, outlining the remarkable effects of development in the American South. Retarded by the effects of a slave economy and defeat in the Civil War, after Reconstruction the southern states languished as a sort of internal colony. Only outside intervention broke this cycle. Federal largess made possible land reform, conservation, and electrification and other activities beyond the capacity of existing southern institutions. Success in the American South had a "direct parallel with the economic development of the former colonial regions of the world." Yet, the South's achievement was a reminder that built-in disadvantages of poverty and underdevelopment stood in the way of modernization. In Goldschmidt's own words, "no amount of bootstrap-pulling" would assure growth. He felt the "pacemaking" organization was the TVA, setting standards with economic effects far beyond its own immediate area of operation. The best hope lay in using these developmental tools to support integration of emerging nations into the global economy.[56]

Meeting with Johnson over hamburgers and Cokes in 1961, Goldschmidt urged the vice president to visit the Mekong Committee to see what a TVA-style program could do in Asia. Support would provide growth while training "representatives of four countries with differing political views, to work together effectively even in a period otherwise characterized by a lot of fussing."[57] Johnson took Goldschmidt's personal advice, confiding to him later, "We are in a better position to handle some of the problems of the developing countries because of the problems we faced so recently in developing our own."[58] During his Asian trip the vice president made a point of stopping at the Mekong Commission's offices in Bangkok. He displayed his "keen interest" by overstaying his appointment by an hour, keeping the prime minister of Thailand waiting. As he lingered, Johnson declared to U Nyun, the commission's executive secretary, that "all my life I have been interested in rivers and their development."[59]

The urgings of Goldschmidt and Bangkok statements aside, Lyndon Johnson hardly needed convincing on the appeal of large-scale development projects. The Texan had seen for himself the effect of programs that sprang from the New Deal on poor and isolated areas of his home state. Some historians have seen his entire political career as based on the politics of economic development.[60] Nevertheless, his affinities were not remarkably different from other members of the Kennedy administration. Like numerous colleagues, Johnson believed that large-scale programs primed by government intervention could produce remarkable economic change. He was enamored with programs promising development for other parts of the world. Robert Komer, later Johnson's special assistant, good-naturedly recalled his boss "was a fanatic . . . on rural electrification [in Vietnam]. Good God, you could drive me up a wall."[61] Johnson firmly believed that electrification was one step toward leaving the "footprints of America" in Vietnam. Much of this would hinge on efforts to "turn the Mekong into a Tennessee Valley."[62]

Interventions by Lilienthal, White, and Goldschmidt assured the Mekong remained visible at the highest levels of a U.S. government predisposed to its approach to development.[63] In the winter of 1962, Bowles suggested directly to Kennedy the Mekong offered a way out of an "explosive" situation in Southeast Asia. By taking the reins of the existing Mekong plan and creating an "International Lower Mekong Valley Authority," the United States could assert a claim on this positive international vision for the region. Bowles realized that the real power in a comprehensive development plan lay not in the potential for economic growth, but the *"political concept"* surrounding it[64] (emphasis original). Nothing came of the proposal immediately, but Bowles's advocacy does suggest how development was strongly integrated in mainstream policy thinking as a solution to foreign policy questions.

Government lethargy only brought more lobbying. As violence grew in Southeast Asia during the mid-1960s, White continued to see the possibility of international harmony through a developmental lens. He believed that the United States had only three unattractive ways to approach the region—expansion, escalation, or neutralization. The river offered a "Fourth Course" to steer out of the situation. International cooperation for development gave incentives for Southeast Asian nations to tamp down fighting, and North Vietnamese and Soviet affinities for this style of development might bridge political differences. The scheme offered the United States a more "graceful" and cheaper investment than expensive military operations. Armed conflict might give way to a struggle for prosperity waged on the river.[65] White sought to use Lilienthal as a conduit to Johnson to assure his internationalist vision received attention. Although Lilienthal read the article with "fascination," events outpaced action, rendering White's hopes moot.[66]

White might have been disappointed to know that even as he wrote his article, the Mekong was being enlisted into U.S. government service, but as a means to support a more aggressive policy. A program international in its scope and commitment was gradually undone as the Johnson White House utilized development as a tool to shape the situation in Vietnam. In mid-1964, Cleveland suggested to McGeorge Bundy that support for the Mekong project would flex more "muscle" in a confrontation with "Chicoms" in Southeast Asia.[67] As events accelerated, the development program further insinuated itself into American strategy. Johnson's personal fondness for economic development should be emphasized in these decisions, yet he was only one among many in the government who saw large-scale technological-based development as a tool to solve social and political problems. The advisers surrounding him were steeped in the liberal consensus on development. All held a firm belief in the transformative power of development led by the United States. As U.S. policy slid toward overt military action in Southeast Asia during 1964, the Mekong project was pushed forward to highlight U.S. claims to a long-term and peaceful commitment to the region against the backdrop of an expanding war.[68]

In February 1965, the United States unleashed a new series of air strikes on North Vietnam in response to NLF attacks on U.S. forces in South Vietnam. But this intensified military activity had been long debated as a means to prop up the flagging Saigon government. Assuming a close connection between the NLF and the North Vietnamese government, the Americans hoped a gradually escalated bombing campaign against the North might constrict aid to the insurgents while bolstering the morale of the South Vietnamese. Modernization formed part of the rationale of Johnson's advisers for the attacks. With his political star on the rise, Rostow's modernization thinking had influence on the shape of the military response. Rostow observed through modernization lenses, "Ho has an industrial complex to protect; he is no longer a guerrilla fighter with nothing to lose." This formulation became known around Washington as the "Rostow Thesis" and gained adherents in the corridors of power.[69] So when the NLF shelled the American-occupied base at Pleiku in February, killing eight U.S. advisers, it provided justification to put into action the pre-existing bombing plan against the North.[70]

Bombing was a double-edged sword. Air attacks provided military benefits but had negative effects, as many American allies were critical of such escalation. Johnson felt trapped. Sectors of the administration pushed the president to announce a "Johnson Doctrine" that would bring the benefits similar to America's own domestic efforts to achieve a "Great Society" to the peoples of Asia.[71] Such emphasis would placate world opinion, while demonstrating the enduring U.S. commitment to its Southeast Asian allies.[72] Bundy and Rostow wanted something with the political impact of the Marshall Plan to drive home the point. There were discussions about creating a "Southeast Asia Economic Development Plan" with the needs of developing states in mind to fill this role. Bundy summarized the rationale thus: "We do not want it thought that we are interested in economic development only because we are trying somehow to get out of our mess in Vietnam. The Marshall Plan was helpful in dealing with Soviet pressure on Europe, but it was not designed or presented to the *Europeans* in those terms"[73] (emphasis original).

Formulations from the 1940s still held. A Marshall Plan per se was not what was needed, but a type of development program that offered the extensive development poorer nations were believed to require. Johnson and his close aides eventually nominated the TVA inspired Mekong project as the vessel for their hopes. Goldschmidt was called to the White House to consult on what was fast becoming a major policy statement. His presence was perhaps unnecessary, as many key officials were already Mekong club initiates. Cleveland had exposed a cross-section of key government policymakers—including Bundy—to the live enthusiasm of Goldschmidt, White, and C. Hart Schaaf (the U.S. Mekong Committee representative) at a meeting in June 1964.[74] When the critical moment arrived in 1965, the Mekong plan, reassuringly grounded in the liberal development consensus, was easily pulled off the shelf. As Johnson began swinging a big stick in Southeast Asia, the Mekong plan became, as it was succinctly phrased, the desperately sought "carrot."[75]

On April 7, 1965, at Johns Hopkins University, before a packed auditorium lit by television lights, Johnson unveiled the plan. In a measured tone, the president assured allies and enemies alike that the United States would not withdraw from Vietnam. But the address was more concerned with the carrot than the stick. Air strikes against the North had begun only months before, and there was an urgent need to show that the United States had more in store for the region than increased violence. While he emphasized the commitment of the United States to South Vietnam, Johnson linked this to an effort to "improve the life of man in that conflict-torn corner of our world." Emphasizing cooperation, Johnson acknowledged one of the best efforts was already under way, started by the United Nations in the form of the Mekong Committee. Projects centered on the Mekong might "provide food and water and power on a scale to dwarf even our own TVA." Reflexively, the speech referenced the more intimate areas of life that would be touched by the modernization the United States offered. Social change, in line with prevailing views, was a goal. Johnson promised that modern medicine would reach those denied it. Educational programs were part of an agenda "to train people in the skills that are needed to manage the process of development."

The experience of the New Deal and the development it delivered was how Johnson meant to make these promises understood and how he saw them himself. Johnson recalled:

> In the countryside where I was born, and where I live, I have seen the night illuminated, and the kitchens warmed, and the homes heated, where once the cheerless night and the ceaseless

cold held sway. And all this happened because electricity came to our area along the humming wires of the REA [Rural Electrification Administration].[76]

There was substance in the address. The president promised contributions to development efforts in the form of a billion dollars and a team of advisers to be headed by Eugene Black. American action alone was not enough. Johnson called on "all other industrialized nations" to join the cause, "including the Soviet Union." American leadership was vital, but the regional effort in Southeast Asia needed to be seen as multilateral.[77]

For all its gravity, Johnson joked with advisers beforehand that the speech's promises would likely appeal to "sob sisters and peace societies" domestically. Still, the Hopkins address sought real international impact. By offering his "TVA on the Mekong" Johnson could tout American commitment as both one to see a conflict through to victory and an investment in the long-term health of the region. As was hoped, the address drew considerable international attention. In Europe there was general approval of the American proposal. Communist states were generally wary. From the riparian nations there was delight, as the American move promised large-scale support for a project they had long supported. In the short run, this reaction fit the hopes of the Johnson administration. The speech also endeavored to deepen the divisions in the communist world with its offer of participation to the Soviet Union while explicitly attacking China as an instigator of the region's troubles. American planners also hoped it would entice the DRV into negotiations, assuming that as an underdeveloped country, North Vietnam would have a hard time justifying not taking advantage of such a dramatic modernization proposal. However, the DRV denounced it.[78]

American action following the Hopkins speech was significant. The most dramatic initiative was another reversal of U.S. policy. Asian nations had long hoped for a regional development bank on the model of the World Bank. The United States and the World Bank had opposed the creation of such a lender itself—a stance taken by Black when he was at the Bank during the 1950s. But the new tack on the Mekong forced a change in this position. One of the first things Black did was to gather a Consultative Committee and barnstorm around the world, including the Eastern Bloc, to raise support for the enterprise. They found international opinion amenable to the establishment of an Asian bank. There was haggling over the location of the bank and the raising of the institution's capitalization of $1 billion (the United States and Japan each contributed $200 million to this sum), but the Asian Development Bank emerged in December 1966. The formation of the ADB pointed at the regional nature of the effort America wanted to support and acknowledged the critical importance of an economically resurgent Japan as a partner to share burdens. It remains in place today.[79]

The regional commitments the ADB represented did not last in the face of a widening war. In 1966, U.S. contributions to the Mekong Committee itself slid to a paltry $4.9 million. Another casualty of the fighting was the U.S. relationship with Cambodia. Prince Norodom Sihanouk's regime walked a tightrope between both sides in the Cold War. Even as the Mekong project was taking shape in the 1950s, Cambodia was also receiving technical aid from the Soviet Union. As the situation in the region worsened in the 1960s, Sihanouk became increasingly critical of U.S. interference in Cambodia and the region generally. In 1963, he refused all U.S. military and economic aid. At the same time he turned a blind eye to North Vietnamese troop sanctuaries on Cambodian soil. Sihanouk also made demands that the Mekong Committee direct more of its efforts toward his country and shift its headquarters to Phnom Penh.[80] Sihanouk's fears about the U.S. domination of the project eventually led to Cambodia's withdrawal from the Mekong project in 1967. This caused considerable apprehension in the region, Japan (by now a major contributor to the project), and the UN. If Cambodia excluded American aid it was unlikely that many of the projects in that country necessary for the whole program would be completed. These concerns were stilled when relations between Cambodia and the United States improved in 1969. Nevertheless, this fracture had profound effects on the progress of the Mekong effort at an important juncture. Work on several dams was curtailed for a number of years because of these disputes.[81]

Even as increased U.S. activity in the region threw down hurdles for the project, the idea of developing the Mekong remained integral to discussions of regional stability. A series of meetings and speeches in Honolulu, Manila, and Thailand during 1966 were used by Johnson to emphasize that while standing against communism in South Vietnam was the immediate concern, American sponsored development was indispensable as the means to guarantee stability and prosperity in Southeast Asia and around the Pacific Rim. Throughout, the Mekong was highlighted as both an example of American largess and a template for other programs from which a stable, economically advanced (and non-communist) Asia-Pacific would evolve. The irony was the actual program that eventually emerged was not regional but focused on South Vietnam.[82]

These Pacific meetings would lead to a major effort to frame a development plan for a postwar RVN. Based on the reconstruction studies done in South Korea, the goal was a general blueprint for nation building and, perhaps more important, to show that American responsibilities did not end with the conclusion of armed conflict. In 1966, Komer suggested the United States get the South Vietnamese regime to call for such a study,

Figure 6.3. A consensus for war: Lilienthal speaking with Lyndon Johnson on *Air Force One*, 1967. Walt Rostow is third from right. Robert McNamara is seated to the left of Johnson. Courtesy of National Archives, Washington, DC

"led by a prestigious individual, and working jointly with a Vietnamese team." Orchestration took until December, when South Vietnamese President Nguyen Cao Ky officially requested a joint commission. An air force officer, Ky was part of a military-backed regime that the United States hoped would rule with a firm and steady hand. Americans hoped this set of strongmen, availed with significant development aid, could work feats of modernization similar to those unfolding in the ROK. It also showed the comfort of modernization ideas claiming liberal roots with autocratic regimes. When the co-chairs were selected, Johnson spoke of how the American nominee was "admired [for] the programs which he has inaugurated." The president's selection for the high-profile task was, unsurprisingly, David Lilienthal.[83]

"Mr. TVA" Goes to Vietnam

The choice of Lilienthal—or "Mr. TVA" as he was described in the press—was a culmination of attempts to demonstrate that involvement in Southeast Asia was constructive rather than destructive.[84] It also demonstrates how efforts in Vietnam were tightly connected to larger developmental consensus ideas and institutions. But the undertaking Lilienthal joined was already feeling the pressures of war. Tensions pro-

duced within the region by U.S. escalation of the fighting had made work
in the riparian nations difficult. Increasingly, the American government
view of the potentials of the Mekong River shrunk to the confines of the
Republic of Vietnam. The project still inspired hopes outside the administration. Arthur Schlesinger, Jr., loyal to his earlier opinions of the TVA
as a "weapon" to contain communism, looked to the regional Mekong
program as a part of a neutralization scheme. In his eyes, the collective
economic development it promised remained "an honorable resolution to
a tragic situation."[85]

Although its agenda was the fate of South Vietnam, Lilienthal's official
client was USAID. For them Lilienthal brought D&R to bear (for a hefty
fee of $250,000) on long-term economic development planning. Here,
D&R's work demonstrates the extensive cooperation upon which the liberal development consensus was built. As much as the American government required the services of D&R to execute policy, D&R drew on the
expertise of the thicket of other nonstate development institutions committed to modernization work. Lilienthal sent emissaries to the epicenter
of modernization thinking, Cambridge, Massachusetts. There they consulted with Lucian Pye and Max Millikan (who held secret clearance,
allowing access to sensitive material related to the project). Various sa-
trapies including CENIS and the Harvard Development Advisory Service
were also consulted. Delegates from D&R attended SEADAG meetings
to draw on another nexus of academic expertise.[86]

Lilienthal knew victory was not solely a military question. Defeating
an insurgency required providing the Vietnamese with "confidence in the
future" through comprehensive development. It accepted that the center
point of this effort was the state. The commission's work was to be linked
to South Vietnam's ongoing national economic planning. Like many in
the Third World, the RVN had embraced state planning; in fact, it already
had sponsored two five-year plans.[87] The resources available for the mission left Lilienthal optimistic about the Vietnamese and the ability of this
brand of planning, tied to Komer's CORDS and related programs of
USAID, to shorten the conflict. Lilienthal wrote to Johnson of their shared
faith in a development schema, "based on the experience in helping to
liberate the creative energies of people in America and overseas."[88]

Nevertheless, there were concerns at the start. Lilienthal harbored few
illusions; Vietnam was a lightning rod in American public life. Added to
this was the checkered track record of U.S. aid programs in Asia, save
places like Taiwan and South Korea. Instability and violence could not be
ignored. Lilienthal believed there was no perfect historical precedent for
planning for postwar reconstruction while fighting continued. In Korea,
planning had not been completed by the time fighting ended. Initial conceptualization in 1966 assumed fighting would end before D&R implemented its program. This would not be the case, as fighting and the U.S.

military presence only intensified. Still, his boundless optimism prevailed. Although the situation in early 1967 resembled the "French and Indian Wars" it was, nevertheless, unlikely to put the long-term development of the RVN out of reach. With unintended irony, Lilienthal predicted peace would soon be established, although it would contain a significant level of violence.[89]

Politically, the project had to appear a collaborative venture with the Vietnamese. Lilienthal believed the Americans should approach their mission with a sense of "humility." The structure of the commission itself was based on another model of U.S. aid efforts, the Joint Commission on Rural Reconstruction. Linear descendant of the nongovernmental development efforts in interwar China and infused with consensus ideas, the JCRR had continuing influence as an example for American aid efforts worldwide. Just as important as the fact that it was based on collaborative activities was its reputation as a success. Its influence was even more direct: the Assistant Administrator of USAID's Vietnam Bureau, James P. Grant, was a JCRR alumnus and believed something born of its example would work "just fine."[90] While "jointness" was a watchword, Lilienthal and D&R staff saw limitations. In part it was the lack of "suitable talents" among the Vietnamese to perform certain tasks. Added was the intrigue brought by working with another nation. Lilienthal encouraged American staff to keep certain comments and reports out of reach of "literal minded" Vietnamese.[91]

The Joint Development Group (JDG) emerged in early 1967, with visits and surveys beginning that spring. Early impressions by D&R personnel were optimistic, even if some were befuddled by the nature of the conflict going on around them. John L. Swift, a D&R employee with considerable world experience (who later worked on domestic Great Society programs), struggled to understand the ambivalent violence of modern guerrilla war. Outside Pleiku, as an artillery barrage smashed a nearby hill, he noticed the non-reaction of USAID officials and Vietnamese tea-pickers. When he inquired about its military significance, one of his handlers responded, "Oh, nothing really." On a later Air America flight near Saigon he saw

> [A]n airstrike . . . Three fighter bombers flying low below us were dropping bombs on a road in the forest. Orange bursts followed by pillars of smoke came up from the trees. There are, of course, hundreds of such strikes every day . . . against an almost invisible enemy, one who perhaps cannot be beaten by this kind of approach.[92]

For D&R and USAID staff, the approach that could succeed was one infused with modernization. All important national development plans drew from legacies of Lilienthal's long career, reinforced by D&R's experiences in places like Iran and Colombia. Lilienthal connected efforts in Vietnam directly to the TVA creed, envisioning projects that would be decentralized and autonomous. Its program was described as other programs of the era were: the best way to induce national economic growth while imparting modern skills to the Vietnamese.[93] Aid officials began calling the group the "Lilienthal Team." He regularly took his message to the international press and American public on television and in print that Vietnamese reconstruction would work. Despite disagreements between the American and Vietnamese commissioners, he and his company took pains to dramatize the Vietnamese contribution to the operation. The group hammered out an initial document, delivered to the South Vietnamese government in November 1967. It did not go unnoticed. Within the foreign policy establishment there was sincere belief in the importance of what Lilienthal was attempting. At the CFR there was satisfaction that the large-scale development planning the United States should have been doing from the beginning of its commitment to the RVN was being instituted. American officials on the ground in Vietnam also anticipated the final products of the JDG.[94] The extensive reports, surveys, and plans crafted by the JDG and D&R show the seriousness of intent. An action plan for an extensive modernization program was crafted. The question that remained was what impact the war would have on its execution.

While the JDG's mandate was fixed on the fortunes of the Republic of Vietnam, D&R kept an eye on regional opportunities. As planning for South Vietnam picked up speed, the company looked longingly at an "Amplified Basin Plan" for the river system that the ECAFE and the Mekong Committee had hammered out. While D&R was obviously lured by the chance of a new source of contracts and profits, the interest in the amplified plan had a clear connection to the large-scale approaches that guided their basic approach to development. Within the RVN, the lion's share of the JDG's attention was placed on the agricultural sector. This was due to the fact that the majority of the Vietnamese population remained rural. However, it was also an acknowledgment that the war had mauled the countryside. Between 1964 and 1966, paddy rice production fell sharply, from 5.2 to 4.3 million tons, forcing the RVN to import the staple. The situation was so bad that by 1967, the United States sought to change the Vietnamese diet by encouraging the consumption of cheaper imported wheat.[95] Any significant development undertaking would have to contend with critical agrarian shortfalls. Boosting agricultural production was crucial for self-sufficiency and exports necessary for the RVN's balance of payments and place in its regional economy.

From the very beginning the Mekong River was touted as the "No. 1" means to unravel South Vietnam's problems. The head of the USAID mission thought taming the Mekong River was the Vietnamese "national purpose" expressed in a modernization idiom.[96] Lilienthal was enthralled by one of the richest agricultural areas in the world to the point of downplaying the importance of the RVN's growing urban areas. He believed that "properly developed, the Mekong Delta could feed all of Southeast Asia."[97] It was "grossly underutilized," because intensive, modern agriculture had not been able to penetrate the region. In line with the prevailing consensus development, success was a matter of converting natural resources through the application of technology, into commodities. Well-managed development could facilitate a rapid increase of delta rice production and a wide variety of other crops. An expansion of agricultural production demanded greater water control, changes in land management, and even new plants. Strands of "Miracle Rice" emerging from Los Baños were a critical addition in which planners put great stock. Tied to improved chemical fertilizers (research the TVA supported), this comprehensive transformation of the agricultural environment could provide resources to push the wider transformation of Vietnamese life.[98]

To accomplish this, the JDG proposed a Mekong Delta Development Authority (MDDA). The idea was hewn from the TVA model and in keeping with its general philosophy the MDDA was to be separate from but work in cooperation with the government. Although tethered to the regional Mekong project, the MDDA was limited by the boundaries of the RVN. Nevertheless, the MDDA's programs would affect the lives of millions of Vietnamese and serve as a basis for other regional authorities in other parts of Vietnam.[99] Responsible for executing the large-scale plans for the Delta region, it would also oversee a conglomeration of local development associations. These would allow the authority to reach down to the grass roots to educate farmers to change local practices through community development projects that served the larger modernization campaign. This would increase production while transforming the worldview of the villagers. This reformation was to be the bedrock of a larger national reconstruction plan. Vietnamese officials generally accepted the MDDA concept but did so with some reticence about its authority.[100]

While the JDG proposed major changes to village life, it skirted the issue of land tenure. Echoing a favoritism for larger farms and corporate agriculture that had driven many agricultural programs in the American South and overseas, the JDG emphasized that "many crops cannot be grown economically ... other than on a large scale ... land reform should not be carried so far as to make such profitable enterprises and potential employers of labor impossible. The solution to rural poverty in some areas may be found in an efficient farm labor force rather than in small tenant holdings." Development brought change, but social reforms threatening to elites supporting the regime in Saigon were to be avoided.[101]

All views faced the unforgiving reality of civil war. The Tet Offensive in January 1968 smashed assumptions guiding development work. Americans in Saigon were stunned by the audacity of the Viet Cong and North Vietnamese as they struck across the South. D&R staff fumbled through rumor and uncertainty to comprehend the impact of the fighting. Immediate "despair" abated as the smoke cleared, but misgivings lingered. Although D&R later tried to claim there were no illusions to shatter, this could not shade reality. There was an admission that the offensive did "shake our belief in some kinds of programs for which we held great hope." Many elements of the JDG's work had rested on confident security estimates, which, after Tet, "changed by almost 180°." Safety in the countryside, never assured, was now officially in question. Urban areas, long thought of as redoubts, were now uncertain. Essential travel and surveys for the project became difficult, if not impossible. Concerns of the commission aside, the fighting drove a further 700,000 people from their homes. Tragically, refugees were not a new concern, but the scale of this flow of people imposed new burdens on an already taxed infrastructure.[102] Even Lilienthal's reservoir of optimism was sapped. He wondered if the JDG's work could "be kept alive" in light of the "serious setback" of Tet.[103] It took the intervention of Johnson, Rusk, and Clark Clifford to impress upon Lilienthal "the degree to which the entire government is relying on D&R." Confidence restored, he called on staff to "redouble" efforts, convinced that the JDG's significance and "responsibilities have grown rather than diminished."[104]

There was a great deal of effort and more than a touch of hope expended on plans that would shape ongoing U.S. modernization efforts in the RVN. But the question quickly became whether the Lilienthal Team's ideas could be successful. Their implementation faced serious hurdles. While the JDG presumed its operations would take place postwar, the sobering reality was its proposals were made during a conflict nowhere near conclusion. Perhaps most daunting to modernization hopes was refugee relief and resettlement. It swallowed the largest single share of U.S. aid funds. The aftereffects of expanded conflict worked against the implementation of development plans. People were resettled only to be uprooted again by a constantly shifting battlefield. In 1968 alone, over 1 million South Vietnamese were driven from their homes. The scale of this problem, the effects of which would not immediately disappear even if peace came quickly, was one of the largest concerns the JDG's plans faced. Talk of implementing programs at the "grass roots" based on the example of the TVA was complicated by the fact that people on the ground faced lives in a persistent state of flux because of armed conflict.[105]

Political will was waning. In a nationally broadcast speech on March 31, 1968, Johnson yet again offered development as proof of "our determination to build a better land [in Vietnam]." He pleaded with North Vietnam to come to the table and "take its place in this common effort just as soon as peace comes." The North Vietnamese ignored this proposal as they had others. It mattered little, in a way, as in that speech Johnson announced his refusal to seek or accept another term as president.[106]

Even after recusing himself from the presidency, he continued to play up the "fantastic" rewards that remained to be tapped in the Mekong River.[107] Johnson's continued faith was mirrored by his two proconsuls on Southeast Asian Development, Lilienthal and Black. Both men continued to see development in Southeast Asia as vital, but it was less as a tool for victory and increasingly a means to salvage America's reputation. Lilienthal shared these sentiments and stretched them further. On *The Today Show* and other television programs, as well as in prominent publications, he emphasized the importance of reconstructing South Vietnam while relating it to his experiences with the TVA and D&R.[108] He held out the JDG's plan for the Mekong Delta as the primary mechanism to reverse the flagging fortunes of the RVN. Yet, modernization work on the Mekong promised an integrative mechanism that could operate on a number of levels. Successful development was a benchmark as "the future standing and influence of the United States in the Pacific Basin will depend largely on the skill—or lack of it—with which the postwar reconstruction of Viet Nam, both South and North, are carried out." Tied to the larger regional Mekong project, the development of South Vietnam promised to foster cooperation between the sometimes antagonistic riparian nations of Southeast Asia as well as the United States and estranged partners on the Pacific Rim.[109]

To these American allies in Asia, Lilienthal stressed the regional benefits. To a Japanese audience he shared his conviction that the twentieth century had been dominated by Atlantic nations but the twenty-first belonged to the Pacific Basin. The emerging primacy of a new Asia-Pacific with its economic motor revving in Japan assured that "this Pacific Asia will resolve the whole world's future." But this new world in Asia could not be divorced from the vigor and imagination of the United States, whose interests lay on the Pacific's shores. Recent history had shown Lilienthal that military might and adventurism were not the way to progress. It was "trade and technology" that brought the peace and prosperity that "no amount of abstract ideology or of bitterness and hatred and military force" could. In the Mekong project the world had a concrete example (literally and figuratively) of how large-scale development could achieve positive ends. The cooperative efforts of the riparian nations and outside sponsors to harness the rich natural resources of the region promised immediate benefits to the whole Asia-Pacific. In the face of the rancor U.S. involvement had inspired in parts of Asia, Lilienthal clung to a belief that the program provided a lesson of how aid from advanced states like Japan and the United States could weld the region into a viable, interdependent unit that purveyed prosperity to all.[110]

For his part, Black, writing in 1969, saw deeper forces at work. He continued to support the Mekong plan. It was still a demonstration of the U.S. commitment to Southeast Asia, but he increasingly acknowledged that "we have learned the real lesson of the Vietnam war . . . it is futile to try to solve, all at once, the problems that are certain to be with us for a long time." Black saw the end of the 1960s as the finale of the New Deal era. Drawing this curtain meant that the United States had to acknowledge changes in its global position. Black now cast the Mekong project, born of the New Deal, as easing the United States into a different age. The economic power and influence of a reconstructed Japan had to be reconciled within a regional framework, the security needs of Southeast Asia had to be recognized, foreign aid had to be given a new rationale—all of this might be embodied by the Mekong program. The multilateralism that the Mekong once again symbolized was an important means to correcting the "over-involvement" that characterized elements of U.S. foreign policy. Black was voicing an opinion increasingly popular in the late 1960s that by funneling aid to multilateral organizations the United States could lower its political profile and liabilities. It gave an "opportunity to change our policy image . . . where we, in the eyes of too many people, now have the reputation of trouble maker." Black had reversed the project's significance; it was no longer primarily an engine of national or even regional development but a plea to revive America's tattered credibility.[111]

Despite the advocacy, the unending war cast doubts on whether any postwar planning could be put into operation. When the JDG issued its final, massive plan in 1969, a Congress skeptical of aid received it with derision. The plan was downplayed by USAID, and Lilienthal's attempts to get the new Secretary of State, Henry Kissinger, to utilize the report's conclusions were met with evasions.[112] However tepid the administration's response, Nixon did not entirely abandon the Mekong project. Particular segments of the project were emphasized, to gain immediate political or military leverage. At the Paris peace negotiations the Mekong project was mentioned in context with economic aid packages meant to entice the DRV into agreement. By and large, however, the Mekong development program continued its drift into the realm of symbols rather than action. When the tottering regime in South Vietnam collapsed in the face of the DRV's invasion in 1975, the United States gave up its seat on the Mekong Committee.[113] With the strategic situation changed, the United States no longer had a use for the development program.

New Directions and New Concerns for Modernization

The fate of the Lilienthal Team might be seen as a result of fickle policy decisions and contingent events, but it was symptomatic of the stresses Vietnam placed on the existing relationships and assumptions that drove development. One important part of the development community, NGOs, found it harder to cooperate with a foreign policy they found troubling. In South Vietnam, as it had throughout the postwar period, the U.S. government attempted to coordinate the activities of various nongovernmental groups to support nation building. As in Korea, U.S. aid agencies and other government bodies provided logistical and other support to facilitate the missions of these groups. The number of American nonprofit groups providing direct development assistance was somewhat smaller than the total in South Korea but still significant. In 1968, the U.S. government counted sixty American voluntary groups at work in the RVN (there were, apparently, fewer international voluntary groups committed to South Vietnam).[114]

However, war bled the cooperative spirit from the NGO community. The unclear cause and the tremendous violence of the war warped relationships between the government and NGOs that had a long history of cooperation. An example of this unease was the breakup of relations between IVS and the U.S. government in Vietnam. As the intensity of U.S. military activity reached a crescendo, IVS staff observed the masses of refugees, smashed farmland, and "free fire" zones inflicted on the countryside. In 1967, welling resentment burst. Calling the war an "overwhelming atrocity," some of the most experienced staff of IVS in Vietnam resigned en masse. Considering its reputation as a leading NGO, upheaval within IVS grabbed considerable media coverage (including the front page of the *New York Times*), and inspired tough questions on the state of American efforts in Vietnam.[115]

Criticism also was levied against university programs connected to U.S. foreign aid and military policy in Vietnam, cracking close relationships forged over the preceding decades. Michigan State University endured the fallout after its work in South Vietnam was subjected to a critical exposé in *Ramparts* magazine in 1966.[116] By the early 1970s, SEADAG found its research agenda rearranged by the war. With the same analytical brio that its participants had turned on Asian development, SEADAG assessed the considerable impact of the war in Southeast Asia on domestic American institutions. SEADAG's out-of-area inquiry investigating the fallout of the war within the United States was a sign of how deeply the conflict impacted the development community. SEADAG itself contended with views it was a lackey to U.S. government policy that was massively unpopular on most campuses by the late 1960s and led a number of scholars to sever ties with the group. The body did not long outlive the U.S. commitment to Vietnam, ceasing operations in 1976.[117]

Established ideas regarding development were facing effective critiques internationally by the mid-1960s. However, these challenges, particularly in regard to U.S. development efforts, were influenced by the American war in Vietnam. The conflict in Southeast Asia shook all aspects of international affairs, and international development was not exempted. One of the most obvious effects was its reordering of the U.S. budget. As the war hungrily consumed greater and greater swaths of the federal budget, the Great Society, as well as foreign aid, was smothered.

The cumulative effects of the stresses of the 1960s on official policy were expressed by the "Nixon Doctrine." This broad reformulation of U.S. national security posture continued the standing American focus on Asian regionalism but was more skeptical of the capabilities of economic assistance to face down the communist threat. The Nixon White House desired to reduce American obligations in foreign aid and mete them out among other developed countries through multilateral institutions. Its central thesis was, "The United States . . . cannot—and will not—conceive all the plans, design all the programs, execute all the decisions, and undertake all the defense of the free nations of the world."[118]

The position of foreign assistance turned along with U.S. grand strategy. As with other basic components of foreign policy, there was a belief that the "U.S. foreign aid program is in major crisis." A confused program with uncertain goals and successes posed challenges in an area that Kissinger believed was central to U.S. influence in the developing world as well as "leadership in the industrialized world." New options were sought to reenergize a flagging effort. However, the question of how this might be implemented plagued policymakers as USAID's reputation sagged. Still, the larger difficulties the problem development faced could not be "blamed solely on Vietnam and . . . budgetary stringencies"; rather, there were deeper questions about what development was to accomplish.[119] These concerns diffused into doctrine, with Nixon calling for "New Directions" in foreign aid in May 1969. The president turned to old standards, as technical assistance was again deputized as a way to reassert the primacy of the United States. There were also bows to the cultivation of private enterprise in developing nations. The real departure was a call for greater emphasis on multilateral aid through the United Nations, particularly the World Bank.[120]

The call appeared at a time when much of official Washington had become disenchanted with foreign aid policy. Even with these changes, in October 1971 the Senate—for the first time ever—voted down the president's foreign aid request. This action was the result of a number of causes. Part was the increasing discomfort with the blending of military and foreign aid. The yawning credibility gap that had grown around the executive branch did not help matters. A perception took hold that developmental commitments eventually produced the political and military commitments that ended in mire like Vietnam. In 1971, Senator Fulbright declared the overall aid program a "shambles." Across official Washington there were demands for deeper reforms than Nixon proposed. The rejection of the president's aid budget in 1971 was a dramatic sign that Congress would no longer accept the premises that had underpinned U.S. foreign aid activity for over a generation.[121]

Frustrations were stoked by dissatisfaction with the performance of USAID. In its biggest theater of action USAID was tied to the corrupt and often incompetent South Vietnamese government. Money was frittered away on ineffective projects, eroding the agency's credibility. Within USAID there was a backlash against the Saigon government. Staff fumbled for other options, including working more closely with local elites, as a way of distancing themselves from the troubled regime. But more fundamental problems stood out. Security, particularly in rural areas, remained the least common denominator. Veterans of aid work recalled that the "best and brightest of AID went to Vietnam," to face the humbling realization "there was no way anyone could do development in that war zone."[122]

Collective confusion in American aid policy inspired major reviews of the place and purpose of development. The intensity of the debate lay in a power struggle between the executive and legislative branches over Vietnam, but it was waged with the intellectual ammunition that was the product of the crisis that had embraced development in the 1960s. In this sense it was a node of the larger global crisis of development in those years. James Grant and other influential individuals involved in this debate saw the idea of development was in a "growing crisis" even as a "major rethinking" of aid was taking place. Within development circles, there was a growing distrust of bureaucracies and the national planning they conducted. This suspicion of state apparatus segued into an environmental critique that was often opposed to the broadly conceived and implemented technological and infrastructural policies that were commonplace in national planning programs.[123]

"New Directions" was no belt tightening, but a profound change in the agency's philosophy. John Hannah, former president of MSU and Nixon's appointee to head the embattled organization, put forward a new program in line with congressional demands. It reoriented the agency to concentrate on providing for the basic human needs of people in developing countries. USAID declared it would "become less of a general purpose assistance organization and more of a specialized agency. It will seek to combine . . . resources to address a relatively limited group of basic human problems." The core of these "priority problems" Hannah and others outlined was poverty. Instead of "impersonal measures of GNP growth" or "rising national income," staple elements of national economic planning, development in USAID's vision was now conceived as "better food, more education, improved health, and more jobs for all people." Instead of large programs USAID would focus on smaller, discrete programs to foster development.[124] "New Directions" also dramatically changed the capacities of the agency. Worldwide staff was slashed from a high of 18,030 in 1968 to just 8,489 in 1975.[125] It served as basic policy well into the 1980s, leaving lasting effects. Many have seen these changes as fundamental operational abilities of USAID in the decades that followed.[126]

Despite these intellectual and policy shifts, into the early 1970s Lilienthal continued to advocate the type of development he had promoted for much of his life. To him, the Paris agreement of 1973 was the moment to implement the plans of the JDG. Tapping the Mekong would be an effective means to repair the damage of large-scale war. A renewed commitment to the Mekong for reconstruction would provide a "unifying political mechanism" in Southeast Asia but also for the United States itself. Turning to the task of rehabilitation would carry Americans away from the "mutual enmity and vilification of Americans by Americans" that had characterized the war years. This had a personal resonance for Lilienthal. His son, an opponent of the war, had become estranged from a father deeply implicated in Vietnam policy. It adds an aspect to Lilienthal's solemn calls for unity around development. Modernization swung back on the Americans who had for so long sought to make it an export. Lilienthal's plea was that a commitment to it might bring national regeneration and, perhaps, personal reconciliation.[127] But Lilienthal's hopes were no longer with the tenor of the times.

The type of development Lilienthal stood for was now under sustained criticism from once hospitable quarters. In 1971, *The Nation*, once a platform for Stuart Chase's accolades for the TVA, drew a bead on Development and Resources. The corporation and its chairman were cast as "agents of the new empire." Lilienthal himself was emblematic of elites whose "passion for development and . . . fascination with technology" drew the United States into dubious overseas commitments. D&R had made profits not only from its development work but also in training members of a further "agency of empire," the Peace Corps. It had become another part of a parasitic bureaucratic class getting fat at the public's expense. But most important, the development work it supported exacerbated rather than lessened the crisis of global poverty.[128]

These problems and criticism were part of a wider shift in opinion on development that started in the late 1960s. In the United States and internationally, the war in Vietnam had helped undermine the broad consensus that had supported modernization since the 1940s. Within the development community, there was an increasing feeling that the first goal of any project should be to eliminate poverty and meet the "basic needs" among people. This was seen in direct contrast to the urge to impose massive projects focused on raising national economic indicators. In this atmosphere, one of Lilienthal's old adversaries, Arthur E. Morgan, reemerged to condemn many recently constructed dams as unmitigated disasters. He was far from alone. Large-scale, multipurpose development programs the TVA had legitimated, rather than being the keys that unlocked potential, now were complicit in regimes that did damage to peoples' health, social systems, and cultural heritage. Broadly conceived development projects lost favor to the belief that "small is beautiful" in economics and other areas of human activity.[129]

The "TVA on the Mekong" was not immune to this critique. In the late 1960s, some began to ask what impacts such a massive restructuring might have on the river system and the peoples of the riparian nations. Critics pointed out that the construction of one dam (out of a total of thirty-four discussed), the Pa Mong, would require the removal of 250,000 persons from their homes. By the end of the decade, such social and environmental concerns, which previously received scant attention, had been pushed into the limelight. These changes abruptly altered priorities of institutions that had been patrons of the development consensus. Among these was the Ford Foundation, which in the early 1970s began studies to grasp the environmental impacts of the Mekong project.[130]

No one symbolized the change of thinking on development more than Robert McNamara. A former president of the Ford Motor Company and one of Kennedy's "whiz kids," he was a powerful proponent of the capabilities of management and technology to solve problems. He had been a strong supporter of the "Other War" and its emphasis on development in Vietnam. His resignation from the cabinet in 1968 because of his doubts about the war also marked the beginning of a shift in his thinking on development. The whiz kid found himself swayed by the arguments of the dissenters on development. McNamara's conversion led to a push by the Bank to revamp some of its thinking on development. Predecessors had seen large technological projects as the key to economic growth. Raised standards of living and poverty reduction were seen to flow from the economic ripples sent out into societies by these programs. However,

McNamara's Bank began to place much more attention on programs that explicitly aimed at alleviating poverty. Such reform made the World Bank a central character in a larger redefinition of development in the late 1960s and early 1970s.[131] This new intellectual atmosphere pulled McNamara away from positions he held during his days in government (although not far from his faith in technology and management to solve problems). Programs that had been parts of the war he had overseen quickly felt the change. Early in his tenure McNamara made it clear to D&R and USAID that the World Bank would not support further projects on the Mekong.[132]

McNamara's aversion to the Mekong was one part of the reappraisals shaking the liberal development consensus. Vietnam marked the high tide of the large-scale liberal development ideas that had been a powerful element of U.S. foreign policy in the postwar period and the basis of a postwar consensus on development. American-sponsored modernization, with the Mekong project as its standard, was utilized as the means to demonstrate that U.S. involvement in Southeast Asia would be constructive for the whole region, the greater Asia-Pacific, a fractured American society, and the globe. However, the war and upheaval surrounding it served to highlight shortcomings of the Mekong adventure and the larger concepts to which it was beholden. Equally important, the conflict rended existing institutional relationships, integral to implementation of consensus ideas. With long-standing modernization ideas in crisis, the door was opened to more voices, reordering the debate and assuring that the American-dominated consensus which shaped much development activity at home and abroad was no longer tenable.

Chapter 7

"EVERYTHING IS GOING WRONG"

THE CRISIS OF DEVELOPMENT AND THE
END OF THE POSTWAR CONSENSUS

The Seventies have destroyed the old consensus [on development] and, so far, put nothing in its place.
—*Barbara Ward, 1974*

FOLLOWING THE PLEASANTRIES of the conclusion of the Columbia Conference on International Economic Development in February 1970, Robert McNamara found himself with several of the conference organizers on the university's New York City campus. McNamara, the new president of the World Bank, still fresh from his post as Secretary of Defense in the Johnson administration, had been inspired by what he had heard. This was despite the fact that the conference had been a dissent on the Pearson Report, a study of foreign aid commissioned by McNamara's predecessor at the Bank. By and large, the bank's new president had been impressed by what he had heard. In the afterglow of this successful meeting, and with a few hours to spare before his flight, McNamara asked his hosts for a tour of the Ivy League campus. This rather mundane request disquieted McNamara's companions. Over the preceding two years Columbia had been alive with protest against the war in Vietnam with which the former defense secretary had been so intimately connected, and the mood remained tense. On a stroll, McNamara was likely to be recognized and with emotions still raw, the potential confrontation was an unpleasant thought. Dissuading McNamara, they put him in a taxi on Broadway, shuttling him off to the airport and away from a potentially touchy, even dangerous, situation.[1]

McNamara's aborted tour is an individual reflection of the breakdown of collaboration that had made much modernization work possible. A man committed to the development consensus and heading the institution rapidly emerging as the most influential player in the international development scene could not walk freely on the campus of a university. It provides insight into the connection between the war in Vietnam and the shifts in thinking about development that came in the late 1960s and early 1970s. The conference itself was a signal moment for increasingly vocal constituencies dissenting from the consensus. It was a signal that the "Development Decade," by its conclusion, was bedeviled by disagreements, lack of success, and apparently intractable problems. Basic relationships instrumental to the liberal consensus shattered under pressures. New issues and perspectives forced their way into discussions of global development. At home and abroad, ferment brought profound changes in thinking regarding what development was meant to achieve and how it was to accomplish these goals. To be sure, the involvement of the United States in the regional war in Southeast Asia was significant in altering perceptions. But Vietnam was only part of a global crisis of development. It was linked to growing doubt about the promise of modern society. There was increasing sensitivity to the impacts of the technologies and processes lying at the core of development. Critics produced solid evidence of its unforeseen and sometimes negative impacts. By the end of the 1960s, the general consensus on development that had taken form in the Depression, emphasizing large-scale multipurpose technological programs to produce grand social and economic change, was under sustained attack.

Critiques catalyzed a reformulation of development. One avenue emphasized the need for the alleviation of poverty as the fundamental goal of aid.[2] A refrain that development needed to be "sustainable" appeared. This was part of an explicit linkage of development with concerns about environmental impact. The environment was one point of focus that allowed the unintended impacts of modernization programs to be discerned. Indeed, by placing attention on this one node of the modernization process, the environment, the transformation of a spectrum of diverse themes buffeted by a larger international crisis can be seen. A set of new views, discussed in an increasingly global frame, altered long-standing assumptions and policies, but it did not remove technology from a central position. The solution to the environmental problems brought by development was generally seen to be the tempered but continued application of technology. Institutions born of the consensus remained in powerful positions to shape this application. Despite talk that the postwar consensus had been sundered, elements that had long girded international development endured.

MODERNIZATION IN CRISIS: AT HOME AND ABROAD

International development efforts were never divorced from domestic reform, and problems at home would influence debates about modernization abroad. This was true as the United States strove to create a Great Society in the 1960s. Inspired by the "rediscovery" of poverty early in the decade, this domestic reform shared the optimism and grand hopes of the international "Development Decade." Scholars and activists eagerly asserted that a solution to poverty at home could be reached in a few years.[3] While the Kennedy administration took some early steps, poverty reduction found a passionate advocate in Lyndon Johnson. As he advocated uplift abroad he also sought to add domestic improvement to his political legacy that would extend and surpass that of Franklin Roosevelt. But he was far from alone. Many individuals at the high tide of domestic liberal developmentalism flowing from the New Deal were themselves immersed in concepts that had driven international modernization efforts. The universe of reformers behind the Great Society also accepted a consensus view that the state should be the central force behind a broad transformation of society.[4]

In fact, many social issues surrounding economic and social justice at home were viewed through the lenses provided by the social science supporting modernization. Unrest in American cities from 1965 through 1967 was explained with social science theories that had initially emerged to explain developing societies and defang insurrectionist movements.[5] Great Society programs betrayed links to overseas development as well. The "center-piece" of the effort, the Office of Economic Opportunity (OEO), was given at its creation in 1964 to Sargent Shriver, who had just finished putting the Peace Corps together.[6] A basis of the OEO's program was the scanty concept of "community action" reflecting ideas found in "community development" internationally. As in the New Deal, talk of community engagement was meant to tie programs to the totem of localism within American politics.[7]

The institutional sinew that had grown up to support international development work quickly grasped the links to ongoing international programs. Social scientists under the aegis of SEADAG saw foreign and domestic aid linked in their attacks on the "consequences of underdevelopment"—that is, poverty. Acknowledging "Massachusetts and Mississippi" were not "India and Ghana," general assumptions persisted that many theories of development could be applied both at home and abroad. In part, proof was found in the fact that aid staffers and Peace Corps veterans easily transferred into domestic anti-poverty programs like VISTA (Volunteers in Service to America), where personal "experiences seem quite comparable."[8] Some views could be impressionistic, but there were numerous and direct connections between international development and domestic poverty programs.

As with the Peace Corps, the OEO required the support of existing institutions to implement its programs. Among the groups eager to assist was D&R. Following its president's call to "look homeward" in the early 1960s, the firm had consulted on capital-intensive engineering programs from the Ramparts River watershed in Alaska to the Meadowlands in New Jersey. The Great Society offered an array of new opportunities. Using government connections cultivated over the years, Lilienthal eagerly sought contracts for the OEO's community-oriented projects. His firm claimed ability to relate to their community focus because D&R was heir to the "grass roots" approach of the TVA. It was further proof that the lines between domestic and international development were always indistinct when ideas that had been exported since the 1930s returned home in the 1960s.[9]

It won a spectrum of Great Society contracts, and the range of programs D&R undertook was extensive. Jamaica, New York, received aid for a Community Action Plan (CAP) to lower poverty through skills training, education, and economic development. Other parts of its diverse portfolio included the training of low-income "predominantly Mexican-American" rural workers in California. In conjunction with Kaiser Engineering, D&R did work with the Department of Housing and Urban Development. It pitched a regional plan for the economic development of the Ozarks. Lilienthal's firm also offered technical assistance for a national program of "Youth Development" through job training within various Community Action Agencies. Even the evaluation of day care centers established by the OEO was pursued by D&R. Courting these contracts, the firm noted its domestic experience, but it was the overseas work that constituted its hard sell. D&R cited its experience instructing 1,500 Peace Corps volunteers (as of 1972) as an asset in its training hundreds of VISTA cadre who were assumed to face similar challenges. Village-level education, health, agricultural, and other training in Iran as well as similar efforts in Malaya and the Ivory Coast were seen as transferable, in principle, to the United States. Drawing from Lilienthal's TVA creed, D&R stressed a development that would alter peoples' vision of the world and their place in it. This outlook was injected directly into domestic programs by D&R staffers fresh from development adventures in Vietnam, Iran, and elsewhere.[10]

Businesses like D&R along with the various NGOs invested in Great Society programs found government largess fleeting. Controversial from its inception, the OEO was dismantled in 1970 and those programs in its portfolio that were not ended outright were transferred to assorted parts of the government. The fate of the OEO was a barometer for the larger Great Society, which was foundering by the end of the 1960s, even if various programs soldiered on. Always controversial with critics on the right, the OEO was attacked with ammunition similar to that spent on the New Deal. CAP programs were (inaccurately) decried as "retread WPA" and the Job Corps lampooned as an adulterated Civilian Conservation Corps—a sort of travel bureau for deprived youth, providing "sun tans and . . . outdoor living."[11] This was only part of the OEO's troubles. Others were uncomfortable with its support of community programs perceived as havens for radical action. Local and state governments were distrustful of a federal program that skirted and undercut their authority. However, it also had its detractors on the left, who (rather like criticism of Lilienthal run in *The Nation*) saw it as another expression of a corrupted bureaucracy and attached welfare system that was fattened at the public trough. Traditional critiques of wasteful government bureaucracy added burdens even as the financial crisis brought by the Vietnam War sapped its budget. It was not solely outside criticism that caused difficulties. The OEO's own understanding of poverty and its methods to tackle it suffered from "conceptual fuzziness," exacerbated by a diffusion of effort. Taken together, these issues stymied the OEO but also helped hollow out views prevailing since the New Deal that government should be the prime mover in large-scale reform programs.[12] The fate of the Great Society at home landed another blow on consensus perceptions privileging the central government's primary role in economic and social development.

In the same period, an international program epitomizing similar assumptions also failed. In Iran, one of the largest attempts at a regional development program in the image of the TVA foundered. Conceived in the 1950s, a multipurpose plan to develop the Khuzestan region was designated an heir to the TVA tradition. The government of Mohammad Reza Shah Pahlavi enthusiastically supported it as part of a "White Revolution." This ambitious vision framed by Western ideas, experts, and aid used modernization to shore up the regime's legitimacy and power. The Khuzestan scheme's most powerful patron was Abol Hassan Ebtehaj, the head of the government's economic coordination bureaucracy, the Plan Organization. Ebtehaj was a member of a cosmopolitan elite enamored of development invested in state planning as a means to national advancement. Undoubtedly influenced by the Soviet example, he nevertheless asserted the state's role was to prepare the ground for private enterprise. The centerpiece of what became known as the Second Plan was the effort in Khuzestan. As with other programs, water was the underlying "theme." Harnessing five snow-fed rivers for hydroelectric power and irrigation, development efforts would be given the power to reach into village life, transforming agricultural practices and even altering the homes in which local inhabitants lived.[13] The plans were not entirely new, growing out of agricultural projects hatched in World War II and various ambitions to bring TVAs to the Middle East promulgated by the UN, World Bank, and U.S. government in the decade after the war. In fact, the preexisting affinity to the concept assured the Iranians ready support. The World Bank was tapped by Ebtehaj to support the scheme, as was a stream of U.S. aid money that began to flow with Point Four to the strategically important Shah. UN bodies brought its expertise to bear. Its Expanded Technical Assistance Program and the FAO teamed up to provide an early survey. However, the FAO investigators were not sanguine, noting potential problems in the salinity of the soil and water among other harsh environmental conditions in the region.[14]

The energetic Ebtehaj was not dissuaded. He found a like mind in Lilienthal, who met the Persian at a World Bank meeting in 1955 and found him "incandescent." As the Second Plan took form, D&R was hired in 1956 to oversee work of the new Khuzestan Water and Power Authority, with Lilienthal predicting the region would become another "Garden of Eden." Lilienthal reassured Ebtehaj that "what the so-called experts had stated was exactly what every single expert in the United States predicted and proclaimed with regard to the Tennessee Valley project before the work . . . had started."[15] As with other projects, public opinion was actively courted, with Lilienthal carrying his enthusiasm to a collection of audiences. He spoke of it to American television audiences, where Iran as much as any other country came to represent the possibilities of comprehensive development. He and Gordon Clapp wooed foreign affairs grandees at the Council on Foreign Relations in the 1960s. Their message was clear: Iran was to be one of the great symbols of postwar liberal development. A large-scale plan, planting dams across the region, would provide power, agricultural reform, new housing, a platform for international private investment and, with it all, social transformation to the inhabitants.[16]

Instead, D&R's program helped cause a debacle. Technical problems appeared early. On the Dez River, a centerpiece of the hydraulic program, the massive dam was threatened by a "most serious problem" of siltation as early as 1971. However, the cause was blamed on erosion brought by "abuse of the land by farmers and herders" and not any flaw with the blueprint. The scale of this problem required vast new programs just to correct the issue and stabilize the watershed.[17]

Technical concerns lay on the surface of deeper failings with the developmental approach. Politically and socially the program inspired a spectrum of resistance. Favoring large-scale agribusiness in the vast reconfiguration of the life of the region, the government imposed a plan and an administrative hierarchy on the countryside that were unaccountable to

Figure 7.1. Too close to the Shah. Lilienthal (third from right) directly behind the Shah at one of the rural development programs in Iran supported by Development and Resources during the 1960s. Difficulties experienced by programs in Iran reflected larger problems with the consensus approach to development that became apparent in the 1960s and 1970s. David Lilienthal Papers. Public Policy Papers Division. Department of Rare Books and Special Collections. Princeton University Library.

existing local political and social structures. This alienated local elites and created difficulties in implementing aspects of the program. These dissatisfactions flared as the program gained momentum. Like the TVA and scores of other large-scale development projects, work in Iran required intimate changes in the lives of people. Tens of thousands of people were displaced and moved to "model" villages where their labor could be better accessed by corporations. These communities were not well designed for local conditions. In a hot climate the houses lacked effective ventilation and had weak roofs—where people in the region often slept to escape the heat. Villages had inadequate sanitation and services. Resentment grew and critics indicted the activities of both Lilienthal's D&R and the Shah's government. Largely, those on the land were tread upon, as the democratic "grass roots" rhetoric of the TVA model was revealed to be barren. The development programs in Iran were imposed upon the population by an unaccountable state seeking to expand its powers, and whose programs actually served to dissolve crucial local social and cultural structures. The program declined in the 1970s, contributing to a crisis that left gross domestic product in the countryside less than half the level of a decade earlier. The fall was rapid; by the 1980s, an observer noted how housing built for the program's staff sheltered only the growth of wild barley.[18]

Khuzestan was part of a wider unrest in the countryside that helped unravel the Shah's government and bring revolution. For Lilienthal personally, these domestic and international failures were overtures to greater complications. The rapid disappearance of Great Society programs hurt the bottom line at D&R, but revolution in Iran was a body blow. The Shah's abdication meant the end of a long and profitable relationship and sank the corporation into bankruptcy and dissolution. Despite these setbacks, until his death in 1981, Lilienthal advocated technical programs in the service of development, but increasingly, his voice went unheeded.[19]

Iran was one exhibit in the growing case against modernization. That it was put in the dock at all demonstrates the serious shift in perceptions occurring during the 1960s. A major part of this shift was related to modernization's intimate connection to the war in Vietnam which had serious repercussions not only in U.S. foreign policy, but also within the international aid community. The costs of the war were one of the reasons high hopes for the "Development Decade" were brought to earth.

Johnson famously remarked, "If I left the woman I really loved— the Great Society—in order to get involved with that bitch of a war on the other side of the world, then I would lose everything at home."[20] Indeed, Johnson's attentions to the harpy brought trouble at home as well as abroad. Economic effects of the war were not limited to the international economy. Once again, foreign and domestic reform were two sides of the same coin, only this time it was budgetary stringency. Demands of the sprawling war in Southeast Asia throttled the Great Society at home and garroted foreign aid allowances. Activity began to suffer as the Vietnam War greedily consumed dollars. By 1968, the official war budget stood at $25.6 billion for the year (up from $20.1 billion in 1967) and was causing considerable economic strain.[21] Budgetary difficulties increasingly hamstrung the largest single donor in the postwar world. U.S. foreign aid hovered around an average of $3.7 billion a year between 1961 and 1963 and grew an average of $3.9 billion between 1970 and 1972. However, when adjusted for inflation, the latter sum declined to $3.1 billion, meaning U.S. overseas assistance *fell* over the course of the "Development Decade."[22]

Hobbled U.S. foreign aid programs were only part of the story. In the same period, European states and Japan, having finally escaped the burdens of recovery, began to organize their own foreign assistance bureaucracies. Internationally, a gaggle of new development NGOs appeared. This pluralism would have considerable effect on the structure of international developmental aid.[23] The relative decline in American aid dollars made these new actors more important. But perhaps more significant would be the weight this transformation transferred to international organizations, particularly the World Bank.[24] These new actors changed the development landscape, but more important, basic elements behind development, so fondly advocated by an American patron, were under scrutiny from new quarters. The concerns of the global development community mirrored a wider dissatisfaction with concepts of development and economic growth that had predominated in the postwar world. Kennedy's ambitious call to action had given way to disappointment and, in some sectors, recrimination.

THE MODERNIZATION CONSENSUS FRACTURES

In this atmosphere perpetual questions surrounding modernization found renewed relevance. Concerns about the efficacy of the state's role in economic life regained traction. As the decade wore on, many on the right honed their long-standing challenges to the dominant international development ideas. They were joined by a clutch of liberals who were troubled by what they perceived as the excesses of the New Left and the apparent drift of the Democratic Party in the United States from a Cold War hard line. Crucially, they were disenchanted by the government-led social engineering of the Great Society. These "neoconservatives" were one column in a conservative onslaught that remained comfortable with continued military and political adventures in the "Third World." However, development support was sidelined in their worldview because of a lingering distrust of government-based aid. In line with "neoliberal" economic views gaining renewed acceptance growth in poorer countries was to be brought by private investment and the "structural adjustment" of economies to the free market. Although defection of the neoconservatives was not a mortal blow in itself, it does demonstrate the increasing skepticism toward the role of the state in previously supportive constituencies.[25]

There were realignments at the other end of the political spectrum. On the left, the school of "Dependency Theory" gained acceptance with the thesis that established relationships in the capitalist global economy actually promoted stagnation and poverty rather than growth and prosperity. A renewed feminist movement prompted critiques of accepted views of modernization theory that often overlooked women as actors in the development equation. A decline of support on the left helped perpetual questions about the efficacy of the state's role in economic life regain traction. Indeed, it marks a significant moment when assumptions about the state's dominant role in governing economic life prevailing since the Depression began to unravel.[26]

Political defections were just some shards of a fracturing consensus. Concerns about population growth, perennially lurking beneath discussions of development, burst into prominence. An international lobby pushed hard for control. Commentators fretted that such growth was creating new demands that might limit or even undo the promises of development. They gained authority and political support in the 1960s as populations exploded across the developing world.[27]

With these and other limits weighing on the process, disillusionment grew even among partisans. Frustration also lay in the fact that objects of development, the "new nations," had not lived up to expectations. By the late 1960s, numerous postcolonial states had taken on the trappings of autocracy and, perhaps more important, their state-centered approaches to development were not bearing the expected fruit. For some, the statism they had embraced seemed to be the problem. Placing emphasis on central authority opened the door to authoritarianism. From a vantage point in 1975, Clifford Geertz, speaking to a Ford Foundation audience, repeated critiques that had emerged over the preceding decade. The battle cry of development in the 1950s and 1960s had left many high expectations of rapid growth and change unfulfilled. Still, there was an unequivocal accomplishment in the destruction of any legitimacy of the rule of one people by another outside group. Where one could equivocate was on the question whether the local elites who, "having claimed power on the principle that rule that is not inwardly connected to the life around it is not just . . . can now be judged by it."[28]

Apprehension regarding the state was one element of a general anxiety about modern society. There was apprehension about what it wrought globally as well as within the United States. Charles Reich's 1970 bestseller, *The Greening of America*, lamented the rise of a "Corporate State" that dehumanized individual relationships and led to hollow, inauthentic, and unfulfilling existence. Technology continued to transform at frightening speeds, shaking established relationships, transforming people at intimate levels. Reich went as far as to single out the New Deal as part of the problem. Rather than controlling these powerful forces, the reform movement, with its technocratic focus on planning and order, had aided and abetted these trends. In essence, the United States itself was not immune to the diseases springing from the modernizing forces it perpetuated and had claimed to control.[29] More grounded statements saw the emergence of a "post-industrial" society changing the structure of the economy and of knowledge itself. New technologies (particularly information technologies) and organization were seen to be shifting society from a focus on industrial production to one based on services and information. Yet, with these rapid shifts came changes in employment and social life that left individuals in the most developed societies—not unlike counterparts in modernizing countries—unemployed, uprooted, and alienated.[30]

While some statements might be discounted as prognostications made in a fevered time, all speak to real concerns with a modern society producing perpetual change seeming to unfold at an ever-accelerating pace. The dissatisfaction this perception fed was part of a broader crisis of confidence in modernity. Questions and critiques came from diverse directions, and impacts were felt in a host of areas. War, economic stagnation, the realities of racism; changing views of gender; political crisis; spiritual and religious ferment; and environmental despoliation challenged the faith in progress in which modernization was rooted.[31]

By the end of the 1960s, mainstream members of the foreign policy establishment were facing these facts. Once-stable terrain was shifting under their feet. Even in the rarified air of the Council on Foreign Relations there was appreciation that a collection of forces demanded hard and fresh looks at international life. A "malaise" discernable in industrialized countries was a product of forces long at work. In 1969, a spokesman for liberalism, Arthur Schlesinger, Jr., shared his concerns about

> instability generated by an incessant increase in the rate of change. Science changes our environment every day, giving us a sense of an unprecedented velocity of history, of being rushed through life in a terrifyingly palpable way; we feel out of control, unsure of values, ideas, institutions . . . The machinery which modern society has created to bring abundance to the masses also brings anxiety to individuals, who feel powerless in relation to it.[32]

As it had in other situations, the technological elements of modernity were the larger historical forces believed to be behind the various social eruptions of the time. The student upsurge itself was linked to anomie brought by modern society. In fact, the "revolutionary" left was described as a symptom of disconnection brought by industrial society rather than simply political dissatisfaction. The great burdens modern industrial society imparted on the global environment were seen. Also important was the erosion of established political categories, upon which postwar assumptions had rested. Traditional political programs of liberalism were indicted. These seemed impotent in the face of social unrest, the rise of environmental concerns, and the war in Vietnam and a perception that politics was drifting rightward. Domestic racial tension and black "militancy" were seen, in part, as a question of economic rights and development. There were candid admissions that race had not become more important (as it had long lurked in international politics) but with decolonization and the domestic civil rights movement its significance had been revealed. In the dust of "fallen empires" built on white domination, the line between the "have-nations and the have-not nations" could very often be drawn on racial lines, adding "greater explosiveness" to world affairs. The outlines of race war were seen and even if that nightmare was discounted it was privately admitted that "race and color *are* in some degree almost universally present in the great issues . . . resources and development, population, and the shaping of the political institutions . . . that will govern the great majority of men for the next long while."[33]

Altogether, as William Pfaff noted, "the spell is broken" regarding many imperatives that had driven the Cold War. By 1968, any moral claim either side had was shattered on the realities of American involvement in Vietnam and the Soviet invasion of Czechoslovakia. In fact, the "superpowers are not seen as sources of stability but of instability and repression." A fatigued American public was growing disinterested in international issues and backing away from commitments. Not far below the surface lay a fear that liberalism was once again falling into another deep crisis of legitimacy. In fact, some participants saw disturbing similarities between the upheaval of the 1960s and the 1930s (admittedly something significant voices dismissed).[34] Such views called into question long-term assumptions guiding U.S. interaction with the globe. It was increasingly difficult to dramatize its superiority to competing social and political systems. Discomfort with the implications of modern life made the prescriptions for widespread and dramatic social and psychological transformation that lay at the core of modernization less palatable. If the liberal West was modernization's finish line, its condition in the 1960s did not inspire confidence in the race.

Again, the opinions and policies were subject to the blinders and bias shielding commentary on contemporary events. However, they do encapsulate many spoken and unspoken beliefs in mainstream U.S. international affairs circles and contextualize issues careening into discussion on policy questions—especially the increasingly diverse and divisive question of development. There were a variety of issues that stressed the assumptions that had driven so much modernization activity. Global doubts about the march of development emphasize the constellation of areas that development could touch. These sectors were often united in the application of technology. It was often seen as the preeminent means to solve or transform whatever issue stood in the way of the march to modernity. But in the period, growing skepticism toward industrial technology and the modernity surrounding it were a sea change in the relation of individuals and institutions to a theme vital to international life.

STRAINING THE ENVIRONMENTAL ENGINE

A swarm of issues came into play as modernization and the modernity it sought to bring were questioned in new ways across the globe. The transformation of modernization these perspectives brought can be focused by looking at its changing relation to the environment. The transformation of environmental systems was instrumental to extensive development programs even before the Cold War. Negative environmental repercussions brought by such programs became apparent in the 1960s. Yet these also touched a host of other areas bound up in the modernization process. No environmental issue could be entirely divorced from the technological, social, cultural, political (and ideological) issues that were always touched by big development projects. Indeed, worries about nature could unify increasingly divergent discussions. Environmental issues became one pivot on which the cascade of new perspectives moved into international discussion. They were intimately connected to other central questions reshaping development. The environment could not be divorced from concerns about governance, the growing north-south divide, the urge to alleviate poverty, and the growing influence of international institutions.

The unwelcome impact of technologies on the environment became hard to ignore in the 1960s. Ironically, the very importance of development brought increased scrutiny to its impacts. As various constituencies tried to better understand this powerful global theme, its limits were revealed. Scientific research began to unravel causal links, demonstrating how large-scale application of modern technologies could have unintended effects far from their initial point of use. An appreciation of the effects of international development was a function of this growing knowledge of the global impact of technologies. Knowledge came from unexpected quarters. Scientists became aware of the damage being done by atmospheric nuclear testing in the 1950s and 1960s. The effects of radiation and fallout on human populations, traced across borders, built a global view of the consequences of high technology. Exploration of the aftereffects of nuclear weapons was an overture to increased understanding of the impacts of less dramatic technologies at the core of modern life.[35]

Research began to uncover the disturbing effects of more prosaic technologies, including those instrumental to development work. One example was the insecticides integral to extensive development projects. Rachel

Carson's *Silent Spring*, which documented the catastrophic effects of DDT on ecosystems worldwide, was a seminal moment. Carson's best-selling book awakened many to the unforeseen costs of carelessly applied technologies that had come to be seen as mundane. Importantly, these revelations made the global and the local indistinct. Technological crisis abroad could eventually upset ecological relationships uncomfortably close to home. *Silent Spring* has rightly been called one of the most far-reaching and influential books ever written by an American.[36]

Carson's analysis was only part of a growing body of research raising disturbing questions about ecological effects of modern technological society. Paradoxically, some of this research was supported by many foundations and universities firmly committed to the mission of development.[37] Scientists increasingly saw the environmental stresses caused by the extensive resource use required by industrialization.[38] With this increasing knowledge of the effects of technology on the environment and human populations came criticism of development programs that attempted to export those technologies. Impacts of grand multipurpose development plans were hard to miss. The Indus River, which had brought India and Pakistan to the negotiating table in the 1950s, was not immune to destructive salination. More U.S. aid had to be pumped in to save Punjabi farmers suffering from waterlogged and salted soils from complete collapse. India, which had embraced large-scale water resource development with a vengeance, did enjoy the benefits of increased agricultural and industrial production. However, few of the dams, like so many similar endeavors globally, fully delivered on their economic promises. They also left India with chronic problems of siltation, soil degradation, and disease. By the 1980s, they had also inspired vocal and effective local political opposition. The Aswan dam, because of its scale and political profile, attracted a great deal of attention to its impacts. The costs of this program were apparent by the final years of the "Development Decade" as unforeseen problems linked to the dam were revealed, some before it was even complete. Critically, the dam barred silt from passing downstream to the Nile Delta, causing the amount of fertile land there to contract. The changes forced on the river led to a dramatic rise in the rate of schistosomiasis infection that in some communities approached 100 percent. The dam also deprived the Mediterranean Sea of vital nutrients, altering marine life drastically and perhaps permanently.[39]

Growing understanding of unintended consequences forced acknowledgment of the effects and the complexities of extensive modernization. Programs had been undertaken worldwide without an appreciation of their potentially negative political, social, economic, or health effects. A fraternity of examples demonstrated the spectrum of damage wrought by this type of modernization. Water control programs, in particular, regularly demanded the resettlement of peoples in large numbers. Entire communities could be picked up and moved to new locations to make way for the dams, reservoirs, or other elements connected to modernization programs. In some cases, recently moved peoples were subject to bouts of epidemic disease as they were exposed to new pathogens or were forced into new living arrangements. There was often deep sociocultural stress on peoples who were suddenly dependent on government aid to reestablish and sustain their communities. Beyond these concerns, there was economic hardship for peoples who might have lost access to agricultural lands or other resources from which they had long derived their livelihoods.[40] These problems were emblematic of the social upheaval that modernization could bring. More advocates of development soured on the large-scale social change demanded as part of the process. It seemed, too often, to lead to degradation rather than a better order of life for the people involved.

The technologies employed to help catalyze social change as part of the development process were interrogated. An encyclopedic and influential example is a 1969 collection of research by a diverse group of ecologists, scientists, and development specialists who found problems with programs ranging from agriculture to nuclear power. Their inquiries into the effects of a host of different development programs worldwide showed what they termed the "careless" transfer of technology to less developed countries and its unintended and negative impacts. These ran the gamut from irrigation programs that led to the outbreak of epidemic disease to a pest control program in Sarawak, Borneo, that inadvertently killed predators of the region's rats—a situation only remedied by airdropping cats to the infested inhabitants.[41]

Such findings were taken as proof of the "grave and systematic fault in the overall approach that has thus guided most international development programs," which showed a "need to reassess our attitudes toward the natural world on which our technology intrudes." The United States, exponent of the promise of modern society, was now beset with "appalling" environmental problems. The environmental difficulties of the United States itself, brought about by the overuse of insecticides, leaded gasoline, and other polluting fossil fuels (among other issues), became a powerful reason to question the long-standing faith in technologically based progress globally.[42]

The liberal West was not alone. Across the communist world there was shared unease. In the 1970s, the People's Republic of China was emerging from the chastening experiences of the "Great Leap Forward" and Cultural Revolution. Utopian programs conducted with a feverish urgency and under a veil of political repression not only displaced, damaged, or destroyed communities and human life on a vast scale; they also had negative effects on the environment. Even after such upheaval, China had to confront the realities of population growth that might eat away what economic gains had accrued. The response was a rigid 1979 "one child" policy. These and other concerns brought a reevaluation of the PRC's agenda. Some have seen the late 1960s and early 1970s marking a "Great Transformation" where China turned from its revolutionary communist path to one that put great emphasis on economic development, a road that eventually led the country into the liberal world economy.[43]

Soviet experts were aware of the limits development was encountering. At the same moment as Western colleagues, the end of the 1960s, scholars were contending with the fact that few "Third World" states had a "noticeable rise in productive forces."[44] It was grimly noted that they "could only call the present situation of planning in developing countries a crisis if there had been better days in the past." Cautious statements were even ventured that suggested the Soviet economic model might not be universally exportable. Even more disturbing were the environmental difficulties experienced within the Soviet empire. In the German Democratic Republic, the limitations of an economic approach grounded in state communism were visible on the landscape. Industrial and urban blight as well as the degradation of forests and other natural systems marked the failures of one model of modern development.[45]

These man-made problems were not limited to communist competitors or clients; they ate away at the Soviet Union from the inside. Gigantism from Stalin's time persisted in mammoth plans, devised in the 1950s, to exploit natural resources east of the Urals. Among these were ambitions to create a belt of cotton production in Central Asia. Beginning in the 1960s, rivers in the region were bled for irrigation for this purpose. In so doing, the Aral Sea, the world's fourth largest lake when the project started, was abruptly starved of water. By the 1980s, the lake only received one-fifth of the water it had in the 1960s. As the Aral Sea withered, there were catastrophic effects on the economic and environmental life of the region. Fisheries collapsed so drastically that frozen fish was flown in to keep local canneries open. The climate became more extreme as the lake's ability to moderate the weather declined with its size. The region was exposed to airborne salination as salt left by the receding waters was stirred up by the wind. The ironic dusting it left on cotton crops hundreds of kilometers from the lake was only part of the ruination such salted winds brought to agriculture, the power grid, buildings, and human health. The Aral Sea was only one of the egregious examples of environmental decay contributing to the mortal crisis of the Soviet system. To be sure, there were excesses in these communist development schemes not always shared in scale by those undertaken under liberal regimes. What it does demonstrate is the fact that the environmental engine of development was being stressed across the ideological spectrum and across the globe.[46]

Part of the international popular dissatisfaction with modern progress appearing in the 1960s was public restiveness brought by increased knowledge of the impact of industrial society on the global ecumene. The most visible moment was "Earth Day." Momentum for the day was provided by an atmosphere of protest that had grown during the decade. In fact, while inspiration came from Senator Gaylord Nelson, the individual primarily responsible for the organizing effort was Sam Brown, who had gained considerable protest experience opposing the Vietnam War. Turnout on the day itself, April 22, 1970, surprised all observers. Perhaps 100,000 people crowded into New York City's Union Square and tens of thousands gathered for similar rallies in other parts of the country. The rallies showed the depth of domestic public interest in an issue with global resonance.[47]

The shifting intellectual, academic, and public views of the harm being done by modern industrial society did not bypass the international affairs community. Into the early 1970s, there was a burst of attention on the subject of environmental degradation and its impact on international relations. In the pages of various leading journals of international affairs, commentators worried about the transnational impacts of nuclear radiation, pollution, and infectious disease.[48] Much of the concern with these issues lay in their transnational nature. For example, the effects of industrial pollution spilled by one country into the atmosphere were shared by the world community at large in terms of air quality, disease, and climate change. Emerging understanding about human impact on climate change itself exposed the incomplete nature of the understanding of complex natural systems upon which modern society and humankind itself depended for existence.[49]

Increasing calls for control brought remarkable reconsiderations of global affairs. There was a wide-ranging discussion of international governance of environmental issues in the period. These discussions drew the attention of one of the deans of the U.S. foreign policy establishment, George F. Kennan. Long sensitive to the "runaway horse" of technology, Kennan was dragged back to the issue of its governance within a modern society to which he was decidedly ambivalent. What has been termed "organicist conservatism" left him alienated from the modernity exemplified by his own country. Distrustful of mass politics as he was of mass culture and consumerism, the blitz of urbanization connected to these trends also disturbed Kennan. Not unlike some observers on the left, he believed all brought disconnection from nature, bred conformity, and served as a solvent for social relationships. These feelings later joined with worries about the ominous new technology of nuclear energy.[50]

Kennan, therefore, was already primed when he weighed in on a growing debate on the environment and global society. Kennan diverged from most other commentators on implementation of a regime of control. What was needed was a clearinghouse for research and the establishment of international standards, and the creation of rules for the "great international media of human activity" (the seas, stratosphere, outer space, and polar regions). Kennan was skeptical of the UN's ability and believed that most of the smaller and less developed countries "could contribute very little to the solution of the problems at hand."[51] What Kennan suggested was an entity, supported by a small group of the "leading industrial and maritime nations" as the "devastation of the environment is primarily, though not exclusively, a function of advanced industrial and urban society. The correction of it . . . is for the advanced nations." Included in this group would be the nations of the Communist Bloc. The actual members of the organization, however, were to "consist primarily of people of technical and scientific competence" and not bound directly to individual governments. Free of influence of organizations devoted to resource exploitation, the body would operate as follows: "the principle should be that one exploits what a careful regard for the needs of conservation leaves to be exploited, not that one conserves what a liberal indulgence of the impulse to development leaves to be conserved."[52]

Kennan later lamented that his plan was not adopted and disapproved of the coupling of developmental and environmental ideas.[53] Still, his interest in the issues was not passing, as environmental deterioration under the weight of the modern world continued to appear in his writings.[54] He noted in 1977 that it was the issue in American domestic life "which probably exceeds all others." The damage being done might force a "reversal of trends of development which for decades have lain at the very heart of the American idea of progress." Changes at home influenced affairs abroad. Solving domestic issues had an international impact.

If we are to be something more to other peoples than just an intimidating military power, we will have to concern ourselves with the image of our society that is projected to the rest of the world. There is not one of the phenomena [of environmental degradation] listed above that does not affect this image—sometimes in very important ways. One of the first requirements of clear thinking of our part in world affairs is the recognition that we cannot be more to others than we are to ourselves—that we cannot be a source of hope and inspiration to others against a background of resigned failure and deterioration of life here at home.[55]

Although Kennan was not sanguine about the present, he hoped environmental concerns might provide future common ground for international cooperation aimed at "restoring the healthy balance between modern industrial civilization and the natural environment in which it is rooted."[56]

Such commentary bore Kennan's singular perspective, but his concern with the impacts of the imposition of modern, industrial life provides a longer perspective. The "romance of economic development" of which he spoke in the 1930s had given way to an abusive relationship. Environmental elements impressed into service as engines of the large-scale planned modernization had come to suffer. In this sense the natural world was a canary in the mine, exposing the dangers of modern life. In the 1940s, Kennan had seen the governance of the political and social impacts of technology as a fundamental part of the chronic "disease" afflicting the West. The crisis of the 1960s and 1970s revealed to Kennan and others the unexpected virulence of the distemper. Long-held assumptions about how these forces could be tempered had been found wanting and new ideas were needed. His concern about development's impact on the environment was linked to the worries of his contemporaries about the political difficulties surrounding development as well as its human costs. Fresh ideas had to be tried as the existing consensus had been found lacking.

"Everything is Going Wrong": Defending the Consensus

In the West, apprehension on development surged into practical policy concerns. Basic ideas were now in play influencing the institutions and relationships that actually implemented development. Blurring lines of the Cold War fed a "donor fatigue" that was pervasive by the mid-1960s. Within USAID there was nagging concern that the American public was souring on the larger program of foreign aid. This did not bode well, considering segments of the U.S. Congress had long been suspicious of aid. Through the mid-1960s, aid was reconsidered at high levels by leading members of the mainstream development community. By and large they agreed that aid was facing mounting difficulties, not the least of which was pervasive disillusionment with the concept.[57] European states, with their new official foreign aid programs, shared these anxieties. Unease was summarized in a 1967 gathering that was a snapshot of the diverse international and nongovernmental groups comprising the international aid community. Officials from the UN, World Bank, Barclays Bank, and the World Council of Churches gathered in the United Kingdom to share their mounting difficulties. Their language was abrupt, as participants felt "there is a clear and present danger, an emergency" on the question of development. There was broad agreement that there was "paralysis of leadership," feeding a fear that "at present everything is going wrong."[58]

A sign of the validity of these critiques was the rush by mainstream supporters to right the listing vessel of liberal developmentalism. The late 1960s and 1970s were an era of studies on the future of development. Mainstream supporters of development attempted to come to grips with the swelling problem. In 1968, seeing inertia and strife ranging across the development community, the president of the World Bank, George Woods, made an unprecedented call for a "grand assize" to review the preceding twenty years of development assistance.[59] Similar concerns prompted the United Nations to review what some termed its "Frankenstein Monster" of proliferating development bureaucracies.[60] Action to contain criticism was already being taken in some quarters. In late 1967, chastened American advocates rallied behind a proposal for a nongovernmental "Development House."[61] The Ford and Rockefeller Foundations, with their intimate understanding of the agility nongovernmental voices had to shape issues through research and advocacy, helped underwrite the organization. The Overseas Development Council (ODC) emerged. Its authority came in part from its prominent membership that included pillars of what might be called the development establishment. The body brought David Lilienthal, Eugene Black, Edward Mason (a leading scholar on development), and David Rockefeller to its board and was led by James P. Grant. Grant's spectrum of development experience, ranging from work with the UN in China after World War II to high-level positions with U.S. government aid agencies that had culminated with heading USAID's Vietnam office (he would later lead UNICEF), made him an authoritative voice on an increasingly fractious subject.[62]

Unintended consequences being the order of the day, the ODC's advocacy actually served to hasten the fall of the consensus. Grant, joining a growing chorus of critics, asserted the consensus approach to development, with its emphasis on large-scale, often national plans, placed too much emphasis on economic indicators. He aligned with those internationally who agitated for poverty rather than economic growth to be placed at the center of the development mission. Their analysis was closely connected to domestic dialogue on poverty that surrounded the Great Society. Those working on reforming aid felt that most postwar development programs had a tendency to assume that national economic growth would eventually "trickle down" to improve the living standards of the poor. With inequality actually increasing in the developing world, this approach was deemed inadequate.[63] He used his post at the ODC to cultivate ideas gaining credibility internationally. Grant even enlisted SEADAG in his calls for development to turn away from planning and big programs and emphasize smaller scale "appropriate technology" meeting "basic human needs" and focused directly on attacking poverty.[64]

The influence dissenting views had attained assured a harsh assessment of attempts to maintain the status quo. Woods's "grand assize" was to be a high-profile target. It appeared in the form of the 1969 Pearson Report. The study acknowledged existing problems but largely prescribed more of the same as solutions. It urged that the developed nations recommit themselves to foreign aid by establishing a clearer rationale for development, forging new relationships, increasing the volume of aid, improving the administration of aid, and slowing population growth. A basic goal of this new strategy was an annual minimum growth rate of 6 percent in the underdeveloped world.[65]

GLOBAL PERSPECTIVES AND GLOBAL VOICES ON DEVELOPMENT

None of Pearson's conclusions sat well with the already unsettled development community. Critics convened at a conference put together by Barbara Ward at Columbia University (with a session in Williamsburg, Virginia) in 1970. Ward, then a professor at Columbia, had continued her career as a commentator on international development, what she called "*the* central drama of the times"[66] (emphasis original). John F. Kennedy had been just one of Ward's contacts among the influential worldwide. Close to centers of power, she was an ideal individual to bring attention to the limitations of the Pearson report and its remedies rooted in the consensus. The Columbia Conference did just that, convening dissenters from around the world and amplifying their voices. The criticism of the report was sharp, with participants noting that even 6 percent growth would still leave a dangerous and "widening gap" between the rich and poor nations.[67] In this larger critique, environmental factors, while not accentuated, appeared for the first time as an important category of analysis.[68] Alleviation of poverty, too, gained prominence. Their inclusion was part of a call for a fundamental rethinking of international development. Some of the best-honed criticism of the existing order came from Mahbub ul Haq, a Pakistani economist who parodied a Western development mind-set requiring change.[69]

These critiques demonstrate how development discourse was increasingly global. The appreciation of the global impact of technologies employed to support development gave environmental concerns significance internationally as never before. Countries remote from a program of international development now could see themselves threatened by unintended consequences of the technologies bent to these tasks. In 1968, the Swedish government, sensitive to the fundamental shifts occurring on these international topics, called on the United Nations to convene a conference on issues concerning development and the environment in Stockholm during 1972.[70]

Part of the reason that the Stockholm Conference became a focal point for new international perspectives working into the development debate was a change in the orientation of the UN system. The body had become an important site for challenges to conventional wisdom. Organs like the UN Council on Trade and Development (UNCTAD) and the Economic Commission for Latin America (ECLA) had become hives of research and opinion running against accepted views. The ECLA, in particular, provided a platform for critical thinking. These included economist Raul Prebish, who laid out analyses important to dependency theorists and other policies running against consensus thinking.[71] UNCTAD made clear that divergence between the rich and poor nations was increasing but advocated the UN as the mechanism to change this reality. The newly formed UN Development Program also provided a forum for the increasingly plural viewpoints on the issue. These changes were reflective of a sea change within the international body as a whole. A rush of newly independent nations profoundly altered the makeup of the General Assembly and the tone of the institution. A "Group of 77" claiming to speak to the interests of the "Global South" pressed fresh voices into the development debate that were often at odds with reigning assumptions in the West.[72]

These increasingly fractious perspectives were displayed by the realities convening the international conference on development the Swedes had promised. The Cold War made organizing hard enough, but the event now had to navigate a yawning north-south divide. Because of this complexity, planning for the Stockholm Conference drifted for some time after the UN called for it. This changed when Maurice Strong, former chief of the Canadian International Development Agency, was appointed the meeting's Secretary-General in 1970. Strong was adroit at soothing the political concerns of the participants. He reassured the Soviets and allayed fears of smaller developing countries that their viewpoints would be overshadowed by convincing the prime minister of India to attend.[73]

Perhaps more important were his efforts to lay solid intellectual foundations for the conference. The need was not just for scholarly legitimacy but to reconcile new perspectives that had gained increased prominence in the years before the meeting. Strong convened a number of leading scholars at Founex in Switzerland in 1971, including dissenter Mahbub ul Haq. Founex gave full bloom to the environmental ideas germinating in the 1960s while splicing them with other reservations about development. Primary credit for the report lay with ul Haq, who was the driving force behind it and the meeting as a whole.[74] The document quickly emerged as one of the "basic texts" for revised thinking on international development issues. Contributors believed environmental issues could no longer be ignored in the larger calculations of international development. It was seen as one aspect of a general widening of the concept of development. The analysis was yet another blow to the consensus emphasis on large programs aimed at raising broad economic indicators. It urged the goals be pushed away from the "narrowly conceived objective of economic growth as measured by the rise in gross national product" toward "attainment of social and cultural goals as part of the development process."[75] The report was a means to build support in the industrialized countries for including environment in the development calculus. But it also endeavored to preempt growing distrust of environmentalism and other Western critiques of development in the developing world. There were those in poorer countries who felt that anxiety about the environment was a luxury for rich nations (a feeling that has not yet abated). At its worst, concern about the ecological costs of development and growing populations stood as a means to put the brakes on modernization efforts, permanently locking less developed countries into a subordinate position.[76]

Founex also effectively made the link between two powerful issues surrounding development that were often considered at odds—poverty and environmental protection. While all countries were threatened by pollution that did not respect borders, wealthier states were more troubled by environmental questions because their level of industrialization had led directly to environmental degradation at home. Although developing countries shared problems associated with industrialization, many of their immediate environmental concerns stemmed from poverty, which was categorized as caused by a lack of development. Overcoming poverty, therefore, emerged as a means to promote an environmentally sustainable society. Yet, this was best achieved by more development that applied technologies with sensitivity to environmental concerns. Founex demonstrated that environmental and poverty issues could be bound together and subsumed into the larger developmental process. The meeting's conclusions underlay numerous studies in the coming years that linked environmental degradation in poorer countries to underdevelopment.[77]

Strong also commissioned a book to further buttress the Stockholm Conference. He selected the well credentialed Barbara Ward and René Dubos. Ward, by this time, had become president of the new International Institute for Environment and Development. Dubos, a microbiologist and experimental pathologist at the Rockefeller University, had written widely on human behavior, genetics, and the environment. The book, written with the advice of an international committee of consultants (including members from communist states), was part of the efforts begun at Founex to "establish a conceptual frame of reference [to] consider fully environmental problems rooted in poverty as well as those rooted in industrialized societies." It shared the goal of "providing the conceptual basis for synthesizing concerns for economic development with concerns for environmental quality which are so often and so mistakenly assumed to be in conflict."[78] However, the means to achieving this reconciliation would not stray far from accepted mechanisms for implementing development. A major theme was, "science and technology are *indispensable assets* for achieving a dynamic reintegration of man and nature"[79] (emphasis original). On these terms, what emerged, *Only One Earth*, was a success. Indeed, the title became the slogan of the conference and the environmental movement generally. Reviewed worldwide, it received favorable comments from the mainstream press in Europe and the United States. More important, it became a best seller and brought these issues to a wide international audience.[80]

Strong also paraded these issues before American policy elites. At the Council on Foreign Relations in 1971, he debated Kennan. In the course of their discussion, Strong believed he had impressed upon the diplomat the importance of the UN's role in containing the environmental threat. Following Strong's presentation at the Council, David Bell, a former head of USAID and then vice president of the Ford Foundation, designated himself a "fan" of Strong's position. Enthusiasm translated into active support on the part of the Ford Foundation for the Stockholm Conference and indicates the growing appeal of these issues in the wider nongovernmental community. Taken as a whole, the publicity and advocacy surrounding Stockholm tapped existing public and elite concerns with the environment, assuring that the meeting would be a major statement on the issue.[81]

Delegates finally convened in Stockholm in June 1972. The two-week conference was troubled by the typical concerns of international meetings, particularly those called during the Cold War. Despite his diplomacy beforehand, Strong devoted much of his time soothing the concerns of rival blocs and individual states. In spite of these tensions, the conference produced a far-reaching and comprehensive declaration.[82] Perhaps the most concrete accomplishment was the establishment of the United Nations Environment Program. Considering the passions of the period, this was no small achievement. Importantly, the conference also drew the world's attention to the intersection of development and environment. Nevertheless, it did not radically alter the world situation. It did pave the way for considerable activity by NGOs and laid the foundation for a number of international environmental agreements. But looking back, Strong himself thought that Stockholm failed to take issues far enough.[83]

Limitations of the actual meeting aside, the road to the Stockholm Conference was an important moment in terms of reframing the global issues that surrounded development.[84] Stockholm provided a critical synthesis distilled out of the crisis of development. No longer could the various impacts of development programs be ignored in the calculus. Equally important, it would drive and alter the implementation of any number of development programs run not only by national and multinational development organizations but also by the ever-growing numbers of nongovernmental groups involved in development. The new views on development forged en route to Stockholm became the foundations of "sustainable development." This concept would be given full form by the World Commission on Environment and Development's (the Brundtland Commission) 1986 report, *Our Common Future.* Its fundamental demand was that development programs be economically and socially maintainable over the long term as well as achieve environmental equilibrium. Despite the fact that there were good questions about whether this was achievable or even the best course of action in many cases, "sustainable" thinking dominated mainstream discourse into the twenty-first century.[85]

As that term became popular, "modernization" fell into disuse. A term that once suggested the future was gradually consigned to describing an approach receding into the past. It was increasingly seen as a label for a chauvinistic approach too dependence on evolutionary universals, Western examples, and Cold War imperatives. Development, used nearly synonymously with modernization for so long, was decoupled and the two terms were used as distinct from each other. The term "sustainable" increasingly became almost a prefix for development and the compound was used to suggest a fresh approach. However, the popularity of a "sustainable development" paradigm had a great deal to do with its vagueness and the fact that it could coexist with organizational structures created under the postwar consensus. Critics have noted the variability of "sustainable" rhetoric. Rather than offering any concrete guide to action, sustainability offers a politically flexible and acceptable lingua franca on the increasingly disparate issue of development.[86]

Sustainability was related to a sweeping movement in development circles toward programs that focused on tackling the problem of poverty. Focus on the "basic needs"—particularly food and health care—of people in poorer countries became a mantra. For example, the Ford Foundation performed a major review of its development assistance program in 1972 in light of a changing world atmosphere. Its first objective became "that people in the poorer countries should attain better material existences, and the greatest concern should be with the neediest."[87] Accompanying the growing emphasis on poverty reduction in the development community was the idea of using "appropriate technology" to meet these needs. Supporters abjured large programs in favor of projects that fit the immediate demands of poorer societies. Broadly conceived multipurpose development projects lost favor in the face of the belief that "small is beautiful" in economics and other areas of human activity.[88]

It was not only intellectual attacks that ground down the consensus; an unsettled global economy added tremendous burdens as well. One sign of this was a set of meetings convened in 1974 by the ODC to deal with the repercussions of the period's economic upheavals. They brought together representatives from the government, World Bank, Ford Foundation, and other leading members of multisided development community.[89] The roster included individuals instrumental in the creation and maintenance of the postwar development system—David Bell, McGeorge Bundy, Henry Labouisse, Robert McNamara, and David Rockefeller. They understood the burdens of Vietnam and the Watergate scandal, which left the U.S. government in disarray. These seemed to pale before the aftershocks of the 1973 oil embargo, which thrust the international economy "into its most fundamental structural change in decades." These issues created anxiety about what it would take to meet the immediate needs of the poorest areas of the world. The spike in energy was another way environmental resources influenced development. High oil prices brought spectacular leaps in commodity prices, particularly fertilizer and food, dragging many developing nations to financial breaking points.[90]

Food and payment problems in the developing world were, sadly, not novel. What was new was the way such an emergency was conceptualized by elite American policymakers. For these leaders, the food and resources crises of 1973–74 were symbolic moments accompanying the apparent arrival of a "new international economic order"—a concept popular among developing states. Environmental questions seemed to have intruded on basic elements of global economic development. Perhaps having imbibed some elements of the Club of Rome's influential 1972 report, *Limits to Growth*, the participants asserted that the postwar global economy had been characterized by material surpluses that supported economic expansion.[91] However, the advance of modern, technological society brought "ecological overload" reflected in pollution, overuse of resources, and rampant population growth. These bases of the global economy were believed to be stressed to the point of collapse. A catastrophic "system overload" was discussed as a frighteningly real possibility. It was a reversal of the confidence in the march of modern society that characterized the faith in modernization held by boosters like Walt Rostow. Rather than bringing unprecedented bounty, modernity might well be returning humanity to want—or a sort of deprivation never before experienced. Many believed international politics as a whole, not just the theme of development, best abandon existing precepts and prepare for a new regime of scarcity.[92] Some leading figures involved in these debates disputed particular aspects of this analysis. McNamara, for one, questioned whether certain material shortages would be permanent. Nevertheless, concerns about environmental issues—meaning issues including resources as well as the more common connotation of conservation and protection—were now engrained in policy discussions. These were more than worries about commodities as they begged the question whether modern society could govern the use of those natural elements inseparable from its operation.[93]

Increasingly, the pivot for these issues was the World Bank. McNamara, as the Bank's president, had been to Stockholm and described to the assembled delegates the Bank's new environmental initiatives. A Swedish interlude was one stop on McNamara's own journey through these ideas. He came to doubt a war he had done so much to shape, and was forced to resign as Secretary of Defense as Lyndon Johnson came to believe McNamara had "gone dovish on me."[94] The presidency of the World Bank—with its tradition of American occupancy—was offered as a way to ease him out. George Woods, seeking a successor, knew the secretary's interest in the issue, in particular his 1966 Montreal speech, and felt that the job would fit well. After initial hesitation, McNamara accepted the position.[95]

McNamara arrived at the Bank in 1968 at the height of development's crisis and as voices of the old consensus were literally fading away. One of the most powerful, Max Millikan, passed away in 1969 during preparations for meetings at the CFR to examine development's place in U.S. foreign policy. The group pressed on without Millikan, advocating ideas already in discussion. The realization that the contributions of the United States were sliding and that the burdens of Vietnam still weighed heavily brought emphasis on greater coordination and international cooperation. A consensus view had always acknowledged international institutions as part of the development order. Now the tone was changing. Rather than being important adjuncts, these bodies were allowed central roles in the process. Internationalists looked to the UN as one mechanism, but there was greater hope that McNamara's Bank would take the lead on these issues. It looked most attractive to become the global hub for funding, coordination, and research on the question of development.[96]

Enlarging the Bank's role segued well with the "New Directions" U.S. aid policy had taken. This included the Nixon administration's frustration with existing programs and a desire to lower financial commitments and political profile in aid, while retaining the leverage that development provided in international affairs. The decline of USAID was matched by an increased emphasis on funneling funds through multilateral institutions. Talk about enhancing the role of the UN for development had been heard, but the World Bank quickly became the favored instrument. To be sure, the Bank remained a "specialized agency" of the UN. However, in a period where the UN had become restive toward U.S. policy and hospitable to questioning conventional wisdom on development, emphasis on a body that increasingly kept these issues at arm's length was politically palatable. Plus, the organization of the Bank allowed its subscribers influence over the direction of policy, and the tradition of American presidents provided further reassurance. Much has been made of McNamara's work to expand the Bank's lending, structure, and operations, but it was larger shifts in U.S. foreign policy that provided him the slack.

The former head of the Ford Motor Company brought his faith in management and technology to the Bank coupled with zeal to attack the problem of development. Under the leadership of the refugee from the debacle of Vietnam, the Bank, constructed largely through American initiatives and dominated by American capital, staff, and management, was to emerge as the single most significant actor in the recast world of development. McNamara's presidency of the institution stretched from 1968 to 1981. Supporters and detractors alike agree that these were some of the most significant years in the history of the institution. McNamara pushed the institution toward his vision that it become "something more than a bank . . . a Development Agency."[97]

His tenure saw a massive increase in Bank lending to poorer nations. Loans expanded exponentially from $953 million in 1968 to $12.4 billion in 1981.[98] By the late 1990s, the average yearly loan total would be over $20 billion. This assured the Bank was the largest single source of development funds and perhaps the most influential body in the diverse international development community. (By comparison, world development aid in 2000 was calculated at approximately $50 billion with total official U.S. foreign aid at $9.4 billion.)[99] The Bank's staff grew almost as quickly, from a clubby crowd of 767 to an imposing bureaucracy of over 4,000.[100]

Aside from the simple increase in scale of lending, there was a significant shift in how the Bank conceptualized its own operations. McNamara turned his intense personal energy and the growing bureaucratic momentum of the Bank itself to the problem of development. Ideas about poverty and the environment affected him profoundly. Ward and ul Haq became close and trusted advisers (ul Haq would later be instrumental in creating the UN Development Program's hugely influential "Human Development" reports).[101] The changes within his Bank were vital to the broader shift in development that saw poverty and basic human needs as the fundamental issues that development should address.[102] This was part of a shift in the foundational discourse on what development was to accomplish in a changed world. The Bank proved remarkably adept at insinuating into its organizational structure the new rhetoric, if not always the actual practices, that had emerged out of the crisis. Poverty would become a mantra of the Bank as the aid community slunk away from the focus on state planning, vast social change, national programs, and raising of general economic indicators that had dominated discussion since the 1930s. McNamara did gain an enthusiasm for attacking what was termed "absolute poverty." This new focus of development was literally etched into the Bank. At the Bank's gleaming headquarters in Washington, DC—just down the street from the White House and U.S. Treasury—visitors are greeted by its organizational motto, "Our dream is a world free of poverty."[103]

Just how rapidly the landscape of development changed was captured by Barbara Ward. Speaking at yet another UN meeting on the issue—the 1974 Conference on Science and Technology for Development in Vienna—Ward stated the modernization ethos of the preceding three decades had been abruptly superseded. A worldview that linked development with environment and made its primary mission the elimination of poverty had taken its place. Ward asserted that this view

> is the child of present history. . . In the Fifties and Sixties consensus would have been more likely. The countries of Asia and Latin America, feeling themselves freed from direct or indirect colonial control, sought as their highest priority . . . sophisticated science and technology . . . But the latest Conference takes place against an almost completely different historical background. The Seventies have destroyed the old consensus and, so far, put nothing in its place."[104]

Even high priests of modernization theory had to acknowledge that something had gone wrong. CENIS veteran Lucian Pye, in a 1976 establishment review of U.S. foreign policy in the wake of South Vietnam's demise, looked at the state of development aid. Vietnam was a reminder that the "American spirit" had felt that it was speaking for humanity, and how it could be hurt when it did not listen. Continuing to operate in the "Third World" was to "remain crucial to the maintenance of our national sense of self-esteem." Nevertheless, Pye understood that the United States was operating in a changed international situation, altering development and with it one of the basic ways the nation participated in global affairs. Yet he questioned whether the malaise that was constraining development assistance in the United States was purely a product of the Vietnam experience. Overreaching in Vietnam merely highlighted a disjuncture between means and ends. It had touched a domestic nerve, and the reflexive response had been a jump in a strain of American cultural relativism. It questioned the wisdom of the United States tutoring the world when its own house was not in order. He wished that Vietnam's apparent terminus for the "cold war phase of America's approach to development" was more "symbolic than real." Still, he found it impossible to ignore a palpable decline in an "activist instinct." The mid-1970s made clear that "the congeries of sentiments and rationales which sustained and gave respectability to foreign aid during the 1960s have been shattered; and few seem to have the spirit to try to pick up the pieces."[105]

Ward and Pye were right; things had changed. The American war in Vietnam and a host of forces that roared into discussion globally had quickly undone the consensus that had guided liberal development since the Depression. The imperative of promulgating a liberal version of development against "totalitarian" opponents had dissipated when the rigidities of the Cold War buckled as questions of the legitimacy of the superpowers and the systems they advocated became common. Assumptions about the importance of the central state came to be doubted in many quarters, as had faith in large-scale programs guided by the concept of planning. These were tied to profound questions about the nature of modern, high-tech, industrialized society. If the end result was a set of relationships deadening to individual life, social relationships, and the global environment as a whole, was it worth exporting or even maintaining at home?

These fanned the selection of critiques that realigned development thinking. New research and perceptions about the overall environmental impact of the style of development predominating in the postwar period provided a global view of its impact. Appreciation of the effects of "careless" technology pushed assumptions that the issues surrounding it required international governance and management. Such views merged with policy needs of the United States to lower its own commitment and profile on development. More emphasis was placed on international and nongovernmental groups to promulgate the process of development and contain its impacts. Paradoxically, the institutions given this task were not new, but pillars of the old order.

Still, these institutions were vested in the new ideas that had challenged and supplanted the "old consensus." Poverty, population, basic human needs, gender, and a throng of other concerns previously given short shrift found their way under the blanket of "sustainable" development. Sustainability itself became a vehicle for maintaining a new accord among an increasingly global yet disparate development community. The World Bank would emerge as the dominant international development actor. But its roots in the consensus were hard to shake and its continued commitment to certain courses of action has not been lost on its critics.

The crisis years of the 1960s and 1970s have been called the end of the vogue of postwar developmentalism. Others see the period as fathering a commitment to a reformed approach, centered on the concept of sustainability, and marking a distinct era in the career of development aid.[106] These views are half right. Undoubtedly, the period brought an end to a set of approaches and a discourse on the subject but not to a commitment to the idea. Modernization had been cast out of the international lexicon as strategic imperatives demanding its application had dissipated and its unintended consequences could not be ignored. What did matter was that the outlooks and relationships that guided the mainstream of development had been altered irrevocably. However, despite the upheaval, key institutions born of the consensus remained the primary executors of development internationally. Over the coming three decades, development would lack the imperatives and intellectual cohesion that had characterized its role in the mid-twentieth century. But it remained a part of international affairs and a means to understand the problems facing global society. When new problems appeared in a new century, some of the ideas forced into remission by the crisis of development would return.

Chapter 8

NEW DEVELOPMENTS

From the Cold War to the "War on Terror"

The great struggles of the twentieth century between
liberty and totalitarianism ended with a decisive victory
for the forces of freedom—and a single sustainable
model for national success.
—*The National Security Strategy
of the United States, 2002*

In 2000, a remarkable thing happened in Washington, DC: a think tank
closed. In a capital where a culture of influence and advocacy kept many
organizations alive well past their prime, the voluntary liquidation of the
Overseas Development Council was remarked upon. Its end had not come
suddenly. During the 1990s, as the significance of foreign aid declined
and the goals of development grew nebulous, the struggling ODC sought
new partners for its work. After attempts to partner with a university
failed, its management faced the inevitable, phasing out ongoing programs and solemnly closing up shop. Considering that the world still spun
through questions of economic development, global trade, and environmental change, only now these were often grouped under the buzzword
of "globalization," the ODC's demise was perhaps premature. Indeed,
within a year, the scholarly and policy communities would be scrambling
to revive its capacities.[1]

The death of the ODC, given life to sustain the consensus, was a function of the status of development in international life in the 1980s and
1990s. A sketch of the trajectory of institutions, individuals, and ideas
after the crises of 1970 provide a coda for what came before. Basic outlooks and relationships that had supported an extensive approach to modernization had been sundered, while other imperatives lay dormant. However, the importance of certain development ideas as a means to
demonstrate the legitimacy of an ideological system and protect it from
threats lay latent in international life.

Global shifts lessened the primacy of development on the international
scene and its importance in U.S. foreign policy. The plurality of views and
issues that had become part of the discussion had created sensitivity to

the complexity and depth of the issue as well as its profound impacts. But this variety also served to blur the overall goals of the process. The increasing suspicion of the role of the state, once central to both the means and ends to development and the end of the Cold War, only accentuated this drift. The implosion of the ideological opponent of state communism at once vindicated liberalism while removing the strategic imperative that had pushed a liberal variant of development into an important role in U.S. strategy. Development would return to a prominent role in U.S. foreign affairs at the start of a new century, rehabilitated by what was seen as an ideological threat to liberal order. Even so, however forward looking and strategically important that development practice was, it could not escape the burdens of the past.

The upheaval of the 1960s and 1970s brought profound changes. Even as the United States stumbled to defeat in Southeast Asia, South Korea and Taiwan "graduated" from the school of American foreign aid. For the ROK, the move had been slow and fraught with political and social upheaval. Into the 1970s, the Ford Foundation staff described a "bony, war-scarred" country where the society as a whole bore the marks of repression. The Park regime became increasingly authoritarian even as it began a big push to establish heavy industries like steel and automobile production.[2]

Although still dependent on loans and a U.S. security blanket, the ROK no longer required the grants and vast technical assistance characterizing the earlier wave of U.S. aid. The Vietnam War also provided stimulus as the United States procured material from South Korean companies. However, the success of South Korea's export-led economy was linked to an expanding economic partnership with Japan. Investment and expertise flowing from the former colonial power did much to aid the struggling South Korean economy. Japan also provided a development model. Among many other attributes, Japan's state ministries, particularly the storied Ministry of Trade and Industry, were credited with guiding and soothing major economic transitions. South Korea followed this example with heavy state intervention in the economy. The flattery of imitation included the 1988 Olympics in Seoul, patterned on the 1964 Tokyo games, a global declaration of the ROK's economic arrival. Many in the aid community saw it as an example for states in Asia and elsewhere to follow. Liberalization of politics and social life in the ROK, however, would have to wade through turmoil in the 1980s for true democratic pluralism to finally emerge.[3] But well before this the ROK had ceased to be a developmental problem and became a case study in success. By the conclusion of the 1970s, it ran with the "four tigers." It was a pack including Taiwan, Singapore, and Malaysia that had achieved a high level of growth and development. As they became emblems of economic achievement within the liberal camp, an enduring debate began over what social, political, and historical elements contributed to their accomplishments. South Korea's story of social and economic development after World War II alone created a small scholarly industry.[4]

Beyond East Asia, major events reshaped priorities of the already chastened U.S. foreign aid program. The final collapse of South Vietnam in 1975 removed a major theater of action. The oil embargo following the Yom Kippur War of 1973 (and a 1979 sequel) refashioned the international economy.[5] These events brought a strategic reorientation toward the Middle East. Israel, growing in strategic importance to the United States, became the primary destination for military and economic aid funds by the late 1970s. The aftershocks of the 1973 war brought renewed efforts for peace in the region, and with the Camp David Accords of 1979, Egypt also began to receive a sizeable portion of American foreign aid. From the late 1970s to the present, these two nations absorbed the bulk of the U.S. foreign assistance budget.[6] A sign of the lessening importance of development aid in U.S. strategy was the fact Japan emerged as the largest state donor of foreign aid during the 1970s and held the title through the end of the century.

Argument with an End? State-led Development in Eclipse

Ideological terrain continued to shift. Economic malaise in the West during the 1970s increased frustrations with statist approaches to political economy. The failure of postwar era policies to effectively weather the economic storms of the period helped conservative politics rise to ascendancy. Ronald Reagan and Margaret Thatcher embodied movements that celebrated the marketplace and actively denigrated the participation of the state in the economy. Further blows to the role of the state were felt internationally. The surge of petrodollars into world credit markets during the 1970s meant a flood of commercial loans to developing nations. Latin America was a major destination. With shifts in interest rates and declines in commodity prices in the early 1980s, many nations found themselves saddled with obligations they were unable to repay. Mexico's 1982 default on its loans further undercut assumptions about the capacity of states to effectively guide economic life. A debt crisis that eventually encompassed much of Latin America and spilled over into other parts of the world, coupled with continued reservations toward foreign aid in the West, made the 1980s, to some, the "lost decade" of development.[7]

The debt crisis was an overture to an even more dramatic collapse. The strains of producing growth in an inflexible economic and social system began to take their toll on the Soviet empire. The sale of oil on the world market was one way the contradictions in the economy were papered over, but those prices began to sag in the early 1980s. Facing wide-ranging malaise, reformers around Mikhail Gorbachev attempted to check the downward slide. Economic restructuring, *perestroika*, was coupled with a program of social liberalization, *glasnost*. Yet, these attempts to enliven the economic sphere only hastened the USSR's collapse. In part it was contradictions within its planned economy. Perhaps more important was that many within the USSR and its satellites had ceased to believe in the ability of communism to deliver the benefits of the modern world. Openness only allowed many to see plainly what had been known in outline. The already ragged gloss of communist promises to deliver human betterment was permanently stripped away. The liberal West appeared to have delivered the higher standard of living that was the promise of modernity. This helped make the decision easier—when the choice came to stand with the Soviet communist project after 1989, the vast majority of people who lived under the system simply turned their backs on it.[8]

The speed and relative peace with which the Eastern Bloc and then the USSR itself melted away was a surprise to the world community. It set off a wave of liberal self-congratulation that has yet to subside. Lucian Pye took the rapid collapse of these communist states as vindication of modernization theory. The demands of increased flows of trade, finance, information, and communication brought by new technologies burdened all nations, but autocratic (meaning totalitarian) states had been unable to cope.[9] The most telling commentary was not the discussion of the failings of autocrats but the triumph of liberalism. Francis Fukuyama captured the zeitgeist with his 1989 article "The End of History." Alternately hailed and damned, the core of Fukuyama's analysis was, as he later admitted, a modernization argument. With increasing liberalization in the USSR and PRC at the end of the 1980s, the competitors to liberalism had demonstrated the exhaustion of their ideologies and there were no other systems with the global legitimacy necessary to mount a challenge. It was not just the bankruptcy of other options that had brought mankind to this point. In Fukuyama's estimation, the path of modernity inevitably led to liberalism, as it was the one system that acknowledged and fed the needs of consciousness as well as the material desires inspired by the human experience. Humanity had found the one universally legitimate ideology around which societies could be organized. The argument that had roared to life in the 1930s could be considered closed.[10]

The challenge of state communism had fallen away. Through the 1990s, liberal concepts drove discussion of political economy and how global progress would proceed. In the amorphous and sometimes disjointed discussion over what was called "globalization" there was a refrain by supporters of economic liberalization that unfettered free markets and open societies would produce global prosperity and eventually raise the standard of living of all peoples. Much literature carries more than a touch of modernization assumptions, particularly in how human perceptions and institutions needed to change for globalization to succeed. The process was seen as a vindication and extension of liberal concepts worldwide and was frequently discussed as a "natural" process, the logical outgrowth of unfettered human interchange—in other words, a process that did not require a formal program of development as previously understood.[11]

Behind buzzwords globalization had concrete policies. A new consensus on how international economics should be structured was set in international life. The "Washington Consensus," emerging out of the conservative ascendancy and the experience of debt crisis during the 1980s (Japan's long economic malaise in the 1990s further tarnished statist approaches), guided action by the institutions given considerable power to shape the post–Cold War world economy—the U.S. Treasury, IMF, and World Bank.[12] To be sure, these ideas belonged to a particular political pole of liberalism. It was often referred to, or derided, as "neoliberalism" that turned back toward traditions of laissez-faire in international political economy. Many of these principles were set up in opposition to policies that favored statism and economic planning. States emerging from a communist interlude or grappling with a rapidly changing global economy were met by demands for structural adjustment, trade liberalization, fiscal austerity (often putting pressure on state welfare programs), privatization of state enterprises, and deregulation. For many it was a controversial and painful process.[13]

If liberal principles dominated the global economy, actual development doctrine and policy remained in disarray. W. Arthur Lewis lamented the state of the field in 1984. Aid levels had fallen, foundations had changed priorities, and the field no longer seemed as innovative. The canaries in the mine were graduate students (at least those from wealthier nations), who, upon seeing that development economics and other related fields were no longer a center of attention or producing the best jobs, had abandoned it in droves. This academic decline was a sign that there were nagging problems in the intellectual centers that had supported the process. All together this begged serious questions about development economics and the state of development theory in general.[14] Development as a policy device had become prefaced on competition with a competing ideological system. Even before the Soviet collapse, many in the aid community were debating how development should be retooled to face a new global situation. The melting away of the Cold War, the economic stagnation in the USSR, as well as the continuing flux of what the process should accomplish made it apparent to the ODC and other observers that development had few clear goals. Starting in the late 1980s, the official U.S. aid program was subjected to perpetual review and calls for reform, revitalization, or renewal. Despite a cavalcade of task force reports and hearings, aid levels continued to decline (particularly after the arrival of a Republican Congress in 1994) and USAID's reputation remained diminished.[15]

The international development community had to contend with the murkiness of its mission. The UN, like many other bodies, rethought the role of development after the Cold War. Concerned that without Cold War imperatives interest in promoting development might wane, 1994 Secretary-General Boutros Boutros-Ghali reaffirmed the place of development as fundamental to the organization's agenda. His statement reflected the ideas that had come to frame discussion since the consensus collapsed. Poverty remained the paramount issue and sustainability the watchword. Good governance and democracy worked their way into discussion as an important means to shepherd the process along and ensure just outcomes. The effort required public and private action, as "governments can no longer be assumed to be paramount economic agents." The test was "finding the right blend" of government intervention with other actors. And these actors were only increasing and there was a need for greater appreciation of "the many dimensions of development" and the "importance of the various actors" contributing to it. It was here Boutros-Ghali felt the UN might continue to make important contributions.[16]

The UN did indeed remain an arbiter. Boutros-Ghali's successor, Kofi Annan, as part of a 2000 "Millennium Summit," sought to reframe the ambitions of development. The Millennium Development Goals laid out eight targets for the international community to meet by 2015. They included a number of issues insinuated into the development calculus since the 1960s: the eradication of poverty, universal education, gender equity, reduced child mortality, improved maternal health, action against disease, environmental sustainability, and the cultivation of a "global partnership for development."[17] Ambitious if potentially unachievable in the timeframe allowed, the goals studiously avoided basics of the modernization consensus—economic growth, certain state and social institutions, and politics. Years after its announcement it remained unclear whether it provided a new consensus or even a guide to coordinate action on an issue that has to placate a welter of interests. Coordination was easier said than done as the numbers of nongovernmental groups committed to development continued to multiply. The emphasis placed on nonstate actors was another element of the decline of emphasis on the state during the period. Through the 1990s, great hopes were pinned on nongovernmental organizations and civil society generally, rather than the state, to take the lead on development.[18]

Above all other institutions loomed the World Bank. McNamara's tenure had made the Bank into the biggest source of development funds. This persisted into the 1990s, when it was offering $20 billion in development loans and grants. Multilateral aid, most of it through the Bank, took up an increasing percentage of total international development aid. It was now the default center of research and source of technical expertise on a variety of issues, fulfilling McNamara's ambitions to make it a development agency. Ascendancy did mean it became the focus of critics, garnering the Bank an unsavory reputation in certain quarters.

Representative of the fire it came under for being an institution with the wrong priorities for the world's poor was its environmental record. In many respects, the World Bank never fully reconciled environmental concerns with those of its own, mature development apparatus. Over time, various commentators came to doubt the Bank's commitment to environmental concerns. A defining moment for many critics was the massive program to open lands in the Polonoroeste region of Brazil for agricultural use and resettlement sponsored by the World Bank in the late 1970s and early 1980s. The plan was put into action without serious environmental investigations and despite the warnings of Bank staff. Not only was there significant ecological damage as the soil was not suited to agricultural use, but the logging and farming instituted in the region by the native Nambiquara tribe was decimated by epidemic disease and contamination of water supplies in the region by defoliants. By 1984, the Polonoroeste program had become a public scandal for the bank's new president, A. W. Clausen, and this heralded increased criticism of the bank's lending worldwide. Highly touted environmental safeguards established during the 1970s turned out to be ineffective. With the massive expansion of the size of the bank's operations and lending came a corresponding increase in the number of programs it supported worldwide and an intense pressure to make loans quickly. Evaluation of the expanded palette of loans was left to a six-person environmental staff (as of 1983, having grown from one in 1972), which had to review over three hundred lending operations annually. It is perhaps too much to say that the newfound environmental concern at the bank was feigned, but it was undoubtedly subordinated to other institutional imperatives.[19]

Mounting criticism and indistinct goals impelled James Wolfensohn, president of the Bank from 1995 to 2005, to respond to a diverse fraternity of critics. He franchised many dissenting voices into discussion, muting some. Among other reforms, the Bank, from its position as the most influential institution in the development community, proposed a "Comprehensive Development Framework" (CDF) in 1999 to fuse the work of government, international, and civil society groups involved in development in particular countries. It was an acknowledgment of the diversity of actors involved in the process and the need for "holistic long-term strategy" to effectively implement programs. It was also a reflection of the lessons learned during interventions in Bosnia, Somalia, East Timor, Rwanda, and Haiti. However late, incomplete, or ineffective the international community's actions might have been, the overall experience imparted hard lessons on the importance of development in conflict prevention and reconstruction (or "peace building" as it could be known). The array of government institutions, international organizations, and NGOs involved saw the need for development aid to build state capacities and strengthen civil society in troubled areas as a means to prevent conflict and secure peace, agendas that bore a passing resemblance to the developmental "nation building" done during the Cold War. By the start of the new century aid bodies—ranging from the Bank to USAID—clutched the concept of "conflict prevention" as a strategic rationale to justify their operations.[20] The appeal of a comprehensive approach was powerful in a period when precisely what aid for development was to accomplish remained in flux. Even so, such policies had to tread carefully. When the Bank proposed the CDF, it was extraordinarily careful to declare it was not advocating a return to development planning.[21]

The urge to avoid any association with the legacy of planning was reflective of the fact that the term could be one of scorn. Trends showed that elements of the consensus development ethos were still at large, as important and at points indispensable for international actors. Yet, basic elements of the consensus approach remained in disrepute, ensuring that modernization was something to be avoided, in name as well as content. In his 2000 presidential campaign, George W. Bush squeezed a dram of political gain out of distancing himself from the still unpopular concept of "nation building."[22]

DEVELOPMENT AGAIN BECOMES A WEAPON

The ready return of development to a prominent place in U.S. foreign relations after the attacks of September 11, 2001, was a function of its utility. For the government and the public, it was the failure of modernization that often provided a means to understand the pathologies in Middle Eastern societies that terrorist organizations had tapped. The "9/11 Commission" asserted that the extremist views of Osama bin Laden found fertile ground in a Middle East where states once seemingly headed toward "balanced modernization" had been thrown off course in the 1970s and 1980s. As the commission asserted, many "state centered" regimes had been unable to produce dynamic economies necessary to keep up with the needs of their populations, leaving a generation of disaffected young men susceptible to extremist blandishments. Prominent observers agreed, seeing the brand of Islamic radicalism embraced by Al Qaeda as having roots in the upheaval and reaction brought by modernity as it rushed into Egypt and Saudi Arabia.[23] Basic assumptions guiding security strategy were revised in the face of a new and often formless threat, yet development could easily find a task in the new posture. In the much heralded and debated 2002 National Security Strategy (NSS), the Bush administration unveiled a commitment to development aid (with a special emphasis on the World Bank) as a means to raise the standards of living of the world's poorest as part of a general posture that also accepted the United States would consider preemptive war.[24]

The NSS restated assumptions of the 1990s, that the "great struggles of the twentieth century between liberty and totalitarianism ended with a decisive victory for the forces of freedom—and a single sustainable model for national success: freedom, democracy, and free enterprise."[25] However, the administration did believe new ideological threats had appeared. From his 2002 State of the Union Address, where he declared an "axis of evil" opposed to the interests of the United States, onward, Bush defined the threat the United States faced as one from "totalitarian" opponents. It was not solely the Bush administration and its partisans who spoke in these stark terms. Various other commentators, including some to the left on the political spectrum, embraced the need to confront a "totalitarian wave" building in critical parts of the globe—particularly the Middle East. Militant Islamism was described as an heir to the totalitarian ideologies of the 1930s, although critics have seen limits in the comparison.[26] Bush, in a second inaugural dominated by international issues, demanded that in the face of such "tyranny" the United States had to accept that the "survival of liberty in our land increasingly depends on the success of liberty in other lands. The best hope for peace in our world is the expansion of freedom in all the world."[27] Those abroad whose ideology was defined as anathema to the liberal ideals the United States held close had to be confronted and destroyed. Accordingly, building conditions in which democratic societies amenable to U.S. interests could grow was a priority. The speech was a rhetorical reaffirmation of the same brand of globalism foundational to American engagement with the world from the 1930s onward.

Development was again mobilized. The U.S. government moved to implement a larger and more aggressive aid agenda. At a 2002 conference held under UN auspices in Monterrey, Mexico, Bush, along with a collection of world leaders, recommitted themselves to the Millennium Goals and promised more money for poorer areas of the globe.[28] His administration attempted to reform the maligned government foreign aid apparatus. A "Millennium Challenge Corporation," taking its name from the UN's goals, even if it did not always operate in its spirit, was established in 2004. Despite the fanfare, the overall impact of these and other innovations remained unclear as bureaucracies were created and others were shifted even as responsibilities and activities remained convoluted.[29] Still, Bush's then Secretary of State, Colin Powell, made it clear that development was seen as a powerful global agent against extremism and a means to shore up American legitimacy.[30]

The international community also entered the revival. There was a flurry of activity to promote development in the poorest areas of the globe, particularly Africa. As development rose in profile and importance, the policy community took steps to rehabilitate institutional capacity that had atrophied after the Cold War. One example of this rejuvenated interest was the November 2001 founding of the Center for Global Development, a mainstream development think tank seen as an inheritor of the ODC's mantle. A 2005 summit at Gleneagles, Scotland, allowed embattled British Prime Minister Tony Blair to call for a renewed push by the G-8 nations on the Millennium Goals and debt relief for the poorest. Publics in the wealthy nations had rich veins of sympathy for aid to alleviate problems ranging from poverty to HIV/AIDS in poorer nations. A Jubilee movement urging debt forgiveness gained widespread support internationally. Rock stars gathered by Bob Geldof for a London concert with great fanfare in the summer of 2005 gave a "Live 8" to focus attention on the very issues the G-8 leaders discussed at Gleneagles. All showed a continued interest across a spectrum of the international community for the humanitarian elements that always lay in the development calculus.

"Rock star" economist Jeffrey Sachs, who spent the 1990s shocking states of the former Soviet empire into the capitalist market, at the dawn of the new century turned his attentions to bringing *An End To Poverty*. In his writing and advocacy, Sachs claimed the Millennium Goals could be met if the world followed a series of technical steps he proposed. His solutions often assumed that a series of technological fixes (many similar to those long advocated by developmentalists) would free societies of the fetters of poverty. Disease ecology was a focus. Sachs put great stock in health measures similar to those transfixing predecessors, especially malaria eradication. There were often grander ideas just below the surface, with the need to build infrastructure such as roads and ports to facilitate significant transformation of societies. In conjunction with Columbia University, he turned scholarly resources to this project and found donors among international institutions and foundations. Indeed, by the early part of the twenty-first century his ideas had influenced the creation of a set of model villages in Africa. Outside donors provided capital and credit to these communities. Dollops of technical assistance would produce rapid change in public health, agricultural techniques, and education that would lift these people out of a "poverty trap." The "Millennium Village Project" (MVP) was discussed as a novel approach, although the motivations behind it would have excited NGO staff working on "rural reconstruction" in the 1930s, or even Fredrich Wilhelm Raffeisen. But the MVP also would have inspired pride in postwar developmentalists with Sachs's suggestion that it become one component part of a new "green revolution" for African agriculture. He was also adept at using the media to tell audiences in wealthy nations that the goal was within easy reach. Sachs echoed what advocates of the type of technical assistance behind Point Four were fond of saying—that the right technology, applied in the right places, could catalyze massive change. Indeed, technology was the unifying mechanism. It underpinned prosperity and could be applied universally to solve the problems causing poverty. Technology also provided a way to skirt difficult questions of politics and culture. It allowed the promise that by fostering "economic systems that spread the benefits of science and technology to all parts of the world" the "sweetest fruits" of modern prosperity would soon be "within our reach."[31]

Sachs was eager to inform twenty-first century audiences about all of the parts fitting into the development equation. It demanded the negotiation of social, political, environmental, infrastructural, demographic, and health issues. The scale of this application demanded those committed to the program adopt an extensive, even global, view. Bringing all these diverse pieces together would require effort across international boundaries but also among institutions in all quarters of the global community. He saw governments in revived roles working with international institutions, nongovernmental groups, and businesses to implement wide-ranging programs of development that embraced whole nations and regions, to eradicate poverty worldwide. Sachs did understand that such visions required proof to show it could be done. Dipping into the past he plucked out a prime example of "successful regional development programs [that] help us understand how international development can succeed"—the TVA.[32]

Sachs's goal was not officially growth but the alleviation of poverty, and he spoke in the lingo of sustainability. The fact that he grabbed the TVA as a model shows the endurance of long-standing imperatives. In important respects, it was a reinvention of the formula propelling much liberal developmentalism in the twentieth century. This and Sachs's own checkered record from the 1990s made him a particular target for critics. Sachs's bête noir, William Easterly, a former economist at the World Bank, had grown critical of foreign aid's inability to produce sustainable growth. Sachs was a specific target because his "utopian social engineering" was said to depend on top-down approaches. Easterly dismissed Sachs and his acolytes' approach as smacking of Marxist teleology, where a Leninist vanguard followed the march of history to achieve a Final

Cause. In contrast, Easterly promised a market-based approach. He sought "seekers" to find their own solutions to the problem of underdevelopment. Their grassroots ideas would percolate from "bottom up" in a system where local and entrepreneurial efforts were privileged. Easterly slung "planner" as a term of derision. In thrall of the "Big Plan," Sachs and the like-minded were stuck in the past. Their vision was not just ineffective, it was proof they were out of touch.[33]

Judicious commentary came from Amartya Sen. The Nobel Prize–winning economist laid out an attractive rationale for ringing in what an earlier generation of economists had called the "economic millennium." Development could be the means to enhanced human freedom, and freedom, in the form of rights, rule of law, and free speech, was the means to assure that development was effectively and justly implanted. Sen's views were sensible and popular. His emphasis on individual rights and democratic governance for the sprawling process of development link him to twentieth-century assumptions that modernization could best be done in a liberal framework.[34]

It is easy (and perhaps cynical) to dismiss discussions that are earnest attempts to wrestle with the enduring problem of global poverty. That is not the goal here. What should be noticed is the power and persistence of long-standing issues that continued to girdle the development debate. Even with talk of poverty and sustainability, the basic goal of achieving the prosperity that modern life provides remains a basic assumption moving many. In Sachs's vision, it is the wealthy nations (often the West) that should carry the burden to secure justice and stability for global society. His mantra is that it can be done if only the wealthy nations, with the assent of poorer societies, effectively mobilize their resources and capacities. Technology and the way it is employed remains a paramount means to achieve this goal. Well-tried assumptions cannot evade well-worn controversies. The political disputes appearing when development even seems to touch on planning and the state seemingly cannot be transcended. It is a reminder that development can be ideological even when there is no fundamentally different system offering an opposed model for global political and economic life. Debate among those committed to the liberal standards of individual rights, private property, and market economies, of course, break across ideological boundaries. Again, the links between national and international development were exposed. Too often they reflect more on political debates that straddle the domestic and the international rather than realities on the ground. All told, for all the ferment in development in the last decade of the twentieth century and the first years of the twenty-first, global debate over development remains contained in categories that have long set the limits of perception and discussion. This has meant limits in action and perhaps success when ideas are actually applied in any society, rich or poor. Real change may only come when new perspectives, particularly ones reflecting the needs of those peoples who desire assistance, catalyze fresh understandings of the complex realities faced when development is attempted.

Complex realities were in abundance during development's reemergence at the start of a new century as a strategic weapon for the United States. Many who followed the tune of poverty reduction were uncomfortable in areas where development was a powerful refrain in a U.S. strategy to transform societies as part of its "war on terror." After demolishing hostile regimes, the United States sought to "reconstruct" Afghanistan and Iraq into liberal societies, which, like the 1940s Republic of Korea, had never existed as such (at least in the form the United States claimed to seek). In both, efforts clearly reached into the realm of development. Once again the goals embraced the whole country, and phrases like "nation building" and "state building" effortlessly flowed back into public discussions about policy.[35] Aid for development also returned as a political and military lever. For the United States, highlighting the benefits it would bring to both countries was a way of reassuring the world community of its benevolence. Engrained as it was in international discourse, success was discerned by developmental barometers—electric current delivered, schools built, or miles of roads paved. In particular, NATO forces operating against a resurgent Taliban in Afghanistan were explicit about development's use as a means to contain the insurgents' appeal among local people. However, emphasis on development cut both ways. Failure to deliver these benefits highlighted the shortcomings of operations they were supposed to serve.[36]

The reappearance of development and the rehabilitation of some of the vocabulary of modernization did not mean a reestablishment of all the institutions, assumptions, and relationships that drove nation-building efforts during the Cold War. In part this is a reflection of the continued wariness in the development community of large-scale programs. In the U.S. struggle to build a new and viable state in Iraq, a surface hostility to the idea of state planning and control remained. A rigid anti-state rhetoric dominated domestic U.S. politics and spilled into foreign policy. Even among the new converts to nation building in the Bush administration, references remained for the need for privatization in the reconstruction. A blunt U.S. government posture regarding Iraq served to alienate many international and nonstate actors whose predecessors were regular recruits during the Cold War. Accordingly, while some U.S. and international NGOs did venture into Iraq (at least initially), various capable organizations gave the adventure a wide berth. In fact, prominent international aid organizations such as Oxfam emerged as early and vocal critics of the war.[37] Although a selection of businesses quickly jumped into Iraq, they represent only one type of institution among the diverse collection of groups involved in nation building's earlier variations. This corporate-dominated approach attracted criticism for its terrific waste and, perhaps more important, ineffectiveness. As in Vietnam, violence impeded development work. The UN mission to Iraq was withdrawn after insurgents destroyed its headquarters. The security situation degenerated to a point in 2006 where even for profit enterprises were unwilling to take the risk.[38]

The transition from the Bush administration to the presidency of Barack Obama brought renewed focus to the war in Afghanistan. With this came calls for greater collaboration, integration, and scope in the development plans that were widely viewed as the bedrock of the nation building considered central to winning the battle there. Richard Holbrooke, a leading voice (whose early career had been shaped by service as a USAID representative in the Mekong Delta in 1966), was supported by Sarah Chayes, who had years of experience running an NGO that sustained small-scale village and regional development in rural Afghanistan. His views were that for the deep reforms necessary to transform an Afghan society beset with nagging problems, the flagging American aid program there had to be reconceptualized. There needed to be greater integration and a more extensive vision. The Asia Society, an organization that had a legacy of bringing together the various constituencies using development for strategic ends, disseminated his views. Holbrooke, speaking at a roundtable discussion, thought that as a means to win the war and to sell to the American public what was likely to be a long struggle, "the U.S. should consider basically what Roosevelt did with the farmers in America in the 1930s, the Rural Electrification Administration, a massive multibillion dollar program, that involved seeds, water, fertilizer, roads, markets." Chayes agreed "absolutely" with a vision drawing inspiration from the past. After Obama's election, Holbrooke was appointed as the U.S. special representative for Afghanistan and Pakistan.[39]

As development regained a clear geopolitical role, old relationships and formulations that marked its era of strategic relevance began to reappear. The pull for greater state involvement was predictable as development again emerged as a weapon to tamp down the appeal of threatening ideologies and to wage counterinsurgencies. But with this also came an urge to draw in the expertise and resources of NGOs and international organizations and renewed calls for broadly conceived programs to achieve strategic ends. The use of old modernization lingo and examples betrayed the latent imperatives that lay in the use of development for strategic goals. Nevertheless, while nation building and the larger concept of development in which it is subsumed have an enhanced role in the post–

September 11 foreign policy of the United States, there remains no broad international agreement on how it should be implemented.

As difficulties mounted in Iraq and Afghanistan, some who initially supported aggressive posture that had come after September 11 grew disillusioned. Many of the strongest voices for Bush's policies had come from neoconservatives. A movement with origins in the ideological hothouse of the 1930s had found vocal expression during the crisis of the 1960s and 1970s. "Neocon" founding fathers opposed the social engineering of the Great Society while encouraging a vigorous prosecution of the Cold War, believing no accommodation was possible with the state communism represented by the USSR. They remained advocates of the use of U.S. power abroad even after the debacle of Vietnam. Following the USSR's collapse there was vindication among adherents. The relatively easy transition of Eastern Europe to liberal democracy was taken as proof these values could be painlessly transferred to other areas of the globe requiring change.[40] Neoconservatism was a camp of which Fukuyama counted himself a part. However, after seeing the contradictions surrounding the unilateral turn in U.S. foreign policy after September 11, 2001, Fukuyama began to express doubts. The "grinding" occupation of Iraq and the failures there suggested the neoconservatives had ended up engaged in the very sort of social engineering they had once decried. The strong international reaction, even among close allies, to a U.S. foreign policy often characterized as arrogant did damage to American leadership that remained critical to world order. All compelled Fukuyama to defect from the movement and propose a new approach to American foreign affairs. His prescriptions included a profound demilitarization and a move away from preemption that came with a more accurate appraisal of the threat posed by Islamism. At the core of a more subtle policy he labeled "realistic Wilsonianism" was a firm commitment to international development. Fukuyama's development agenda was not solely economic as he emphasized the importance of nurturing institutions that fed democratic inclinations within society. However, this sort of cultivation was always political and required considerable attention, funding, and institutional sinew of its own within the U.S. government and American society. He sounded chords that had been played at other moments of doubt—if successful it would create stable, healthy states that would be contributing members of a global society while stitching together tattered U.S. legitimacy.[41]

Fukuyama's apostasy was another moment that displays the resilience and significance of development as a theme in international life and as a mechanism in U.S. foreign policy. Yet, development had not come full circle back to the assumptions that had driven it during much of the twentieth century. History had made it impossible to do so. To be sure, the roots of many elements (and continuing disputes) recruited for contemporary campaigns flowed from the consensus. These all expose how deeply the concept of development can reach into discussions of how societies understand and attempt to guide change. Accordingly, development lies at the core of questions of legitimacy for social systems and ideologies at home and abroad. But those questions are framed by the events of particular historical moments. In the 1930s, liberals found the legitimacy of their faith challenged by the dynamism of global ideologies with developmental components. To combat this they grasped existing concepts and methods and thrust them into international life. Many of the formulations were products of sometimes rancorous domestic and international debate regarding how the juggernaut of modernity could be effectively applied and controlled. These became the basis of an international consensus on development that accepted massive projects, a focus on state planning that presumed the large-scale application of technology to produce widespread and often intimate social and political change. This consensus dominated the development discourse and worked its way into the foreign policy and then the Cold War strategy of the United States to contain and discredit the appeal of dangerous ideologies. At its very apogee of influence on the world stage, the contradictions and consequences were laid bare. The upheaval around the concept and the waning of the ideological struggles that provided it such meaning sundered the consensus rendering the means and goals of development indistinct.

International crises at the start of the new millennium again found liberals mobilizing the ideas and institutions of development to meet a threat. In what is now a much more plural and international discourse, policymakers and thinkers, implicitly or explicitly, grapple with the question of what and how development will be implemented in an altered world situation. However, this ferment has not produced a new consensus. History left a series of institutions committed to development but also a set of critiques. Service in a struggle again defined as ideological did not remove the baggage development still carries from the twentieth century. This has framed the employment of development in the twenty-first. For all the calls to integrate and cooperate, planning remains discredited, the state is still viewed with suspicion, various practices continue to attract criticism, and the voices invested in the debate often advocate divergent approaches. As the first decade of the new millennium staggered toward conclusion, even well-informed commentators like Easterly called global views of what development aid "is doing, will do, can do, or should do" at best "muddled."[42] A consensus on what constitutes just and effective development remains elusive and may be impossible to achieve. History is complicit in the muddle. Development is a ruthlessly future-oriented concept, looking toward what can be done next rather than gazing back at what has been done. But its past, because of how it shaped the options and views operating in the present, must be apprehended if a powerful force in world affairs is to be effectively bridled.

Nevertheless, the utility of the concept assures it will play a critical role in shaping global affairs. It undoubtedly grips the humanitarian imagination. The impulse to improve the conditions of people seen to be in need still moves many worldwide. Development as a means to further policy and justify political programs will almost certainly remain in a prominent position. It has become indispensable to the organs of global politics, be they nation-states, movements, NGOs, or international institutions. All are expected by an international public to assure that their visions will somehow improve conditions for those who receive. Development will remain a compelling means to demonstrate the validity of their agendas.

NOTES

INTRODUCTION

1. James Ferguson, *The Anti-Politics Machine: "Development," Depoliticization, and Bureaucratic Power in Lesotho* (New York: Cambridge University Press, 1990), 372–75.

2. The core of this scholarly consensus is expressed by John Lewis Gaddis, *The Cold War: A New History* (New York: Penguin Press, 2005); Melvyn P. Leffler, *For the Soul of Mankind: The United States, the Soviet Union, and the Cold War*, 1st ed. (New York: Hill and Wang, 2007); Odd Arne Westad, *The Global Cold War: Third World Interventions and the Making of Our Times* (Cambridge, New York: Cambridge University Press, 2005). Ideology is a contested and varied term. It is used here in a general sense to describe a body of views, assumptions, myths, and beliefs that guide individuals, groups, movements, and institutions in their actions and worldviews. For a discussion of ideology, see Michael Hunt, *Ideology and U.S. Foreign Policy* (New Haven, CT: Yale University Press, 1987), and Michael Hogan and Thomas G. Paterson, *Explaining the History of American Foreign Relations* 2nd ed. (New York: Cambridge University Press, 2004), 222.

3. Michael H. Hunt, *The American Ascendancy: How the United States Gained and Wielded Global Dominance* (Chapel Hill: University of North Carolina Press, 2007); Westad, *Global Cold War*.

4. This work is best exemplified by Odd Arne Westad, "The New International History of the Cold War: Three (Possible) Paradigms," *Diplomatic History* 24 (Fall 2000): 551–65; Nils Gilman, *Mandarins of the Future: Modernization Theory in Cold War America*, New Studies in American Intellectual and Cultural History (Baltimore, London: Johns Hopkins University Press, 2003); Michael E. Latham, *Modernization as Ideology: American Social Science and "Nation Building" in the Kennedy Era* (Chapel Hill: University of North Carolina Press, 2000). Nick Cullather, "Development: It's History," *Diplomatic History* 24 (Fall 2000): 641–53; Nicole Sackley, "Passage to Modernity: American Social Scientists, India, and the Pursuit of Development, 1945–1961," Ph.D. diss. Princeton University, 2004.

5. Carol Lancaster, *Foreign Aid: Diplomacy, Development, Domestic Politics* (Chicago: University of Chicago Press, 2007), 28–29.

6. Wolfgang Sachs, "The Archaeology of the Development Idea," *INTERculture* 23 (Fall 1990): 2–3; Gilbert Rist, *The History of Development: From Western Origins to Global Faith* (New York: Zed Books, 1997), 70–75; Gustavo Esteva, "Development," in Wolfgang Sachs, ed., *The Development Dictionary: A Guide to Knowledge as Power* (New York: Zed Books, 1992), 6–7; Arturo Escobar, *Encountering Development: The Making and Unmaking of the Third World*, (Princeton, NJ: Princeton University Press, 1995); H. W. Arndt, *Economic Development: The History of An Idea* (Chicago: University of Chicago Press, 1987), 9–48.

7. Gaddis, *The Cold War*, 27.

8. David Engerman, "The Romance of Economic Development and New Histories of the Cold War," *Diplomatic History* 28 (Jan. 2004): 24–54.

9. See Anders Stephanson, *Manifest Destiny: American Expansionism and the Empire of Right*, 1st ed. (New York: Hill and Wang, 1995).

10. Michael Adas, *Dominance by Design: Technological Imperatives and America's Civilizing Mission* (Cambridge, MA: Belknap Press of Harvard University Press, 2006), 246–51.

11. David Armitage and M. J. Braddick, *The British Atlantic World, 1500–1800* (New York: Palgrave Macmillan, 2002), 21–27. See also Bernard Bailyn, *Atlantic History: Concept and Contours* (Cambridge, MA: Harvard University Press, 2005).

12. Joyce Appleby, Lynn Hunt, and Margaret Jacob, *Telling the Truth About History* (New York: Norton, 1994), 87–88.

13. In this study I have followed no particular romanization format for terms and names from Asian languages. I have tended to use the more common forms for some words and names (e.g., Chiang Kai-shek as opposed to Jiang Jeishi) or terms that are regularly written in one manner in sources or secondary materials. I have also chosen not to capitalize the term "communist" as, rather like the term "liberal," it refers to a multiplicity of movements, parties, and individuals rather than one monolithic group. Finally, I use the term "American" or "America" as synonymous with "citizen of the United States" and "the United States" respectively. This is purely for the sake of variation within the text, as there are many others who can rightly be called Americans beyond those from the United States.

14. *The Encyclopedia of the Social Sciences* (New York: Macmillian, 1933); *International Encyclopedia of the Social Sciences* 10 (New York: Macmillian, 1968), 386–409.

15. David Harrison, *The Sociology of Modernization and Development* (London: Routledge, 1991), 155.

16. Alex Inkeles, *Becoming Modern: Individual Change in Six Developing Countries* (Cambridge, MA: Harvard University Press, 1974), 3–5.

17. Ibid., 5.

18. Harrison, *Sociology of Modernization*, 154–55.

CHAPTER 1
THE RISE OF AN AMERICAN STYLE OF DEVELOPMENT, 1914–1937

1. M. P. Cowen and R. W. Shenton, *Doctrines of Development* (New York: Routledge, 1996), 35.

2. Ibid., 24–36.

3. John F. Kasson, *Civilizing the Machine: Technology and Republican Values in America, 1776–1900*, 2d ed. (New York: Hill and Wang, 1999), 8. For an overview of the place of technology in U.S. foreign relations see Walter LaFeber, "Technology and U.S. Foreign Relations," *Diplomatic History* 24 (Winter 2000): 1–19.

4. Drew R. McCoy, *The Elusive Republic: Political Economy in Jeffersonian America* (New York: Norton, 1980).

5. Kasson, *Civilizing the Machine*, 28–32.

6. Ibid., 112–135.

7. Cecelia Tichi, *Shifting Gears: Technology, Literature, Culture in Modernist America* (Chapel Hill: University of North Carolina Press, 1987).

8. Eric Foner, *Reconstruction: America's Unfinished Revolution, 1863–1877* (New York: Harper and Row, 1988), 346–411; Edward Ayers, "The First Occupation," *New York Times Magazine*, May 29, 2005.

9. Louis Menand, *The Metaphysical Club*, 1st ed. (New York: Farrar, Straus and Giroux, 2001), 372–75. On American progressives in the world see Alan Dawley, *Changing the World: American Progressives in War and Revolution, Politics and Society in Twentieth-Century America* (Princeton, NJ: Princeton University Press, 2003).

10. J. F. Dashiell, "Some Psychological Phases of Internationalism," *American Journal of Sociology* 25 (May 1920): 757.

11. Walter Lippmann, *Drift and Mastery* (reprint 1914; Madison: University of Wisconsin Press, 1985), 150–51; Steven J. Diner, *A Very Different Age: Americans of the Progressive Era* (New York: Hill and Wang, 1998), 229–30.

12. Ordway Tead, "The British Reconstruction Programs," *Political Science Quarterly* 33 (March 1918): 56–76; R. L. Schyler, "The Reconstruction of the British Empire," *Political Science Quarterly* 31 (Sept. 1916): 445–52. Raymond Leslie Buell, "Political and Social Reconstruction in France," *American Political Science Review* 15 (Feb. 1921): 27–51; J. A. Salter, "The Reconstruction of Hungary," *Journal of the Royal Institute of International Affairs* 3 (July 1924): 190–202.

13. Edwin Maxey, "The Reconstruction of Korea," *Political Science Quarterly* 25 (Dec. 1910): 673–87; Ulysses G. Weatherly, "Haiti: An Experiment in Pragmatism," *American Journal of Sociology* 32 (Nov. 1926): 353–66; Oswald Garrison Villard, "Reconstruction in Puerto Rico," April 4, 1937, *The Nation*, 408.

14. Robert W. Rydell, *All the World's a Fair: Visions of Empire at American International Expositions, 1876–1916* (Chicago: University of Chicago Press, 1984), 38–71; Kasson, *Civilizing*, 183–234.

15. Josiah Strong, *Our Country* (reprint 1885, Cambridge: Belknap Press, 1963), 213–17; Anders Stephanson, *Manifest Destiny: American Expansionism and the Empire of Right*, 1st ed. (New York: Hill and Wang, 1995), 79–80.

16. Michael Adas, *Machines as the Measure of Men: Science, Technology, and Ideologies of Western Dominance* (Ithaca, NY: Cornell University Press, 1989), 271–342. See also Daniel Headrick, *Tools of Empire: Technology and European Imperialism in the Nineteenth Century* (New York: Oxford University Press, 1981).

17. Adas, *Machines*, 206–207; James C. Thompson, Peter Stanley, and John C. Perry, *Sentimental Imperialists: The American Experience in East Asia* (New York: Harper and Row, 1981), 50–52.

18. Glenn Anthony May, *Social Engineering in the Philippines: The Aims, Execution, and Impact of American Colonial Policy, 1900–1913* (Westport: Green-

wood Press, 1980), 8–10; Frank Ninkovich, *The United States and Imperialism* (Malden, MA: Blackwell, 2001), 55.

19. W. Cameron Forbes, *The Philippine Islands*, vol. 1 (New York: Houghton Mifflin, 1928), 330, 368–69; Michael Adas, *Dominance by Design: Technological Imperatives and America's Civilizing Mission* (Cambridge, MA: Belknap Press of Harvard University Press, 2006), 145–49.

20. Adas, *Machines*, 406–407.

21. Peter W. Stanley, *A Nation in the Making: The Philippines and the United States, 1899–1921* (Cambridge, MA: Harvard University Press, 1974), 98.

22. Forbes, *The Philippine Islands*, vol. 2, 390–94.

23. C. H. Forbes-Lindsay, *America's Insular Possessions*, vol. 2 (Philadelphia: John C. Winston Co., 1906), 420–22; "Plans of Manila, P.I.," Official Plans furnished by D. H. Burnham, Daniel H. Burnham Papers, Art Institute of Chicago, Chicago, Illinois (hereafter AIC).

24. *Annual Report of the Consulting Architect for the Period Extending from November 17th, 1905 to June 30th, 1906*, Burnham Papers, AIC; W. Cameron Forbes, Typescript Journals, vol. 1, W. Cameron Forbes Papers, Houghton Library, Harvard University, 123, 125 (hereafter HLH).

25. Quoted in May, *Social Engineering*, 139; Stanley, *A Nation*, 98–100, 102–106.

26. Forbes, *The Philippine Islands*, vol. 1, 408–409.

27. Adas, *Dominance by Design*, 148–49.

28. May, *Social Engineering*, 78–79, 93, 111–26.

29. Soma Hewa and Philo Hove, *Philanthropy and Cultural Context: Western Philanthropy in South, East, and Southeast Asia in the 20th Century* (New York: University Press of America, 1997), 47.

30. Stanley Karnow, *In Our Own Image: America's Empire in the Philippines* (New York: Random House, 1989), 196–97.

31. Hewa and Hove, *Philanthropy and Cultural Context*, 53.

32. May, *Social Engineering*, 182.

33. Stanley, *A Nation*, 205, 226.

34. Adas, *Dominance by Design*, 177–78.

35. More Rockefeller family foundations would follow. These would include the Rockefeller Brothers Fund (1940) and the Rockefeller Family Fund (1967). This roster, of course, does not include universities, such as the University of Chicago and the Rockefeller University, or nonprofit groups aimed at specific issues, such as the Bureau of Social Hygiene, the Population Council, Colonial Williamsburg, or the Council on Economic and Cultural Affairs, all founded with Rockefeller money.

36. David Nasaw, *Andrew Carnegie* (New York: Penguin Press, 2006), 671, 742–45, 66–67. Carnegie money would also establish, among other organizations, the Carnegie Institution of Washington, the Teachers Insurance and Annuity Association (now TIAA-CREF), and the Carnegie Institute of Technology (now Carnegie-Mellon University).

37. Lloyd E. Ambrosius, *Wilsonian Statecraft: Theory and Practice of Liberal Internationalism During World War I* (Wilmington, DE: Scholarly Resources Books, 1991), 1–28.

38. Donald Fisher, "The Role of Philanthropic Foundations in the Reproduction and Production of Hegemony: Rockefeller Foundations and the Social Sciences," *Sociology* 17 (May 1983): 206–33; Daniel T. Rodgers, *Atlantic Crossings: Social Politics in a Progressive Age* (Cambridge, MA: Belknap Press, 1998).

39. Hewa and Hove, *Philanthropy and Cultural Context*, 58–60.

40. On the American occupation of Haiti, see Mary A. Renda, *Taking Haiti: Military Occupation and the Culture of U.S. Imperialism, 1915–1940* (Chapel Hill: University of North Carolina Press, 2001); Lester D. Langley, *The Banana Wars: An Inner History of American Empire, 1900–1934* (Lexington: University Press of Kentucky, 1983).

41. Arthur Chester Millspaugh, *Haiti under American Control, 1915–1930* (Westport, CT: Negro Universities Press, 1970), 139; Robert M. Spector, *W. Cameron Forbes and the Hoover Commissions to Haiti* (New York: University Press of America, 1985), 210.

42. Herbert Hoover, "The Nation and Science," *Science* 65 (Jan. 1927): 26–29; Herbert Hoover, *An American Epic* (Chicago: H. Regnery Co., 1959). William O. Walker III, "Crucible for Peace: Herbert Hoover, Modernization, and Economic Growth in Latin America," *Diplomatic History* 30 (Jan. 2006): 83–117; Nick Cullather, "The Foreign Policy of the Calorie," *American Historical Review* 112 (April 2007): 336–64; Emily S. Rosenberg, *Spreading the American Dream: American Economic and Cultural Expansion, 1890–1945* (New York: Hill and Wang, 1982).

43. Thomas J. McCormick, *The China Market: America's Quest for Informal Empire, 1893–1901* (Chicago: Quadrangle, 1967); T. Christopher Jespersen, *American Images of China, 1931–1949* (Stanford, CA: Stanford University Press, 1996), 3; Frank Ninkovich, *The United States and Imperialism* (Malden: Blackwell, 2001), 153–54; Adas, *Machines*, 285, 291, 307.

44. William R. Hutchinson, *Errand into the World: American Protestant Thought and Foreign Missions* (Chicago: University of Chicago Press, 1987), 146–83; James C. Thompson, Jr., Peter W. Stanley, and John Curtis Perry, *Sentimental Imperialists: The American Experience in East Asia* (New York: Harper, 1981), 50–52.

45. Dwight W. Edwards, "Progress and Opportunity," n.d. [1911], box 6, Dwight W. Edwards Papers, Yale Divinity Library Special Collections, Yale University (hereafter YDSL).

46. Julean Arnold, "China's Economic Problems and Christian Missionary Effort," *The Chinese Recorder*, Aug. 1919, 515.

47. Randall E. Stross, *The Stubborn Earth: American Agriculturalists on Chinese Soil, 1898–1937* (Berkeley: University of California Press, 1986), 92–115.

48. Peking Union International Famine Relief Committee, *The North China Famine of 1920–1921 With Special Reference to the West Chihli Area, Being the Report of the Peking United International Famine Relief Committee* (Peking, 1922), 2–5, 45–48, 167. With this comparison the PUIFRC may have been exaggerating its success. The 1920–1921 famine was massive but still smaller than the catastrophic 1877–1878 event. Perhaps 90 million persons were affected by the earlier hunger, and some estimates put deaths as high as 13 million. For a discussion of the human costs of the 1877–1878 famine in China and its connection to

global weather patterns, as well as international political and social upheaval, see Mike Davis, *Late Victorian Holocausts: El Niño Famines and the Making of the Third World* (New York: Verso, 2001), 64–79, 113.

49. Walter Mallory, *China: Land of Famine* (New York: American Geographical Society, 1926), 1–2, 64–83, 84–106. Mallory served as secretary of the CIFRC during the 1920s and would later serve as secretary of the Council on Foreign Relations.

50. "The Famine of 1920–1921, Achievements, Lessons and Christian Participation," n.d. [1923]; Dwight Edwards, "Don't Blame it on the Crops," 1925, box 7, Dwight Edwards Papers, YDSL.

51. The National Christian Conference on Modern Industry, "The Church and China's Economic and Industrial Problems," *The Chinese Recorder,* April 1922, 257–64.

52. Edwards, "Crops." On the economics of famine, see Amartya Kumar Sen, *Poverty and Famines: An Essay on Entitlement and Deprivation* (New York: Oxford University Press, 1981).

53. Mallory, *Land of Famine,* 189.

54. Ibid., 2–3, 29–30; Dwight W. Edwards, "Recent Experience and Future Plans for Rural Reconstruction by the China International Famine Relief Commission," *The Chinese Recorder,* Dec. 1936, 1; Andrew Nathan, *A History of the China International Famine Relief Commission* (Cambridge, MA: Harvard University Press, 1965), 11–12, 23–24; CIFRC, *Annual Report, 1922,* 1; PUIFRC, *The North China Famine,* 9–10, 31; and CIFRC, *History, Organization, and Policy* (Peking, 1923), 9.

55. Daniel T. Rodgers, *Atlantic Crossings,* 321, 327–28.

56. CIFRC, *Herr Raffeisen among Chinese Farmers, 1922–1934* (reprint, 1935, DaCapo, 1980), 5, 15–17.

57. CIFRC, *Annual Report, 1935,* 18.

58. Nathan, *History,* 38.

59. CIFRC, *Herr Raffeisen,* 24–25; Nathan, *History,* 33, 38.

60. Stross, *Stubborn Earth,* 60–65.

61. O. J. Todd, "Assuring China's Food Supply," *China,* 1935, 302; "A Practical Educational Movement," *China Weekly Review,* Jan. 26, 1929, 316–319; "Engineering and Altruism in China," 1929, 324; "Agricultural Engineering in China," *Journal of the Association of Chinese and American Engineers* (Nov. 1933): 341; all reprinted in O. J. Todd, *Two Decades in China* (Peking: Association of Chinese and American Engineers, 1938). See also Jonathan Spence, *To Change China: Western Advisors in China, 1620–1960* (reprint, 1969, New York: Penguin Books, 1980), 203–16.

62. G. E. Hubbard, "Financial Reconstruction for China," *Journal of the Royal Institute of International Affairs* 9 (Sept. 1930): 636–37; Frank Ninkovich, "The Rockefeller Foundation, China, and Cultural Change," *Journal of American History* 70 (March 1984): 799–820.

63. Lossing J. Buck, *Land Utilization in China,* 3 vols. (Nanking: University of Nanking, 1937); Stross, *Stubborn Earth,* 169, 186–87.

64. Jespersen, *American Images,* 24–44.

65. Yat-sen Sun, *The International Development of China,* 2d ed. (New York: Da Capo Press, 1975).

66. Wen-Hsin Yeh, ed., *Becoming Chinese: Passages to Modernity and Beyond* (Berkeley: University of California Press, 2000), 137–53.

67. Margherita Zanasi, "Exporting Development: The League of Nations and Republican China," *Comparative Studies in Society and History* 49 (January 2009): 143–69.

68. Soma Hewa and Philo Hove, eds., *Philanthropy and Cultural Context: Western Philanthropy in South, East, and Southeast Asia in the 20th Century* (New York: University Press of America, 1997), 26–31; Ninkovich, "Rockefeller Foundation," 801–804.

69. Hewa and Hove, *Philanthropy and Cultural Context*, 35; Ninkovich, "Rockefeller Foundation," 808–809; John Jordan, *Machine-Age Ideology: Social Engineering and American Liberalism, 1911–1939* (Chapel Hill: University of North Carolina Press, 1994), 129–31; and Judith Sealander, *Private Wealth and Public Life: Foundation Philanthropy and the Reshaping of American Social Policy from the Progressive Era to the New Deal* (Baltimore: Johns Hopkins University Press, 1997), 34–78; Dorothy Ross, *The Origins of American Social Science* (New York: Cambridge University Press, 1991), 467–68.

70. Yung-Chen Chiang, *Social Engineering and the Social Sciences in China, 1919–1949* (New York: Cambridge University Press, 2001), 224–227; J. B. Condliffe, ed., *Problems of the Pacific, 1929: Proceedings of the Third Conference of the Institute of Pacific Relations* (Chicago: University of Chicago Press, 1930), 3–35, 660; Lawrence T. Woods, *Asia-Pacific Diplomacy: Nongovernmental Organizations and International Relations* (Vancouver, University of British Columbia Press, 1993), 30–33. From 1931 to 1934, the IPR would disperse over $164,000 for research on China. After China came the United States and Japan, research on which received $66,000 and $36,000 respectively. Carter to Mason, Nov. 11, 1935, box 292, Institute of Pacific Relations Papers, Rare Book and Manuscript Library, Columbia University.

71. Address by Raymond Fosdick, "The Individual's Place in the Age of Machines," June 22, 1930, *New York Times*; Raymond Blaine Fosdick, *Our Machine Civilization* (New York: Eilert, 1922). Jordan, *Machine-Age Ideology*, 137.

72. Selskar M. Gunn, "Report on Visit to China, June 9–July 30, 1931," box 12, Series 601 China, RG 1.1, RAC, 5–6; and James C. Thomson, Jr., *While China Faced West: American Reformers in Nationalist China, 1928–1937* (Cambridge, MA: Harvard University Press, 1969), 126–28.

73. Selskar M. Gunn, "China and the Rockefeller Foundation," January 23, 1934, box 12, Series 601 China, RG 1.1, RAC; and Thompson, *While China Faced West*, 130; Rockefeller Foundation Annual Report, 1935, http://www .rockfound.org/library/library.shtml, accessed May 16, 2007, 317. Thompson, *While China Faced West*, 139; Gregg to Greene, March 20–21, 1934, box 13, Roger S. Greene Papers, Houghton Library, Harvard University (hereafter HLH).

74. Day to Gunn, June 25, 1935, box 12, Series 601 China, RG 1.1, RAC; Greene to Gunn, Jan. 12, 1934; Greene to Liu, Oct. 16, 1934, box 13, Greene Papers, HLH.

75. "The Mass Education Movement in China, 1929–1939: A Constructive Decade," July 1939, box 3, United China Relief Papers, NYPL; "North China Council for Rural Reconstruction, Report, 1936," box 11, Series 601 China, RG 1.1, RAC; and Ninkovich, "Rockefeller Foundation," 810–11; See also Charles

W. Hayford, *To the People: James Yen and Village China* (New York: Columbia University Press, 1990).

76. "China Program Preliminary Interim Statement," October 1935, box 12, Series 601 China, RG 1.1, RAC.

77. Grant #8, July 22, 1936; Grant #9, July 7, 1937; Grant #13, Nov. 2, 1936; Grant #14, Nov. 2, 1936, box 10, Series 601 China, RG 1.1, RAC.

78. Grant #15, Nov. 15, 1936, box 10, Series 601 China, RG 1.1, RAC; Ninkovich, "Rockefeller Foundation," 815–16; John De Francis, *Nationalism and Language Reform in China* (reprint 1950, New York: Octagon Books, 1972). On the complications of structuring languages and dialects to convey technological and scientific ideas, see Eric Hobsbawm, *Nations and Nationalism Since 1780: Programme, Myth, Reality* (New York: Cambridge University Press, 1990), 55–56.

79. Frederick Cooper, *Decolonization and African Society: The Labor Question in French and British Africa* (New York: Cambridge University Press, 1996), 1–20.

80. Oliver J. Todd, "As an Engineer Sees America in 1935," *Journal of the Association of Chinese and American Engineers* (Nov.–Dec. 1935 and Jan.–Feb. 1936): 369–71; Oliver J. Todd, "The Development of a Profession," *Journal of the Association of Chinese and American Engineers* (May–June 1937): 383–84, reprinted in Todd, *Two Decades in China*.

81. Todd to Snow, June 28, 1937, box 50, Oliver J. Todd Papers, Hoover Institution on War Revolution and Peace, Stanford University (hereafter HIA); Oliver J. Todd, *The China that I Knew* (Palo Alto, 1973), 121–22.

82. "Shanghai Leaders Organize International Red Cross to Cope with Unprecedented Refugee Situation; Aim to Coordinate Relief Efforts Now Being Made Here," *CIFRC News Bulletin*, Dec. 1, 1937, box 14, Dwight Edwards Papers, YDSL; Nathan, *History,* 68–69; Y. S. Djang to ad interin [sic] Committee Members, CIFRC, "Liquidation," Aug. 24, 1949, box 14, Dwight Edwards Papers, YDSL; Rockefeller Foundation Annual Report, 1938, http://www.rockfound.org/library/library.shtml, accessed May 16, 2007, 361–62. Nathan notes in his history of the CIFRC that it apparently dissolved with the start of the Sino-Japanese War, as he could find no further references to its operation. However, the Commission was officially terminated in 1949, when it formally handed over its obligations and assets to the International Relief Committee of China. Whether the body was active in the intervening years is unclear, but it did exist as a formal organization.

CHAPTER 2

THE ONLY ROAD FOR MANKIND, 1933–1944

1. Odette Keun, *A Foreigner Looks at the TVA* (New York: Longmans, 1937), 5.

2. Ibid., 5.

3. George F. Kennan, "Memorandum for the Minister," August 19, 1932, reprinted in the *New York Review of Books,* April 26, 2001.

4. On this scholarly consensus, see John Lewis Gaddis, *The Cold War: A New History* (New York: Penguin Press, 2005); Melvyn P. Leffler, *For the Soul of Mankind: The United States, the Soviet Union, and the Cold War*, 1st ed. (New York: Hill and Wang, 2007); Odd Arne Westad, *The Global Cold War: Third World Interventions and the Making of Our Times* (Cambridge, New York: Cambridge University Press, 2005). See also David Engerman, "The Romance of Economic Development and New Histories of the Cold War," *Diplomatic History* 28 (Jan. 2004): 23–54.

5. Quoted in David Reynolds, *From Munich to Pearl Harbor: Roosevelt's America and the Origins of the Second World War* (Chicago: Ivan R. Dee, 2001), 30–31.

6. Mark Mazower, *Dark Continent: Europe's Twentieth Century*, 1st American ed. (New York: Knopf: Distributed by Random House, 1999), 3–17. Reinhold Niebuhr, *Reflections on the End of an Era* (New York, London: C. Scribner's Sons, 1934), 23. Harold Joseph Laski, *Democracy in Crisis* (Chapel Hill: University of North Carolina Press, 1933), 16–19, 237. See also Akira Iriye, *Cultural Internationalism and World Order* (Baltimore: Johns Hopkins University Press, 1997).

7. Raymond Blaine Fosdick, *Companions in Depression: The International Implications of the Business Slump* (New York: League of Nations Association, 1930).

8. James Thomson Shotwell and Raymond Blaine Fosdick, *The Conditions of Enduring Prosperity* (New York: Carnegie Endowment for International Peace, 1931).

9. Richard Pells, *Radical Visions and American Dreams: Culture and Social Thought in the Depression Years* (New York: Harper & Row, 1973).

10. Mazower, *Dark Continent*, 104–15. See also Wolfgang Schivelbusch, *Three New Deals: Reflections on Roosevelt's America, Mussolini's Italy, and Hitler's Germany, 1933–1939* (New York: Metropolitan Books, 2006); Robert O. Paxton, *The Anatomy of Fascism* (New York: Knopf, 2004), 32–42. R. J. Overy, *The Dictators: Hitler's Germany and Stalin's Russia*, 1st American ed. (New York: Norton, 2004).

11. Sinclair Lewis, *It Can't Happen Here* (1935, New York: Signet edition, 2005), 30.

12. *Official Guide Book of the Fair* (Chicago: A Century of Progress, 1933), 11; J. M. Winter, *Dreams of Peace and Freedom: Utopian Moments in the Twentieth Century* (New Haven, CT: Yale University Press, 2006). Lewis Mumford, *Technics and Civilization* (New York: Harcourt Brace & World, 1963), 3, 6.

13. John P. Diggins, *Mussolini and Fascism: The View from America* (Princeton, NJ: Princeton University Press, 1972).

14. *Official Guide*, 93.

15. R.J.B. Bosworth, *Mussolini's Italy: Life under the Dictatorship* (London: Allen Lane, 2005), 436–40. Frank M. Snowden, *The Conquest of Malaria: Italy, 1900–1962* (New Haven, CT: Yale University Press, 2006), 142–80.

16. Richard J. Evans, *The Third Reich in Power, 1933–1939* (New York: Penguin Press, 2005), 45–50, 322–28, 707–709. Mazower, *Dark Continent*, 133–37; Dan P. Silverman, *Hitler's Economy: Nazi Work Creation Programs, 1933–1936* (Cambridge, MA: Harvard University Press, 1998), 244–46; Schivelbusch, *Three*

New Deals, 173–83; Jeffry A. Frieden, *Global Capitalism: Its Fall and Rise in the Twentieth Century*, 1st ed. (New York: Norton, 2006), 214–15.

17. David Engerman, *Modernization from the Other Shore: American Intellectuals and the Romance of Russian Development* (Cambridge, MA: Harvard University Press, 2003), 153–93.

18. Stephen Kotkin, *Magnetic Mountain: Stalinism as a Civilization* (Berkeley: University of California Press, 1995); 21–35; Orlando Figes, *The Whisperers: Private Life in Stalin's Russia* (New York: Metropolitan Books, 2007).

19. Kotkin, *Magnetic Mountain*, 363; Soviet Union, "USSR in Construction" (Moscow: State Art Publishing House, 1930); William Henry Chamberlin, *The Soviet Planned Economic Order* (Boston: World Peace Foundation, 1931). See also Paul R. Josephson, *Industrialized Nature: Industrialized Nature Brute Force Technology and the Transformation of the Natural World* (Washington, DC: Island Press, 2002).

20. Martin Malia, *Russia Under Western Eyes: From the Bronze Horseman to the Lenin Mausoleum* (Cambridge, MA: Belknap Press, 1999), 314–56. See also Peter G. Filene, *Americans and the Soviet Experiment, 1917–1933* (Cambridge, MA: Harvard University Press, 1967).

21. Stuart Chase, *A New Deal* (New York: Macmillian, 1932), 235–41, 252.

22. Stuart Chase, "TVA: The New Deal's Best Asset, The Great Transition," *The Nation*, June 24, 1936, 804–805; Stuart Chase, "TVA: The New Deal's Best Asset, Broadening the Exchange Base," *The Nation*, June 10, 1936, 738–41; Stuart Chase, "TVA: The New Deal's Best Asset, Planning by Consent," *The Nation*, June 17, 1936, 775–77; Stuart Chase, "TVA: The New Deal's Best Asset, Landscape and Background," *The Nation*, June 3, 1936, 702–705.

23. Julian Huxley, *Africa View* (London: Chatto & Windus, 1931). Julian Huxley, *A Scientist Among the Soviets* (New York: Harper and Brothers, 1932), 60–61. On the international intellectual economy feeding the New Deal, see Daniel T. Rodgers, *Atlantic Crossings: Social Politics in a Progressive Age* (Cambridge, MA: Belknap Press, 1998), 409–84.

24. Huxley, *A Scientist*, 6, 14–15, 18, 34.

25. Julian Huxley, *If I Were Dictator* (New York: Harper and Brothers, 1935), 154–55; Huxley, *A Scientist*, 129–31.

26. Huxley, *Dictator*, 99–100.

27. Julian Huxley, "Plans for Tomorrow: The Tennessee Valley Authority," *The Listener*, Nov. 20, 1935, 897–900.

28. Julian Huxley, "The TVA: A Great American Experiment," *The Times*, May 21, 1935; and Julian Huxley, "The TVA—A Town in the Making," *The Times*, May 22, 1935.

29. James Scott, *Seeing Like a State: How Certain Schemes to Improve the Human Condition Have Failed* (New Haven, CT: Yale University Press, 1998), 6; David Nye, *Electrifying America: Social Meanings of a New Technology, 1880–1940* (Cambridge, MA: MIT Press, 1990), 298; David Kennedy, *Freedom from Fear: The American People in Depression and War, 1929–1945* (New York: Oxford University Press, 1999), 147–49; Erwin C. Hargrove and Paul K. Conkin, eds., *TVA: Fifty Years of Grass-Roots Bureaucracy* (Urbana: University of Illinois Press, 1983), 3–34.

30. Jordan A. Schwarz, *The New Dealers: Power Politics in the Age of Roosevelt* (New York: Vintage, 1993), xi–xii; Anthony J. Badger, *The New Deal: The Depression Years, 1933–1940* (New York: Basic books, reprint, Chicago: Ivan Dee, 2002), 169, 175–77; and "Tennessee Valley Authority Act," May 18, 1933, *New Deal Network*, http://newdeal.feri.org/html, Dec. 12, 2001; "Problem No. 1," *Time*, July 18, 1938; National Emergency Council, *Report on Economic Conditions of the South* (U.S. Government Printing Office, 1938).

31. Donald Worster, *Rivers of Empire: Water, Aridity, and the Growth of the American West* (New York: Pantheon Books, 1985), 5–15; World Commission on Dams, *Dams and Development: A New Framework for Decisionmaking* (Sterling: 2000), xxix; Richard White, *The Organic Machine: The Remaking of the Columbia River* (New York: Hill and Wang, 1995), 55–58; J. R. McNeill, *Something New Under the Sun: An Environmental History of the Twentieth Century World* (New York: Norton, 2000), 149–91; Earle S. Draper, "Regional Planning and the Tennessee Valley Authority," Jan. 14, 1935, box 242, RG 142 Records of the Tennessee Valley Authority, National Archives Southeast Region, Atlanta, Georgia (hereafter NAGA).

32. David Blackbourn, *The Conquest of Nature: Water, Landscape, and the Making of Modern Germany*, 1st American ed. (New York: Norton, 2006).

33. Milton to Arnett, May 22, 1933, box 159, RG 1, General Education Board, Series 1, RAC; Paul Hutchinson, "Revolution by Electricity," *Scribner's Magazine*, Oct. 1934, 194; Comments of A. S. Jandrey, Feb. 20, 1943, box 79, RG 142 Records of the Tennessee Valley Authority, NAGA; "Roosevelt's Development Plan Seen as Boon to South," *Greensboro Daily News*, April 3, 1933; Dewey W. Grantham, "TVA and the Ambiguity of American Reform," in Hargrove and Conkin, eds., *TVA*, 325.

34. Roy Talbert, Jr., *FDR's Utopian: Arthur Morgan of the TVA* (Jackson: University Press of Mississippi, 1987), 3–21, 59, 69–107, 111.

35. Badger, *New Deal*, 175; Jordan, *Machine-Age Ideology*, 245–47; and Talbert, *FDR's Utopian*, 110–14.

36. Richard A. Colignon, *Power Plays: Critical Events in the Institutionalization of the Tennessee Valley Authority* (Albany: State University of New York Press, 1997); Thomas K. McCraw, *TVA and the Power Fight, 1933–1939* (Philadelphia: Lippincott, 1971).

37. Ronald C. Tobey, *Technology as Freedom: The New Deal and Electrical Modernization* (Berkeley: University of California Press, 1996), 48, 50–51.

38. TVA Agricultural Engineering Department, "Community Refrigerators," Jan. 1941, box 160, Clapp to Mann, Dec. 18, 1941, box 159, RG 1, General Education Board, Series 1.1, Rockefeller Archive Center, North Tarrytown, New York (hereafter RAC).

39. Tennessee Valley Authority, *Communities for Living* (Tennessee Valley Authority, 1941); Talbert, *FDR's Utopian*, 116–22; Rodgers, *Crossings*, 462–68.

40. Advisory Committee on Education, "Regional and National Problems and Education's Contribution to their Solution," Sept. 21, 1937, box 13, President's Advisory Committee on Education, Franklin D. Roosevelt Library, Hyde Park, New York (hereafter FDRL), 22.

41. Tennessee Valley Authority Training Program, "A Tentative and Unofficial Statement of Work, Aims, and Objectives," March 21, 1935, box 160, RG 1, General Education Board, Series 1, RAC.

42. Advisory Committee on Education, "Educational Activities of the Tennessee Valley Authority," Aug. 27, 1937, box 13, President's Advisory Committee on Education, FDRL, 7–11; Talbert, *FDR's Utopian*, 118.

43. Nancy L. Grant, *TVA and Black Americans: Planning for the Status Quo* (Philadelphia: Temple University Press, 1990), 134. On racial exclusion and the New Deal, see Ira Katznelson, *When Affirmative Action Was White: An Untold History of Racial Inequality in Twentieth-Century America*, 1st ed. (New York: Norton, 2005).

44. Charles H. Houston and John P. Davis, "TVA: Lily-White," *Crisis* (October 1934): 290–91, 311; and Cranston Clayton, "The TVA and the Race Problem," *Opportunity* (April 1934), *New Deal Network*, http://newdeal.feri.org/texts/121.htm (last accessed Feb. 19, 2002).

45. Grant, *TVA and Black Americans*, 113.

46. Daniel Klingensmith, *"One Valley and a Thousand": Dams, Nationalism, and Development* (New Delhi: Oxford University Press, 2007).

47. Patrick D. Reagan, *Designing a New America: The Origins of New Deal Planning, 1890–1943* (Amherst: University of Massachusetts Press, 2000), 5–7.

48. T. Levron Howard, "The Social Scientist in the Tennessee Valley Authority Program," *Social Forces* 15 (Oct. 1936): 29–34; E. S. Wengert, "TVA Enlists Local Cooperation," *Public Opinion Quarterly* 1 (April 1937): 97–101; "Work Memorandum on the Plan of the Tennessee Valley Study," May 20, 1933; Odum to Walker, June 17, 1933, Thompson to Crane June 20, 1933, box 407, RG 1.1 Projects, Series 200 Social Science Research Council—Tennessee Valley Authority Administrative Development, 1935–1937, RAC.

49. E. L. Bishop, Director of Health, TVA, "The Health Program as a Contribution to the Population Engaged in the Economies of the Tennessee Valley," Feb. 1, 1937, box 132, RG 2, RAC.

50. Reagan, *Designing*, 224–25.

51. Walter Lippmann, *An Inquiry into the Principles of the Good Society* (Boston: Little, Brown, 1937), 3–4.

52. James Burnham, *The Managerial Revolution: What Is Happening in the World* (New York: John Day, 1941). Karl Mannheim and Edward Shils, *Man and Society in an Age of Reconstruction: Studies in Modern Social Structure* (New York: Harcourt, 1940), 6. Tony Judt, *Postwar: A History of Europe since 1945* (New York: Penguin Press, 2005), 68–70.

53. On the place of planning, see Guy Alchon, *The Invisible Hand of Planning: Capitalism, Social Science, and the State in the 1920s* (Princeton, NJ: Princeton University Press, 1985); John M. Jordan, *Machine-Age Ideology: Social Engineering and American Liberalism, 1911–1939* (Chapel Hill: University of North Carolina Press, 1994); McCraw, *TVA and the Power Fight, 1933–1939*; Edwin Vennard, "The Case Against TVA," 1943; Edwin Vennard, "Supplement to The Case Against TVA," 1944; Edwin Vennard, "Dangers of the TVA Method of River Control," 1945; box 1, Office of the Chairman and the Board of Directors, Records of David E. Lilienthal, RG 142, NAGA; David Nye, *Electrifying America,*

308–309; Donald Davidson, *The Tennessee,* vol. 2, *The New River: Civil War to TVA* (reprint, Nashville, 1992). Most Agrarians were optimistic about the effects of the TVA. See Edward Shapiro, "The Southern Agrarians and the Tennessee Valley Authority," *American Quarterly* 22 (Winter 1970): 791–806. See also Otis L. Graham, *Toward a Planned Society: From Roosevelt to Nixon* (New York: Oxford University Press, 1976).

54. Rodgers, *Crossings,* 452–61; Anthony Badger, *New Deal: The Depression Years* (New York: Hill and Wang, 2002), 176.

55. Neuse, *David E. Lilienthal,* 131, ch. 3–4.

56. "Digest of TVA," September–October 1933, box 407, RG 1.1 Projects, Series 200, RAC; Jordan, *Machine-Age Ideology,* 243–45; Talbert, *FDR's Utopian,* 169–94; Neuse, *David E. Lilienthal,* 93–108; Badger, *New Deal,* 175.

57. Remarks of Lilienthal, "For This We Fight: Public Works in Postwar America," Oct. 30, 1943, Audio Recording, RWA 8617B3–4, NBC Collection, Motion Picture, Broadcasting and Recorded Sound Division, Library of Congress, Washington, DC; quoted in John Gunther, *Inside U.S.A.* (New York, 1947), 748; David E. Lilienthal, "The TVA: An Experiment in the 'Grass Roots' Administration of Federal Functions," Nov. 10, 1939, box 20, David E. Lilienthal Papers, Mudd Library, Princeton University (hereafter MLP). For a later and broader discussion of this concept, see David E. Lilienthal, "The TVA and Decentralization," *Survey Graphic,* June 1, 1940, *New Deal Network,* http://newdeal.feri.org/texts/ 262.htm (last accessed Feb. 19, 2002).

58. Anthony Giddens, *The Consequences of Modernity* (Stanford: Stanford University Press, 1990), 151; Daniel Bell, *The Winding Passage: Sociological Essays and Journeys* (New Brunswick, NJ: Transaction Publishers, 1991), 69–70.

59. William E. Leuchtenberg, *Franklin D. Roosevelt and the New Deal, 1932–1940* (New York: Harper & Row, 1963), 345; Neuse, *David E. Lilienthal,* 131–32; Roosevelt to Morgan, May 15, 1936, box 166, Subject Files, President's Secretary's File, FDRL; Nye, *Electrifying America,* 343–44.

60. Alan Brinkley, *The End of Reform: New Deal Liberalism in Recession and War,* 1st Vintage Books ed. (New York: Vintage Books, 1996), 3–14. See also Thomas Bender, *A Nation among Nations: America's Place in World History,* 1st ed. (New York: Hill and Wang, 2006); Alan Brinkley, *Voices of Protest: Huey Long, Father Coughlin, and the Great Depression,* 1st Vintage Books ed. (New York: Vintage Books, 1983); Nancy Cohen, *The Reconstruction of American Liberalism, 1865–1914* (Chapel Hill: University of North Carolina Press, 2002).

61. John Dewey, *Liberalism and Social Action* (New York: G. P. Putnam, 1935), 41–62, 91–92. John Dewey, "Why I Am Not a Communist," *Modern Monthly* 8 (April 1934): 135–37; See also Robert B. Westbrook, *John Dewey and American Democracy* (Ithaca, NY: Cornell University Press, 1991).

62. Benjamin Alpers, *Dictators, Democracy, and American Public Culture: Envisioning the Totalitarian Enemy, 1920s–1950s* (Chapel Hill: University of North Carolina Press, 2003), 2–4; Iriye, *Cultural Internationalism and World Order.*

63. Mallory to Stolper, Dec. 15, 1936; "Rise of Dictator States in Europe, First Meeting," Jan. 6, 1937, box 39, Study Groups, Council on Foreign Relations Archives, MLP. On the Council, see Robert D. Schulzinger, *The Wise Men of*

Foreign Affairs: The History of the Council on Foreign Relations (New York: Columbia University Press, 1984).

64. Thomas R. Maddux, "Red Fascism and Brown Bolshevism: The American Image of Totalitarianism in the 1930s," *The Historian* 40 (Nov. 1977): 85–103; Les K. Adler and Thomas G. Paterson, "Red Fascism: The Merger of Nazi Germany and Soviet Russia in the American Image of Totalitarianism, 1930's–1950's," *American Historical Review* 75 (April 1970): 1046–1064.

65. Inderjeet Parmar, " 'To Relate Knowledge to Action' The Impact of the Rockefeller Foundation on Foreign Policy Thinking During America's Rise to Globalism, 1939–1945," *Minerva* 40 (2002): 235–63; Inderjeet Parmar, "The Carnegie Corporation and the Mobilization of Opinion in the United States' Rise to Globalism, 1939–1945," *Minerva* 37 (1999): 355–78.

66. Memo from Willits, Sept. 16, 1940, box 11, Rockefeller Foundation, RG 3, Series 910, RAC.

67. For Cold War views of totalitarianism, see Carl J. Friedrich, Michael Curtis, and Benjamin R. Barber, *Totalitarianism in Perspective: Three Views* (New York: Praeger, 1969); and Carl J. Friedrich, ed., *Totalitarianism: Proceedings of a Conference Held at the American Academy of Arts and Sciences* (Cambridge, MA: Harvard University Press, 1954).

68. "Studies of the Nature of Totalitarian Societies," Oct. 3, 1940; Memo from Willits, Aug. 19, 1940, box 11, Rockefeller Foundation, RG 3, Series 910, RAC.

69. Lasswell's analysis was inspired by the 1937 Sino-Japanese War and the role of Japanese military elites in its origins. Harold Dwight Lasswell and Jay Stanley, *Essays on the Garrison State* (New Brunswick, NJ; London: Transaction Publishers, 1997). Reynolds, *Roosevelt*, 180.

70. Ross A. Kennedy, "Woodrow Wilson, World War I, and an American Conception of National Security," *Diplomatic History* 25 (Winter 2001): 1–31.

71. On the idea's importance in the Cold War, see Aaron L. Friedberg, *In the Shadow of the Garrison State: America's Anti-Statism and Its Cold War Grand Strategy*, (Princeton, NJ: Princeton University Press, 2000). Melvyn Leffler, *The Specter of Communism: The United States and the Origins of the Cold War* (New York: Hill and Wang, 1994).

72. Akira Iriye, *The Cambridge History of American Foreign Relations*, vol. 3, *The Globalizing of America, 1913–1945* (New York: Cambridge University Press, 1993); 164–169; and David Reynolds, *From Munich to Pearl Harbor: Roosevelt's America and the Origins of the Second World War* (New York: Hill and Wang, 2001), 69–101, 102–32; Barbara Rearden Farnham, *Franklin Roosevelt and the Munich Crisis: A Study in Political Decision Making* (Princeton, NJ: Princeton University Press, 1997); Iriye, *Cultural Internationalism and World Order.* Frank Ninkovich, *Diplomacy of Ideas: U.S. Foreign Policy and Cultural Relations, 1938–1950* (New York: Cambridge University Press, 1981).

73. Frank A. Ninkovich, *The Wilsonian Century: U.S. Foreign Policy since 1900* (Chicago: University of Chicago Press, 1999), 124–25. J. B. Condliffe, *War and Depression* (Boston: World Peace Foundation, 1935); Henry A. Wallace, *America Must Choose* (New York: Foreign Policy Association, 1934). On the impact of nationalism and planning internationally, see Walter Lippmann, "Self-Sufficiency: Some Random Reflections," *Foreign Affairs* 12 (January 1934);

G.D.H. Cole, "Planning and International Trade," *Foreign Affairs* 12 (January 1934); Franklin Roosevelt, "Address at Chautauqua, New York," Aug. 14, 1936, American Presidency Project, http://www.presidency.ucsb.edu/ws/index .php?pid=15097&st=Chautauqua&st1=, accessed June 8, 2007.

74. Eugene Staley, "Cancellation of Allied War Debts," 1923; Eugene Staley, "Social and Economic Theories of Beatrice and Sidney Webb," 1926; Eugene Staley, "A Scheme for Reforming Economics and for Making it a Hypothetical Science," n.d., box 1; Eugene Staley Papers, HIA.

75. Simeon Strunsky, "Machines: The Threat Appraised," *New York Times*, Jan. 29, 1933; Raymond Blaine Fosdick, *The Old Savage in the New Civilization* (Garden City, NY: Doubleday Doran, 1928).

76. Eugene Staley, "What Price Self Sufficiency?" *Christian Science Monitor*, Sept. 22, 1937; Eugene Staley, *World Economy in Transition* (New York: Council on Foreign Relations, 1939), 206–22; Eugene Staley, *Raw Materials in Peace and War* (New York: Council on Foreign Relations, 1937).

77. Eugene Staley, "Power Economy versus Welfare Economy," *Annals of the American Academy of Political and Social Science* 198 (July 1938): 9–14; Staley, *World Economy*, 327–30.

78. Eugene Staley, "Economic Foundations of a Just and Enduring Peace," May 30, 1941, box 3, Staley Papers, HIA; Staley, *Raw*, 55–69.

79. Eugene Staley, "What Types of Economic Planning are Compatible with Free Institutions?" *Plan Age*, Feb. 1940, 33–50.

80. Staley, *World Economy*, 279–81.

81. Ibid., 68, 269–86, 333.

82. "Speech to Massachusetts League of Women Voters," Jan. 23, 1940, box 3, Transcripts of Radio Broadcasts, "University of Chicago Round Table," NBC Radio Network, various dates between 1938–1941, box 4; Eugene Staley, "Answer to Lindbergh," July 2, 1941, box 3, Staley Papers, HIA.

83. Charles Beard, *A Foreign Policy for America* (New York: Knopf, 1940); Jerome Frank, *Save America First* (New York: Harper and Brothers, 1938). See also Ronald Radosh and ebrary Inc., *Prophets on the Right: Profiles of Conservative Critics of American Globalism* (Cybereditions, 2001); available from http:// site.ebrary.com/lib/yale/Doc?id=10041217, online book.

84. Eugene Staley, "The Myths of Continents," in Hamilton Fish Armstrong, ed., *The Foreign Affairs Reader* (New York: Harper and Brothers, 1947), 318–33. Armstrong helped Staley refine his argument and the article was initially published in April 1941. Armstrong to Staley, March 29, 1941, box 3, Eugene Staley, "Can Capitalism Survive the War?" June 25, 1941, box 3, Eugene Staley, "The World is Round," Oct. 23, 1942, box 3; Staley Papers, HIA; Henry Luce, "The American Century," [1941], reprinted in *Diplomatic History*, Spring 1999, 159–71.

85. H.W. Arndt, "Development Economics Before 1945," in Jagdish Bhagwati and Richard Eckaus, eds., *Development and Planning: Essays in Honor of Paul Rosenstein Rodan*: (London: Allan and Unwin, 1972), 26; H. W. Arndt, "Economic Development: A Semantic History," *Economic Development and Cultural Change* 29 (April, 1981): 465.

86. Odette Keun, *My Adventures in Bolshevik Russia* (New York: Dodd, Mead, 1923). Julian Huxley, *Memories* (London: Allen and Unwin, 1970), 166; Odette Keun, *Darkness from the North* (London: Brinton, 1935).

87. Monique Reintjes, *Odette Keun: 1888–1978* (Netherlands: M. Reintjes, 2000). Keun, *Foreigner*, 5.

88. Keun, *Foreigner*, 4–5.

89. Odette Keun, *I Think Aloud in America* (New York: Longmans, 1939), 331, 336–37.

90. Keun, *Foreigner*, 89.

91. "Notes on a Luncheon Meeting between Arthur E. Morgan, Lewis Meriam, and Charles Ascher," Feb. 5, 1936, box 407, RG 1.1, Series 200, RAC; Frank Ninkovich, "The Rockefeller Foundation, China, and Cultural Change," *Journal of American History* 70 (March 1984): 799–820.

92. "Report on Administrative Organization of the Tennessee Valley Authority and Future Regional Authorities," May 14, 1937, box 166, President's Secretary's File, Franklin D. Roosevelt Library; William E. Leuchtenburg, "Roosevelt, Norris and the 'Seven Little TVAs,' " *Journal of Politics* 14 (Aug. 1952): 418–41.

93. J. B. Grant, "Tennessee Valley Authority," Dec. 19, 1934, box 407, RG 1.1, Series 200, RAC; May to Gough, June 9, 1937, box 147, RG 2, Series, 248, RAC.

94. Robert Rook, "Race, Water, and Foreign Policy: The Tennessee Valley Authority's Global Agenda Meets 'Jim Crow,' " *Diplomatic History* 28 (Jan. 2004): 55–81; Visitors six months of 1937, Nov. 30, 1937, box 620, RG 142, National Archives, NAGA; Leonard S. Hsu, "A Sociological View on Rural Reconstruction," *China Critic*, Dec. 26, 1935; Hayford, *To the People*, 177. See also Leonard S. Hsu, "Rural Reconstruction in China," *Pacific Affairs* 10 (Sept. 1937): 249–65.

95. "China Program Progress Report," April 15, 1936, box 12, Series 601 China, RG 1.1; Gunn to Fosdick, Dec. 9, 1936; Gunn to Sawyer, Oct. 19, 1937, box 13, Series 601 China, RG 1.2; Favrot to Gunn, March 31, 1937, box 1, Series 601 China, RG 1.2, RAC.

96. Memorandum "Policy Re China," Jan. 4, 1944, box 13, Series 601 China, RG 1.1, RAC.

97. Claude C. Erb, "Prelude to Point Four: The Institute of Inter-American Affairs," *Diplomatic History* 9 (Fall 1985): 249–69; Darlene Rivas, *Missionary Capitalist: Nelson Rockefeller in Venezuela* (Chapel Hill: University of North Carolina Press, 2002), 39–41.

98. Memorandum, Dec. 9, 1939; "Final Report on Visit to USA," Dec. 1939–Feb. 1940; "Interim Report on Visit to USA," Nov. 28–Dec. 1939, box 14.4, Isaiah Bowman Papers, Special Collections, Milton S. Eisenhower Library, Johns Hopkins University; R. L. Duffus, "Blueprint for a Post-War World," *New York Times*, Jan. 28, 1940.

99. Conference Proceedings, "The Economic and Political Bases of Durable Peace," April 1940, box 12, World Peace Foundation Papers, Swarthmore College Peace Collection. On the Nazi "New Order" in Europe, see Mark Mazower, *Hitler's Empire: How the Nazis Ruled Europe* (New York: Penguin Press, 2008).

100. Eugene Staley, "Toward a Durable Peace," *Common Sense Magazine*, April 2, 1942; Eugene Staley, "Economic Aspects of Relief and Rehabilitation," Aug. 26, 1943; Eugene Staley, "Foreign Investment as an Economic Investment," Jan. 5, 1944, box 3, Staley Papers, HIA; Percy Ellwood Corbett, *Post-War Worlds* (New York, London: Farrar and Rinehart, 1942); E. F. M. Durbin, *The Economic Basis of Peace* (London: National Peace Council, 1942); Henry P. Jordan and American Council on Public Affairs, *Problems of Post-War Reconstruction* (Washington, DC: American Council on Public Affairs, 1942). On the emphasis on prosperity in the postwar settlement see Elizabeth Borgwardt, *A New Deal for the World: America's Vision for Human Rights* (Cambridge, MA: Belknap Press of Harvard University Press, 2005).

101. Eugene Staley, *World Economic Development: Effects on Advanced Industrial Countries* (Montreal: International Labour Office, 1944), 15–20. Staley would put some of his conclusions about technical assistance into action while part of an UNRRA mission to China in 1944. See Eugene Staley, *Far Eastern Survey*, 13 (Oct. 1944), 183–85.

102. Staley, *Economic Development*, 5.

103. Staley to Rogers, Aug. 16, 1944, box 1, Staley Papers, HIA; Staley, *Economic Development*, 8, 190. Interestingly, a study instrumental to Staley's understanding of the significance of the TVA was by Herman Finer, a professor at the London School of Economics, whose research on the authority was funded by the Rockefeller Foundation.

104. Staley, *Economic Development*, 31–32.

CHAPTER 3
A GOSPEL OF LIBERALISM, 1943–1952

1. Harry S. Truman, "Inaugural Address," Jan. 20, 1949, *Public Papers of the Presidents of the United States, Harry S. Truman, 1949*, 112–16; and Truman "Inaugural Address," Jan. 20, 1949, video recording, Harry S. Truman Library, Independence Missouri (hereafter HTL).

2. Oral History Interview, Clark Clifford with Jerry Hess, March 16, 1972, http://www.trumanlibrary.org/oralhist/cliford6.htm, accessed Feb. 1, 2002, HTL.

3. Truman, "Inaugural Address," 116.

4. Robert Latham, *The Liberal Moment: Modernity, Security, and the Making of the Postwar International Order* (New York: Columbia University Press, 1997), 60–61.

5. David Reynolds, *One World Divisible: A Global History Since 1945* (New York: Norton, 2000), 9–11.

6. Richard Rhodes, *The Making of the Atomic Bomb* (New York: Simon & Schuster, 1986), 486–87; David Kennedy, *Freedom from Fear: The American People in Depression and War, 1929–1945* (New York: Oxford, 1999), 664–65; Erwin C. Hargrove, Paul Keith Conkin, and Vanderbilt Institute for Public Policy Studies, *TVA, Fifty Years of Grass-Roots Bureaucracy* (Urbana: University of Illinois Press, 1983).

7. Foreign Visitor Story, Dec. 24, 1943; File, April 12, 1943; box 619; Memo: Visit of French Journalists to the TVA, Jan. 30, 1945, box 346; File on Postwar Program for Visitors, August 7, 1945, box 619, Records of the General Manager, RG 142, NAGA.

8. Quoted in Charles Maier, "The Politics of Productivity: Foundations of American International Economic Policy After World War II," *International Organization* 31 (Autumn 1977), 615.

9. David E. Lilienthal, *TVA: Democracy on the March*, rev. ed. (New York: Harper, 1953), 196–200, 203–209. Ideas quoted here did not change from the first edition, published in 1944.

10. Steven M. Neuse, *David E. Lilienthal: The Journey of an American Liberal* (Knoxville: University of Tennessee Press, 1996), 135; and Erwin C. Hargrove, *Prisoners of Myth: The Leadership of the Tennessee Valley Authority, 1933–1990* (Princeton, NJ: Princeton University Press, 1994), 49.

11. Guinzburg to Lilienthal, June 19, 1945, box 288, Records of the General Manager, RG 142, NAGA.

12. Fairbank to Lilienthal, Nov. 8, 1944, box 288, Records of the General Manager, RG 142, NAGA; Lockhart to Collado, 27 April 1945, Office Files of the Asst. Sec. of State for Economic Affairs, 1944–1950 and the Under Secretary of State for Economic Affairs, 1946–1947, box 1, Record Group 59, HTL; Fairbank to Greene, May 19, 1944, box 23, Roger Sherman Greene Papers, HLH; Lilienthal, *Journals*, vol. 1, 696, 701; Chinese News Service Press Release, "Y.V.A. Project to be Carried out on Smaller Scale Within Six Years," 4 December 1945, box 1, John D. Sumner Papers, HTL; and Arthur N. Young, *China and the Helping Hand, 1937–1945* (Cambridge, MA: Harvard University Press, 1963), 393.

13. David Lilienthal, "Machines and the Human Spirit," Address at Radcliffe College, June 27, 1945, box 109 Lilienthal Papers, MLP.

14. Lilienthal, "Machines," 7.

15. David Lilienthal, "An American Development Program," Address at the University of North Carolina, Jan. 30, 1945, box 109, Lilienthal Papers, MLP.

16. David Lilienthal, "Will We Have a World TVA?" *Magazine Digest*, March 1945.

17. Julian Huxley, *On Living in a Revolution* (New York: Harper and Brothers, 1942), 139–46.

18. Julian Huxley, *Democracy Marches* (London: Chatto and Windus, 1941), 77–79, 92–93; Huxley, *Revolution*, 156–61. The two boosters likely cross-fertilized each other. *Democracy Marches* may have influenced Lilienthal's choice of *Democracy on the March* as the title of his 1944 book.

19. Julian Huxley, *TVA: Adventure in Planning* (London: Architectural Press, 1944), 7, 136.

20. Laski to Lilienthal, July 14, 1945, box 109, Lilienthal Papers, MLP; Herman Finer, *The TVA: Lessons for International Application* (Montreal: International Labour Office, 1944), i. On Wallace's view of how American "know-how" could contribute to an international New Deal for the postwar world, see Alonzo L. Hamby, *Beyond the New Deal: Harry S. Truman and American Liberalism* (New York: Columbia University Press, 1973), 22–27; Mark L. Kleinman,

A World of Hope, a World of Fear: Henry A. Wallace, Reinhold Niebuhr, and American Liberalism (Columbus: Ohio State University Press, 2000), 153–56.

21. Georg Brochmann, *The Adventure of TVA* Translation (Tiden Norsk Forlag: Oslo, 1945), box 1, Office of the Chairman and the Board of Directors, Records of David E. Lilienthal, RG 142, NAGA, 2, 4–5; F. A. Hayek, *The Road to Serfdom* (Chicago: University of Chicago Press, 1944), 247–48; "TVA for Wales," n.d. [1946], box 116, Lilienthal Papers, MLP; Wistrand to Lilienthal, May 25, 1944, box 348, Records of the General Manager, RG 142, NAGA; Commission on Palestine Surveys, Office Memo, Nov. 28, 1942, box 54, Records of the General Manager, RG 142, NAGA; Peter B. D. de la Mare, 'Working at the Grass Roots': A Forward Policy for New Zealand, A Digest of David E. Lilienthal's *TVA*, 1946, box 116, Lilienthal Papers, MLP; Indian Scientists Delegation—Visit to TVA, Dec. 19, 1945; Hume to Lilienthal, Jan. 17, 1944, box 347, Records of the General Manager, RG 142, NAGA.

22. Stuart Chase, "The New Energy," *The Nation*, Dec. 22, 1945.

23. Vannevar Bush, *Science—The Endless Frontier: Report to the President on a Program of Postwar Scientific Research* (Washington, DC: Government Printing Office, 1945), 1–7; G. Pascal Zachary, *Endless Frontier: Vannevar Bush: Engineer of the American Century* (New York: Free Press, 1997), 189–217, 257–59, 331–32; National Planning Association, "American Technologies in World Affairs," May 2, 1947, box 680, Office File, OF 129–B, HTL.

24. Dean Acheson, *Present at the Creation: My Years in the State Department* (New York: Norton, 1969), 68–69; "Notes on the Definition of Relief and Rehabilitation," May 23, 1943, box 263, Philip C. Jessup Papers, Manuscript Division, Library of Congress. It should be noted that at this point UNRRA was part of the "United Nations," the designation for the alliance waging war against the Axis powers. UNRRA would later fall under the banner of the United Nations Organization created in 1945.

25. Lehman to Clapp, Jan. 6, 1944, box 4, Gordon Clapp Papers, HTL; Timothy Walch and Dwight M. Miller, *Herbert Hoover and Harry S. Truman: A Documentary History* (Worland, WY: High Plains, 1992).

26. Dean Acheson, "U.S. Position Regarding UNRRA," Dec. 7, 1946, Decimal File, 1950–54, 800.49, RG 59, NAMD; William Adams Brown, Jr. and Redvers Opie, *American Foreign Assistance* (Washington, DC: Brookings Institution, 1953), 109–11.

27. Brown and Opie, *American Foreign Assistance*, 111; and George Woodbridge, *UNRRA*, vol. 3 (1950), 476–80.

28. Akira Iriye, *Cultural Internationalism and World Order* (Baltimore: Johns Hopkins University Press, 1997), 146–47.

29. United Nations Charter, Chapter IX, Article 55(a), http://www.un.org/aboutun/charter/chapter9.htm, accessed January 23, 2002; Paul Kennedy, *The Parliament of Man: The Past Present and Future of the United Nations* (New York: Random House, 2006), 115–17; Gary Ostrower, *The United Nations and the United States* (New York: Twayne, 1998), 35; Prasad Singh, *The Politics of Economic Cooperation in Asia: A Study of Asian International Organizations* (Columbia: University of Missouri Press, 1966), 53, 58.

30. Gove Hambidge, *The Story of FAO* (New York: Van Nostrand, 1955), 73–74; Malcom Gladwell, "The Mosquito Killer," *The New Yorker*, July 2, 2001, 42.

31. Frank M. Snowden, *The Conquest of Malaria: Italy, 1900–1962* (New Haven, CT: Yale University Press, 2006). Hughes Evans, "European Malaria Policy in the 1920s and 1930s," *Isis* 80 (1989): 40–59; Socrates Listos, "Malaria Control, the Cold War, and the Postwar Reorganization of International Assistance," *Medical Anthropology* 17 (1997): 265–67.

32. United Nations Preparatory Educational Scientific and Cultural Commission and Henry W. Holmes, *Fundamental Education, Common Ground for All Peoples; Report of a Special Committee to the Preparatory Commission of the United Nations Educational, Scientific and Cultural Organization, Paris, 1946* (New York,: Macmillan, 1947).

33. "UNESCO World Review," Radio Broadcast Transcript, April 9, 1949; "Is UNESCO the Key to International Understanding?" Radio Broadcast Transcript, NBC University of the Air, June 1, 1946.

34. Devesh Kapur, John P. Lewis, and Richard Webb, *The World Bank: Its First Half Century*, vol. 1 (Washington, DC: Brookings Institution Press, 1997), 68–69.

35. H. D. White, "Proposal for a Bank for Reconstruction and Development of the United and Associated Nations," March 1942; Henry Dexter White, "Proposal for United Nations Stabilization Fund and a Bank for Reconstruction and Development of the United and Associated Nations," April 1942, box 8 Harry Dexter White Papers, MLP, 3–5.

36. Jochen Kraske et al., *Bankers with a Mission: The Presidents of the World Bank, 1946–1991* (New York: Oxford University Press, 1996), 76. See also Kapur, Lewis, and Webb, *The World Bank: Its First Half Century*.

37. P. S. Lokanathan to Chief Diplomatic Officer, SCAP, September 17, 1948, reel 136, Subject File of the Secretariat General, 1945–1952, RG 43, NAMD. See also Harald Fuess, ed., *The Japanese Empire in East Asia and Its Postwar Legacy* (Munich: Iudicium, 1998).

38. United Nations, *United Nations Work and Programs for Technical Assistance* (New York: United Nations, 1952), 6–7.

39. *Technical Assistance for Economic Development: Plan for an Expanded Programme Through the United Nations and the Specialized Agencies* (Lake Success: United Nations, 1949), 10, 21; Department of State Policy Statement Regarding the United Nations, Sept. 18, 1950, *Papers Relating to the Foreign Relations of the United States* (hereafter FRUS), 1950, vol. 2, *The United Nations; The Western Hemisphere* (Washington, DC: GPO, 1976), 29–46; and Ostrower, *United Nations*, 151.

40. Gant to Bass, Sept. 14, 1948, box 216, Files of the General Manager, RG 142, NAGA.

41. Lilienthal to Wallace, June 19, 1945, box 222, Files of the General Manager, RG 142, NAGA.

42. Clapp to Barrett, Aug. 23, 1949, box 216; Barrett Shelton, "The Decatur Story," Address to the UN Scientific Conference on the Conservation and Utilization of Resources, Sept. 5, 1949; Gordon R. Clapp, "The Experience of the Tennessee Valley Authority in the Comprehensive Development of a River Basin,"

United Nations Scientific Conference on the Conservation and Utilization of Resources, Sept. 5, 1949, box 217, Files of the General Manager, RG 142, NAGA.

43. United Nations Visit, Aug. 19, 1949, box 217, Files of the General Manager, RG 142, NAGA. Acheson to Lilienthal, July 3, 1946; Memo: Gant to Clapp, "Arrangements for Assistance to the United Nations," July 11, 1946; Fletcher to Lilienthal, Sept. 12, 1946; Memo of Caso, "Meeting of TVA Staff With Mr. Howard K. Menhinick," Jan. 29, 1947; box 217, Files of the General Manager, RG 142, NAGA.

44. Michael Hogan, *The Marshall Plan: America, Britain and the Reconstruction of Western Europe, 1947–1952* (New York: Cambridge University Press, 1987), 5–25; Charles Maier, "The Politics of Productivity: Foundations of American International Economic Policy After World War II," *International Organization* 31 (Autumn, 1977): 607–33.

45. Report to the International Secretariat to the Pacific Council, vol. 1, August 1947, box 471, Institute of Pacific Relations Papers, RBML.

46. IPR Pacific Council Minutes, Stratford-upon-Avon, 1947, box 470, Institute of Pacific Relations Papers, RBML, 74.

47. H. Belshaw, "Agricultural Reconstruction in the Far East," paper given at Stratford Conference, Sept. 1947, box 471, Institute of Pacific Relations Papers, RBML.

48. See also John De Francis, "Japanese Language Reform: Politics and Phonetics," and Daniel C. Holtom, "Ideographs and Ideas," *Far Eastern Survey*, Nov. 5, 1947, 217–23.

49. Shirley Jenkins, "The Stratford Conference," *Far Eastern Survey*, Oct. 15, 1947, 209–213.

50. "Memorandum on Far Eastern Economic Policy," March 23, 1948, reel 151, U.S. Delegation Subject Files, 1945–1952, RG 43 Records of International Conferences, Commissions, and Exhibitions, NAMD, 1–2, 4–5, 8–10, 16.

51. "Preliminary Proposals for an Economic Coordination Program for the Far East," Oct. 14, 1948; "Far Eastern Recovery Program," Oct. 14, 1948, reel 151, U.S. Delegation Subject Files, 1945–1952, RG 43 Records of International Conferences, Commissions, and Exhibitions, NAMD.

52. Nitze to Butterworth, "A Coordinated Economic Policy for the Far East," Oct. 26, 1948, reel 151, U.S. Delegation Subject Files, 1945–1952, RG 43, NAMD.

53. Butterworth, Satterthwaite, Labouisse, and Nitze, "Coordinated Policy for the Far East," Nov. 22, 1948, reel 151, U.S. Delegation Subject Files, 1945–1952, RG 43, NAMD.

54. "Coordinated Policy for the Far East."

55. For a discussion of the IIAA's programs, see Cary Reich, *The Life of Nelson Rockefeller: Worlds to Conquer, 1908–1958* (New York: Doubleday, 1996) and Claude C. Erb, "Prelude to Point Four: The Institute of Inter-American Affairs," *Diplomatic History* 9 (Fall 1985): 249–69.

56. Sergei Shenin, *The United States and the Third World: The Origins of Postwar Relations and the Point Four Program* (Commack, NY: Nova Science, 2000), 8–12.

57. Hardy to Russell, "Use of U.S. Technological Resources as a Weapon in the Struggle with International Communism," Nov. 23, 1948, box 1, Hardy Papers, HTL.

58. Shenin, *United States and the Third World*, 12–13; Ken Hechler, *Working with Truman: A Personal Memoir of the White House Years* (New York: Putnam, 1982), 118.

59. Clark Clifford and Richard C. Holbrooke, *Counsel to the President: A Memoir* (New York: Random House, 1991), 251. Clifford claimed that Acheson read the draft speech including the technical assistance plan and proclaimed it "splendid."

60. Harry Truman, *Memoirs*, vol. 2, *Years of Trial and Hope, 1946–1952* (New York: Doubleday, 1956), 231.

61. Office of Public Affairs, Dept. of State, "Point Four" (Washington, DC, Feb. 1949); Shenin, *United States and the Third World*, 13–14; Discussion Meeting Report, June 10, 1949, box 3.7, Isaiah Bowman Papers, Special Collections, Johns Hopkins University; Merle Curti, *Prelude to Point Four: American Technical Missions Overseas, 1838–1938* (Madison: University of Wisconsin Press, 1954).

62. Harry S. Truman, "Remarks at the Women's National Democratic Club Dinner," Nov. 8, 1949, *Public Papers, Harry S. Truman, 1949*, 557 and "Point IV," *Fortune*, Feb. 1950, 88–89.

63. Advisory Committee on Technical Assistance, "Objectives and Nature of the Point IV Program," April 19, 1949, box 86, Records of Interagency Mobilization Planning Committee on the Framework of International Economic Cooperation, RG 353, NAMD.

64. Richard Pells, *The Liberal Mind in a Conservative Age: American Intellectuals in the 1940s and 1950s*, 2nd ed. (Middletown, CT: Wesleyan University Press, 1989), 52–116; Alonzo Hamby, *Beyond the New Deal: Harry S. Truman and American Liberalism* (New York: Columbia University Press, 1973).

65. Gunther, *Inside U.S.A.*, 748; Visitor File, John Gunther, March 27, 1945, box 619, Records of the General Manager, RG 142, NAGA.

66. Henry Steele Commager, *The American Mind: An Interpretation of American Thought and Character Since the 1880's* (New Haven, CT: Yale University Press, 1950), 344–45.

67. Morris Llewellyn Cooke, "Down to Earth with Point Four," *The New Republic*, July 11, 1949, 18–21.

68. Arthur Schlesinger, Jr., *The Vital Center: The Politics of Freedom* (Boston: Houghton Mifflin, 1949), 183–86, 230–34.

69. Walter Lippmann, "Two Approaches to the Misery of Asia," *Washington Post*, Jan. 25, 1950. See also *Final Report of the United Nations Economic Survey Mission for the Middle East* (Lake Success, 1949).

70. Henry Hazlitt, *Illusions of Point Four* (Irvington-on-Hudson, NY: Foundation for Economic Education, 1950), 31, 44–46.

71. Willard R. Espy, *Bold New Program* (New York: Harper, 1950), 14, 201–202; Pells, *The Liberal Mind*, 76–83; and Brinkley, *End of Reform*, 154–64. On the TVA as an export commodity of the New Deal, see Jordan A. Schwartz, *The*

New Dealers: Power Politics in the Age of Roosevelt (New York: Vintage, 1993), 324–42.

72. George F. Kennan, "Where Do We Stand," Dec. 21, 1949; George F. Kennan "Problems of Far Eastern Policy," Jan. 14, 1948, box 17, George F. Kennan Papers, MLP; John Lewis Gaddis, *Strategies of Containment: A Critical Appraisal of Postwar American National Security Policy During the Cold War* rev. ed. (New York: Oxford University Press, 2005), 34–41.

73. George F. Kennan, "Basic Objectives of United States Foreign Policy," Foreign Service Institute, Jan. 19, 1949, box 17, Kennan Papers, MLP. On Kennan's views of the developing world, see George F. Kennan, *Memoirs, 1925–1960* (Boston: Little Brown, 1967); George F. Kennan, *Realities of America Foreign Policy* (Princeton, NJ: Princeton University Press, 1954); See also Anders Stephanson, *Kennan and the Art of Foreign Policy* (Cambridge, MA: Harvard University Press, 1989).

74. Melvyn Leffler, *A Preponderance of Power: National Security, the Truman Administration, and the Cold War* (Stanford, CA: Stanford University Press, 1992), 291.

75. Waldo to Clapp, Nov. 13, 1950, box 620, Records of the General Manager's Office, Administrative Files, 1933–1957, RG 142, NAGA.

76. A. M. Rosenthal, "Nehru Sees Defeat for One Ideology," *New York Times*, Oct. 20, 1949.

77. Committee on Policy and Program Report, Dec. 3–4, 1946, box 60, RG 3.2, Series 900, RAC.

78. Problems of Less Industrialized Areas, Feb. 17, 1948, box 60, RG 3.2, Series 900, RAC.

79. Memo: SS and Under-developed Areas, March 10, 1948, box 60, RG 3.2, Series 900, RAC.

80. Memo: SS and Under-developed Areas, March 10, 1948.

81. Memo: Comments on a Policy of SS Operational Programs in the World's Backwards Areas, March 21, 1949, box 60, RG 3.2, Series 900, RAC.

82. Rough Draft of Notes on Backward Areas Discussion, April 5, 1949; Philip Mosley, Feb. 3, 1949, box 60, RG 3.2, Series 900, RAC; Edward H. Berman, "Rockefeller Philanthropy and the Social Sciences: International Perspectives," in Theresa Richardson and Donald Fisher, eds., *The Development of the Social Sciences in the United States and Canada: The Role of Philanthropy* (Stamford, CT: Ablex Publishing, 1999), 199.

83. Study of Efforts to Help Backwards Peoples Help Themselves, June 22, 1949, box 60, RG 3.2, Series 900, RAC.

84. Fosdick to Clapp, Jan. 19, 1950, box 3, Clapp Papers, HTL.

85. For a discussion of the larger effort the survey mission was attached to, see Rebekah C. Beatty Davis, "Development as a Tool of Diplomacy: The Domestic Models for United States Policy in the Jordan River Valley, 1939–1956," Ph.D. diss. Georgetown University, 1999.

86. Gordon Clapp, "TVA: A Democratic Method for the Development of a Region's Resources," Feb. 10, 1948, box 2, Clapp Papers, HTL.

87. Memo: Meeting with the Voluntary Interests, Sept. 1, 1949, box 3, Clapp Papers, HTL.

88. Acheson to Truman, March 14, 1949, box 679, Truman Papers–Official File, HTL.

89. Advisory Committee on Technical Assistance, "Enlisting and Aiding Participation by Private Non-Profit Groups in Point IV Program," May 31, 1949, box 86, Records of Interagency Mobilization Planning Committee on the Framework of International Economic Cooperation, RG 353, NAMD.

90. Black to Lloyd, "Study of Voluntary Activities in Underdeveloped Areas," Nov. 20, 1950, box 19, David Lloyd Papers, HTL.

91. Technical Cooperation Administration, "Voluntary Groups and Private Organizations in the Point 4 Program," April 1952, box 20, Lloyd Papers, HTL.

92. Amanda Kay Mcvety, "Pursuing Progress: Point Four in Ethiopia," *Diplomatic History* 32 (Summer 2008): 371–403.

93. James Dahir, *Region Building: Community Development Lessons from the Tennessee Valley* (New York: Harper, 1955) 158–76.

94. Charnow to Shaffer, March 8, 1946, box 4144; Gates to Wood, April 22, 1946, box, 4147, Decimal File, 1950–54, 800.49, RG 59, NAMD.

95. Charles Bloomstein, "History of CARE," chapter 15 (unpublished manuscript), 1955, box 1, CARE Archives, Manuscripts Division, New York Public Library, New York City. As its role changed, so would CARE's title, with the "R" altered to "Relief" and the "E" edited to reflect a mission to "Everywhere."

96. Hooper to Stokes, Jan. 18, 1946, box 26, Phelps-Stokes Fund Papers, Schomburg Center for Research in Black Culture, New York City (hereafter SCR).

97. Report of the Executive Secretary for 1949–1950, Agricultural Missions Inc., Sept. 1950, box 49, Phelps-Stokes Fund Papers, SCR.

98. Laubach to Truman, Feb. 6, 1952; Laubach to Truman, Dec. 13, 1952, box 680, Harry S. Truman Papers–Official File, HTL; *Doorway to the 20th Century*, Nov. 15, 1955.

99. Cambell to Lloyd, Nov. 20, 1950, box 19, Lloyd Papers, HTL.

100. Nelson Rockefeller, "Comments on Foreign Aid," April 9, 1951, Meeting Reports, CFR Archives, MLP.

101. Charles Collingwood, CBS News Transcript, Nov. 29, 1949, box 679, Truman Papers–Official File, HTL.

102. Steward Alsop, "Point 4 Began as a 'Punchline,'" *Washington Post*, Jan. 30, 1949; *Worcester Telegram*, Jan. 28, 1949, cited in "Information Demands on Point Four Program," Feb. 8, 1949, box 1, Hardy Papers, HTL; Thomas G. Patterson, *Meeting the Communist Threat: Truman to Reagan* (New York: Oxford University Press, 1988), 152.

103. Shenin, *United States and the Third World*, 55.

104. Quoted in ibid., 60.

105. Ibid., 64.

106. Patterson, *Meeting the Communist Threat*, 157.

107. Joseph V. Kennedy and Vernon W. Ruttan, "A Reexamination of Professional and Popular Thought on Assistance for Economic Development: 1949–1952," *Journal of Developing Areas* 20 (April 1986): 311–15.

108. U.S. Special Assistant to the President [Gordon Gray], *Report to the President on Foreign Economic Policies* (Washington, DC: GPO, 1950).

109. Report to the President by the International Development Advisory Board, *Partners in Progress* (March 1951), 26–27, 62–68, 70. The Rockefeller report met a cool reception, meaning thousands of copies simply sat in storage. See Reich, *Nelson Rockefeller*, 461.

110. Brown and Opie, *American Foreign Assistance,* 508; Charles Wolf, Jr., *Foreign Aid: Theory and Practice in Southeast Asia* (Princeton, NJ: Princeton University Press, 1960), 53–55; and Chester J. Pach, Jr., *Arming the Free World: The Origins of the United States Military Assistance Program, 1945–1950* (Chapel Hill: University of North Carolina Press, 1991).

111. Mutual Security Program, *Second Report to Congress on the Mutual Security Program* (Washington, DC: GPO, 1952).

112. Harriman to Truman, Jan. 5, 1952, box 1024, Truman Papers–Official File, HTL.

113. Brien McMahon, August 27, 1951, box 1023, Truman Papers–Official File, HTL.

114. Collingwood to Short, May 1, 1952, box 680, Truman Papers–Official File, HTL; Jonathan Bingham, *Shirtsleeve Diplomacy: Point Four in Action* (New York: John Day, 1953), xi.

115. Eugene Staley, *The Future of Underdeveloped Countries: Political Implications of Economic Development*, rev. ed. (New York: Council on Foreign Relations, 1960). The revised edition included a new afterword; however, Staley did not think the core issues had changed since the book's initial publication in 1954, so the sections on which this discussion was based were not altered for the revised edition.

116. "Political Implications of Economic Development," Fourth Meeting, June 5, 1952, Study Groups, box 46; Eugene Staley, Working Paper, Study Group on Political Implications of Economic Development, Oct. 28, 1952, Study Groups, box 46, CFR, MLP; Staley, *Future*, 5–6, 40, 119–120.

117. Staley, *Future*, 195.

118. Ibid., 94–95, 173.

119. Ibid., 29–35, 190, 236.

CHAPTER 4
"THE PROVING GROUND," 1945–1960

1. Andrew John Rotter, *The Path to Vietnam: Origins of the American Commitment to Southeast Asia* (Ithaca, NY: Cornell University Press, 1987), 191; and Samuel P. Hayes, *The Beginnings of American Aid to Southeast Asia: The Griffin Mission of 1950* (Lexington, MA: Heath Lexington Books, 1971), 8–9, 12–13; Annex to Memo for the President, "Allocation of Section 303 Funds to Provide Economic Assistance for Indochina," April 17, 1950, box 25, Central File, HTL; Record of an Interdepartmental Meeting on the Far East at the Department of State, May 11, 1950 *FRUS 1950* vol. 6, 87–90; R. A. Griffin, "Challenge of Southeast Asia," June 24, 1950, box 12, R. Allen Griffin Papers, Hoover Institution. Marginal notes on this document state that the speech was concluded with the news that North Korea had attacked the South.

2. Chinese News Service Press Release, "Y.V.A. Project to be Carried out on Smaller Scale Within Six Years," Dec. 4, 1945, box 1, John D. Sumner Papers, HTL; Arthur N. Young, *China and the Helping Hand, 1937–1945* (Cambridge, MA: Harvard University Press, 1963), 393; "Program and Estimated Requirements for Relief and Rehabilitation in China Presented to the United Nations Relief and Rehabilitation Administration by the Government of the Republic of China," Sept. 1944, box 1, UNRRA China Office Papers, HI, 7.

3. *UNRRA: The History of the United Nations Relief and Rehabilitation Administration*, vol. 2 (New York: Columbia University Press, 1950), 401, 417–19, 424–25, 430–31; William Adams Brown, Jr., and Redvers Opie, *American Foreign Assistance* (Washington, DC: Brookings Institution, 1953), 111; and United Nations Relief and Rehabilitation Administration, *UNRRA in China, 1945–1947* (Washington, DC: United Nations, 1948), 199–200, 232.

4. Memorandum by the Staff Committee of the National Advisory Council on International Monetary and Financial Problems to the National Advisory Council, Feb. 14, 1947, *FRUS 1947*, vol. 1, *General: The United Nations* (Washington, DC: GPO, 1973), 1031. However, this did not mean the United States wanted to abandon entirely multilateral means to deliver aid and technical assistance.

5. Robert A. Packenham, *Liberal America and the Third World: Political Development Ideas in Foreign Aid and Social Science* (Princeton, NJ: Princeton University Press, 1973), 35; and C. X. George Wei, "The Economic Cooperation Administration, the State Department, and the American Presence in China, 1948–1950," *Pacific Historical Review* 70 (Aug. 2001): 21–53.

6. Memo, March 30, 1949, box 1 Roger D. Lapham Papers, HIA; Memorandum for Mr. Hoffman, Dec. 11, 1948, box 16, Dwight Edwards Papers, YDSL; Harlan Cleveland, "Where do we go From Here?" July 31, 1948, box 3, R. Allen Griffin Papers, HIA, 9; and Economic Cooperation Administration China Program Division, "A Brief Summary of the Background and Programs of the Chinese-American Joint Commission for Rural Reconstruction," n.d. (1948), box 3, Griffin Papers, HI, 1–2.

7. Hayford, *To the People*, 212–13; Raymond T. Moyer, "Recommendations for Rural Reconstruction," July 24, 1948, box 6, John D. Sumner Papers, HTL. Moyer was later a commissioner on the Joint Commission for Rural Reconstruction.

8. "Objectives and Principles of the Program of the Joint Commission on Rural Reconstruction," box 40, Chang Fu-liang Papers, YSDL; Economic Cooperation Administration China Program Division, "A Brief Summary of the Background and Program of the Chinese-American Joint Commission for Rural Reconstruction," Sept. 1949, box 21, Fosdick Papers, MLP; Chang Fu-liang, "Working Together for the Common Good," Report for the Officers and Directors of the Rockefeller Foundation, box 40, Chang Fu-liang Papers, YSDL; Memo for the President, Sept. 13, 1948, box 536, Official File, OF-150F, HTL; Irrigation Engineering Division, Joint Commission on Rural Reconstruction, "History of JCRR Engineering Program," n.d. [1950], box 46, Todd Papers, HIA; and Todd, *The China that I Knew*, 162–66.

9. Grant to Cleveland, Sept. 13, 1949, box 21, Fosdick Papers, MLP; Economic Cooperation Administration, *The Program of the Joint Commission on*

Rural Reconstruction in China: Its Organization, Accomplishments, and Lessons for Rural Reconstruction Elsewhere in Asia, 1951, 4–5, 29; Raymond W. Miller, "Our Economic Policy in Asia," *Harvard Business Review* 4 (July 1951): 52–70; Melvin Conant, Jr., "JCRR: An Object Lesson," *Far Eastern Survey*, May 2, 1951, 88; Barbara Ward, "Recipe for a Victory in the Far East," *New York Times*, March 25, 1951; Richard Lee Hough, "Models of Rural Development Administration: The JCRR Experience in Taiwan," May 1968, SEADAG Paper, USAID Library Doc., PN–ABI–359.

10. *The Program of the Joint Commission on Rural Reconstruction in China*, 19–26; Joseph A. Yager, *Transforming Agriculture in Taiwan: The Experience of the Joint Commission on Rural Reconstruction* (Ithaca, NY: Cornell University Press, 1988), 210–11.

11. Robert L. Beisner, *Dean Acheson: A Life in the Cold War* (New York: Oxford University Press, 2006), 120, 86.

12. Fosdick to Webb, Sept. 18, 1949; Fosdick, "Memorandum for Mr. Jessup," Dec. 2, 1949; Cleveland to Fosdick, Sept. 8, 1949; Du Bois to Fosdick, Oct, 26, 1949, box 21, Fosdick Papers, MLP; Raymond Fosdick, "Asia's Challenge to Us—Ideas, Not Guns," Feb. 12, 1950, *New York Times*.

13. Fosdick to Jessup, "Some Random Thoughts on the Far East," Dec. 2, 1949; Lapham and Griffin to Jessup, "Opinions Relative to a Continuing U.S. Policy in the Far East," Sept. 14, 1949, box 21, Fosdick Papers, MLP; Hayes, *Beginnings of American Aid to Southeast Asia*, 4–6.

14. Charlton Ogburn, Memorandum of Conversation, "Oral Report by Ambassador-at-Large Philip C. Jessup upon his Return from the East," April 3, 1950, *FRUS, 1950*, vol. 6, *East Asia and the Pacific*, 69, 75.

15. Harlan Cleveland, "Problems of Economic Development in the Far East," in John K. Fairbank, ed., *Next Step in Asia* (Cambridge, MA: Harvard University Press, 1949), 26–28; Harland Cleveland, "Economic Aid to China," *Far Eastern Survey*, Jan. 12, 1949, 1–6.

16. Cleveland, "Problems," 26, 40.

17. Bruce Cumings, *Origins of the Korean War*, vol. 1 (Princeton, NJ: Princeton University Press, 1981), 102.

18. Ibid., 104, 107.

19. Spencer Coxe, "Korea's Relief Needs," July 6, 1945, reel FE/4, UNRRA Papers, Lehman Suite, Columbia University.

20. UNRRA, *UNRRA: The History of the United Nations Relief and Rehabilitation Administration*, 462–64. Most supplies sent to the North were medicines, railroad supplies, and trucks, while the South mainly received medicines, agricultural supplies, and textiles.

21. Cumings, *Origins*, vol. 1, 114–21, 124–29.

22. Ibid., 54–60; Ronald H. Spector, *In the Ruins of Empire: The Japanese Surrender and the Battle for Postwar Asia* (New York: Random House, 2007).

23. Bruce Cumings, *Korea's Place in the Sun: A Modern History* (New York: Norton, 1997), 142–43.

24. *Report on the Occupation Area of South Korea Since Termination of Hostilities*, Part I, Political, Sept. 1947, reel 15, RG 59, Records of the Bureau of Far

Eastern Affairs, Records of the Directors of Northeast Asia Affairs, Records of Northeast Asian Affairs relating to Foreign Policy Decisions, Records of the Office of Northeast Asian Affairs (Briefing Books), 1943–1956, NAMD, 4.

25. *Report on the Occupation*, Part I, 5–6.

26. Ibid., 4–5.

27. Pauly to Truman, June 22, 1946, *FRUS, 1946*, vol. 8, 706–709, 713–14; Ronald L. McGlothlen, *Controlling the Waves: Dean Acheson and U.S. Foreign Policy in Asia* (New York: Norton, 1993), 56–57; William Stueck, *The Wedemeyer Mission: American Politics and Foreign Policy During the Cold War* (Athens: University of Georgia Press, 1984), 64.

28. *Report on the Occupation Area of South Korea Since Termination of Hostilities*, Part II Economic, "Rehabilitation Program for South Korea," 1–4.

29. McGlothlen, *Controlling the Waves,* 58.

30. "Memorandum for Lt. Gen. A. C. Wedemeyer," July 28, 1947, box 95, Albert C. Wedemeyer Papers, HIA.

31. *Report to the President Submitted by Lt. Gen. A. C. Wedemeyer,* September 1947 (Washington, DC: GPO, 1951), 7, 5–6, 13–14, 17, 21, 22–23.

32. Mason et al., *Economic and Social Modernization,* 169.

33. Noel F. McGinn, Donald R. Snodgrass, Yung Bong Kim, Shin-Bok Kim, and Quee-Young Kim, *Education and Development in Korea* (Cambridge, MA: Harvard University Press, 1980), 81–84; UNESCO, *Rebuilding Education in the Republic of Korea* (Frankfurt, 1954), 23–24; Mason et al., *Economic and Social Modernization,* 344; Don Adams and Esther E. Gottlieb, *Education and Social Change in Korea* (New York: Garland, 1993), 12.

34. McGinn et al., *Education and Development,* 12, 86–87; HUSAFIK, vol. 4, 524, 544; Mason et al., *Economic and Social Modernization,* 344–45.

35. "Overall Statement on the Far East," July 29, 1947, box 12, RG 1.1 Projects, Series 601, RAC, 3; HUSAFIK, vol. 4, 525, 531.

36. HUSAFIK, vol. 4, 602–604.

37. Grant, Nov. 5, 1945, and Grant, June 27, 1946, box 1, RG 1.1 Projects, Series 613 Korea, RAC; Adams and Gottlieb, *Education and Social Change,* 106.

38. HUSAFIK, vol. 4, 499; Ross Harold Cole, "The Koreanization of Elementary Citizenship education in South Korea, 1948–1974," Ph.D. diss. Arizona State University, 1975, 402.

39. John Lie, *Han Unbound: The Political Economy of South Korea* (Stanford, CA: Stanford University Press, 1998), 17; McGinn et al., *Education and Development,* 241.

40. HUSAFIK, vol. 4, 302; Address given by Robert Kinney, U.S. Economic Advisory Staff, U.S. Army Military Government in Korea, "The Food Position of South Korea as of 1 May, 1946," reel FE/4, UNRRA Papers, Lehman Suite.

41. Atul Kohli, "Where Do High-Growth Political Economies Come From? The Japanese Lineage of Korea's 'Developmental State,'" in Meredith Woo-Cumings, ed., *The Developmental State* (Ithaca, NY: Cornell University Press, 1999), 115; HUSAFIK, vol. 4, 353–86.

42. HUSAFIK, vol. 4, 436–40; Anne O. Krueger, *The Developmental Role of the Foreign Sector and Aid* (Cambridge, MA: Harvard University Press, 1982), 16–17. Yearly imports of fertilizer were (in 1,000MT) 1946=171.4; 1947=419.1;

1948=529.3; 1949=766.1. As Korean farmers received a subsidy for farm-produced fertilizer use during the colonial period, the earlier average may be higher due to over-reporting. However, most reports from the period discern an overall decline in the use of fertilizer in Korea, regardless of the degree.

43. United States Army Military Government in Korea, "Present Economic Conditions in South Korea," August 1947; Seoul to SecState, "Semi-Monthly Economic Review," May 23, 1948; Department of Commerce, United States Army Military Government in Korea, "Report on Electric Power Generation and Distribution and Present Power Emergency in South Korea," June 23, 1948; Seoul (Hodge) to SecState, May 15, 1948; Rozier, "Republic of Korea (Summary of Current Economic Conditions)," April 5, 1949, reel 8, Records Relating to the Internal Affairs of Korea, 1945–49, Decimal File 895, RG 59, NAMD.

44. Bunce to SecState, National Economic Board Reports, Oct. 11, 1947, reel 8, Records Relating to the Internal Affairs of Korea, 1945–49, Decimal File 895, RG 59, NAMD.

45. *Report on the Occupation Area of South Korea Since Termination of Hostilities*, Part II, Economics, Sept. 1947, 9–11.

46. "Administrative Arrangements for Continuation of United States Assistance to Korea," June 1, 1948, reel 8, Records Relating to the Internal Affairs of Korea, 1945–49, Decimal File 895, RG 59, NAMD. Packenham, *Liberal America and the Third World*, 36; NSC 8/2, March 22, 1949, *FRUS, 1949*, vol. 7, 969–78; McGlothlen, *Controlling the Waves*, 76–77. See also Michael Schaller, *The American Occupation of Japan: The Origins of the Cold War in Asia* (New York: Oxford University Press, 1985).

47. Cumings, *Korea's Place in the Sun*, 255; and Woo, *Race to the Swift*, 50; Comments of Biddle, "Briefing Session with Paul Hoffman—Banto Hotel," Dec. 16, 1948; Paul G. Hoffman, "Address to the Entire Staff of ECA Mission," Dec. 16, 1948, reel 8, Records Relating to the Internal Affairs of Korea, 1945–49, Decimal File 895, RG 59, NAMD, 5.

48. Mason et al., *Economic and Social Modernization*, 174; Economic Cooperation Administration, "ECA Recovery Program for 1950" (Washington, DC: 1950), quoted in Krueger, *Developmental Role*, 15.

49. Press Conference, Dec. 16, 1948, reel 8, Records Relating to the Internal Affairs of Korea, 1945–49, Decimal File 895, RG 59, NAMD; Economic Cooperation Administration, *The Economy of South Korea: Basic Survey*, March 1950.

50. Krueger, *Developmental Role*, 17–19.

51. Louis K. Benjamin, "Memorandum," Jan. 20, 1950, box 5, Division of Korea Program, Subject Files, 1948–1951, RG 469, NAMD.

52. William Stueck, *The Korean War: An International History* (Princeton, NJ: Princeton University Press, 1995), 47–48.

53. Statement of Warren F. Austin, July 11, 1950, box 679, OF 192-A, Truman Papers—Official File, HTL.

54. Merchant to Jessup, "Korean Relief and Rehabilitation," Sept. 9, 1950, reel 32, Records Relating to the Internal Affairs of Korea, 1950–54, RG 59, NAMD; "UN Action on Korean Relief and Reconstruction: Background and Suggestions," Sept. 8, 1950, box 9, Subject files of Durward V. Sandifer, Deputy Assistant Secretary of State for United Nations Affairs, 1944–1954, RG 59, NAMD.

55. Remarks of Dean Acheson, UN General Assembly, Fifth Session, Plenary Meetings, vol. 1, *Official Records*, 279th meeting, Sept. 20, 1950, 26–27.

56. "Departmental Committee for United Nations Program in Korea," Nov. 1, 1950, box 9, Subject files of Durward V. Sandifer, Deputy Assistant Secretary of State for United Nations Affairs, 1944–1954, RG 59, NAMD.

57. Memorandum of Conversation, Nov. 20, 1950, box 76, Dean Acheson Papers, HTL; Rusk and Sandifer to Secretary of State, "UN Agent General for Korean Relief and Rehabilitation," Oct. 25, 1950; Hickerson to Acting Secretary, "United Nations Agent General for Korean Reconstruction," Dec. 13, 1950, box 9, Subject files of Durward V. Sandifer, Deputy Assistant Secretary of State for United Nations Affairs, 1944–1954, RG 59, NAMD. There were good technical reasons to appoint Clapp to run UNKRA. Clapp had become an expert on electrification, something undoubtedly useful in power-starved South Korea. Part of the reason Clapp was not sent to Korea may touch on domestic development. In 1949, Truman had proposed a Columbia Valley Authority for the Pacific Northwest. Keeping Clapp at his post may have been to keep him in a position to intervene in domestic debate.

58. M. Whittaker, "UNKRA Draft History," Feb. 9, 1961, box 1 United Nations Korean Reconstruction Agency, 1950–1960, ROAG 2/5, UNA, 3; Gene M. Lyons, *Military Policy and Economic Aid: The Korean Case, 1950–1953* (Columbus: Ohio State University Press, 1961), 33; United States Representative at the United Nations (Austin) to the Secretary of State, Dec. 9, 1950, *FRUS, 1950*, VII *Korea*, 1489; Chen Jian, *China's Road to the Korean War: The Making of the Sino-American Confrontation* (New York: Columbia University Press, 1994), 136–37, 209; Stueck, *The Korean War*, 127–30.

59. Johnson to Porter, April 12, 1951; Colman to Johnson, May 17, 1951, box 1, Division of Korea Program, Subject Files, 1948–1951, RG 469, NAMD; Gene M. Lyons, "American Policy and the United Nations' Program for Korean Reconstruction," *International Organization* 12 (Spring 1958): 180–92; and Whittaker, "UNKRA History," 12.

60. Summary Record of 4th Meeting of UNKRA Advisory Committee, May 23, 1951, box 9, ROAG 2/5, United Nations Reconstruction Agency, 1950–1960, UNA.

61. "UNKRA, The Guest Forgets the Koreans, the Owner Spending 8 million Dollars Per Year Completes only 20 million Dollars Project," Jan. 31, 1954, *Pyung Wha Shin Moon*, translation, box 2, Frank A. Crampton Papers, HIA; Summary Record of 16th Meeting of UNKRA Advisory Committee, 29 July 1952, box 9, ROAG 2/5, United Nations Reconstruction Agency, 1950–1960, UNA; Robert R. Nathan Diary, Korea-Burma, October–November 1952, Robert Nathan Papers, Division of Rare and Manuscript Collections, Cornell University, Ithaca NY, [hereafter MCC], 10.

62. *Strengthening the Korean Economy: Report to the President* [Tasca Report], June 15, 1953, box 60, White House Office—National Security Staff Papers, Disaster File, Dwight D. Eisenhower Library, Abilene, Kansas (hereafter DEL), ii–vi, vii–viii, 19, 90. See also "Relief and Rehabilitation Recommendations Contained in the Report to the President by Dr. Henry J. Tasca," June 15, 1953, Mission to Vietnam, Office of the Director, Subject Files, RG 469, NAMD. It is

worth noting that the American technical assistance mission to French Indochina was closely watching the activities of UNKRA in Korea.

63. *Strengthening the Korean Economy*, v–vi, 1–3, 72, 90.

64. NSC 156/1, Note to the Executive Secretary of the National Security Council on *Strengthening the Korean Economy*, July 17, 1953, box 60, White House Office—National Security Staff Papers, Disaster File, DEL, 4, 6, 14–16.

65. Burton I. Kaufman, *Trade and Aid: Eisenhower's Foreign Economic Policy, 1953–1961* (Baltimore: Johns Hopkins University Press, 1982), 12–33; Memo of discussion at the 267th Meeting of the NSC, Camp David Maryland, Nov. 21, 1955, *FRUS*, vol. 10, 1955–1957, *Foreign Aid and Economic Defense Policy*, 33–37.

66. *Strengthening the Korean Economy*, vii–viii, xi, 75, 90.

67. Summary Record of 22nd Meeting of UNKRA Advisory Committee, 13 May 1953, box 9, ROAG 2/5, United Nations Reconstruction Agency, 1950–1960, UNA; Coulter to Persons, Nov. 22, 1954; Memorandum, Nov. 20, 1954, box 331, Official File, White House Central Files, 1953–1961, DEL. Kingsley went on to work for the Ford Foundation.

68. Summary Record of 17th Meeting of UNKRA Advisory Committee, 29 July 1952, box 9, ROAG 2/5, United Nations Reconstruction Agency, 1950–1960, UNA; Nathan Diary, "Korea–Burma, October–November 1952," MCC, 17, 21; Robert R. Nathan Associates, *An Economic Programme for Korean Reconstruction: Prepared for the United Nations Korean Reconstruction Agency* (Washington, DC: 1954), ix. R. R. Nathan and Associates were selected by UNKRA in 1952 for the task and paid an initial sum of $125,000 for their work.

69. Nathan, *Economic Programme*, xxv.

70. Ibid., 19.

71. Ibid., 21,vii, xiv, xxv–xxvii.

72. Food and Agriculture Organization, *Rehabilitation and Development of Agriculture, Forestry, and Fisheries in South Korea: Report Prepared for the United Nations Korean Reconstruction Agency by a Mission Selected by the Food and Agriculture Organization of the United Nations* (New York: Columbia University Press, 1954); UNESCO, *Rebuilding Education in the Republic of Korea* (Frankfurt, 1954); and Nathan, *Economic Programme*, 417.

73. Nathan, *Economic Programme*, xxii–xxiii.

74. International Cooperation Agency, *Evaluation of Korea Program*, April 1958 (USAID Doc # PJ-ABP-462), 6; FAO, *Rehabilitation and Development*, 3–8, 184–185; Nathan, *Economic Programme*, 261, 268–69, 279–80. The FAO believed nearly 20,000 new agricultural technicians were required to support the recovery and development of the agricultural sector.

75. Nathan, *Economic Programme*, 270, 273, 351, 355, 358.

76. Ibid., 417.

77. Ibid., 423, 425.

78. UNESCO, *Rebuilding Education*, 171.

79. Ibid., 104; Amembassy, Pusan to Dept. of State, "Summary of Korean Educational Developments in April and May 1952," June 11, 1952, reel 32, Records Relating to the Internal Affairs of Korea, 1955–1959, Decimal File 895, RG 59, NAMD; Adams and Gottlieb, *Education and Social Change*, 106.

80. UNESCO, *Rebuilding Education*, 124; Nathan, *Economic Programme*, 426; M. Whittaker, "UNKRA Draft History," Feb. 9, 1961, box 1, United Nations Korean Reconstruction Agency, 1950–1960, ROAG 2/5, UNA.

81. McGinn et al., *Education and Development*, 14, 101–104, 214–15, 241.

82. John P. Lewis, *Reconstruction and Development in South Korea* (Washington, DC: National Planning Association, 1955), 4, 5–6, 109.

83. UNKRA Activities Monthly Report, Korea HQ, 1–31 March 1953, box 4, ROAG 2/5, United Nations Reconstruction Agency, 1950–1960, UNA. See also Gregg Brazinsky, *Nation Building in South Korea: Koreans, Americans, and the Making of a Democracy* (Chapel Hill: University of North Carolina Press, 2007), 189–222.

84. Whittaker, "Assistance Through Voluntary Agency Programs," in "UNKRA History," 1. Amembassy, Seoul, "US-ROK Agreement on Voluntary Relief Activities" May 10, 1955, reel 22, Records Relating to the Internal Affairs of Korea, 1955–1959, RG 59, NAMD. UNKRA would give some $1.4 million in grants to voluntary agencies.

85. Korean Association of Voluntary Agencies, *KAVA Personnel Directory* (1958); Address of William E. Warne, May 23, 1957, reel 21, Records Relating to the Internal Affairs of Korea, 1955–1959, RG 59, NAMD.

86. Address of Warne, 4; William E. Warne, "The Place and Function of the Voluntary Agency in Korea," *Technical Assistance Quarterly Bulletin* 4 (May 1958): 18; Vaughn Mechan, *Economic Assistance to Korea and Aid Accomplishments*, 1954–1960, International Cooperation Agency, 1960, USAID Doc # PN–ABK–610, 49.

87. Glen Leet, "Community Development in Korea as Practiced by Save the Children Federation," *Technical Assistance Quarterly Bulletin* 4 (May 1958): 35–42; Address of Warne, 4.

88. "The Voluntary Agency—What is it?" May 22, 1957; "Official Aid Agencies Vis-à-vis or in Cooperation with Voluntary Agencies," May 22, 1957, reel 21, Records Relating to the Internal Affairs of Korea, 1955–1959, RG 59, NAMD.

89. International Cooperation Agency, *Evaluation of Korea Program*, April 1958, USAID Doc # PJ-ABP-462, 88–89; "Annual Economic Report 1955, Republic of Korea," March 19, 1956; "Annual Economic Review, ROK, 1956," May 21, 1957; "Quarterly Economic Summary," June 10, 1958, reel 16, Records Relating to the Internal Affairs of Korea, 1955–1959, Decimal File 895, RG 59, NAMD.

90. ICA, *Evaluation*, 31; McClurkin to Robertson, "Appraisal of Progress toward Viability in Korea"; Carey to Smith, July 11, 1955; Damon to Carey, "Alleged Power Shortage in Korea," July 11, 1955, reel 16, Records Relating to the Internal Affairs of Korea, 1955–1959, Decimal File 895, RG 59, NAMD.

91. Woo, *Race to the Swift*, 46.

92. ICA, *Evaluation*, 26–27; Rhee to Eisenhower, Dec. 29, 1954, *FRUS, 1952–1954* vol. 15, *Korea*, 1940; Woo, *Race to the Swift*, 56–57.

93. Woo, *Race to the Swift*, 47–48, 56, 65–66; Lie, *Han Unbound*, 20, 26.

94. Woo, *Race to the Swift*, 71–72; Lie, *Han Unbound*, 37; Cumings, *Korea's Place*, 343–45.

95. CINCUNC Seoul Korea to Joint Chiefs of Staff, April 29, 1960, box 3, OCB Series, Subject Subseries, White House Office—National Security Staff Papers, DEL; Cumings, *Korea's Place*, 346; Lie, *Han Unbound*, 45.

96. Letter from the Assistant Secretary of State for Far Eastern Affairs (Parsons) to the Ambassador in Korea (McConaughy), Aug. 12, 1960, *FRUS, 1958–1960*, vol. 18, *Japan and Korea*, 682–83.

97. NSC 5817, "U.S. Policy Toward Korea," NSC Policy Papers, box 25, DEL; Charles Armstrong, "'Fraternal Socialism': The International Reconstruction of North Korea, 1953–62," *Cold War History* 5 (May 2005): 161–87.

98. "Future United States Economic Assistance for Asia," Jan. 21, 1955, box 4, CFEP, NSC, DEL; "Highlights of Mr. Dodge's Report," March 20, 1956; "The Nature and Problems of Soviet Economic Penetration of Underdeveloped Areas," March 14, 1956, box 8, CFEP, NSC, DEL, 7

99. Memorandum of Discussion at the 44th Meeting of the National Security Council, June 8, 1960, *FRUS, 1958–1960*, vol. 17, *Japan and Korea*, 665.

CHAPTER 5
"THE GREAT AMERICAN MISSION," 1952–1960

1. *Romanoff and Juliet*, dir. Peter Ustinov, 1961.

2. Harry S. Truman, Interview, Kansas City, Aug. 28, 1953, box 4, Harry S. Truman Papers, Post Presidential Files, Memoirs, HTL.

3. Commission on Foreign Economic Policy Report to the President and Congress [Randall Commission], Jan. 1954, box 4, Council on Foreign Economic Policy, NSC Papers, DEL. See also Burton I. Kaufman, *Trade and Aid: Eisenhower's Foreign Economic Policy, 1953–1961* (Baltimore: Johns Hopkins University Press, 1982), 21–23. See also Sergei Y. Shenin, *America's Helping Hand: Paving the Way to Globalization (Eisenhower's Foreign Aid Policy and Politics)* (New York: Nova Science, 2005).

4. "Stassen's Role in Foreign Aid," *Newsweek*, Dec. 8, 1952, 25; Arthur Krock, "The Future of Point Four: Two Views," *New York Times Magazine*, Sept. 26, 1954; Harold Stassen, "Remarks at a Press Conference," *Doorway to the 20th Century*, Dec. 15, 1954.

5. Stanley Andrews, "Foreign Operations Administration: Point 4 Streamlined or Submerged?" *Doorway to the 20th Century*, Sept. 7, 1953, 1.

6. William E. Warne, *Mission For Peace: Point 4 in Iran* (Bobbs-Merrill, 1956, reprint Bethesda, MD: IBEX Publishers, 1999), 12.

7. Kaufman, *Trade and Aid*, 63–65; Dulles to Ohly, Aug. 5, 1954; Ohly to Stassen, Sept. 24, 1954, box 90, Ohly Papers, HTL; United Nations, "Special United Nations Fund For Economic Development," General Assembly, Official Records: 10th Session, 1955; Hoover comments, box 90, Ohly Papers, HTL; Memo, "U.S. Position Paper on SUNFED for 20th Session of ECOSOC," June 23, 1955, box 12, Randall Subject Files, DEL; Gary Ostrower, *The United Nations and the United States* (New York: Twayne Publishers, 1998), 151.

8. Reuther to Eisenhower, Sept. 30, 1955, box 90, Ohly Papers, HTL.

9. Report of a Group of Experts Appointed by the Secretary-General of the United Nations, *Measures for the Economic Development of Under-Developed Countries* (New York: United Nations, 1951), 13–15, 28–29, 55, 66–68.

10. Edwin A. Bock, *Fifty Years of Technical Assistance: Some Administrative Experiences of US Voluntary Agencies* (Chicago: Public Administration Clearing House, 1953), iii, 2–3; Morris E. Opler, *Social Aspects of Technical Assistance in Operation* (Amsterdam: Drukkerij for UNESCO, 1954), 5.

11. Margaret Mead, *Cultural Patterns and Technical Change* (New York: UNESCO, 1955), preface, 11–13, 16.

12. "Author! Author! Where's the Author?" *New Yorker*, April 19, 1952; John Brooks, "Profiles: A Second Sort of Life," *New Yorker*, April 29, 1961; Neuse, *David E. Lilienthal*, 247–49; and *House Beautiful*, August, 1947, 65–67.

13. David Eli Lilienthal, *Big Business: A New Era*, 1st ed. (New York: Harper, 1953); Alice Teichova, Maurice Lévy-Leboyer, and Helga Nussbaum, *Multinational Enterprise in Historical Perspective* (New York: Cambridge University Press, 1986), 24.

14. Brooks, "A Second Sort of Life," 78; Neuse, *David E. Lilienthal*, 264–66; and Grace Goodell, *The Elementary Structures of Political Life: Rural Development in Pahlavi Iran* (New York: Oxford University Press, 1986).

15. John L. Swift, "International Development," May 26, 1967, box 562, Development and Resources Archives, MLP.

16. David E. Lilienthal, "The Road to Change," *International Development Review* 6 (Dec. 1964): 13.

17. Ibid., 12.

18. Lilienthal, "Road to Change" and David E. Lilienthal, "Overseas Development as a Humanist Art," in *Management: A Humanist Art* (Carnegie Institute of Technology, Distributed by Columbia University Press, 1966), 46–67.

19. Transcript, Eugene R. Black Oral History Interview by Robert Oliver, Aug. 6, 1961, interview I, tape I, Oral History Research Office, Columbia University, 46–48. See also Eugene R. Black, *The Diplomacy of Economic Development* (Cambridge, MA: Harvard University Press, 1960). On the Bank's internationalist pose, see Amy L. S. Staples, *The Birth of Development: How the World Bank, Food and Agriculture Organization, and World Health Organization Changed the World, 1945–1965* (Kent, OH: Kent State University Press, 2006). Feliks Bochenski and William Diamond, "TVA's in the Middle East," *Middle East Journal* 4 (Jan. 1950): 51–82. Both authors were staff members of the International Bank.

20. David E. Lilienthal, "Another 'Korea' in the Making?" *Colliers*, Aug. 4, 1951, 57–58.

21. Diane Raines Ward, *Water Wars: Drought, Flood, Folly, and the Politics of Thirst* (New York: Riverhead Books, 2002), 83–84.

22. Black to Ali Khan, Sept. 6, 1951; Black to Nehru, Sept. 6, 1951, box 364, Lilienthal Papers, MLP.

23. "Terms of Reference in Exchange of Letters Between President Black and the Two Prime Ministers," box 25, Wheeler Papers, HIA; Edward Mason and Robert Asher, *The World Bank Since Bretton Woods* (Washington, DC: Brookings Institution, 1973), 610–27; Jochen Kraske et al., *Bankers with a Mission: The*

Presidents of the World Bank, 1946–1991 (New York: Oxford University Press, 1996), 95; and J. R. McNeill, *Something New under the Sun: An Environmental History of the Twentieth-Century World* (New York: Norton, 2000), 159–62.

24. David E. Lilienthal, "Are We Losing India?" *Colliers,* June 23, 1951, 44; Balkrishna Govind Gokhale, "Nehru and History," *History and Theory* 17 (October 1978): 311–22; Judith M. Brown, *Nehru: A Political Life* (New Haven, CT: Yale University Press, 2003).

25. On Lilienthal, the TVA, India, and hydraulic development, see Daniel Klingensmith, *"One Valley and a Thousand": Dams, Nationalism, and Development* (New Delhi: Oxford University Press, 2007).

26. Kanwar Sain, *America Through Indian Eyes* (Lahore: Uttar Chand Kapur, 1943), 33, 234, 229–53.

27. Henry Hart, *Administrative Aspects of River Valley Development* (New York, 1962), v, 1–24; Henry Hart, *New India's Rivers* (Bombay: Orient Longmans, 1956), 72–79.

28. Jawaharlal Nehru, "Temples of the New Age," July 8, 1954, *Jawarharlal Nehru's Speeches,* vol. 3 (Calcutta, 1958), 1–4.

29. James T. Patterson, *Grand Expectations: The United States, 1945–1971* (New York: Oxford University Press, 1996), 270.

30. Humphrey to Cabot-Lodge, Dec. 20, 1956; Humphrey to Randall, March 20, 1957, box 5, Randall Series; Subject Subseries, U.S. Council on Foreign Economic Policy, Office of the Chairman: Records, 1954–1961, DEL.

31. Karl Mannheim, *Freedom, Power, and Democratic Planning* (New York: Oxford University Press, 1950).

32. Gunnar Myrdal, *Development and Underdevelopment: A Note on the Mechanism of National and International Economic Inequality* (National Bank of Egypt, Cairo, 1956), 62; W. Arthur Lewis, *The Theory of Economic Growth* (Homewood, IL: Richard D. Irwing, 1955); Alexander Gerschenkron, *Economic Backwardness in Historical Perspective* (Cambridge, MA: Belknap Press, 1962); John K. Galbraith, *Economic Development* (New York: Houghton Mifflin, 1962). For the thinking of Lewis, see Robert Tignor, *W. Arthur Lewis and the Birth of Development Economics* (Princeton, NJ: Princeton University Press, 2005).

33. Daniel Bell, *The End of Ideology; on the Exhaustion of Political Ideas in the Fifties* (Glencoe, IL: Free Press, 1960), 30, 373–74.

34. Robert Jacob Alexander Skidelsky, *The Road from Serfdom: The Economic and Political Consequences of the End of Communism,* 1st American ed. (New York: Allen Lane/Penguin Press, 1996), 70–95.

35. W. Arthur Lewis, "Development Planning," *International Encyclopedia of the Social Sciences,* vol. 12, 118–25.

36. His views are well summarized in P. T. Bauer, *Dissent on Development: Studies and Debates in Development Economics* (London: Weidenfeld and Nicolson, 1971).

37. Dulles to Embassy in Israel, Sept. 12, 1953, 1310–11; and Report by the President's Special Representative to the President, Nov. 17, 1953, 1418–23; *Papers Relating to the Foreign Relations of the United States* (hereafter *FRUS*),

1952–1954, vol. 9, *The Near and Middle East, Part 1* (Washington: GPO, 1986). See also Charles T. Main, Inc., *The Unified Development of the Water Resources of the Jordan Valley Region, Prepared at the Request of UNRWA under the Direction of the Tennessee Valley Authority* (Boston, 1953).

38. Hiroshi Hori, *The Mekong: Environment and Development* (New York: United Nations University Press, 2000), 93–94.

39. Thi Dieu Nguyen, *The Mekong River and the Struggle for Indochina: War, Water, Peace* (Westport, CT: Praeger, 1999), 52–56.

40. Barbara Ward, "In the Snowy Mountains, a Great Portent," *New York Times*, Sept. 23, 1951; Barbara Ward, "Australia Seeks a Bigger World Role," *New York Times*, June 15, 1952.

41. McNeill, *Something New*, 157–58; Robert R. Bowie, "Eisenhower, Dulles, and the Suez Crisis," in William Roger Louis and Roger Owen, eds., *Suez, 1956: The Crisis and its Consequences* (New York: Oxford University Press, 1989), 190. The United States and Britain jointly promised up to $200 million. Egypt, obviously, carried the greatest burden, allocating $900 million for the program.

42. McNeill, *Something New*, 170.

43. Frank X. Sutton, correspondence with author, October 26, 2006; Chester Bowles, "Ways for More Effective Technical Assistance by Three Experts," *Doorway to the 20th Century*, July 1, 1953; Robert R. Nathan, *Doorway to the 20th Century*, May 15, 1954.

44. Warren I. Cohen, *Dean Rusk* (Totowa, NJ: Cooper Square, 1980), 82; James Lang, *Feeding a Hungry Planet: Rice, Research, and Development in Asia and Latin America* (Chapel Hill: University of North Carolina Press, 1996); Dean Rusk with Richard Rusk and Daniel S. Papp, *As I Saw It* (New York: Norton, 1990), 183–84.

45. Merle Curti, *American Philanthropy Abroad*, rev. ed. (New Brunswick, NJ: Transaction, 1988), 580–81; Berman, *Ideology of Philanthropy*, 2–3; Volker Berghahn, *America and the Intellectual Cold Wars in Europe: Shepherd Stone Between Philanthropy, Academy, and Diplomacy* (Princeton, NJ: Princeton University Press, 2001); Ford Foundation Press Release, Aug. 1, 1951, box 4, Bureau of Far Eastern Affairs, 1953, Records Relating to Economic Aid, 1948–1958, RG 59, NAMD. "Details of the trip are in Summary Report on Visit to Near East, South Asia, and Far East," Oct. 1, 1951, Report 002576, FF; Alan R. Raucher, *Paul G. Hoffman: Architect of Foreign Aid* (Lexington: University Press of Kentucky, 1985), 80–99; Dwight Macdonald, *The Ford Foundation: The Men and the Millions* (New York: Reynal, 1956), 153–54.

46. Grant, Nov. 26, 1956, box 840, Carnegie Corporation of New York Archives, Rare Book and Manuscript Library, Columbia University (hereafter CC-RBML); To the frustration of McGraw-Hill, the publisher of *The Overseas Americans* (published in 1960), much of the book's content and conclusions were taken directly from *The Art of Overseasmanship* (published in 1957) which itself was based on early studies and conferences organized by the "Carnegie Project." This was even more disappointing, considering it was an academic book of "mild prestige," arriving after the sensation of *The Ugly American* but not capturing the same audience. Benjamin to Mahoney, June 15, 1959, box 840, CC-RBML.

47. Carnegie hatched the idea internally, initially hoping Daniel Lerner, Henry Kissinger, or Max Millikan would head the inquiry. Record of Interview, March 6, 1956; and Record of Interview, March 14, 1956, box 840, CC–RBML.

48. Cleveland to Diebold, March 7, 1963, box 19, Staley Papers, HIA.

49. David Engerman, "The Romance of Economic Development," 24; Harlan Cleveland, *The Theory and Practice of Foreign Aid: A Paper Prepared for the Special Studies Project of the Rockefeller Brothers Fund* (New York: Syracuse University Press, 1956), 4–7. See also John W. McDonald, Jr., "Secretariat Note: The Theory and Practice of Foreign Aid," Dec. 31, 1956, box 184, Ohly Papers, HTL.

50. Cleveland, *Theory and Practice*, 13–20, 43.

51. Ibid., 12, 43–48, 86.

52. Ibid., 31, 92.

53. Harland Cleveland and Gerard J. Mangone, eds., *The Art of Overseasmanship* (Syracuse, NY: Syracuse University Press, 1957), 11–29. The 100,000 in 1956 broken down, in round figures:

U.S. Government (and those on government contracts)	37,000
Religious and Missionary Organizations	28,000
American Business Enterprises	24,000
Students	10,000
Teachers and Scholars	1,500
Voluntary Agencies and Philanthropic Foundations	1,000

54. Harland Cleveland, Gerard J. Mangone, and John Clarke Adams, eds., *The Overseas Americans* (New York: McGraw-Hill, 1960), 4–7.

55. Cleveland and Mangone, eds., *Art of Overseasmanship*, 1–7, 31–50, 63, 65–79.

56. Cleveland et al., *Overseas Americans*, 291–305; Cleveland and Mangone, eds., *Art of Overseasmanship*, 129–34.

57. "Role of American Universities in Technical Cooperation Continues to Grow," *Doorway to the 20th Century*, Oct. 21, 1954; John Ernst, *Forging a Fateful Alliance: Michigan State University and the Vietnam War* (East Lansing: Michigan State University Press, 1998), 7.

58. Ernst, *Forging*, 7–8, 21–36, 41–84; David L. Anderson, *Trapped by Success: The Eisenhower Administration and Vietnam, 1953–1961* (New York: Columbia University Press, 1991).

59. Noam Chomsky et al., *The Cold War and the University: Toward an Intellectual History of the Postwar Years* (New York: New Press, 1997), 24; Christopher Simpson, ed., *Universities and Empire: Money and the Social Sciences during the Cold War* (New York: New Press, 1998), 163.

60. John W. Gardner, *Aid and the Universities* (Education and World Affairs, 1964); *Evaluation of the Southeast Asia Development Advisory Group*, 1972, USAID Library Doc. PD-AAA-433, 1.

61. Nils Gilman, *Mandarins of the Future: Modernization Theory in Cold War America, New Studies in American Intellectual and Cultural History* (Baltimore, London: Johns Hopkins University Press, 2003), 156–60.

62. Daniel Lerner, *The Passing of Traditional Society: Modernizing the Middle East* (New York: Free Press, 1958), 46, 397–99.

63. Kaufman, *Trade and Aid*, 73.

64. "The Crisis of 1954," n.d., box 83, C.D. Jackson Papers, DEL; Pearce, *Rostow, Kennedy, and the Rhetoric of Foreign Aid*, 51.

65. Millikan and Rostow to Allen Dulles, "Notes on Foreign Economic Policy," May 21, 1954, Box 83, DEL.

66. Jackson to Princeton Attendees, May 14, 1954, box 82, C. D. Jackson Papers, DEL; Pearce, *Rhetoric*, 60–61.

67. Walt W. Rostow, *An American Policy in Asia* (Cambridge, MA: MIT Press, 1955); and Max Millikan and Walt W. Rostow, *A Proposal: Key to an Effective Foreign Policy* (New York: Harper 1957).

68. Catholic Association for International Peace, "Economic Aid to Underdeveloped Areas"; and National Study Conference on the Churches and World Order, "Protestant Viewpoint," Oct. 27–30, 1953, *Doorway to the 20th Century*, Jan. 15, 1954, 2–3. The Catholic statement was an extension of earlier Church views that connected equitable economic growth to a struggle against communism. Pope Pius XI had issued a 1937 encyclical on "Atheistic Communism" that emphasized the importance of economic development in confronting the threat it posed. He acknowledged the importance of technical aid in this task. The Church "in the sphere of social economics, although *the Church has never proposed a definite technical system*, she has nevertheless clearly outlined the guiding principles, which, while susceptible to varied concrete applications according to the diversified conditions of times and places and peoples, indicate the safe way of securing the happy progress of society" (emphasis original). See Pius XI, "Encyclical on Atheistic Communism" (*Divini Redemptoris*), March 19, 1937, reprinted in Joseph Husslein, *Social Wellsprings: Eighteen Encyclicals of Social Reconstruction by Pope Pius XI* (Milwaukee: Bruce Publishing, 1942), 355.

69. Cleveland and Mangone, eds., *The Art of Overseamanship*, 54–55.

70. On the developmental "great game" in Afghanistan, see Nick Cullather, "Damming Afghanistan: Modernization in a Buffer State," *Journal of American History*, September 2002, http://www.historycooperative.org//journals/jah/89.2/cullather.html; accessed Nov. 21, 2006.

71. Foreign Service Institute, "Relating Religious Leaders and Beliefs to Country Development," n.d. [1958], box 125, Ohly Papers; Dana Reynolds, "Utilizing Religious Principles and Leadership in Rural Improvement," n.d., Ohly Papers, HTL.

72. Foreign Service Institute, "Relating Religious Leaders and Beliefs to Country Development," n.d. [1958], box 125, Ohly Papers, HTL.

73. Arthur F. Raper, "The Unique Role of the Church in the Improvement of Village Life," Dec. 5, 1958, box 125, Ohly Papers, HTL, 1–4.

74. Ibid., 5–8.

75. Wayland Zwayer, *Directory of American Voluntary and Non-Profit Agencies Interested in Technical Assistance* (New York: Technical Assistance Information Clearing House, 1960).

76. Statement of Mrs. Paul Hartz of the General Federation of Women's Clubs before the Senate Foreign Relations Committee Subcommittee on Technical Assistance Programs, Feb. 23, 1955.

77. ACVA, "Foreign Policy Objectives and the Voluntary Sector of Overseas Activities," Nov. 12, 1958.

78. Winbun T. Thomas, *The Vietnam Story of International Voluntary Service, Inc.,* June 1972, USAID Library Doc. PN-ABI-170, 49, 77. IVS Vietnam Newsletter, August 1959, box 3, White House Office, OCB Series, NSC Papers.

79. Thomas, *Vietnam Story,* 55, 113–14.

80. Statement of Louis Schneider, Secretary of Foreign Service Section of the American Friends Service Committee before the Senate Committee on Foreign Relations, May 19, 1955, 1–3.

81. Statement of Howard M. Teaf, Jr., Chairman, Subcommittee on Social and Technical Assistance of the American Friends Service Committee before the Subcommittee on Technical Assistance Programs of the Senate Committee on Foreign Relations, Feb. 24, 1955, 2–3.

82. William J. Lederer and Eugene Burdick, *The Ugly American* (New York: Norton, 1958). The authors would collaborate again with the novel *Sarakan* (New York: McGraw Hill, 1965); Christian Appy, ed., *Cold War Constructions: The Political Culture of United States Imperialism, 1945–1966* (Amherst: University of Massachusetts Press, 2000), 132–54. Recent work has shown the Soviets were perhaps not as good as the Americans feared. For example, Soviet advisers in China often had difficulties with the language and culture, further complicating a strained relationship. See Odd Arne Westad, ed., *Brothers in Arms: The Rise and Fall of the Sino-Soviet Alliance* (Stanford, CA: Stanford University Press, 1998), 117–40.

83. Lederer and Burdick, *Ugly American,* 77–82.

84. Ibid., 205–38, 283–85.

85. Today the phrase "ugly American" often is used as shorthand for a U.S. citizen who is insensitive or callous in the face of other cultures. This sort of behavior was a major theme in the novel; however, the title actually applies to how Homer Atkins looked physically. What mattered was not Atkins' appearance but his earnestness and skill in working with people in another country.

86. International Cooperation Agency, *Reply to the Criticism in the Ugly American* (Washington, DC: ICA, 1959).

87. Speech of Senator J. W. Fulbright on "The Ugly American," Sept. 7, 1959, box 120, Ohly Papers, HTL.

88. Owen to Hoffman, June 5, 1956, box 76, Paul G. Hoffman Papers, HTL.

89. *The Ugly American,* dir. George Englund, 1963.

90. Graham Greene, *The Quiet American* (New York: Viking, 1956); *The Quiet American,* dir. Joseph L. Mankiewicz, 1958; and James T. Fisher, "'A World Made Safe for Diversity': The Vietnam Lobby and the Politics of Pluralism, 1945–1963," in Appy, ed., *Cold War Constructions,* 230–31.

91. *The King and I,* dir. Walter Lang, 1956; David Engerman et al., *Staging Growth: Modernization, Development and the Global Cold War* (Amherst: University of Massachusetts Press, 2003), 129–64.

92. *Wild River*, dir. Elia Kazan, 1960; Kazan to Lilienthal, May 2, 1960, box 419, Lilienthal Papers, MLP

93. U.S. Department of State, *The Communist Economic Threat* (Washington, DC, 1959), 4–5.

94. Memo of Discussion at the 273d Meeting of the National Security Council, Washington, Jan. 18, 1956, *FRUS, 1955–1957*, vol. 10, *Foreign Aid and Economic Defense Policy* (Washington, DC: GPO, 1989), 64–66; Walt W. Rostow, *Eisenhower, Kennedy and Foreign Aid* (Austin: University of Texas Press, 1985), 16. See also Peter W. Rodman, *More Precious than Peace: The Cold War and the Struggle for the Third World* (New York: Scribner's, 1994), 52–74.

95. Robert A. Divine, *Eisenhower and the Cold War* (New York: Oxford University Press, 1981), 80–81; and Walter McDougall, *The Heavens and the Earth: A Political History of the Space Age* (New York: Basic Books, reprint, Baltimore: Johns Hopkins University Press, 1997), 142–44.

96. Statement of Representative Henry S. Reuss, Dec. 6, 1957, box 120, John H. Ohly Papers, HTL; Office of Research and Analysis, "Impact of US and Soviet Space Programs on World Opinion, July 7, 1959, Skolnikoff to Nielson, July 1, 1960, Memo from Coffey, "The Impact of Science and Technology Upon the Image Abroad of the United States," box 6, Presidents' Committee on Information Activities Abroad, Records, 1959–1961, DEL.

97. Gordon Chang, *Friends and Enemies: The United States, China, and The Soviet Union, 1948-1972* (Stanford, CA: Stanford University Press, 1990), 167-68; Rostow, *Foreign Aid*, 32; Bradley R. Simpson, *Economists with Guns: Authoritarian Development and U.S.-Indonesian Relations, 1960-1968* (Stanford, CA: Stanford University Press, 2008), 26-27; Jeffery James Byrne, "Our Own Special Brand of Socialism: Algeria and the Contest of Modernities in the 1960s," *Diplomatic History* 33 (Summer 2009): 427–47. See also Jian Chen, *Mao's China and the Cold War, The New Cold War History* (Chapel Hill: University of North Carolina Press, 2001); Werner Klatt, *The Chinese Model: A Political, Economic and Social Survey* (Hong Kong: Hong Kong University Press, 1965).

98. Mao Tse-Tung, "Speech at the Moscow Meeting of the Communist and Workers' Parties," Nov. 18, 1957, in Mao Tse-Tung, *Mao Tse-Tung's Quotations: The Red Guard's Handbook* (Nashville, TN: Peabody International Center, 1967), 81.

99. Kaufman, *Trade and Aid*, 95.

100. Reinhold Niebuhr, *The Irony of American History* (New York: Scribner, 1952), 209–29.

101. Walter Lippmann, "Unique and Inimitable," *Washington Post*, Jan. 26, 1956; Walter Lippmann, *The Communist World and Ours*, 1st ed. (Boston: Little, 1959), 36–43.

102. "Psychological Aspects of United States Strategy," box 2, White House Office—National Security Staff Papers, DEL, 1, 11.

103. Quoted in James M. Hagen and Vernon W. Ruttan, "Development Policy Under Eisenhower and Kennedy," *Journal of Developing Areas* 23 (October 1988): 5.

104. International Development Advisory Board, "U.S. Foreign Economic Policy Objectives," Oct. 30, 1956, box 7, White House Office—National Security Staff Papers, Council on Foreign Economic Policy, box 8, DEL.

105. "The Nature and Problems of Soviet Economic Penetration of Underdeveloped Areas," March 14, 1956, White House Office—National Security Staff Papers, Council on Foreign Economic Policy, box 8, 1–2; Memo for Anderson, "The Nature and Problems of Soviet Economic Penetration of Underdeveloped Areas," White House Office—National Security Staff Papers, Council on Foreign Economic Policy, box 1, DEL; Memo, Mrozinski to Dearborn, Oct. 17, 1957; "Economic Problems Facing the USSR," Aug. 15, 1957, White House Office—National Security Staff Papers, Council on Foreign Economic Policy, box 8, DEL.

106. "Soviet Economic Penetration" March 12, 1958, White House Office—National Security Staff Papers, Council on Foreign Economic Policy, box 1, DEL; "Sino-Soviet Bloc Economic Activities in Underdeveloped Areas, 1 October–31 December 1957," March 6, 1958, 9–10; and "The Nature of the Sino-Soviet Bloc Economic Threat in the Underdeveloped Areas," Aug. 5, 1958, 33–35, *FRUS, 1958–1960*, vol. 4, *Foreign Economic Policy*; Caldwell, "Pitfalls in re 'Soviet Economic Penetration,'" Dec. 12, 1957, box 90, Ohly Papers, HTL.

107. "Report of the Working Group of the Subcommittee on Soviet Economic Penetration Proposing An Action Program on Increasing Efforts of Private Industry in Underdeveloped Areas to Strengthen Such Areas Against Soviet Penetration," March 11, 1957; Memo from Randall, April 17, 1957, White House Office—National Security Staff Papers, Council on Foreign Economic Policy, box 8, DEL; Bevan Sewell, "A Perfect (Free Market) World? Economics, the Eisenhower Administration, and the Soviet Economic Offensive in Latin America," *Diplomatic History*, 32 (November 2008): 841–68.

108. U.S. Congress, Senate, Special Committee to Study the Foreign Aid Program, *Foreign Aid Program: Compilation of Studies and Surveys*, 85th Cong., 1st sess., 1957; Center for International Studies, "The Objective of United States Economic Assistance Programs"; and Kaufman, *Trade and Aid*, 95–97.

109. Max Millikan and Walt W. Rostow, *A Proposal: Key to an Effective Foreign Policy* (New York: Harper 1957), 34–41.

110. Ibid., 50, 60–63, 126–27.

111. Ibid., 8.

112. Carnegie awarded Rostow a "Reflective Year Fellowship," a relatively new program, to support "creative individuals." The $10,000 award was to support work at Cambridge University on *The Stages of Economic Growth* during the 1958–1959 academic year. Rostow later groused that the fellowship had been too small. Carnegie staff believed this was "not quite fair" as they provided the sum Rostow initially requested for his sabbatical. Grant, May 27, 1958; Gardner to Rostow, May 7, 1958; Rostow to Cawes, Feb. 1, 1966; Rostow to Marvel, Aug. 5, 1957; Grant Files, box 796, CC-RBML; W. W. Rostow, *The Stages of Economic Growth, a Non-Communist Manifesto* (Cambridge: Cambridge University Press, 1960), 42, 62, 130–36.

113. Kaufman, *Trade and Aid*, 110; Gary Ostrower, *The United Nations and the United States* (New York, Twayne, 1998), 151–53; and Raucher, *Paul Hoffman*, 143; Nyguen, *Mekong River*, 52–56.

114. "Advisory Committe on Voluntary Foreign Aid," Foreign Operations Administration, Sept. 15, 1953, box 2, James M. Lambie, Jr. Papers, DEL; "The Psychological Impact of American Voluntary Aid," June 2, 1960, box 5, U.S. Presidents' Committee on Information Activities Abroad, Records, 1959–1961, DEL.

115. President's Committee on Information Activities Abroad, "The Psychological Impact of American Voluntary Aid," June 6, 1960, box 22, "American Voluntary Agency Overseas Services: Their Objectives, Relationships and Accomplishments," n.d., box 5, "Impact of Voluntary American Organizations in South Asia," n.d., box 5; "Instances of the Activities of US Humanitarian Organizations Affecting the Image of the US in Latin America," April 29, 1960, box 5; ICA and US Voluntary Agencies, ICA, 1959, box 5; "The Non-Profit Sector of American Private Enterprise," Nov. 20, 1960; box 5; President's Committee on Information Activities Abroad, "Psychological and Informational Aspects of Foreign Economic Aid," June 6, 1960, box 22; Presidents' Committee on Information Activities Abroad, Records, 1959–1961. DEL.

116. Harlan Cleveland, "The Convalescence of Foreign Aid," *American Economic Review* 49 (May 1959): 216–31; David Lilienthal, "Needed: A New Credo for Foreign Aid," *New York Times Magazine*, June 26, 1960; Paul Hoffman, "Operation Breakthrough," *Foreign Affairs* 38 (October 1959): 37; Barbara Ward, "The Other Foreign Aid Program," *New York Times Magazine*, July 13, 1962.

CHAPTER 6
A TVA ON THE MEKONG, 1960–1973

1. Akira Iriye, *Global Community: The Role of International Organizations in the Making of the Contemporary World* (Berkeley: University of California Press, 2002), 77–84.

2. Steven Rabe, *Eisenhower in Latin America: The Foreign Policy of Anti-Communism* (Chapel Hill: University of North Carolina Press, 1988), 103.

3. David Milne, *America's Rasputin: Walt Rostow and the Vietnam War* (New York: Hill and Wang, 2008), 9.

4. Rostow, *Foreign Aid*, 156–57.

5. Quoted in John Lewis Gaddis, *Strategies of Containment: A Critical Appraisal of Postwar American National Security Policy* (New York: Oxford University Press, 1982), 176.

6. Report of the Task Force on Foreign Economic Policy, Dec. 31, 1960, box 287, National Security File, JFKL; Walt Rostow, "The Strategy of Foreign Aid, 1961"; Message to Congress, Special Message on Foreign Aid, March 22, 1961; John Kenneth Galbraith to Bundy, "A Positive Approach to Foreign Aid," Feb. 1, 1961, box 297, National Security File, JFKL; Staley to Bowles, "Taking Economic and Social Development Out of the Cold War," Nov. 1, 1960, box 3, Staley Papers, HIA; Memo, "Growth for Peace," Feb. 20, 1961, box 37, Henry R. Labouisse Papers, MLP.

7. Michael Latham, *Modernization as Ideology: American Social Science and 'Nation Building' in the Kennedy Era* (Chapel Hill: University of North Carolina Press, 2000), 113–15; Remarks of Senator John F. Kennedy, University of Michi-

gan, Oct. 14, 1960, www.jfklibrary.org/speeches.htm, accessed Nov. 19, 2001; "Youth Corps Idea Popular Abroad," *New York Times*, Jan. 12, 1961; Gertrude Samuels, "A Force of Youth as a Force for Peace," Feb. 5, 1961, *New York Times*.

8. Peter L. Hahn and Mary Ann Heiss, eds., *Empire and Revolution: The United States and the Third World Since 1945* (Columbus: Ohio State University Press, 2001), 123–33.

9. Lilienthal to Kennedy, Sept. 6, 1960, box 419, Lilienthal Papers, MLP; Kennedy to Lilienthal, April 10, 1961, President's Name File, File LILI, JFKL; Memo from Murphy, June 20, 1969, box 452, Development and Resources Papers, MLP; The Committee on the Peace Corps, American Council of Voluntary Agencies for Foreign Service, March 13, 1961, box 1146, CARE Archives, Manuscripts Division, New York Public Library, New York City; Shriver to Vogel, June 7, 1962, box 17, Lee C. White Papers, JFKL.

10. TVA, National Fertilizer Development Center, "World Supplies of Phosphorus Fertilizers," 1966, PN-ABJ-271; USAID, "Country Assistance Program: Korea, Part II, FY 1966," USAID Library.

11. Roland A. Kampmeier, *Ways to Share Experience with Less Developed Countries: A Case Study of TVA* (Washington, DC: Brookings Institution, 1961).

12. James C. Baird, "Proposal for Expanding the use of TVA's Knowledge and Experience in the U.S. Aid Programs Overseas by the Agency of International Development," Feb. 1963, Tennessee Valley Authority Records, JFKL, 36–38.

13. John F. Kennedy, "Statement by the President Upon Announcing the Appointment of Aubrey J. Wagner as a Member of the Board of Directors, Tennessee Valley Authority," February 11th, 1961, American Presidency Project, http://www.presidency.ucsb.edu/ws/index.php?pid=8256, accessed January 18, 2007.

14. John F. Kennedy, "Remarks at Muscle Shoals, Alabama, at the 30th Anniversary Celebration of the TVA," May 18, 1963, *Public Papers of the Presidents, John F. Kennedy, 1963* (Washington: GPO, 1963), 409–11.

15. E. W. Kenworthy, "Foreign Aid Faces New Battle," *New York Times*, June 4, 1961.

16. David E. Lilienthal, "Look Homeward America," May 17, 1963, box 339, Lilienthal Papers, MLP.

17. David R. Farber, *The Sixties: From Memory to History* (Chapel Hill: University of North Carolina Press, 1994), 11–44.

18. Michael Harrington, *The Other America: Poverty in the United States*, rev. ed. (New York: Penguin Books, 1981), 161. Oscar Lewis, *Five Families: Mexican Case Studies in the Culture of Poverty* (New York: New American Library, 1959); Oscar Lewis, *La Vida: A Puerto Rican Family in the Culture of Poverty—San Juan and New York* (New York: Random House, 1966).

19. John F. Kennedy, "Address at a White House Reception for Members of Congress and for the Diplomatic Corps of the Latin American Republics," March 13, 1961, www.jfklibrary.org/speeches.htm, Oct. 16, 2001; Jeffrey F. Taffet, *Foreign Aid as Foreign Policy: The Alliance for Progress in Latin America* (New York: Routledge, 2007).

20. John F. Kennedy, "Address before the General Assembly of the United Nations," Sept. 25, 1961, www.jfklibrary.org/speeches.htm, Oct. 16, 2001.

21. Hahn and Heiss, eds., *Empire and Revolution*, 242; and Nancy Bernkopf Tucker, *Taiwan, Hong Kong, and the United States: Uncertain Friendships* (New York: Twayne, 1994), 61–62.

22. David Bell, "Countries Receiving Substantial Aid Have Scored Successes," April 24, 1963, box 120, Ohly Papers, HTL.

23. Barbara Ward, "Foreign Aid has Succeeded," *New York Times Magazine*, July 12, 1964.

24. Walt W. Rostow, interview with author, June 17, 2000; Walt W. Rostow, unpublished chapter manuscript, 2000.

25. Tae-Gyun Park, "Change in U.S. Policy Toward South Korea in the Early 1960s," *Korean Studies* 23 (1999): 94–120.

26. William Bundy, "East Asia in the Fall of 1964," box 1, NSF—Papers of William F. Bundy, LBJL.

27. Yuen Foong Khong, *Analogies at War: Korea, Munich, Dien Bien Phu, and the Vietnam Decisions of 1965* (Princeton, NJ: Princeton University Press, 1992); Woo, *Race to the Swift*, 78. For a discussion of the rise and fall of the democratic regime, see Sungjoo Han, *The Failure of Democracy in South Korea* (Berkeley: University of California Press, 1974).

28. Report by Hugh D. Farley, "International Cooperation Admin. Situation in Korea," February 1961, March 6, 1961, FRUS, 1961–1963, XXII Northeast Asia, 424–25; "Prospects for the Republic of Korea," Nov. 22, 1960, FRUS, 1958–1960, XVIII, Japan and Korea, 697–98; National Security Action Memorandum 151, "Impasse Between Japan and South Korea," April 24, 1962, http://www.jfklibrary.org/Historical+Resources/Archives/Reference+Desk/NSAMs.htm, accessed Nov. 30, 2006.

29. Memo to the President, W.W.R. (Rostow), March 15, 1961; Komer to Rostow, March 9, 1961; Robert Johnson, Memo For Mr. Rostow, March 15, 1961; Memo: Komer to Rostow, March 15, 1961, box 127, National Security Files, JFKL; Memo: Komer to Bundy and Rostow, "Relative Priority of Military vs. Reconstruction," June 12, 1961, box 127A, National Security File, JFKL.

30. Bromley Smith to O'Donnell, May 17, 1961, box 127, National Security Files, JFKL; Cumings, *Korea's Place in the Sun*, 347.

31. "Memo from the Ambassador to Korea (Berger) to Dean Rusk," Dec. 15, 1961; "Telegram from the Department of State to the Embassy in Korea," Aug. 5, 1962, FRUS, 1961–1963, 22 Northeast Asia, 591–94.

32. John Kie-Chiang Oh, *Korea: Democracy on Trial* (Ithaca, NY: Cornell University Press, 1968), 174–75; Gregg Brazinsky, *Nation Building in South Korea: Koreans, Americans, and the Making of a Democracy* (Chapel Hill: University of North Carolina Press, 2007), 161–88.

33. Woo, *Race to the Swift*, 87–88; Berger "Transformation," 23.

34. Brazinsky, *Nation Building*, 125.

35. Samuel D. Berger, "The Transformation of Korea—1961–1965," Jan. 1, 1966, box 102, Dean Acheson Papers, HTL, 3–4, 25. Berger's analysis, in some respects, foreshadows Samuel Huntington's thesis that strong central authority is a prerequisite for effective modernization. See Samuel P. Huntington, *Political Order in Changing Societies* (New Haven, CT: Yale University Press, 1968).

36. Berger to Acheson, "Further Observations on the Changing Situation in the Far East," July 14, 1966, box 102, Acheson Papers, HTL; Simpson, *Economists with Guns*, 15, 67–86.

37. Memo for the President (Rostow), "The Shape of World Politics," Oct. 8, 1965; Memo for the President (Rostow), "Foreign Aid and the Politics of Moderation," Oct. 29, 1965; Rostow to Bell, "Foreign Aid: Economic Development, Politics and the U.S. Interest," Oct. 28, 1965, box 44, WHCF, LBJL.

38. Rostow, "Foreign Aid."

39. Steven Hugh Lee, *Outposts of Empire: Korea, Vietnam and the Origins of the Cold War in Asia, 1949–1954* (Montreal and Kingston: McGill-Queens, 1995), 125; John Ernst, *Forging a Fateful Alliance: Michigan State University and the Vietnam War* (East Lansing Michigan State University Press, 1998).

40. Robert McNamara, "Security in the Contemporary World," *Department of State Bulletin*, June 6, 1966, 878; James M. Carter, *Inventing Vietnam: The United States and State Building, 1954–1968* (New York: Cambridge University Press, 2008).

41. Joint Action Program Proposed by the Viet Nam-United States Special Financial Groups [Staley Report], July 25, 1961, box 231, National Security File, JFKL; Memo: Rostow to President, August 4, 1961; Memo: Rusk to President, July 28, 1961; box 23, Staley Papers HIA.

42. For the modernization ideas lying beneath the "strategic hamlets," see Michael Latham, *Modernization as Ideology: American Social Science and 'Nation Building' in the Kennedy Era* (Chapel Hill: University of North Carolina Press, 2000), 167–207. See also Douglas A. Blaufarb, *The Counterinsurgency Era: US Doctrine and Performance, 1950 to the Present* (New York: Free Press, 1977), 116–18.

43. Jeremy Suri, *Power and Protest: Global Revolution and the Rise of Détente* (Cambridge, MA: Harvard University Press, 2005), 138–42. See also Jeffrey Race, *War Comes to Long An: Revolutionary Conflict in a Vietnamese Province* (Berkeley: University of California Press, 1972).

44. Memo: Komer to the President, "The Other War in Vietnam: A Progress Report," Sept. 13, 1966, NSF, Files of Robert Komer, box 1–2, LBJL; Robert Komer, "The Other War in Vietnam: A Progress Report," *Department of State Bulletin*, 1966.

45. *The Pentagon Papers: The Defense Department History of United States Decisionmaking on Vietnam*, Senator Gravel Edition, vol. 2 (Boston: Beacon Press, 1971), 595–97 (hereafter PP).

46. Christopher Fisher, "The Illusions of Progress: CORDS and the Crisis of Modernization in South Vietnam, 1965–1968," *Pacific Historical Review* 75 (1): 25–51.

47. *Agency for International Development: Program Presentation to the Congress, Proposed FY 1969 Program*, USAID Library, H–5.

48. John O'Donnell and Harvey C. Neese, *Prelude to Tragedy: Vietnam, 1960–1965* (Annapolis, MD: Naval Institute Press, 2001), 102.

49. Winbun T. Thomas, *The Vietnam Story of International Voluntary Service, Inc.*, June 1972, USAID Library Doc. PN-ABI-170, 17; O'Donnell, *Prelude*, 104, 237, 242.

50. Blaufarb, *Counterinsurgency Era*, 232.

51. Thi Dieu Nguyen, *The Mekong River and the Struggle for Indochina: War, Water, Peace* (Westport, CT: Praeger, 1999), 52–55; Hiroshi Hori, *The Mekong: Environment and Development* (New York: United Nations University, 2000), 93–94.

52. Nguyen, *Mekong River*, 55–56.

53. "Wheeler Heads Study of Mekong Project," *Washington Post*, Nov. 16, 1957, and "Wheeler Named by UN to Study Plan to Develop an Asian 'TVA,'" *New York Times*, Nov. 16, 1957.

54. Request for Foundation-Administered Project Action, June 30, 1960, grant PA 60–370, reel R-0819, Grant Files, FF; Gilbert F. White, Egbert de Vries, Harold B. Dunkerley, and John V. Krutilla, *Economic and Social Aspects of Lower Mekong Development*, Report to the Committee for Coordination of Investigations of the Lower Mekong Basin, 1962, Report 000369, FF, 25; Franklin P. Huddle, *The Mekong Project: Opportunities and Problems of Regionalism* (Washington, DC, 1972), 25–28; Kanwar Sain, *Informal Consultation Concerning Comprehensive Development of the Lower Mekong Basin as TVA-Type River Basin Development Project*, May 21, 1965, box 29, Wheeler Papers, HIA.

55. Lilienthal to Bowles, Feb. 9, 1961, box 424; Lilienthal to Bowles, Jan. 24, 1962, box 433, Lilienthal Papers, MLP; and Lloyd Gardner, "From the Colorado to the Mekong," in Lloyd Gardner and Ted Gittinger, eds., *Vietnam: The Early Decisions* (Austin: University of Texas Press, 1997), 44; Cleveland to White, Jan. 5, 1962, box 20, Thomson Papers, JFKL.

56. Arthur Goldschmidt, "The Development of the US South," *Scientific American* 209 (Sept. 1963), 225–32.

57. Arthur Goldschmidt Oral History, 28–29; Memo: Goldschmidt to the Vice President, May 4, 1961, Confidential File, Oversize Attachments, box 167, LBJ Library, Austin, Texas.

58. Johnson to Goldschmidt, Sept. 24, 1963, Confidential File, Oversize Attachments, box 167, LBJ Library, Austin, Texas.

59. Press Release ECAFE/88, May 17, 1961; Memo: Cesar Ortiz-Tinoco, n.d. Vietnam Country File, NSF, box 202, LBJ Library.

60. Lloyd C. Gardner, *Pay Any Price: Lyndon Johnson and the Wars for Vietnam* (New York: Ivan Dee, 1995), 193.

61. Komer oral history, vol. 1, 55.

62. Doris Kearns, *Lyndon Johnson and the American Dream* (New York: Harper & Row, 1976), 267.

63. "Briefing Paper for Mr. Bowles' Trip, Feb. 1962; USAID, "Briefing: Lower Mekong River Basin Development with Special Reference to Cambodia," March 1962, box 20, Thomson Papers, JFKL.

64. Bowles, "Memorandum for the President," box 20, Thomson Papers, JFKL.

65. Gilbert White, "Vietnam: The Fourth Course," *Bulletin of the Atomic Scientists* 20 (Dec. 1964), 6–10.

66. Lilienthal to White, Jan. 22, 1965; White to Lilienthal, March 22, 1965; Lilienthal to White, April 27, 1965; White to Lilienthal, May 5, 1965, box 454, Lilienthal Papers, MLP.

67. Memo: Cleveland to Bundy, "Strengthening the Confrontation with China in Southeast Asia: Some Thoughts on the Mekong," July 2, 1964, box 20, James C. Thomson Papers, JFKL.

68. For a discussion of the influence of modernization on American policy and policy makers in the 1960s, see Latham, *Modernization as Ideology.*

69. PP, vol. 3, 153; and Marilyn Young, *The Vietnam Wars, 1945–1990* (New York: Harper, 1991), 122–23; Milne, *America's Rasputin,* 148.

70. Robert D. Schulzinger, *A Time for War: The United States and Vietnam, 1941–1975* (New York: Oxford University Press, 1997), 165–72; George C. Herring, *America's Longest War: The United States in Vietnam, 1950–1975,* 3rd ed. (New York: McGraw Hill, 1996), 137–41; David Kaiser, *American Tragedy: Kennedy, Johnson, and the Origins of the Vietnam War* (Cambridge, MA: Belknap Press, 2000), 341–411.

71. Memo from Rostow, March 30, 1965, Foreign Affairs (1964–1965), White House Confidential File, box 44, LBJ Library; Gardner, *Pay Any Price,* 176.

72. Gardner, *Pay Any Price,* ch. 9.

73. Memo for the President, April 1, 1965, Bundy Memos, box 3, LBJL; and Gardner, *Pay Any Price,* 190.

74. Cleveland to Bundy, "Meeting on the Mekong," June 17, 1964, box 20, Thomson Papers, JFKL.

75. Memo from Barnett, "The 'Carrot,'" March 31, 1965, box 20, Thomson Papers, JFKL.

76. Lyndon Johnson, "Address at Johns Hopkins University: 'Peace Without Conquest,'" April 7, 1965, *Public Papers of the Presidents of the United States, Lyndon B. Johnson, 1965,* vol. 1 (Washington, DC, 1966), 398; CBS Television Coverage of the Johns Hopkins Speech, April 7, 1965, video recording, Museum of Television and Radio, New York City.

77. Johnson, "Peace Without Conquest," 397; and Gardner, *Pay Any Price,* 196–97.

78. Milne, *America's Rasputin,* 151; Research Report, Foreign Press Reaction to President Johnson's Johns Hopkins Speech on Viet-Nam, WHCF, box 168, LBJL; Fredrik Logevall, *Choosing War* (Berkeley, London: University of California Press, 1999), 372; Nguyen, *Mekong River,* 110–16; Kaiser, *American Tragedy,* 424–27.

79. Po-Wen Huang, *The Asian Development Bank: Diplomacy and Development in Asia* (New York: Vantage, 1975), 11–23, 59–80, 108; and Nguyen, *Mekong River,* 122.

80. Nguyen, *Mekong River,* 129–32; Robert J. McMahon, *The Limits of Empire: The United States in Southeast Asia Since World War II* (New York: Columbia University Press, 1999), 138, 161.

81. Nguyen, *Mekong River,* 133–34.

82. "Declaration of Honolulu," Feb. 8, 1966, NSF—National Security Council Histories, box 44, LBJL; Memo: Komer to the President, "The Other War in Vietnam: A Progress Report," Sept. 13, 1966, NSF, Files of Robert Komer, box 1–2, LBJ Library; and Robert Komer, "The Other War in Vietnam: A Progress Report," *Department of State Bulletin,* 1966; Lyndon Johnson, "Remarks to the American Alumni Council: United States Asian Policy," July 12, 1966, *Public*

Papers of the Presidents of the United States, Lyndon B. Johnson, 1966, vol. 2 (Washington, DC, 1967), 721; "Manila Declaration," Oct. 25, 1966, NSF—National Security Council Histories, box 45, LBJL; Cable State (Wm. Bundy) to Moyers, Oct. 11, 1966 and Cable Moyers to Bundy, Oct. 12, 1966, Manila Conference and President's Asian Trip Oct. 17–Nov. 2, 1966, vol. 4, Backup Material not Referenced in Narrative [III], National Security File—National Security Council History, Manila Conference and Presidential Asian Trip, Oct. 17–Nov. 2, 1966, box 46, LBJ Library; Lyndon Johnson, "Remarks at Chulalongkorn University," Oct. 29, 1966, in The U.S. Department of State, *The Promise of the New Asia: United States Policy in the Far East as Stated by President Johnson on his Pacific Journey* (Washington, DC, 1966), 44–45.

83. Richard Moorsteen to Robert Komer, "Study of Postwar Reconstruction and Development in Vietnam," Aug. 17, 1966, Komer-Leonhart File (1966–1968), NSF, box 21, LBJL; and Nguyen, *Mekong River*, 153.

84. North American Newspaper Alliance, Press Release, Dec. 19, 1967, box 472, Lilienthal Papers, MLP.

85. "What Should We Do Now: Five Experts Give Their Answer," *Look*, Sept. 9, 1966, 31.

86. Frederick T. Moore, "Meeting on Vietnam at MIT and Harvard," Jan. 27, 1967, box 561, Development and Resources Archives, MLP; D&R staff were regular attendees of SEADAG meetings between 1966 and 1970, particularly its "Mekong Seminar." The larger seminar drew the participation of Gilbert White, C. Hart Schaaf, and "Tex" Goldschmidt, as well as representatives of the U.S. Army and USAID. See "SEADAG" folder, box 564, Development and Resources Archives, MLP.

87. Asia Bureau, "Development Planning," *Vietnam Terminal Report*, USAID, Dec. 31, 1975, USAID Library Doc., PN-ABH-875, 2.

88. Lilienthal to President (Johnson), March 8, 1967, box 561, Development and Resources Archives, MLP.

89. Wood Tate, "Meeting on Vietnam," March 21, 1967, box 561, Development and Resources Archives, MLP.

90. Memo from Moore, "Meeting with Jim Grant, USAID," June 16, 1967, box 561, Development and Resources Archives, MLP.

91. Tate, "Meeting on Vietnam." There is suspicion that the records of Development and Resources were culled by corporation veterans before they were delivered to the Mudd Library, with some potentially embarrassing materials removed.

92. John L. Swift, "Viet Nam Journal," May 5, 1967, box 562, Development and Resources Archives, MLP, 11–12.

93. Lilienthal to Lodge, Sept. 7, 1967, box 581, Development and Resources Archives, MLP; Martin Skala, "Old Hand at Development," *Christian Science Monitor*, March 20, 1967.

94. Discussion Meeting Report: Special Discussion Group on Vietnam's Post–Conflict Prospects, June 19, 1967, box 60, CFRA, MLP; Memo from Michael J. Deutch, June 19, 1967, box 11, David Bell Papers, FF.

95. Joint Development Group, *The Postwar Development of South Vietnam: Policies and Programs* (New York, 1970), 17; Agency for International Development, Asia Bureau, "Economic Context United States Economic Assistance to Viet

Nam, 1954–1975," *Vietnam Terminal Report*, Dec. 1975, 6; Memorandum to the President, Attachment A: Vietnam Rice Situation, Aug. 7, 1967, Vietnam 1B(1)a Economic Activity File, box 58, NSF, LBJL.

96. Letter to Lilienthal, March 12, 1968; Lilienthal to Mead, March 21, 1968, box 577, Development and Resources Archives, MLP.

97. Lilienthal to Seymour, March 29, 1967, box 581, Development and Resources Archives, MLP; "Selling Self-Help—at a Profit," *Business Week*, Aug. 12, 1967, 54–60.

98. Swift, "VIET NAM—Supplementary Mekong Delta Study," May 17, 1967, box 561, Development and Resources Archives, MLP; Memo, Leonhart to Johnson, Dec. 26, 1967, Vietnam 1B(1)a Economic Activity File, box 58, NSF, LBJL; Joint Development Group, *Postwar Development*, 517. On Los Baños, the "Green Revolution," and the Cold War, see Nick Cullather, "Miracles of Modernization: The Green Revolution and the Apotheosis of Technology," *Diplomatic History* 28 (April 2004): 227–54.

99. "Lilienthal Team—Number of People, Cost, Man-Hours, Field and Progress," May 24, 1968, box 562, Development and Resources Archives, MLP.

100. Memo, Mead to O'Brien, "Institutional Development," Oct. 23, 1968, box 569, Development and Resources Archives, MLP; Joint Development Group, *Postwar Development*, 520, 529, 531–32.

101. Joint Development Group, *Postwar*, 545.

102. Mead to Burnett, Feb. 8, 1968; Stinson to Mead, " 'Tet Offensive' bearing on P.P.G. Transportation Study," n.d. [Feb. 1968]; box 562, Development and Resources Archives, MLP.

103. Moore to Lilienthal, "Notes on Vietnam Program," Feb. 26, 1968, box 552; Lilienthal to Mead, Feb. 27, 1968; Lilienthal to Mead, Feb. 28, 1968, box 562; Lilienthal to Mead, Feb. 27, 1968, box 562, Development and Resources Archives, MLP.

104. Lilienthal to Mead, March 21, 1968, box 577, Development and Resources Archives, MLP.

105. Joint Development Group, *Postwar,* 134; and Agency for International Development, Asia Bureau, "War Victims and Relief and Rehabilitation: United States Economic Assistance to Vietnam, 1954–1975," *Vietnam Terminal Report*, Dec. 1975, 1, 3, 19.

106. Lyndon Johnson, "President's Address to the Nation," March 31, 1968, *Public Papers of the Presidents of the United States, Lyndon B. Johnson, 1968–1969*, vol. 1 (Washington, DC, 1970), 469–76.

107. Lyndon Johnson, "Remarks at the Korean Consulate in Honolulu," April 17, 1968, *Public Papers, Lyndon B. Johnson, 1968–1969*, vol. 1, 515.

108. Transcript, *Speaking Freely*, NBC Television Network, March 6, 1969; and Transcript, *The Today Show*, NBC Television Network, May 26, 1967, box 343, Lilienthal Papers, MLP.

109. David Lilienthal, "Postwar Development in Viet Nam," *Foreign Affairs* (January 1969), 321–33.

110. David Lilienthal, "Japan and the New World of the Pacific," May 21, 1968, box 343, Lilienthal Papers, MLP.

111. Eugene Black, *Alternative in Southeast Asia* (New York: Praeger, 1969), 145–46, 150–51.

112. Lilienthal to Kissinger, April 14, 1969; Lilienthal to Kissinger, May 21, 1969; Kissinger to Lilienthal, June 10, 1969, box 483, Lilienthal Papers, MLP; Neuse, *David E. Lilienthal*, 278–79.

113. Nguyen, *Mekong River*, 169–72, 177–79, 186.

114. *Report on Voluntary Agency Assistance in South Vietnam*, Jan. 8–19, 1967, box 25, NSF, LBJL, 12–13; Amembassy Saigon to State, Nov. 14, 1967, box 25, NSF, LBJL; American Association of Voluntary Agencies for Foreign Service, *South Vietnam: Assistance Programs of U.S. Non-Profit Organizations* (New York: Technical Assistance Clearing House, 1968).

115. Bernard Weinraub, "Volunteer Aides in Saigon Dispute," Sept. 15, 1967, *New York Times*; Bernard Weinraub, "4 Chiefs of Volunteer Unit In Vietnam Quit Over War," Sept. 20, 1967, *New York Times*; "I Have Seen the 'Destruction of a People I Love,'" Sept. 24, 1967, *New York Times*; "Are We Losing the 'Other War'?" Sept. 25, 1967, *New York Times*; Thomas, *Vietnam Story*, 17, 37–38; Don Luce and John Sommer, *Viet Nam: The Unheard Voices* (Ithaca, NY: Cornell University Press, 1969).

116. Ernst, *Forging*, 115–16.

117. McAlister Brown, "The Impact of the Indochina Involvement on American Political Institutions," May 1971, SEADAG Paper, USAID Library Doc., PN-ABI-180; Eric R. Wolf and Joseph G. Jorgensen, "Anthropology on the Warpath in Thailand," Nov. 19, 1970, *New York Review of Books*, 26–35; *Evaluation of the Southeast Asia Development Advisory Group*, 2; Bordonaro to Boylan, June 15, 1977, Unprocessed Materials, Asia Society Papers, RAC.

118. Richard M. Nixon, "U.S. Foreign Policy for the 1970's, a New Strategy for Peace," *Public Papers of the Presidents: Richard Nixon, 1970* (Washington, DC: GPO), 116–90; William Bundy, *A Tangled Web: The Making of Foreign Policy in the Nixon Presidency* (New York: Hill and Wang, 1998), 67–68.

119. Action Memorandum, Kissinger to Nixon, "NSC Meeting on Foreign Aid," March 26, 1969; Action Memorandum Greenwald to Rogers, March 25, 1969, http://www.state.gov/r/pa/ho/frus/nixon/iv/15558.htm, January 22, 2007.

120. President Nixon's Message to Congress, "New Directions in Foreign Aid," May 28, 1969, USAID Library Doc., PCAAA-593.

121. Felix Belair, Jr., "Foreign Aid Bill Beaten," Oct. 30, 1972, *New York Times*; Felix Belair, "Foreign Aid Setup Called 'Shambles' by Senate Group," April 26, 1971, *New York Times*; Vernon W. Ruttan, *United States Development Assistance Policy: The Domestic Politics of Foreign Economic Aid* (Baltimore: Johns Hopkins University Press, 1996), 102.

122. Abraham M. Hirsch, *The USAID Program and Vietnamese Reality*, June 1968, USAID Library Doc., PN-ABS-391; Reminiscences of John H. Sullivan, Oct. 29, 1996, Foreign Affairs Oral History Project, USAID Library.

123. Ruttan, *Development Assistance*, 105; M. Taghi Farvar and John P. Milton, eds., *The Careless Technology: Ecology and International Development* (New York: Natural History Press, 1969).

124. Agency for International Development, *Introduction to the FY 1973 Development and Humanitarian Assistance Program Presentation to Congress*, USAID Library Doc., 1–2.

125. Agency for International Development, *Introduction to the FY 1974 Development Assistance Program Presentation to Congress*, USAID Library, 6.

126. For example, see Nicholas Eberstadt, *Foreign Aid and American Purpose* (Washington, DC: American Enterprise Institute, 1988), 50–52.

127. David E. Lilienthal, "Reconstruction Days," *New York Times*, Jan. 13, 1973.

128. Marshall Windmiller, "Agents of the New Empire," *The Nation*, May 10, 1971, 592–96.

129. Martha Finnemore, "Redefining Development at the World Bank," in *International Development and the Social Sciences: Essays in the History and Politics of Knowledge*, ed. Frederick Cooper and Randall Packard (Berkeley: University of California Press, 1998), 208–10; Gunnar Myrdal, *Asian Drama: An Inquiry into the Poverty of Nations*, 3 vols. (New York: Twentieth Century Fund, 1968); Arthur E. Morgan, *Dams and Other Disasters: A Century of the Army Corps of Engineers in Civil Works* (Boston: Porter Sargent, 1971); Pete S. Michaels and Steven F. Napolitano, "The Hidden Costs of Hydroelectric Dams," *Cultural Survival Quarterly* 12 (1988): 2–4.

130. Thayer Scudder, "The Human Ecology of Big Projects: River Basin Development and Resettlement," *Annual Review of Anthropology* 2 (1973): 45–55; Farvar and Milton, eds., *Careless Technology*, 236–44; Agency for International Development, *To Tame a River* (Washington, DC, 1968), 13; Pfanner to van der Oord, May 28, 1973; Mekong Committee, *Plan of Operation for Environmental Research for Lower Mekong Basin Development*, April 16, 1973, grant 73–567, reel R-3367, Grant Files, FF.

131. Finnemore, "Redefining Development," 203–27.

132. Mead, "Memorandum for Files," June 20, 1969, box 559, Development and Resources Archives, MLP; David E. Lilienthal, *The Journals of David E. Lilienthal*, vol. 7, *Unfinished Business, 1968–1981* (New York, 1983), 131–32.

CHAPTER 7

THE CRISIS OF DEVELOPMENT

1. Deborah Shapley, *Promise and Power: The Life and Times of Robert McNamara* (New York: Little Brown, 1993), 507–508.

2. Frederick Cooper and Randall Packard, eds., *International Development and the Social Sciences: Essays in the History and Politics of Knowledge* (Berkeley: University of California Press, 1998), 203–27.

3. James T. Patterson, *America's Struggle against Poverty, 1900–1994* (Cambridge, MA: Harvard University Press, 1994), 105–14. Michael B. Katz, *In the Shadow of the Poorhouse: A Social History of Welfare in America*, 10th anniversary ed. (New York: Basic Books, 1996).

4. James T. Patterson, *Grand Expectations: The United States, 1945–1974* (New York: Oxford University Press, 1996), 530–31.

5. Ellen Herman, *The Romance of American Psychology: Political Culture in the Age of Experts* (Berkeley: University of California Press, 1995), 208–10.

6. Patterson, *America's Struggle against Poverty, 1900–1994*, 142.

7. Patterson, *Grand Expectations*, 535–36.

8. John D. Montgomery, "Transferability of What?: The Relevance of Foreign Aid to the Domestic Poverty Program," May 16, 1969, SEADAG Paper, USAID Doc. PN-ABI-414.

9. Lilienthal to Shriver, April 20, 1965, box 456, Lilienthal Papers, MLP.

10. "Develop a Twelve Month National Training Program for Youth Development," June 11, 1970, box 483; "Proposal to the Office of the Economic Opportunity, Technical Assistance and Support of OEO/CAP," June 1969; Pre-Service Training for VISTA Volunteers, March 1972, box 476; "The Ozarks Region–Planning for Development: Proposal to the Ozarks Regional Commission," February 17, 1969, box 475; "Proposal to Department of Housing and Urban Development for Program of Technical Assistance and Training," May 1969; "Proposal to Office of Economic Opportunity for Development and Conduct of an In-Service Training Program for Approximately 184 VISTA Volunteers," Sept. 1969; "Proposal to Office of Economic Opportunity for Evaluation of Exemplary OEO Day Care Centers," June 18, 1970, box 474, Development and Resources Papers, MLP.

11. Patterson, *America's Struggle against Poverty, 1900–1994*, 144.

12. Patterson, *Grand Expectations*, 589–92.

13. Westad, *Global Cold War*, 289–90; Clapp to Ebtehaj, March 10, 1959, box 162, "Public and Private Enterprise in the Development of Iran," Oct. 17, 1957, box 1, D&R, "Unified Development of the Khusetan Region," 1958, Memo: Village Development, Aug. 8, 1958, box 1, D&R, Housing in Khuzestan: Problems—Policies—Programs, Preliminary Report," Jan. 14, 1958, box 1, Development and Resources Papers, MLP; Frances Bostock and Geoffrey Jones, *Planning and Power in Iran: Ebtehaj and Economic Development under the Shah* (London, Totowa, NJ: F. Cass, 1989), 88, 133–36.

14. Roland Popp, "An Application of Modernization Theory During the Cold War?: The Case of Pahlavi Iran," *International History Review* 30 (March 2008): 76–98; Expanded Technical Assistance Program/FAO, "The Development of Land and Water Resources in Khuzistan," 1956, box 161, Development and Resources Papers, MLP.

15. Bostock, *Planning and Power*, 136, 156–57. Ebtehaj would not see Khuzestan take form, as the Shah would remove him from his post in 1959; he would later be briefly imprisoned for criticizing the regime.

16. Transcript: *Today Show*, NBC, Jan. 6, 1959, box 335, Lilienthal Papers, MLP; David Lilienthal and Gordon Clapp, Meeting Report, Jan. 12, 1959, box 128, CFR Archives, MLP.

17. D&R, "Dez River Watershed Stabilization Program," March 1971; box 506, Development and Resources Papers, MLP; Imperial Government of Iran, Ministry of Agriculture and Natural Resources, "Dez Watershed Resource Management Plan," n.d. [1973], box 508, Development and Resources Papers, MLP.

18. Grace Goodell, *The Elementary Structures of Political Life: Rural Development in Pahlavi Iran* (New York: Oxford University Press, 1986), 8, 15, 24–32, 302–303, 343. On Lilienthal's relation to the Pahlavi regime, see James A. Bill, *The Eagle and the Lion: The Tragedy of American–Iranian Relations* (New Haven, CT: Yale University Press, 1988).

19. Steve Neal, "The Man Behind the Mighty TVA Now Sees Energy in Our Streams," *Philadelphia Inquirer*, June 5, 1977; Neuse, *Lilienthal*, 307, 310.

20. Doris Kearns, *Lyndon Johnson and the American Dream* (New York: Harper & Row, 1976), 251.

21. Gabriel Kolko, *Anatomy of a War: Vietnam, the United States and the Modern Historical Experience* (New York: New Press, 1985), 287; James T. Patterson, *Grand Expectations: The United States, 1945–1971*, 597–98; Charles R. Frank and Mary Baird, "Foreign Aid: Its Speckled Past and Future Prospects," *International Organization* 29 (Winter 1975): 140.

22. Kolko, *Anatomy*, 286–87, 314–15; Diane B. Kunz, ed., *The Diplomacy of the Crucial Decade: American Foreign Relations During the 1960s* (New York: Columbia University Press, 1994), 105–107; Organization for Economic Cooperation for Development, *Development Assistance: Efforts and Policies of the Developmental Assistance Committee* (Paris: OECD, 1973), 176.

23. Carol Lancaster, *Foreign Aid: Diplomacy, Development, Domestic Politics* (Chicago: University of Chicago Press, 2007), 29–38; Brian H. Smith, *More Than Altruism: The Politics of Private Foreign Aid* (Princeton, NJ: Princeton University Press, 1990), 75–111.

24. Frank and Baird, "Foreign Aid," 137–40. For information on the Scandinavian countries (Norway, Sweden, and Denmark) see OECD, 181.

25. Jacob Heilbrunn, *They Knew They Were Right: The Rise of the Neocons*, 1st ed. (New York: Doubleday, 2008); Michael H. Hunt, *The American Ascendancy: How the United States Gained and Wielded Global Dominance* (Chapel Hill: University of North Carolina Press, 2007).

26. An early and defining work of this school is Andre Gunder Frank, "The Development of Underdevelopment," *Monthly Review* 18 (4), 23–28; Ester Boserup, *Woman's Role in Economic Development* (New York: St. Martin's, 1970); Daniel Yergin and Joseph Stanislaw, *The Commanding Heights: The Battle between Government and the Marketplace That Is Remaking the Modern World* (New York: Simon & Schuster, 1998), 91–124. For a discussion of the discontent with modernization on all sides of the political spectrum in this period, see Howard Brick, *Age of Contradiction: American Thought and Culture in the 1960s* (New York: Twayne, 1998), 44–65.

27. Cooper and Packard, eds., *International Development*, 176–202; Matthew Connelly, *Fatal Misconception: The Struggle to Control World Population* (Cambridge, MA: Belknap Press, 2008). See also Paul R. Ehrlich, *The Population Bomb* (New York: Ballantine Books, 1968).

28. Clifford Geertz, "Judging Nations: Some Comments on the Assessment of Regimes of the New States," report # 002919, FF, 24–25.

29. Charles A. Reich, *The Greening of America: How the Youth Revolution Is Trying to Make America Livable*, 1st ed. (New York: Random House, 1970).

30. Perhaps the most cogent statement of these views is Daniel Bell, *The Coming of Post-Industrial Society: A Venture in Social Forecasting* (New York: Basic Books, 1973).

31. Gilman, *Mandarins*, 241–51.

32. Discussion Meeting Report, "New Forces in World Politics," First Meeting Dec. 11, 1969, box 63, CFR, MLP. While certainly not a complete representation of the liberal internationalist establishment, meetings on "New Forces" were attended by a remarkable cross-section of influential individuals. A sampling includes Arthur Schlesinger, Fritz Stern, William Pfaff, Daniel Bell, James Chace, Stanley Hoffman, Francis Keppel, Ronald Steele, Adam Walinsky, August Heckscher, Richard Holbrooke, Joseph Kraft, and James H. Billington.

33. Harold R. Isaacs, "Race and Color in World Affairs," Discussion Group on Color in International Affairs," n.d. [October 1969], box 62, CFR, MLP. On social unrest, elite anxiety, and international politics in the period, see Suri, *Power and Protest*, 164–269.

34. William Pfaff, "The Scope of Our Discussions," Dec. 11, 1969; Discussion Meeting Report, "New Forces in World Politics," Second Meeting, Jan. 15, 1970; Discussion Meeting Report, "New Forces in World Politics," Third Meeting, Feb. 12, 1970; box 63, CFR, MLP.

35. Donald Worster, *Nature's Economy: A History of Ecological Ideas*, 2nd ed. (New York: Cambridge University Press, 1994), 342–46.

36. Rachel Carson, *Silent Spring* (reprint, New York: Houghton Mifflin, 1987); J. R. McNeill, *Something New Under the Sun: An Environmental History of the Twentieth Century World* (New York: Norton, 2000), 339.

37. E. M. Nicholson, "Ecological Research: An Approach to the Understanding and Management of Man's Natural Environment," presented at the Conference on Natural Resources, Feb. 27–March 1, 1964, Report 002657, FF.

38. Edward H. Graham, "Environmental Resources and the Man-Nature Relationship," Presented at the Conference on Natural Resources, Feb. 27–March 1, 1964, Report 002657, FF.

39. McNeill, *Something New*, 160–61, 166–71.

40. Thayer Scudder, "The Human Ecology of Big Projects," 45–55; Patricia L. Rosenfield and Blair T. Bower, "Management Strategies for Mitigating Adverse Health Impacts of Water Resource Development Projects," *Progress in Water Technology* 11 (1979): 285–301.

41. M. Taghi Farvar and John P. Milton, eds., *The Careless Technology: Ecology and International Development* (New York: Natural History Press, 1969), 484.

42. Ibid., xvii, xxiii–xxiv, xxix.

43. Connelly, *Fatal Misconception*, 327–369; Judith Shapiro, *Mao's War against Nature: Politics and the Environment in Revolutionary China* (New York: Cambridge University Press, 2001), 195–215; Chen Jian, "The Great Transformation: How China Changed in the Long 1970s," London School of Economics, January 22, 2009, http://www.lse.ac.uk/collections/LSEPublicLecturesAndE vents/events/2008/20081203t1253z001.htm, accessed February 3, 2009.

44. A. P. Kolontaev and V. I. Pavlov, "V.I. Lenin o preobrazovanii mnogouklad-nykh struktur i chastnogo sektora (na primer razvivaiushchikhia stran)," *Narody Azii i Afriki* 2 (1970), 23.

45. S. Bessonov, "Real'nye predposylki i vozmozhnosti planirovaniia," *Mirovaia ekonomika i mezhdunarodnye otnosheniia* 12 (1969), 90–92; Jerry F. Hough, *The Struggle for the Third World: Soviet Debates and American Options* (Washington, DC: Brookings Institution, 1986); Arvid Nelson, *Cold War Ecology: Forests, Farms, and People in the East German Landscape, 1945–1989* (New Haven, CT: Yale University Press, 2005).

46. McNeill, *Something New*, 163–66.

47. Adam Rome, "Give Earth a Chance: The Environmental Movement and the Sixties," *Journal of American History*, September 2003, http://www.history cooperative.org/cgi-bin/justtop.cgi?act=justtop&url=http://www.historycooperat ive.org/journals/jah/90.2/rome.html, accessed 13 Oct. 2008; Suri, *Power and Protest*, 164–66; Worster, *Nature's Economy*, 347–59; Thomas Robertson, "'This Is the American Earth': American Empire, the Cold War, and American Environmentalism," *Diplomatic History* 32 (September 2008): 561–84; J. Brooks Flippen, *Nixon and the Environment* (Albuquerque: University of New Mexico Press, 2000), 1–16.

48. Lord Ritchie-Calder, "Mortgaging the Old Homestead," *Foreign Affairs* 48 (Jan. 1970): 207–20; Eugene B. Skolnikoff, "The International Functional Implications of Future Technology," *Journal of International Affairs* 25 (1971): 274; Wayland Kennet, "The Stockholm Conference on the Human Environment," *International Affairs* 48 (Jan. 1972): 33–45; David Kay and Eugene B. Skolnikoff, "International Institutions and the Environmental Crisis: A Look Ahead" *International Organization* 26 (Spring 1972): 469–78; Eugene B. Skolnikoff, "Science and Technology: The Implications for International Institutions," *International Organization* 25 (Autumn 1971): 759–75; Richard N. Gardner, "The Role of the UN in Environmental Problems," *International Organization* 26 (Spring 1972): 237–54; International Institute for Environmental Affairs, *The Human Environment: Science and International Decision-Making, A Basic Paper, Prepared for the Secretariat of the United Nations Conference on the Human Environment* (1971). See also Eugene B. Skolnikoff, *The Elusive Transformation: Science, Technology, and the Transformation of International Politics* (Princeton, NJ: Princeton University Press, 1993).

49. *Inadvertent Climate Modification*, Report of the Study of Man's Impact on the Climate (Cambridge, MA: MIT Press, 1971).

50. Anders Stephanson, *Kennan and the Art of Foreign Policy* (Cambridge, MA: Harvard University Press, 1989), 215–38.

51. By the late 1970s, Kennan thought the UN, after the rapid expansion of its membership in the preceding three decades, retained only a "modicum of usefulness." See George F. Kennan, *Cloud of Danger: Some Current Problems of American Foreign Policy* (London: Hutchinson, 1977), 30.

52. George F. Kennan, "To Prevent a World Wasteland," *Foreign Affairs* 48 (April 1970): 401–13.

53. Kennan, *Cloud*, 35.

54. George F. Kennan, *Sketches From a Life* (New York: Pantheon, 1989), 225–26, 354–55.

55. Kennan, *Cloud*, 24–25.

56. Ibid., 233–34.

57. Memo for Administrator: Memorandum on the Foreign Aid Studies, Sept. 22, 1965, box 23, David Bell Papers, JFKL; Kaysen to Bell, Nov. 11, 1966, box 11, David Bell Papers, FF; Discussion Meeting Report, Foreign Aid Policy, First Meeting, Nov. 29, 1966; Discussion Meeting Report, Foreign Aid Policy, Second Meeting, Feb. 1, 1967; Discussion Meeting Report, Foreign Aid Policy, Fourth Meeting, April 4, 1967; Discussion Meeting Report, Foreign Aid Policy, Fifth Meeting, May 2, 1967, box 11, David Bell Papers, FF.

58. Davidson Summers, "Report on trip to Europe," June 6, 1967, box 13; Summary of Discussions, Meeting on Aid and Development, April 20, 1967, box 13, David Bell Papers, FF.

59. Address by George Woods to the UN Conference on Trade and Development, Feb. 9, 1968, box 483, David E. Lilienthal Papers, MLP.

60. *A Study of the Capacity of the United Nations Development System* (UN Doc. DP/5) [Jackson Report] (2 vols.; Geneva: United Nations, 1969).

61. Murden and Company, "Toward the Establishment of a National Nongovernmental Program on International Economic Development" ["Murden Report"], Dec. 29, 1967; Report of President's General Advisory Committee on Foreign Aid, April 1968, box 1, Overseas Development Council Papers. These were unarchived papers in storage when viewed by the author. They have since been transferred to the Rockefeller Archive Center.

62. "Overseas Development Council Prospectus," June 1968; Rockefeller to Harrar, Oct. 7, 1968, box 2507, RG 2, RAC.

63. James P. Grant, "Beyond Economic Growth or SEADAG's Unique Opportunity," August 1972, Asia Society Papers, RAC; James P. Grant, "Growth from Below: A People Oriented Development Strategy," Overseas Development Council, Dec. 1973.

64. Edgar Owens and Robert Shaw, *Development Reconsidered: Bridging the Gap Between Government and People* (Lexington, MA: Lexington Books, 1972); Ruttan, *Development Assistance*, 107.

65. Commission on International Development, *Partners in Development* (New York: Praeger, 1969), 14–22.

66. Speech written by Barbara Ward and given by George Woods, 1967, quoted in Kraske et al., 155.

67. Barbara Ward, Lenore D'Anjou, and J. D. Runnals, eds., *The Widening Gap: Development in the 1970s* (New York: Columbia University Press, 1971), 11.

68. Max Nicholson, "Environment" paper no. 32, *Columbia Conference on International Economic Development, Documents, Papers, and Addresses, Feb. 15–21, 1970*, vol. 2; and Max Nicholson, "Environment," in Ward et al., eds., 147–51.

69. Mahbub ul Haq, "Mr. Polanski's Dilemma," in Ward et al., eds., 278–82.

70. Peter Stone, *Did We Save the Earth at Stockholm?* (London: Earth Island, 1973), 18–19; Maurice Strong, *Where on Earth are We Going?* (New York: Texere, 2000), 120.

71. Cooper and Packard, eds., *International Development*, 228–58.

72. Paul M. Kennedy, *The Parliament of Man: The Past, Present, and Future of the United Nations* (New York: Random House, 2006), 126–29.

73. Strong, *Where on Earth*, 129–30.

74. Mahbub ul Haq, *Reflections on Human Development* (New York: Oxford University Press, 1995), ix; and Strong, *Where on Earth*, 127–28.

75. "Development and Environment: The Founex Report," in *In Defense of the Earth: The Basic Texts on Environment* (Nairobi: United Nations Environment Programme, 1981), 4–5.

76. Igancy Sachs, "Environmental Quality, Management and Development Planning: Some Suggestions for Action," in *Development and Environment: Report and Working Papers of a Panel of Experts Convened by the Secretary-General of the United Nations Conference on the Human Environment* (Geneva: United Nations, 1972), 123–24.

77. "Founex Report," 5–7. A good example of the link made between poverty and environmental degradation is Wilson, Francis, and Mamphela Ramphele, *Uprooting Poverty: The South African Challenge*, 1st American ed. (New York: Norton, 1989).

78. Strong to Dubos, n.d. (1971), box 1, Barbara Ward Jackson Papers, RBML.

79. "A Discussion Note," n.d. [1971], box 1, Barbara Ward Jackson Papers, RBML.

80. Barbara Ward and Rene Dubos, *Only One Earth: The Care and Maintenance of a Small Planet* (New York: Norton, 1972); Strong, *Where on Earth*, 128–29.

81. Maurice Strong, interview with author, June 7, 2001; Bell to Strong, April 22, 1971, box 35; Bell to Bundy, April 17, 1971, box 35, David Bell Papers, FF.

82. "Declaration on the Human Environment" (Stockholm Declaration), *In Defense of the Earth*, 41–106. See also *Report of the United Nations Conference on the Human Environment*, July 3, 1972, UN Doc. A/CONF.48/14, UNA.

83. Maurice Strong, interview with author, June 7, 2001.

84. Worster, *Nature's Economy*, 358; Strong, *Where on Earth*, 136.

85. World Commission on Environment and Development, *Our Common Future* (New York: Oxford, 1987), 43–65.

86. Sharachchandra M. Lélé, "Sustainable Development: A Critical Review," *WorldDevelopment* (June 1991): 607–21. An example of research that questions whether it is best for development programs to seek sustainability in all cases is Michael Kramer and Edward Miguel, "The Illusion of Sustainability," in William Easterly, ed., *Reinventing Foreign Aid* (Cambridge, MA: MIT University Press, 2008), 201–53.

87. Staff Working Paper, "The Foundation and the Less Developed Countries: The Decade of the Seventies," April 1972, Report 003307, FF, 13.

88. E. F. Schumacher, *Small is Beautiful: Economics As If People Mattered* (London: Blond and Briggs, 1973).

89. Bell to Goodwin, "Meeting on Foreign Aid," April 11, 1974, box 37, David Bell Papers, JFKL.

90. James P. Grant, "Century Club Meeting—April 9, 1974," April 9, 1974; "Energy, Food, and Fertilizer Crisis, the New Politics of Resource Scarcity and What Might We Do," April 3, 1974, box 37; David Bell Papers, JFKL.

91. Donella H. Meadows et al., *Limits to Growth: A Report for the Club of Rome's Project on the Predicament of Mankind* (New York: Universe Books, 1972).

92. "Energy, Food, and Fertilizer Crisis," 1–3. Scarcity would emerge as an important theme in international affairs during the 1970s; see Dennis Pirages, "Scarcity and International Politics," *International Studies Quarterly* 21 (Dec. 1977), 563–67.

93. Bell, "Meeting on Foreign Aid," 2.

94. David Halberstam, *The Best and the Brightest* (Greenwich, CT: Fawcett Crest, 1972), 783.

95. Robert McNamara and Brian VanDeMark, *In Retrospect: The Tragedy and Lessons of Vietnam* (New York: Vintage, 1996), 312–13; Jochen Kraske, William H. Becker, William Diamond, and Louis Galambos, *Bankers with a Mission: The Presidents of the World Bank, 1946–1991* (New York, 1996), 160–61.

96. Discussion Meeting Report, "Multilateral Development Issues," Fourth Meeting, March 3, 1970, box 63, CFR, MLP.

97. Kraske et al., *Bankers with a Mission,* 209; Bruce Rich, *Mortgaging the Earth: The World Bank, Environmental Impoverishment, and the Crisis of Development* (Boston: Beacon Press, 1994), 81; Shapley, *Promise and Power,* 477, 498.

98. Bruce Rich, "World Bank/IMF: 50 Years is Enough," in *50 Years is Enough: The Case Against the World Bank and International Monetary Fund* (Boston: South End Press, 1994), 9.

99. Carol Lancaster, *Transforming Foreign Aid: United States Assistance in the 21st Century* (Washington, DC: Institute for International Economics, 2000), 10–11. Total World Bank Group lending for 1999 was $28.9 billion, World Bank *Annual Report* 1999, http://www.worldbank.org/html/extpb/annrep/pdf/tab1_1 .pdf, accessed Sept. 18, 2001. The U.S. foreign aid sum also includes an $811 million allocation for the World Bank itself and a further $301 million for the regional banks.

100. Shapley, *Promise and Power,* 477.

101. Ibid., 506–507; ul Haq, *Reflections,* 10.

102. Cooper and Packard, eds., *International Development,* 210–17.

103. Robert McNamara, "Address to the United Nations Conference on the Human Environment," June 9, 1972, in *The McNamara Years at the World Bank: Major Policy Addresses of Robert S. McNamara, 1968–1981* (Baltimore: Johns Hopkins University Press, 1981), 191–206; Robert McNamara, interview with author, June 5, 2005.

104. Barbara Ward, "Science and Technology: For What?" box 11, Barbara Ward (Baroness Jackson) Papers, Special Collections, Georgetown University.

105. Anthony Lake, *The Vietnam Legacy: The War, American Society, and the Future of American Foreign Policy* (New York: New York University Press, 1976), 374–86.

106. David Rieff, *A Bed for the Night: Humanitarianism in Crisis* (New York: Simon & Schuster, 2002), 100–102. Lancaster, *Foreign Aid*, 43–44.

CHAPTER 8

NEW DEVELOPMENTS

1. "Death of a Think Tank," *Washington Post*, Nov. 10, 2000; author's interview with John Sewell, June 16, 2005.

2. Staples to Bell, "A Note on Asia," March 26, 1970, report # 005117; Finkelstein to Bundy, June 24, 1975, report # 002044, FF.

3. F. X. Sutton, "Reflections on a Visit to Japan," n.d., report # 009080; Jung-en Woo, *Race to the Swift: State and Finance in Korean Industrialization* (New York: Columbia University Press, 1991), 73–117.

4. A sampling of this vast literature includes Edward S. Mason, Mahn Je Kim, Dwight H. Perkins, Kwang Suk Kim, and David C. Cole, *The Economic and Social Modernization of the Republic of Korea* (Cambridge, MA: Harvard University Press, 1980), 2; Jung-en Woo, *Race to the Swift: State and Finance in Korean Industrialization* (New York: Columbia University Press, 1991), Bruce Cumings, "The Origins and Development of the Northeast Asian Political Economy: Industrial Sectors, Product Cycle, and Political Consequences," *International Organization* 38 (Winter 1984): 1–40; John Lie, *Han Unbound: The Political Economy of South Korea* (Stanford, CA: Stanford University Press, 1998); Alice Amsden, *Asia's Next Giant: South Korea and Late Industrialization* (New York: Oxford University Press, 1989); Robert Wade, *Governing the Market: Economic Theory and the Role of Government in East Asian Industrialization* (Princeton, NJ: Princeton University Press, 1990); David C. Cole and Princeton N. Lyman, *Korean Development: The Interplay of Politics and Economics* (Cambridge, MA: Harvard University Press, 1971).

5. James E. Cronin, *The World the Cold War Made: Order, Chaos, and the Return of History* (New York: Routledge, 1996), 163–96.

6. Carol Lancaster, *Transforming Foreign Aid: United States Assistance in the 21st Century* (Washington, DC: Institute for International Economics, 2000), 18–19.

7. Jeffry A. Frieden, *Global Capitalism: Its Fall and Rise in the Twentieth Century*, 1st ed. (New York: Norton, 2006), 374–75.

8. E. J. Hobsbawm, *The Age of Extremes: A History of the World, 1914–1991*, 1st Vintage Books ed. (New York: Vintage Books, 1996), 488–89. Stephen Kotkin, *Armageddon Averted: The Soviet Collapse, 1970–2000* (Oxford: Oxford University Press, 2001). Tony Judt, *Postwar: A History of Europe since 1945* (New York: Penguin Press, 2005), 627–33.

9. Lucian Pye, "Political Science and the Crisis of Authoritarianism," *The American Political Science Review* 84 (March 1990): 3–19.

10. Francis Fukuyama, "The End of History," *National Interest* (Summer 1989): 3–18; Nils Gilman, *Mandarins of the Future: Modernization Theory in Cold War America* (Baltimore, London: Johns Hopkins University Press, 2003), 267–69; Francis Fukuyama, *America at the Crossroads: Democracy, Power, and the Neoconservative Legacy, The Castle Lectures in Ethics, Politics, and Economics* (New Haven, CT: Yale University Press, 2006), 53–54.

11. Two leading examples of such pro-globalization literature are Thomas L. Friedman, *The Lexus and the Olive Tree* (New York: Farrar, Straus & Giroux, 1999); John Micklethwait and Adrian Wooldridge, *A Future Perfect: The Challenge and Hidden Promise of Globalization* (London: Heinemann, 2000).

12. John Williamson, *Latin American Adjustment: How Much Has Happened* (Washington, DC: Institute for International Economics, 1990).

13. Joseph E. Stiglitz, *Globalization and Its Discontents*, 1st ed. (New York: Norton, 2002).

14. W. Arthur Lewis, "The State of Development Theory," *American Economic Review* 74 (March 1984): 1.

15. Overseas Development Council, "US Development Cooperation Assistance and the Third World: Issues and Options for the 1990s," Nov. 1988, box 1318, CC-RBML.

16. *An Agenda for Development: Report of the Secretary General*, May 6, 1994, UN Doc. A/48/935. This report followed the 1992 UN Conference on Environment and Development convened in Rio de Janeiro that was an heir to the issues raised at Stockholm in 1972.

17. "UN Millennium Development Goals," http://www.un.org/millennium goals/, accessed May 12, 2007.

18. Jessica T. Matthews, "Power Shift," *Foreign Affairs* 76 (January/February 1997): 50–66.

19. Rich, *Mortgaging*, 112–15; Shapley, *Promise and Power*, 578.

20. USAID, *The Role of Foreign Assistance in Conflict Prevention*, Conference Report, Jan. 8, 2001. For a discussion of the role development could play in an international regime of prevention, see David A. Hamburg, *No More Killing Fields: Preventing Deadly Conflict* (Lanham, MD: Rowman & Littlefield, 2002).

21. World Bank, "Overview and Background of the CDF" (World Bank, 1999); James Wolfensohn, "Discussion Paper on the Comprehensive Development Framework" (World Bank, 1999). For a general discussion of the changes in Bank policy during the 1990s, see Sebastian Mallaby, *The World's Banker: A Story of Failed States, Financial Crises, and the Wealth and Poverty of Nations* (New York: Penguin Press, 2004).

22. Comments of George W. Bush, Presidential Candidates Debate, October 3, 2000, Transcript, http://www.cnn.com/ELECTION/2000/debates/transcripts/u221003.html, accessed August 30, 2006.

23. National Commission on Terrorist Attacks upon the United States, *The 9/11 Commission Report: Final Report of the National Commission on Terrorist Attacks Upon the United States: Official Government Edition* (Washington, DC: U.S. GPO, 2004), 52–54; Lawrence Wright, *The Looming Tower: Al–Qaeda and the Road to 9/11*, 1st ed. (New York: Knopf, 2006).

24. *National Security Strategy of the United States*, September 2002, http://www.whitehouse.gov/nsc/nss.html, accessed Feb. 10, 2007. See also John Lewis

Gaddis, *Surprise, Security, and the American Experience* (Cambridge, MA, London: Harvard University Press, 2004).

25. *National Security Strategy*, "Introduction."

26. Paul Berman, "Liberal Hawks Reconsider the Iraq War," Jan. 13, 2004, http://www.slate.com/id/2143331/entry/2093867/, accessed May 10, 2007; Paul Berman, *Terror and Liberalism*, 1st ed. (New York: Norton, 2003); Ian Buruma and Avishai Margalit, *Occidentalism: The West in the Eyes of Its Enemies* (New York: Penguin Press, 2004). For the comparison's limits, see Anson Rabinbach, "Totalitarianism Revisited," *Dissent* (Summer 2006), http://www.dissentmagazine.org/article/?article=660, accessed October 12, 2006.

27. George W. Bush, "Inaugural Address," Jan. 20, 2005, http://www.whitehouse.gov/inaugural/, accessed Feb. 10, 2007.

28. United Nations, *Report of the International Conference on Financing for Development*, March 18–22, 2002, UN Doc. A/Conf.198/11.

29. Carol Lancaster and Ann Van Dusen, *Organizing U. S. Foreign Aid: Confronting the Challenges of the 21st Century* (Washington, DC: Brookings Institution Press, 2005), 18–25.

30. Colin Powell, "How Bush Should Win the War on Terror," *Foreign Policy*, Jan./Feb. 2005.

31. Jeffrey Sachs, *The End of Poverty: Economic Possibilities for Our Time* (New York: Penguin Press, 2005), 352; Gaby Woods, "Can the U.S. Change its Spots?" *The Guardian*, March 27, 2005, http://books.guardian.co.uk/departments/politicsphilosophyandsociety/story/0,6000,1446179,00.html, accessed May 30, 2007; Victoria Schlesinger, "The Continuation of Poverty: Rebranding Foreign Aid in Kenya," *Harpers*, May 2007, 58–66.

32. Jeffrey Sachs, *Common Wealth: Economics for a Crowded Planet* (New York: Penguin Press, 2008).

33. William Easterly, ed., *Reinventing Foreign Aid* (Cambridge, MA: MIT Press, 2008), 4–5. William Easterly, "A Modest Proposal," *Washington Post*, March 13, 2005; William Russell Easterly, *The Elusive Quest for Growth: Economists' Adventures and Misadventures in the Tropics* (Cambridge, MA: MIT Press, 2001); Easterly, *The White Man's Burden: Why the West's Efforts to Aid the Rest Have Done So Much Ill and So Little Good* (New York: Penguin Press, 2006).

34. Amartya Kumar Sen, *Development as Freedom*, 1st. ed. (New York: Knopf, 1999).

35. Samuel R. Berger and Brent Scowcroft, "The Right Tools to Build Nations," *Washington Post*, July 27, 2005.

36. "Force 'Cannot Solve Afghanistan,'" May 8, 2007, BBC News Online, http://news.bbc.co.uk/2/hi/south_asia/6636703.stm, accessed May 8, 2007; James Glanz and Erik Eckholm, "Reality Intrudes on Promises in Rebuilding of Iraq," *New York Times*, June 30, 2004; Carlotta Gall, "More G.I.s to go to Insecure Afghan Areas to Permit Aid Work," *New York Times*, Dec. 21, 2003. It is interesting to note one body initially involved in bringing increased electricity to Iraqis was the TVA. See James Glanz, "In Race to Give Power to Iraqis, Electricity Lags," *New York Times*, June 14, 2004.

37. David Rieff, *A Bed for the Night: Humanitarianism in Crisis*, updated ed. (New York: Simon & Schuster, 2002), 345.

38. Paul Krugman, "As Bechtel Goes," Nov. 3, 2006, *New York Times*. One example of criticism of Iraq's reconstruction is T. Christian Miller, *Blood Money: Wasted Billions, Lost Lives, and Corporate Greed in Iraq*, 1st ed. (New York: Little, Brown, 2006).

39. "Afghanistan and Pakistan: Uneasy Neighbors," Panel Discussion at the Asia Society, February 14, 2008, www.asiasociety.org/resources/uneasy _neighbors_021408.html, accessed February 3, 2009.

40. See Jim Mann, *Rise of the Vulcans: The History of Bush's War Cabinet* (New York, London: Viking, 2004). Stefan A. Halper and Jonathan Clarke, *America Alone: The Neo-Conservatives and the Global Order* (Cambridge; New York: Cambridge University Press, 2004).

41. Fukuyama, *America at the Crossroads: Democracy, Power, and the Neo-conservative Legacy*, 155–94. For Fukuyama's views on building institutional capacity within states, see Francis Fukuyama, *State-Building: Governance and World Order in the 21st Century* (Ithaca, NY: Cornell University Press, 2004).

42. Easterly, ed., *Reinventing Foreign Aid*, 2.

BIBLIOGRAPHY

ARCHIVE AND MANUSCRIPT COLLECTIONS

Art Institute of Chicago, Chicago, Illinois
  Daniel Burnham Papers

Cornell University, Division of Rare and Manuscript Collections, Ithaca,
    New York
  Robert R. Nathan Papers

Dwight D. Eisenhower Presidential Library, Abilene, Kansas
  Christian Herter Papers
  C. D. Jackson Papers
  Central Files
  Dennis A. Fitzgerald Papers
  Dwight D. Eisenhower: Papers as President of the United States, 1953–1961
  James M. Lambie, Jr., Papers
  U.S. Council on Foreign Economic Policy, Office of the Chairman: Records,
    1954–1961
  U.S. Presidents' Committee on Information Activities Abroad Papers
  White House Office—National Security Staff Papers

Ford Foundation Archives, New York, New York
  David Bell Papers
  Grant Files
  Oral Histories
  Report Files

Franklin Delano Roosevelt Presidential Library, Hyde Park, New York
  John M. Carmody Papers
  Official File
  President's Advisory Committee on Education Records
  President's Secretary's File
  Morgenthau Diaries
  Rexford Tugwell Papers

Georgetown University, Special Collections, Washington, DC
  Barbara Ward (Baroness Jackson) Papers
  Samuel D. Berger Papers

Harry S. Truman Presidential Library, Independence, Missouri
  Walter S. Salant Papers
  Dean Acheson Papers
  Benjamin Hardy Papers

David Lloyd Papers
E. A. Johnson Papers
George Elsey Papers
Gordon Clapp Papers
Edwin A. Locke Papers
Harry S. Truman Papers
Harry S. Truman Papers—Official File
Theodore Tannenwald, Jr., Papers
Albert H. Huntington, Jr., Papers
John H. Oly Papers
Paul Hoffman Papers
John Sumner
William Clayton Papers
White House Central File
Records of the Committee for the Marshall Plan
General Records of the U.S. Department of State

Herbert Lehman Suite, Columbia University, New York, New York
    Herbert Lehman Papers
    United Nations Relief and Rehabilitation Administration Collection

Hoover Institution Archives, Stanford University, Palo Alto, California
    Albert Wedemeyer Papers
    Arthur B. McCaw Papers
    Daniel Lerner Papers
    Eugene Staley Papers
    Michele Fisher Papers
    Frank A. Crampton Papers
    George Fox Mott Papers
    Harold H. Fisher Papers
    Herbert Hoover Papers
    J. Franklin Ray Papers
    Oliver J. Todd Papers
    Raymond A. Wheeler Papers
    Robert Allen Griffin Papers
    Roger D. Lapham
    Sidney R. Hinds
    UNRRA China Office Papers

Houghton Library, Harvard University, Cambridge, Massachusetts
    Roger S. Green Papers
    W. Cameron Forbes Papers

John F. Kennedy Presidential Library, Boston, Massachusetts
    Agency for International Development Records
    David Bell Papers
    James C. Thomson Papers
    Lee C. White Papers

Max Millikan Papers
National Security File
Office File
Tennessee Valley Authority Records
Walt W. Rostow Papers

Johns Hopkins University, Special Collections, Baltimore, Maryland
Isaiah Bowman Papers

Library of Congress, Manuscript Division, Washington, DC
Philip C. Jessup Papers

Library of Congress, Motion Picture, Broadcasting and Recorded Sound Division, Washington, DC
National Broadcasting Company Archives

Lyndon Baines Johnson Presidential Library, Austin, Texas
Oral History Collection
National Security File
White House Name File
Confidential File

Museum of Television and Radio, New York, New York
Columbia Broadcast System Television Collection

National Archives and Records Administration, Atlanta, Georgia
Record Group 142 Records of the Tennessee Valley Authority

National Archives and Records Administration, College Park, Maryland
Record Group 43 Records of International Conferences, Commissions, and Exhibitions
Record Group 59 General Records of the U.S. Department of State
Record Group 286 Records of the Agency for International Development
Record Group 306 Records of the United States Information Agency
Record Group 353 Interdepartmental and Intradepartmental Committees
Record Group 469 Records of U.S. Foreign Assistance Agencies, 1948–1961
Record Group 490 Records of the Peace Corps

New York Public Library, Manuscript Division, New York, New York
CARE Archives
United China Relief Papers

Rare Book and Manuscript Library, Columbia University, New York, New York
Barbara Ward Jackson Papers
Carnegie Corporation of New York Archives
Institute of Pacific Relations Archives
Oral History Collection

Rockefeller Archive Center, North Tarrytown, New York
Asia Society Archives

General Education Board Records
Overseas Development Council Archives
Record Group 1 Projects
Record Group 2 Rockefeller Foundation Correspondence
Record Group 3 Administration, Program, and Policy
Record Group 4 Nelson A. Rockefeller, Personal Files
Social Science Research Council Records

Schomburg Center for Research in Black Culture, New York, New York
Phelps-Stokes Fund Papers

Seeley G. Mudd Manuscript Library, Princeton University, Princeton, New Jersey
Development and Resources Corporation Archives
George F. Kennan Papers
Council on Foreign Relations Archives
Hamilton Fish Armstrong Papers
Harry Dexter White Papers
Henry Labouisse Papers
John Foster Dulles Papers
Raymond B. Fosdick Papers
W. Arthur Lewis Papers
William Bundy Papers
David E. Lilienthal Papers

Swarthmore College Peace Collection, McCabe Library, Swarthmore,
    Pennsylvania
World Peace Foundation Archives

Tufts University, Digital Collections and Archives, Medford, Massachusetts
World Peace Foundation Archives
Tufts University Archives

United Nations Archives, Long Island City, New York
Records of the United Nations Reconstruction Agency, 1950–1960

United Nations Educational, Scientific, and Cultural Organization Archives,
    Paris, France
Correspondence Files

United States Agency for International Development Library, Washington, DC
Reports

World Bank Archives, Washington, DC
Presidential Oral History Collection

Yale University, Manuscripts and Archives, New Haven, Connecticut
Dean Acheson Papers
Harold Lasswell Papers
Institute of International Studies Records

Yale University, Yale Divinity Library Special Collections, New Haven,
    Connecticut
  Chang Fu-liang Papers
  Dwight Edwards Papers

PERIODICALS

Business Week

Chinese Recorder

Christian Science Monitor

Colliers

Doorway to the Twentieth Century

Far Eastern Survey

Foreign Affairs

Foreign Policy

Harpers

Look

The Nation

Newsweek

New Yorker

New York Times

Philadelphia Inquirer

Technical Assistance Quarterly Bulletin

Washington Post

PUBLISHED PRIMARY AND SECONDARY SOURCES

Acheson, Dean. *Present at the Creation: My Years in the State Department*. 1st
    ed. New York: Norton, 1969.
Adams, Donald K., and Esther E. Gottlieb. *Education and Social Change in
    Korea*. New York: Garland, 1993.
Adas, Michael. *Machines as the Measure of Men: Science, Technology, and Ideolo-
    gies of Western Dominance*, Cornell Studies in Comparative History. Ithaca,
    NY: Cornell University Press, 1989.

Adas, Michael. *Dominance by Design: Technological Imperatives and America's Civilizing Mission.* Cambridge, MA: Belknap Press of Harvard University Press, 2006.

Adler, Les K., and Thomas G. Paterson. "Red Fascism: The Merger of Nazi Germany and Soviet Russia in the American Image of Totalitarianism, 1930s–1950s." *American Historical Review* 75 (April 1970): 1046–64.

Akin, William E. *Technocracy and the American Dream: The Technocrat Movement, 1900–1941.* Berkeley: University of California Press, 1977.

Alchon, Guy. *The Invisible Hand of Planning: Capitalism, Social Science, and the State in the 1920s.* Princeton, NJ: Princeton University Press, 1985.

Alexander, Jeffrey C. *Twenty Lectures: Sociological Theory since World War II.* New York: Columbia University Press, 1987.

Alpers, Benjamin Leontief. *Dictators, Democracy, and American Public Culture: Envisioning the Totalitarian Enemy, 1920s–1950s,* Cultural Studies of the United States. Chapel Hill: University of North Carolina Press, 2003.

Ambrosius, Lloyd E. *Wilsonian Statecraft: Theory and Practice of Liberal Internationalism During World War I.* Wilmington, DE: SR Books, 1991.

Amsden, Alice H. *Asia's Next Giant: South Korea and Late Industrialization.* New York: Oxford University Press, 1989.

Anderson, David L. *Trapped by Success: The Eisenhower Administration and Vietnam, 1953–1961,* Contemporary American History Series. New York: Columbia University Press, 1991.

Appleby, Joyce Oldham, Lynn Avery Hunt, and Margaret C. Jacob. *Telling the Truth About History.* 1st ed. New York: Norton, 1994.

Appy, Christian G. *Cold War Constructions: The Political Culture of United States Imperialism, 1945–1966,* Culture, Politics, and the Cold War. Amherst: University of Massachusetts Press, 2000.

Armitage, David, and M. J. Braddick. *The British Atlantic World, 1500–1800.* New York: Palgrave Macmillan, 2002.

Armstrong, Charles. "'Fraternal Socialism': The International Reconstruction of North Korea, 1953–62." *Cold War History* 5 (May 2005): 161–87.

———. *The North Korean Revolution, 1945–1950.* Ithaca, NY: Cornell University Press, 1994.

Armstrong, Hamilton Fish. *The Foreign Affairs Reader.* New York: Harper, 1947.

Arndt, H. W. *Economic Development: The History of an Idea.* Chicago: University of Chicago Press, 1987.

Arndt, H. W., and Royal Institute of International Affairs. *The Economic Lessons of the Nineteen-Thirties.* London, New York: Oxford University Press, 1944.

Asian Peoples' Anti-Communist League Republic of China. *Soviet Economic Aid to Underdeveloped Countries.* Taipei: Taiwan, 1958.

Badger, Anthony J. *The New Deal: The Depression Years, 1933–40.* Basingstoke, Hampshire: Macmillan, 1989.

Bailyn, Bernard. *Atlantic History: Concept and Contours.* Cambridge, MA: Harvard University Press, 2005.

Ban, Sung Hwan, Pal-lyong Mun, and Dwight H. Perkins. *Rural Development,* Studies in the Modernization of the Republic of Korea, 1945–1975. Cambridge, MA: Harvard University Press, 1980.

Bauer, P. T. *Dissent on Development: Studies and Debates in Development Economics*. London: Weidenfeld and Nicolson, 1971.

Beard, Charles Austin. *A Foreign Policy for America*. New York: Knopf, 1940.

Beard, Charles Austin, and William Beard. *The American Leviathan: The Republic in the Machine Age*. New York: Macmillan, 1930.

Beisner, Robert L. *Dean Acheson: A Life in the Cold War*. New York: Oxford University Press, 2006.

Bell, Daniel. *The End of Ideology: On the Exhaustion of Political Ideas in the Fifties*. Glencoe, IL: Free Press, 1960.

———. *The Coming of Post-Industrial Society: A Venture in Social Forecasting*. New York: Basic Books, 1973.

———. *The Winding Passage: Sociological Essays and Journeys*. New Brunswick, NJ: Transaction Publishers, 1991.

Bender, Thomas. *A Nation among Nations: America's Place in World History*. 1st ed. New York: Hill and Wang, 2006.

Berghahn, Volker Rolf. *America and the Intellectual Cold Wars in Europe: Shepard Stone between Philanthropy, Academy, and Diplomacy*. Princeton, NJ: Princeton University Press, 2001.

Berliner, Joseph S. *Soviet Economic Aid: The New Aid and Trade Policy in Underdeveloped Countries*. 1st ed. New York: F. A. Praeger, 1958.

Berman, Edward H. *The Ideology of Philanthropy: The Influence of the Carnegie, Ford, and Rockefeller Foundations on American Foreign Policy*. Albany: State University of New York Press, 1983.

Berman, Paul. *Terror and Liberalism*. 1st ed. New York: Norton, 2003.

Bessonov, S. "Real'nye predposylki i vozmozhnosti planirovaniia." *Mirovaia ekonomika i mezhdunarodnye otnosheniia* 12 (1969): 90–92.

Bill, James A. *The Eagle and the Lion: The Tragedy of American-Iranian Relations*. New Haven, CT: Yale University Press, 1988.

Bingham, Jonathan B. *Shirt-Sleeve Diplomacy: Point 4 in Action*. New York: J. Day Co., 1954.

Black, Cyril Edwin. *The Dynamics of Modernization: A Study in Comparative History*. New York Harper & Row, 1966.

Black, Eugene R. *The Diplomacy of Economic Development*. Cambridge, MA: Harvard University Press, 1960.

———. *Alternative in Southeast Asia*. New York: Praeger, 1969.

Blackbourn, David. *The Conquest of Nature: Water, Landscape, and the Making of Modern Germany*. 1st American ed. New York: Norton, 2006.

Blackburn, Robert M. *Mercenaries and Lyndon Johnson's "More Flags": The Hiring of Korean, Filipino, and Thai Soldiers in the Vietnam War*. Jefferson, NC: McFarland, 1994.

Blaufarb, Douglas S. *The Counterinsurgency Era: U.S. Doctrine and Performance, 1950 to the Present*. New York: Free Press, 1977.

Bock, Edwin A., and Public Administration Clearing House. *Fifty Years of Technical Assistance: Some Administrative Experiences of U.S. Voluntary Agencies*. Chicago: Public Administration Clearing House, 1954.

Borgwardt, Elizabeth. *A New Deal for the World: America's Vision for Human Rights*. Cambridge, MA: Belknap Press of Harvard University Press, 2005.

Borkenau, Franz, Julian Huxley, and Geoffrey Crowther. *After Peace, What? A Program for Counter-Revolution*. Norman, OK: Cooperative Books, 1941.

Boserup, Ester. *Woman's Role in Economic Development*. New York: St. Martin's Press, 1970.

Bostock, Frances, and Geoffrey Jones. *Planning and Power in Iran: Ebtehaj and Economic Development under the Shah*. London, Totowa, NJ: F. Cass, 1989.

Bosworth, R. J. B. *Mussolini's Italy: Life under the Dictatorship*. London: Allen Lane, 2005.

Bradley, Mark. *Imagining Vietnam and America: The Making of Postcolonial Vietnam, 1919–1950*, The New Cold War History. Chapel Hill: University of North Carolina Press, 2000.

Brazinsky, Gregg. *Nation Building in South Korea: Koreans, Americans, and the Making of a Democracy*, The New Cold War History. Chapel Hill: University of North Carolina Press, 2007.

Bremner, Robert Hamlett. *American Philanthropy*. 2nd ed. The Chicago History of American Civilization. Chicago: University of Chicago Press, 1988.

Brick, Howard. *Age of Contradiction: American Thought and Culture in the 1960s*, Twayne's American Thought and Culture Series. New York, London: Twayne Publishers, 1998.

Brinkley, Alan. *Voices of Protest: Huey Long, Father Coughlin, and the Great Depression*. 1st Vintage Books ed. New York: Vintage Books, 1983.

———. *The End of Reform: New Deal Liberalism in Recession and War*. 1st Vintage Books ed. New York: Vintage Books, 1996.

Brown, Judith M. *Nehru: A Political Life*. New Haven, CT: Yale University Press, 2003.

Brown, William Adams, and Redvers Opie. *American Foreign Assistance*. Washington, DC: Brookings Institution, 1953.

Buck, John Lossing. *Land Utilization in China, a Study of 16,786 Farms in 168 Localities, and 38,256 Farm Families in Twenty-Two Provinces in China, 1929–1933*. Shanghai, China: Commercial Press, 1937.

Buck, Pearl S. *The Good Earth*. New York: John Day, 1931.

Buell, Raymond Leslie. "Political and Social Reconstruction in France." *American Political Science Review* 15 (February 1921): 27–51.

Bundy, William P. *A Tangled Web: The Making of Foreign Policy in the Nixon Presidency*. 1st ed. New York: Hill and Wang, 1998.

Burnham, James. *The Managerial Revolution: What Is Happening in the World*. New York: John Day, 1941.

Buruma, Ian, and Avishai Margalit. *Occidentalism: The West in the Eyes of Its Enemies*. New York: Penguin Press, 2004.

Byrne, Jeffery James. "Our Own Special Brand of Socialism: Algeria and the Contest of Modernities in the 1960s." *Diplomatic History* 33 (Summer 2009): 427–447.

Carnegie Commission on Science, Technology, and Government. *A Science and Technology Agenda for the Nation: Recommendations for the President and Congress: A Report of the Carnegie Commission on Science, Technology, and Government*. New York: The Commission, 1992.

————. *Science, Technology, and Government for a Changing World: The Concluding Report of the Carnegie Commission on Science, Technology, and Government.* New York: The Commission, 1993.

————. *Facing toward Governments: Nongovernmental Organizations and Scientific and Technical Advice.* New York: The Commission, 1993.

Carson, Rachel. *Silent Spring.* Boston: Houghton Mifflin, 1962.

Carter, James M. *Inventing Vietnam: The United States and State Building, 1954–1968* (New York: Cambridge University Press, 2008).

Catholic Church, and Joseph Casper Husslein. *Social Wellsprings.* Milwaukee: Bruce Publishing, 1940.

Chamberlin, William Henry. *The Soviet Planned Economic Order.* Boston: World Peace Foundation, 1931.

Chang, Gordon H. *Friends and Enemies: The United States, China, and the Soviet Union, 1948–1972.* Stanford, CA: Stanford University Press, 1990.

Chapin, F. Stuart, and Sam Schiller. *Communities for Living, Prepared for the Advisory Panel on Regional Materials of Instruction for the Tennessee Valley.* Athens: University of Georgia Press, 1941.

Chas. T. Main Inc. *The Unified Development of the Water Resources of the Jordan Valley Region.* Boston, 1953.

Chase, Stuart. *A New Deal.* New York: Macmillan, 1932.

Chen, Jian. *China's Road to the Korean War: The Making of the Sino-American Confrontation.* New York: Columbia University Press, 1994.

————. *Mao's China and the Cold War,* The New Cold War History. Chapel Hill: University of North Carolina Press, 2001.

Chiang, Yung-chen. *Social Engineering and the Social Sciences in China, 1919–1949,* Cambridge Modern China Series. Cambridge, UK, New York: Cambridge University Press, 2001.

China International Famine Relief Commission. *Herr Raiffeisen among Chinese Farmers.* New York: Garland, 1980.

Chomsky, Noam. *The Cold War and the University: Toward an Intellectual History of the Postwar Years.* New York: New Press; distributed by Norton, 1997.

Clapp, Gordon Rufus. *The TVA: An Approach to the Development of a Region,* Charles R. Walgreen Foundation Lectures. Chicago: University of Chicago Press, 1955.

————. *The TVA and Its Critics.* New York: League for Industrial Democracy, 1955.

Clapp, Gordon Rufus, and C. Hart Schaaf. *An Approach to Economic Development in the Middle East,* International Conciliation, No. 460. New York: Carnegie Endowment for International Peace, 1950.

Cleveland, Harlan. "The Convalescence of Foreign Aid." *The American Economic Review* 49 (May 1959): 216–31.

Cleveland, Harlan, and Gerard J. Mangone. *The Art of Overseasmanship.* Syracuse, NY: Syracuse University Press, 1957.

Cleveland, Harlan, Gerard J. Mangone, and John Clarke Adams. *The Overseas Americans.* 1st ed. New York: McGraw-Hill, 1960.

Cleveland, Harlan, and Maxwell Graduate School of Citizenship and Public Affairs. *The Theory and Practice of Foreign Aid*. New York: Syracuse University Press, 1956.

Clifford, Clark M., and Richard C. Holbrooke. *Counsel to the President: A Memoir*. 1st ed. New York: Random House, 1991.

Cobbs Hoffman, Elizabeth. *All You Need Is Love: The Peace Corps and the Spirit of the 1960s*. Cambridge, MA: Harvard University Press, 1998.

Cohen, Nancy. *The Reconstruction of American Liberalism, 1865–1914*. Chapel Hill: University of North Carolina Press, 2002.

Cohen, Warren I. *The Chinese Connection: Roger S. Greene, Thomas W. Lamont, George E. Sokolsky and American-East Asian Relations*, Studies of the East Asian Institute. New York: Columbia University Press, 1978.

——. *Dean Rusk*, The American Secretaries of State and Their Diplomacy; V. 19. Totowa, NJ: Cooper Square Publishers, 1980.

Colignon, Richard A. *Power Plays: Critical Events in the Institutionalization of the Tennessee Valley Authority*. Albany: State University of New York Press, 1997.

Columbia Conference on International Economic Development, Documents Papers, and Addresses, Feb. 15–21, 1970, 2 vols. New York: Columbia University, 1970.

Commager, Henry Steele. *The American Mind: An Interpretation of American Thought and Character since the 1880's*. New Haven, CT: Yale University Press, 1950.

Commission on International Development and Lester B. Pearson. *Partners in Development: Report*. New York: Praeger, 1969.

Condliffe, J. B. *Problems of the Pacific: Proceedings of the Second Conference of the Institute of Pacific Relations, Honolulu, Hawaii, July 15 to 29, 1927*. Chicago: University of Chicago Press, 1928.

——. *Problems of the Pacific, 1929: Proceedings of the Third Conference of the Institute of Pacific Relations, Nara and Kyoto, Japan, October 23 to November 9, 1929*. Chicago: University of Chicago Press, 1930.

——. *The Pacific Area in International Relations*, Reading with a Purpose, No. 44. Chicago: American Library Association, 1931.

——. *War and Depression*. Boston: World Peace Foundation, 1935.

——. *Agenda for a Postwar World*. New York: Norton, 1942.

Condliffe, J. B., and Commission to Study the Organization of Peace. *Problems of Economic Reorganization*. New York: Commission to Study the Organization of Peace, 1943.

Condliffe, J. B., and Harold Hutcheson. *Point Four and the World Economy: Point Four; Economic Development*, Headline Series, No. 79. New York: Foreign Policy Association, 1950.

Condliffe, J. B., and World Peace Foundation. *China to-Day: Economic*. Boston: World Peace Foundation, 1932.

Conference on North Atlantic Relations. *Note as to Some Post-War Economic Problems*, Conference on North Atlantic Relations (September 4–9, 1941: Prout's Neck, ME) Documents; No. 19. London: Royal Institute of International Affairs, 1941.

Connelly, Matthew James. *Fatal Misconception: The Struggle to Control World Population*. Cambridge, MA: Belknap Press of Harvard University Press, 2008.

Cooper, Frederick. *Decolonization and African Society: The Labor Question in French and British Africa*. New York: Cambridge University Press, 1996.

Cooper, Frederick, and Randall Packard, eds. *International Development and the Social Sciences: Essays on the History and Politics of Knowledge*. Berkeley: University of California Press.

Corbett, Percy Ellwood. *Post-War Worlds*. New York, London: Farrar and Rinehart, 1942.

Council on World Tensions. *Restless Nations: A Study of World Tensions and Development*. New York: Dodd, Mead, 1962.

Cowen, Michael, and Robert W. Shenton. *Doctrines of Development*. London, New York: Routledge, 1996.

Cronin, James E. *The World the Cold War Made: Order, Chaos and the Return of History*. New York: Routledge, 1996.

Crush, J. S. *Power of Development*. London, New York: Routledge, 1995.

Cullather, Nick. "Development: It's History." *Diplomatic History* 24 (Fall 2000): 641–53.

———. "Damming Afghanistan: Modernization in a Buffer State." *Journal of American History* 89 (September 2002): 512–37.

———. "Miracles of Modernization: The Green Revolution and the Apotheosis of Technology." *Diplomatic History* 28 (April 2004): 227–54.

———. "The Foreign Policy of the Calorie." *American Historical Review* 112 (April 2007): 336–64.

Cumings, Bruce. *The Origins of the Korean War*. Princeton, NJ: Princeton University Press, 1981.

———. *Korea's Place in the Sun: A Modern History*. 1st ed. New York: Norton, 1997.

———. "The Origins and Development of the Northeast Asian Political Economy: Industrial Sectors, Product Cycle, and Political Consequences." *International Organization* 38 (Winter 1984): 1–40.

Curti, Merle Eugene. *Prelude to Point Four*. Madison: University of Wisconsin Press, 1954.

———. *American Philanthropy Abroad*, Society and Philanthropy Series. New Brunswick, NJ: Transaction Books, 1988.

Curti, Merle Eugene, and Roderick Nash. *Philanthropy in the Shaping of American Higher Education*. New Brunswick, NJ: Rutgers University Press, 1965.

Dahir, James. *Region Building: Community Development Lessons from the Tennessee Valley*. New York: Harper, 1955.

Danaher, Kevin. *50 Years Is Enough: The Case against the World Bank and the International Monetary Fund*. Boston, MA: South End Press, 1994.

Dashiell, J. F. "Some Psychological Phases of Internationalism." *American Journal of Sociology* 25 (May 1920): 757.

Davidson, Donald. *The Tennessee*. Lanham, MD: J. S. Sanders, 1991.

Davis, Mike. *Late Victorian Holocausts: El Niño Famines and the Making of the Third World*. New York: Verso, 2001.

Davis, Rebekah C. Beatty. "Development as a Tool of Diplomacy: The Domestic Models for United States Policy in the Jordan River Valley, 1939–1956," Ph.D. diss. Georgetown University, 1999.

Dawley, Alan. *Changing the World: American Progressives in War and Revolution*, Politics and Society in Twentieth-Century America. Princeton, NJ: Princeton University Press, 2003.

DeFrancis, John. *Nationalism and Language Reform in China*. Princeton, NJ: Princeton University Press, 1950.

Department of State. *Papers Relating to the Foreign Relations of the United States*. Washington, DC: Government Printing Office, various dates.

Dewey, John. *Liberalism and Social Action*. New York: G. P. Putnam, 1935.

———. "Why I am Not a Communist." *Modern Monthly* 8 (April 1934): 135–37.

Diggins, John P. *Mussolini and Fascism: The View from America*. Princeton, NJ: Princeton University Press, 1972.

Diner, Steven J. *A Very Different Age: Americans of the Progressive Era*. 1st ed. New York: Hill and Wang, 1998.

Divine, Robert A. *Eisenhower and the Cold War*. New York: Oxford University Press, 1981.

Dower, John W. *Embracing Defeat: Japan in the Wake of World War II*. 1st ed. New York: W.W. Norton and Company/ New Press, 1999.

Duffett, John. *Against the Crime of Silence: Proceedings*. New York: Simon & Schuster, 1970.

Durbin, E.F.M. *The Economic Basis of Peace*. London: National Peace Council, 1942.

Easterly, William Russell. *The Elusive Quest for Growth: Economists' Adventures and Misadventures in the Tropics*. Cambridge, MA: MIT Press, 2001.

———. *The White Man's Burden: Why the West's Efforts to Aid the Rest Have Done So Much Ill and So Little Good*. New York: Penguin Press, 2006.

———, ed., *Reinventing Foreign Aid*. Cambridge, MA: MIT University Press, 2008.

Eberstadt, Nicholas. *Foreign Aid and American Purpose*. Washington, DC: American Enterprise Institute, 1988.

Ebtehaj, A. H., and Sāazmāan-i Barnāamah (Iran). *The Plan Organization of Iran: Historical Review, September 25, 1955–March 20, 1958*. Tehran: Public Relations Bureau, Plan Organization, 1958.

Ehrlich, Paul R. *The Population Bomb*. New York: Ballantine Books, 1968.

Eisenstadt, S. N. *Modernization: Protest and Change*, Modernization of Traditional Societies Series. Englewood Cliffs, NJ: Prentice-Hall, 1966.

Engerman, David C. *Staging Growth: Modernization, Development, and the Global Cold War*, Culture, Politics, and the Cold War. Amherst: University of Massachusetts Press, 2003.

———. *Modernization from the Other Shore: American Intellectuals and the Romance of Russian Development*. Cambridge, MA: Harvard University Press, 2003.

———. "The Romance of Economic Development and New Histories of the Cold War." *Diplomatic History* 28 (January 2004): 23–54.

Ernst, John. *Forging a Fateful Alliance: Michigan State University and the Vietnam War.* East Lansing: Michigan State University Press, 1998.

Escobar, Arturo. *Encountering Development: The Making and Unmaking of the Third World*, Princeton Studies in Culture/Power/History. Princeton, NJ: Princeton University Press, 1995.

Espy, Willard R. *Bold New Program.* 1st ed. New York: Harper, 1950.

Evans, Richard J. *The Third Reich in Power, 1933–1939.* New York: Penguin Press, 2005.

Fairbank, John King. *Next Step in Asia.* Cambridge, MA: Harvard University Press, 1949.

Farber, David R. *The Sixties: From Memory to History.* Chapel Hill: University of North Carolina Press, 1994.

Farnham, Barbara. *Roosevelt and the Munich Crisis: A Study of Political Decision-Making.* Princeton, NJ: Princeton University Press, 1997.

Farvar, M. Taghi, John P. Milton, *The Careless Technology: Ecology and International Development; the Record.* 1st ed. Garden City, NY: Natural History Press, 1972.

Ferguson, James. *The Anti-Politics Machine: 'Development,' Depoliticization, and Bureaucratic Power in Lesotho.* Minneapolis: University of Minnesota Press, 1994.

Figes, Orlando. *The Whisperers: Private Life in Stalin's Russia.* New York: Metropolitan Books, 2007.

Filene, Peter G. *Americans and the Soviet Experiment, 1917–1933.* Cambridge, MA: Harvard University Press, 1967.

Finer, Herman. *The T.V.A.: Lessons for International Application.* Montreal: International Labour Office, 1944.

Fisher, Christopher. "The Illusions of Progress: CORDS and the Crisis of Modernization in South Vietnam, 1965–1968." *Pacific Historical Review* 75 (1): 25–51.

Flippen, J. Brooks. *Nixon and the Environment.* 1st ed. Albuquerque: University of New Mexico Press, 2000.

Florini, Ann, Nihon Kokusai Kāoryāu Sentāa., and Carnegie Endowment for International Peace. *The Third Force: The Rise of Transnational Civil Society.* Tokyo: Japan Center for International Exchange; Washington, DC: Carnegie Endowment for International Peace: Brookings Institution Press Distributor, 2000.

Foner, Eric. *Reconstruction: America's Unfinished Revolution, 1863–1877.* 1st ed. New American Nation Series. New York: Harper and Row, 1988.

Food and Agriculture Organization of the United Nations, and United Nations. Korean Reconstruction Agency. *Rehabilitation and Development of Agriculture, Forestry, and Fisheries in South Korea: Report Prepared for the United Nations Korean Reconstruction Agency.* New York: Columbia University Press, 1954.

Forbes, W. Cameron. *The Philippine Islands.* Boston, New York: Houghton Mifflin, 1928.

Forbes-Lindsay, Charles Harcourt Ainslie. *America's Insular Possessions.* Philadelphia: J. C. Winston Co., 1906.

Fosdick, Raymond Blaine. *Our Machine Civilization*. New York: Eilert, 1922.
Fosdick, Raymond Blaine. *Companions in Depression: The International Implications of the Business Slump*. Margaret C. Peabody Fund, 1930.
———. *The Old Savage in the New Civilization*. Garden City, NY: Doubleday Doran, 1928.
———. *The Story of the Rockefeller Foundation*. 1st ed. New York: Harper, 1952.
Frank, Andre Gunder. "The Development of Underdevelopment," *Monthly Review* 18 (4): 23–28.
Frank, Charles R., and Mary Baird. "Foreign Aid: Its Speckled Past and Future Prospects." *International Organization* 29 (Winter 1975): 140.
Friedberg, Aaron L. *In the Shadow of the Garrison State: America's Anti-Statism and Its Cold War Grand Strategy*, Princeton Studies in International History and Politics. Princeton, NJ: Princeton University Press, 2000.
Frieden, Jeffry A. *Global Capitalism: Its Fall and Rise in the Twentieth Century*. New York: Norton, 2006.
Friedman, Thomas L. *The Lexus and the Olive Tree*. New York: Farrar, Straus & Giroux, 1999.
Friedrich, Carl J. *Totalitarianism: Proceedings of a Conference Held at the American Academy of Arts and Sciences, March 1953*. Cambridge, MA: Harvard University Press, 1954.
Friedrich, Carl J., Michael Curtis, and Benjamin R. Barber. *Totalitarianism in Perspective: Three Views*. New York: Praeger, 1969.
Fuess, Harald. *The Japanese Empire in East Asia and Its Postwar Legacy*. Munich: Iudicium, 1998.
Fukuyama, Francis. "The End of History." *National Interest* (Summer 1989): 3–18.
———. *The End of History and the Last Man*. New York: Avon Books, 1993.
———. *The Great Disruption: Human Nature and the Reconstitution of Social Order*. New York: Free Press, 1999.
———. *State-Building: Governance and World Order in the 21st Century*. Ithaca, NY: Cornell University Press, 2004.
———. *Nation-Building: Beyond Afghanistan and Iraq*, Forum on Constructive Capitalism. Baltimore: Johns Hopkins University Press, 2006.
———. *America at the Crossroads: Democracy, Power, and the Neoconservative Legacy*, The Castle Lectures in Ethics, Politics, and Economics. New Haven, CT: Yale University Press, 2006.
Gaddis, John Lewis. *The United States and the Origins of the Cold War, 1941–1947*. New York: Columbia University Press, 1972.
———. *Strategies of Containment: A Critical Appraisal of Postwar American National Security Policy*. New York: Oxford University Press, 1982.
———. *We Now Know: Rethinking Cold War History*. New York: Oxford University Press, 1997.
———. *Surprise, Security, and the American Experience*. Cambridge, MA: Harvard University Press, 2004.
———. *The Cold War: A New History*. New York: Penguin Press, 2005.

Galbraith, John Kenneth. *Economic Development in Perspective*. Cambridge, MA: Harvard University Press, 1962.

Gardner, Lloyd C. *Approaching Vietnam: From World War II through Dienbienphu, 1941–1954*. 1st ed. New York: Norton, 1988.

———. *Pay Any Price: Lyndon Johnson and the Wars for Vietnam*. Chicago: I. R. Dee, 1995.

Gardner, Lloyd C., and Ted Gittinger. *Vietnam: The Early Decisions*. Austin: University of Texas Press, 1997.

Gardner, Richard N. "The Role of the UN in Environmental Problems." *International Organization* 26 (Spring 1972): 237–54.

Gerschenkron, Alexander. *Economic Backwardness in Historical Perspective*. Cambridge, MA: Belknap Press, 1962.

Gibson, James William. *The Perfect War: Technowar in Vietnam*. 1st ed. Boston: Atlantic Monthly Press, 1986.

Gilman, Nils. *Mandarins of the Future: Modernization Theory in Cold War America*, New Studies in American Intellectual and Cultural History. Baltimore, London: Johns Hopkins University Press, 2003.

Gleason, Abbott. *Totalitarianism: The Inner History of the Cold War*. New York: Oxford University Press, 1995.

Goodell, Grace E. *The Elementary Structures of Political Life: Rural Development in Pahlavi Iran*. New York: Oxford University Press, 1986.

Goodwin, Doris Kearns. *Lyndon Johnson and the American Dream*. 1st ed. New York: Harper & Row, 1976.

Graham, Otis L. *Toward a Planned Society: From Roosevelt to Nixon*. New York: Oxford University Press, 1976.

Grant, Nancy. *TVA and Black Americans: Planning for the Status Quo*. Philadelphia: Temple University Press, 1990.

Gray, Gordon. *Report to the President on Foreign Economic Policies*. Washington, DC: U.S. Government Printing Office, 1950.

Greene, Graham. *The Quiet American*. New York: Viking Press, 1956.

Gunther, John. *Inside U.S.A.* New York: Harper, 1947.

———. *The Story of TVA*. Rev. ed. New York: Harper, 1953.

Hagen, James M., and Vernon W. Ruttan, "Development Policy Under Eisenhower and Kennedy." *Journal of Developing Areas* 23 (October 1988): 5.

Hahn, Peter L., and Mary Ann Heiss. *Empire and Revolution: The United States and the Third World since 1945*. Columbus: Ohio State University Press, 2000.

Halberstam, David. *The Best and the Brightest*. Greenwich, CT: Fawcett Publications, 1973.

Halper, Stefan A., and Jonathan Clarke. *America Alone: The Neo-Conservatives and the Global Order*. Cambridge, New York: Cambridge University Press, 2004.

Hambidge, Gove. *The Story of FAO*. New York: Van Nostrand, 1955.

Hamburg, David A. *No More Killing Fields: Preventing Deadly Conflict*. Lanham, MD: Rowman and Littlefield, 2002.

Hamby, Alonzo L. *Beyond the New Deal: Harry S. Truman and American Liberalism*, Contemporary American History Series. New York: Columbia University Press, 1973.

Hamby, Alonzo L. *Liberalism and Its Challengers: From F.D.R. to Bush*. 2nd ed. New York: Oxford University Press, 1992.

———. *For the Survival of Democracy: Franklin Roosevelt and the World Crisis of the 1930s*. New York, London: Free Press, 2004.

Han, Sæung-ju. *The Failure of Democracy in South Korea*. Berkeley: University of California Press, 1974.

Haq, Mahbub ul. *The Poverty Curtain: Choices for the Third World*. New York: Columbia University Press, 1976.

———. *Reflections on Human Development: How the Focus of Development Economics Shifted from National Income Accounting to People-Centered Policies, Told by One of the Chief Architects of the New Paradigm*. New York: Oxford University Press, 1995.

Hargrove, Erwin C. *Prisoners of Myth: The Leadership of the Tennessee Valley Authority, 1933–1990*, Princeton Studies in American Politics. Princeton, NJ: Princeton University Press, 1994.

Hargrove, Erwin C., Paul Keith Conkin, and Vanderbilt Institute for Public Policy Studies. *TVA, Fifty Years of Grass-Roots Bureaucracy*. Urbana: University of Illinois Press, 1983.

Harrington, Michael. *The Other America: Poverty in the United States*. Rev. ed. New York: Penguin Books, 1981.

Harrison, David. *The Sociology of Modernization and Development*. London: Routledge, 1991.

Hart, Henry C. *New India's Rivers*. Bombay: Orient Longmans, 1956.

———. *Administrative Aspects of River Valley Development*. New York: Asia Pub. House, 1962.

Hatcher, Patrick Lloyd. *The Suicide of an Elite: American Internationalists and Vietnam*. Stanford, CA: Stanford University Press, 1990.

Hayek, Friedrich A. von. *The Road to Serfdom*. Chicago: University of Chicago Press, 1944.

Hayes, Samuel P. *The Beginning of American Aid to Southeast Asia: The Griffin Mission of 1950*. Lexington, MA: Heath Lexington Books, 1971.

Hayford, Charles Wishart. *To the People: James Yen and Village China*, The U.S. and Pacific Asia—Studies in Social, Economic, and Political Interaction. New York: Columbia University Press, 1990.

Hazlitt, Henry. *Illusions of Point Four*. Irvington-on-Hudson, NY: Foundation for Economic Education, 1950.

Headrick, Daniel R. *The Tools of Empire: Technology and European Imperialism in the Nineteenth Century*. New York: Oxford University Press, 1981.

Hechler, Ken. *Working with Truman: A Personal Memoir of the White House Years*. New York: Putnam, 1982.

Heilbrunn, Jacob. *They Knew They Were Right: The Rise of the Neocons*. 1st ed. New York: Doubleday, 2008.

Herman, Ellen. *The Romance of American Psychology: Political Culture in the Age of Experts*. Berkeley: University of California Press, 1995.

Herring, George C. *America's Longest War: The United States and Vietnam, 1950–1975*. 3rd ed. America in Crisis. New York: McGraw-Hill, 1996.

Hewa, Soma, and Philo Hove. *Philanthropy and Cultural Context: Western Philanthropy in South, East, and Southeast Asia in the 20th Century.* Lanham, MD: University Press of America, 1997.

History of United States Armed Forces in Korea, 4 vols. Seoul, 1988.

Hobsbawm, E. J. *Nations and Nationalism Since 1780: Programme, Myth, Reality.* New York: Cambridge University Press, 1990.

———. *The Age of Extremes: A History of the World, 1914–1991.* New York: Vintage Books, 1996.

Hogan, Michael J. *The Marshall Plan: America, Britain, and the Reconstruction of Western Europe, 1947–1952,* Studies in Economic History and Policy. Cambridge, Cambridgeshire, New York: Cambridge University Press, 1987.

Hogan, Michael, and Thomas G. Paterson. *Explaining the History of American Foreign Relations.* 2nd ed. New York: Cambridge University Press, 2004.

Holland, W. L., and Kate Louise Mitchell. *Problems of the Pacific, 1936. Aims and Results of Social and Economic Policies in Pacific Countries: Proceedings of the Sixth Conference of the Institute of Pacific Relations, Yosemite National Park, California, 15–29 August 1936.* Chicago: University of Chicago Press, 1937.

Hoover, Herbert. "The Nation and Science," *Science* 65 (Jan. 1927): 26–29.

———. *An American Epic.* Chicago: H. Regnery Co., 1959.

Hori, Hiroshi. *The Mekong: Environment and Development.* Tokyo, New York: United Nations University Press, 2000.

Hough, Jerry F. *The Struggle for the Third World: Soviet Debates and American Options.* Washington, DC: Brookings Institution, 1986.

Howard, T. Levron. "The Social Scientist in the Tennessee Valley Authority Program." *Social Forces* 15 (October 1936): 29–34.

Huang, Po-Wen. *The Asian Development Bank: Diplomacy and Development in Asia.* 1st ed. New York: Vantage Press, 1975.

Hubbard, G. E. "Financial Reconstruction for China," *Journal of the Royal Institute of International Affairs* 9 (September 1930): 636–37.

Hunt, Michael H. *Ideology and U.S. Foreign Policy.* New Haven, CT: Yale University Press, 1987.

———. *Lyndon Johnson's War: America's Cold War Crusade in Vietnam, 1945–1968.* 1st ed. A Critical Issue. New York: Hill and Wang, 1996.

———. *The American Ascendancy: How the United States Gained and Wielded Global Dominance.* Chapel Hill: University of North Carolina Press, 2007.

Huntington, Samuel P., and Harvard University Center for International Affairs. *Political Order in Changing Societies.* New Haven, CT: Yale University Press, 1968.

Huxley, Julian. *Africa View.* London: Chatto & Windus, 1931.

———. *A Scientist among the Soviets.* New York: Harper & Brothers, 1932.

———. *If I Were Dictator.* New York, London: Harper, 1934.

———. *Democracy Marches.* London: Chatto & Windus, 1941.

———. *Reconstruction and Peace.* New York: New Republic, 1942.

———. *TVA, Adventure in Planning.* Cheam, Surrey: Architectural Press, 1943.

Huxley, Julian. *On Living in a Revolution*. New York: Harper, 1944.

———. *Memories*. 1st U.S. ed. New York: Harper & Row, 1970.

Inkeles, Alex, and David Horton Smith. *Becoming Modern: Individual Change in Six Developing Countries*. Cambridge, MA: Harvard University Press, 1974.

Institute of Economic Affairs (Great Britain), Barbara Ward, and P. T. Bauer. *Two Views on Aid to Developing Countries*. London: Institute of Economic Affairs, 1966.

Institute of Pacific Relations, Bruno Lasker, and W. L. Holland. *Problems of the Pacific, 1933: Economic Conflict and Control. Proceedings of the Fifth Conference of the Institute of Pacific Relations, Banff, Canada, 14–26 August, 1933*. Chicago: University of Chicago Press, 1934.

International Institute for Environmental Affairs. *The Human Environment: Science and International Decision-Making, A Basic Paper, Prepared for the Secretariat of the United Nations Conference on the Human Environment*, 1971.

Iriye, Akira. *The Cold War in Asia: A Historical Introduction*. Englewood Cliffs, NJ: Prentice-Hall, 1974.

———. *Cultural Internationalism and World Order*. Baltimore: Johns Hopkins University Press, 1997.

———. *Global Community: The Role of International Organizations in the Making of the Contemporary World*. Berkeley: University of California Press, 2002.

Isaacs, Harold Robert. *Two-Thirds of the World: Problems of a New Approach to the Peoples of Asia, Africa, and Latin America*. Washington, DC: Public Affairs Institute, 1950.

Jespersen, T. Christopher. *American Images of China, 1931–1949*. Stanford, CA: Stanford University Press, 1996.

Joint Commission on Rural Reconstruction, and United States Economic Cooperation Administration. *The Program of the Joint Commission on Rural Reconstruction in China: Its Organization, Accomplishments and Lessons for Rural Reconstruction Elsewhere in Asia*. Washington, DC: Economic Cooperation Administration, 1951.

Jordahl, Brian D., and Vernon W. Ruttan. *Universities and Aid: A History of Their Partnership in Technical Assistance for Developing Countries*. St. Paul Department of Agricultural and Applied Economics, University of Minnesota, 1991.

Jordan, Henry P., and American Council on Public Affairs. *Problems of Post-War Reconstruction*. Washington, DC: American Council on Public Affairs, 1942.

Jordan, John M. *Machine-Age Ideology: Social Engineering and American Liberalism, 1911–1939*. Chapel Hill: University of North Carolina Press, 1994.

Josephson, Paul R. *Industrialized Nature: Brute Force Technology and the Transformation of the Natural World*. Washington, DC: Island Press, 2002.

Judt, Tony. *Postwar: A History of Europe since 1945*. New York: Penguin Press, 2005.

Kaiser, David E. *American Tragedy: Kennedy, Johnson, and the Origins of the Vietnam War*. Cambridge, MA: Belknap Press of Harvard University Press, 2000.

Kampmeier, Roland A. *Ways to Share Experience with Less Developed Countries: A Case Study of TVA*. Washington, DC: Brookings Institution, 1961.

Kanwar, Sain. *America through Indian Eyes, by Kanwar Sain ... With a Foreword by the Hon'ble Khan Bahadur, Lt.-Col., Sirdar Sir Sikander Hyat Khan.* Lahore: Uttar Chand Kapur & Sons, 1943.

Kapur, Devesh, John Prior Lewis, and Richard Charles Webb. *The World Bank: Its First Half Century.* Washington, DC: Brookings Institution, 1997.

Karnow, Stanley. *In Our Image: America's Empire in the Philippines.* 1st ed. New York: Random House, 1989.

Kasson, John F. *Civilizing the Machine: Technology and Republican Values in America, 1776–1900.* New York: Hill and Wang, 1999.

Katz, Michael B. *In the Shadow of the Poorhouse: A Social History of Welfare in America.* 10th anniversary ed. New York: Basic Books, 1996.

Katznelson, Ira. *When Affirmative Action Was White: An Untold History of Racial Inequality in Twentieth-Century America.* 1st ed. New York: Norton, 2005.

Kaufman, Burton Ira. *Trade and Aid: Eisenhower's Foreign Economic Policy, 1953–1961.* Baltimore: Johns Hopkins University Press, 1982.

Kay, David, and Eugene B. Skolnikoff. "International Institutions and the Environmental Crisis: A Look Ahead." *International Organization* 26 (Spring 1972): 469–78.

Kennan, George Frost. *Realities of American Foreign Policy.* Princeton, NJ: Princeton University Press, 1954.

———. *Memoirs, 1925–1950.* 1st ed. Boston: Little, 1967.

———. *The Cloud of Danger: Current Realities of American Foreign Policy.* 1st ed. Boston: Little Brown, 1977.

———. *Sketches from a Life.* New York: Pantheon Books, 1989.

Kennedy, David M. *Freedom from Fear: The American People in Depression and War, 1929–1945.* New York: Oxford University Press, 1999.

Kennedy, Paul M. *The Parliament of Man: The Past, Present, and Future of the United Nations.* New York: Random House, 2006.

Kennedy, Ross A. "Woodrow Wilson, World War I, and an American Conception of National Security." *Diplomatic History* 25 (Winter 2001): 1–31.

Kennet, Wayland. "The Stockholm Conference on the Human Environment." *International Affairs* 48 (January 1972): 33–45.

Keun, Odette. *My Adventures in Bolshevik Russia.* New York: Dodd, Mead, 1923.

———. *Darkness from the North.* London: Brinton, 1935.

———. *A Foreigner Looks at the TVA.* New York, Toronto: Longmans, Green, 1937.

———. *I Think Aloud in America.* London, New York: Longmans, Green, 1939. Microform by Odette Keun.

———. *And Hell Followed ... A European Ally Interprets the War for Ordinary People Like Herself.* London: Constable and Company, 1942.

———. *Continental Stakes; Marshes of Invasion, Valley of Conquest and Peninsula of Chaos.* London: Letchworth Herts, 1944.

Khong, Yuen Foong. *Analogies at War: Korea, Munich, Dien Bien Phu, and the Vietnam Decisions of 1965.* Princeton, NJ: Princeton University Press, 1992.

Klatt, Werner. *The Chinese Model: A Political, Economic and Social Survey.* Hong Kong: Hong Kong University Press, 1965.

Kleinman, Mark L. *A World of Hope, a World of Fear: Henry A. Wallace, Reinhold Niebuhr, and American Liberalism*. Columbus: Ohio State University Press, 2000.

Klingensmith, Daniel. *"One Valley and a Thousand": Dams, Nationalism, and Development*. New Delhi: Oxford University Press, 2007.

Kolko, Gabriel. *Confronting the Third World: United States Foreign Policy, 1945–1980*. 1st ed. New York: Pantheon Books, 1988.

———. *Anatomy of a War: Vietnam, the United States, and the Modern Historical Experience*. New York: New Press; distributed by Norton, 1994.

Kolontaev, A. P., and V. I. Pavlov. "V.I. Lenin o preobrazovanii mnogoukladnykh struktur i chastnogo sektora (na primer razvivaiushchikhia stran)." *Narody Azii i Afriki* 2 (1970): 23.

Kotkin, Stephen. *Magnetic Mountain: Stalinism as a Civilization*. Berkeley: University of California Press, 1995.

———. *Armageddon Averted: The Soviet Collapse, 1970–2000*. Oxford: Oxford University Press, 2001.

Kotkin, Stephen, and David Wolff. *Rediscovering Russia in Asia: Siberia and the Russian Far East*. Armonk, NY: M. E. Sharpe, 1995.

Kraske, Jochen, William H. Becker, William Diamond, and Louis Galambos. *Bankers with a Mission: The Presidents of the World Bank, 1946–91*. New York: Oxford University Press.

Krueger, Anne O. *The Developmental Role of the Foreign Sector and Aid*, Studies in the Modernization of the Republic of Korea, 1945–1975. Cambridge: Harvard University Press, 1979.

Kunz, Diane B. *The Diplomacy of the Crucial Decade: American Foreign Relations During the 1960s*. New York: Columbia University Press, 1994.

LaFeber, Walter. *America, Russia, and the Cold War, 1945–1996*. 8th ed. America in Crisis. New York: McGraw-Hill, 1997.

———. "Technology and U.S. Foreign Relations." *Diplomatic History* 24 (Winter 2000): 1–19.

Lagemann, Ellen Condliffe. *The Politics of Knowledge: The Carnegie Corporation, Philanthropy, and Public Policy*. Middletown, CT: Wesleyan University Press, 1989.

Lake, Anthony. *The Vietnam Legacy: The War, American Society, and the Future of American Foreign Policy*. New York: New York University Press, 1976.

Lancaster, Carol. *Foreign Aid: Diplomacy, Development, Domestic Politics*. Chicago: University of Chicago Press, 2007.

Lancaster, Carol, and Institute for International Economics (U.S.). *Transforming Foreign Aid: United States Assistance in the 21st Century*. Washington, DC: Institute for International Economics, 2000.

Lancaster, Carol, and Ann Van Dusen. "Organizing U. S. Foreign Aid: Confronting the Challenges of the 21st Century." Washington, DC: Brookings Institution Press, 2005.

Lang, James. *Feeding a Hungry Planet: Rice, Research & Development in Asia and Latin America*. Chapel Hill: University of North Carolina Press, 1996.

Langley, Lester D. *The Banana Wars: An Inner History of American Empire, 1900–1934*. Lexington: University Press of Kentucky, 1983.

Lasker, Bruno, and William L. Holland. *Problems of the Pacific, 1931: Proceedings of the Fourth Conference of the Institute of Pacific Relations, Hangchow and Shanghai, China, October 21 to November 2.* Chicago: University of Chicago Press, 1932.

Laski, Harold Joseph. *Democracy in Crisis.* Chapel Hill: University of North Carolina Press, 1933.

Lasswell, Harold Dwight, and Jay Stanley. *Essays on the Garrison State.* New Brunswick, NJ, London: Transaction Publishers, 1997.

Latham, Michael E. *Modernization as Ideology: American Social Science and "Nation Building" in the Kennedy Era,* The New Cold War History. Chapel Hill: University of North Carolina Press, 2000.

Latham, Robert. *The Liberal Moment: Modernity, Security, and the Making of Postwar International Order,* New Directions in World Politics. New York: Columbia University Press, 1997.

League of Nations, Economic Financial and Transit Department, Klaus Eugen Knorr, and Eugene Staley. *Raw-Material Problems and Policies.* Geneva: League of Nations, 1946.

Lederer, William J., and Eugene Burdick. *The Ugly American.* 1st ed. New York: Norton, 1958.

Lee, Steven Hugh. *Outposts of Empire: Korea, Vietnam, and the Origins of the Cold War in Asia 1949–1954.* Montreal: McGill-Queen's University Press, 1995.

Leffler, Melvyn P. *A Preponderance of Power: National Security, the Truman Administration, and the Cold War.* Stanford, CA: Stanford University Press, 1992.

———. *The Specter of Communism: The United States and the Origins of the Cold War, 1917–1953.* New York: Hill and Wang, 1994.

———. *For the Soul of Mankind: The United States, the Soviet Union, and the Cold War.* 1st ed. New York: Hill and Wang, 2007.

Lélé, Sharachchandra M. "Sustainable Development: A Critical Review." *World Development* (June 1991): 607–21.

Lerner, Daniel, and Massachusetts Institute of Technology. Center for International Studies. *The Passing of Traditional Society: Modernizing the Middle East.* New York: Free Press, 1958.

Leuchtenburg, William E. "Roosevelt, Norris and the 'Seven Little TVAs.'" *Journal of Politics* 14 (August 1952): 418–41.

———. *Franklin D. Roosevelt and the New Deal, 1932–1940.* 1st ed. New York: Harper & Row, 1963.

Lewis, John Prior. *Reconstruction and Development in South Korea, an International Committee Report,* Planning Pamphlets, No. 94. Washington, DC: National Planning Association, 1955.

Lewis, Oscar. *Five Families: Mexican Case Studies in the Culture of Poverty.* New York: New American Library, 1959.

———. *La Vida: A Puerto Rican Family in the Culture of Poverty—San Juan and New York.* New York: Random House, 1966.

Lewis, Robert A. *Science and Industrialisation in the USSR.* New York: Holmes & Meier, 1979.

Lewis, Sinclair, and Jay Richard Kennedy. *It Can't Happen Here*. New York: New American Library, 1970.

Lewis, W. Arthur. "The State of Development Theory." *The American Economic Review* 74 (March 1984): 1.

Lie, John. *Han Unbound: The Political Economy of South Korea*. Stanford, CA: Stanford University Press, 1998.

Lilienthal, David Eli. *This I Do Believe*. 1st ed. New York: Harper, 1949.

———. *TVA: Democracy on the March*. New York: Harper, 1953.

———. *Big Business: A New Era*. 1st ed. New York: Harper, 1953.

———. "The Road to Change." *International Development Review* 6 (December 1964): 13.

———. *Management: A Humanist Art*. New York: Columbia University Press, 1967.

Lilienthal, David Eli, and Helen M. Lilienthal. *The Journals of David E. Lilienthal*. 1st ed. New York: Harper & Row, 1964.

Lippmann, Walter. *An Inquiry into the Principles of the Good Society*. Boston: Little, Brown, 1937.

———. *In the Service of Freedom*. New York: Freedom House, 1940.

———. *The Cold War: A Study in U.S. Foreign Policy*. New York: Harper, 1947.

———. *The Communist World and Ours*. 1st ed. Boston: Little, 1959.

———. *Drift and Mastery: An Attempt to Diagnose the Current Unrest*. Madison: University of Wisconsin Press, 1985.

Lippmann, Walter, and G.D. H. Cole. *Self-Sufficiency: Some Random Reflections*, International Conciliation, No. 299. Worcester, MA, New York: Carnegie Endowment for International Peace, 1934.

Listos, Socrates. "Malaria Control, the Cold War, and the Postwar Reorganization of International Assistance." *Medical Anthropology* 17 (1997): 265–67.

Logevall, Fredrik. *Choosing War: The Lost Chance for Peace and the Escalation of War in Vietnam*. Berkeley, London: University of California Press, 1999.

Louis, William Roger, and Roger Oowen. *Suez 1956: The Crisis and Its Consequences*. Oxford, New York: Clarendon Press; Oxford University Press, 1989.

Luce, Don, and John Sommer. *Viet Nam: The Unheard Voices*. Ithaca, NY: Cornell University Press, 1969.

Lundestad, Geir. *The United States and Western Europe since 1945: From "Empire" by Invitation to Transatlantic Drift*. Oxford, New York: Oxford University Press, 2003.

Lyons, Gene Martin. *Military Policy and Economic Aid: The Korean Case, 1950–1953*. Columbus: Ohio State University Press, 1961.

Macdonald, Dwight. *The Ford Foundation: The Men and the Millions*. New York: Reynal, 1956.

Maddux, Thomas R. "Red Fascism and Brown Bolshevism: The American Image of Totalitarianism in the 1930s." *The Historian* 40 (November 1977): 85–103.

Maier, Charles S. "The Politics of Productivity: Foundations of American International Economic Policy After World War II." *International Organization* 31 (Autumn 1977): 607–33.

———. *Among Empires: American Ascendancy and Its Predecessors*. Cambridge, MA: Harvard University Press, 2006.

Malia, Martin E. *Russia under Western Eyes: From the Bronze Horseman to the Lenin Mausoleum.* Cambridge, MA: Belknap Press of Harvard University Press, 1999.

Mallaby, Sebastian. *The World's Banker: A Story of Failed States, Financial Crises, and the Wealth and Poverty of Nations.* New York: Penguin Press, 2004.

Mallory, Walter. *China: Land of Famine.* New York: American Geographical Society, 1926.

Mann, Jim. *Rise of the Vulcans: The History of Bush's War Cabinet.* New York, London: Viking, 2004.

Mannheim, Karl. *Freedom, Power, and Democratic Planning.* New York: Oxford University Press, 1950.

Mannheim, Karl, and Edward Shils. *Man and Society in an Age of Reconstruction.* New York: Harcourt, 1940.

Mannheim, Karl, Louis Wirth, and Edward Shils. *Ideology and Utopia: An Introduction to the Sociology of Knowledge.* New York: Harcourt, Brace, 1936.

Mason, Edward S. *The Economic and Social Modernization of the Republic of Korea,* Studies in the Modernization of the Republic of Korea, 1945–1975. Cambridge, MA: Harvard University Press, 1980.

Mason, Edward S., and Robert E. Asher. *The World Bank since Bretton Woods; the Origins, Policies, Operations, and Impact of the International Bank for Reconstruction and Development and the Other Members of the World Bank Group: The International Finance Corporation, the International Development Association and the International Centre for Settlement of Investment Disputes.* Washington, DC: Brookings Institution, 1973.

Massachusetts Institute of Technology, Kungl. Svenska vetenskapsakademien, and Ingenjèorsvetenskapsakademien (Sweden). *Inadvertent Climate Modification: Report.* Cambridge, MA: MIT Press, 1971.

May, Glenn Anthony. *Social Engineering in the Philippines: The Aims, Execution, and Impact of American Colonial Policy, 1900–1913.* Contributions in Comparative Colonial Studies, No. 2. Westport, CT: Greenwood Press, 1980.

Maxey, Edwin. "The Reconstruction of Korea." *Political Science Quarterly* 25 (December 1910): 673–87.

Mazower, Mark. *Dark Continent: Europe's Twentieth Century.* 1st American ed. New York: A.A. Knopf; distributed by Random House, 1999.

McCormick, Thomas J. *China Market; America's Quest for Informal Empire, 1893–1901.* Chicago: Quadrangle Books, 1967.

McCormick, Thomas J. *America's Half-Century: United States Foreign Policy in the Cold War and After.* 2nd ed. Baltimore: Johns Hopkins University Press, 1995.

McCoy, Drew R. *The Elusive Republic: Political Economy in Jeffersonian America.* Chapel Hill: University of North Carolina Press, 1980.

McCraw, Thomas K. *TVA and the Power Fight, 1933–1939.* Critical Periods of History. Philadelphia: Lippincott, 1971.

McDougall, Walter A. *The Heavens and the Earth: A Political History of the Space Age.* Baltimore: Johns Hopkins University Press, 1997.

McGinn, Noel F. *Education and Development in Korea.* Studies in the Modernization of the Republic of Korea, 1945–1975. Cambridge, MA: Council on

East Asian Studies, Harvard University; distributed by Harvard University Press, 1980.

McGlothlen, Ronald L. *Controlling the Waves: Dean Acheson and U.S. Foreign Policy in Asia.* New York: Norton, 1993.

McMahon, Robert J. *The Limits of Empire: The United States and Southeast Asia since World War II.* New York: Columbia University Press, 1999.

McNamara, Robert S. *The Essence of Security; Reflections in Office.* 1st ed. New York: Harper & Row, 1968.

McNamara, Robert S., and Brian VanDeMark. *In Retrospect: The Tragedy and Lessons of Vietnam.* 1st ed. New York: Vintage Books, 1996.

McNamara, Robert S. *The McNamara Years at the World Bank: Major Policy Addresses of Robert S. McNamara, 1968–1981.* Baltimore: Johns Hopkins University Press, 1981.

McNeill, J. R. *Something New under the Sun: An Environmental History of the Twentieth-Century World.* 1st ed. New York: Norton, 2000.

Mead, Margaret. *Cultural Patterns and Technical Change.* Paris: UNESCO, 1953.

Meadows, Donella H. et al. *Limits to Growth: A Report for the Club of Rome's Project on the Predicament of Mankind.* New York: Universe Books, 1972.

Meinig, D. W. *The Shaping of America: A Geographical Perspective on 500 Years of History.* 4 vols. New Haven, CT: Yale University Press, 1986.

Menand, Louis. *The Metaphysical Club.* 1st ed. New York: Farrar, Straus and Giroux, 2001.

Michaels, Pete S., and Steven F. Napolitano. "The Hidden Costs of Hydroelectric Dams." *Cultural Survival Quarterly* 12 (1988): 2–4.

Micklethwait, John, and Adrian Wooldridge. *A Future Perfect: The Challenge and Hidden Promise of Globalization.* London: Heinemann, 2000.

Miller, T. Christian. *Blood Money: Wasted Billions, Lost Lives, and Corporate Greed in Iraq.* 1st ed. New York: Little, Brown, 2006.

Millikan, Max F., and W. W. Rostow. *A Proposal: Key to an Effective Foreign Policy.* 1st ed. New York: Harper & Bros., 1957.

Millspaugh, Arthur Chester. *Haiti under American Control, 1915–1930.* Westport, CT: Negro Universities Press, 1970.

Milne, David. *America's Rasputin: Walt Rostow and the Vietnam War.* New York: Hill and Wang, 2008.

Mitchell, Kate Louise, and W. L. Holland. *Problems of the Pacific, 1939: Proceedings of the Study Meeting of the Institute of Pacific Relations, Virginia Beach, Virginia, November 18–December 2, 1939.* New York: Institute of Pacific Relations, 1940.

Mitchell, Timothy. *Colonising Egypt.* Berkeley: University of California Press, 1988.

Morgan, Arthur Ernest. *The Philosophy of Edward Bellamy.* New York: King's Crown Press, 1945.

———. *Dams and Other Disasters: A Century of the Army Corps of Engineers in Civil Works.* Boston: P. Sargent, 1971.

Mumford, Lewis. *Technics and Civilization.* New York: Harcourt Brace & World, 1963.

Myrdal, Gunnar. *Population, a Problem for Democracy.* Cambridge, MA: Harvard University Press, 1940.

Myrdal, Gunnar, and Twentieth Century Fund. *Asian Drama: An Inquiry into the Poverty of Nations.* New York: Twentieth Century Fund, 1968.

Nagai, Yōonosuke, and Akira Iriye. *The Origins of the Cold War in Asia.* New York: Columbia University Press, 1977.

Nasaw, David. *Andrew Carnegie.* New York: Penguin Press, 2006.

Nathan, Andrew J. *A History of the China International Famine Relief Commission.* Cambridge, MA: Harvard University Press, 1965.

National Commission on Terrorist Attacks upon the United States. *The 9/11 Commission Report: Final Report of the National Commission on Terrorist Attacks Upon the United States: Official Government Edition.* Washington, DC: U.S. Government Printing Office, 2004.

Nelson, Arvid. *Cold War Ecology: Forests, Farms, and People in the East German Landscape, 1945–1989.* New Haven, CT: Yale University Press, 2005.

Neuse, Steven M. *David E. Lilienthal: The Journey of an American Liberal.* 1st ed. Knoxville: University of Tennessee Press, 1996.

Nguyen, Thi Dieu. *The Mekong River and the Struggle for Indochina: Water, War, and Peace.* Westport, CT: Praeger, 1999.

Niebuhr, Reinhold. *Reflections on the End of an Era.* New York, London: C. Scribner's Sons, 1934.

———. *The Irony of American History.* New York: Scribner, 1952.

Nielsen, Waldemar A. *The Big Foundations.* New York: Columbia University Press, 1972.

Ninkovich, Frank A. *The Diplomacy of Ideas: U.S. Foreign Policy and Cultural Relations, 1938–1950.* Cambridge, New York: Cambridge University Press, 1981.

———. "The Rockefeller Foundation, China, and Cultural Change." *Journal of American History* 70 (March 1984): 799–820.

———. *Modernity and Power: A History of the Domino Theory in the Twentieth Century.* Chicago: University of Chicago Press, 1994.

———. *The Wilsonian Century: U.S. Foreign Policy since 1900.* Chicago, London: University of Chicago Press, 1999.

———. *The United States and Imperialism,* Problems in American History. Malden, MA: Blackwell Publishers, 2001.

Njilstad, Olav. *The Last Decade of the Cold War: From Conflict Escalation to Conflict Transformation,* Cass Series—Cold War History, 5. London: Frank Cass, 2004.

Nye, David E. *Electrifying America: Social Meanings of a New Technology, 1880–1940.* Cambridge, MA: MIT Press, 1990.

———. *American Technological Sublime.* Cambridge, MA: MIT Press, 1994.

———. *Narratives and Spaces: Technology and the Construction of American Culture.* New York: Columbia University Press, 1997.

———. *Consuming Power: A Social History of American Energies.* Cambridge, MA: MIT Press, 1998.

O'Donnell, John, and Harvey C. Neese. *Prelude to Tragedy: Vietnam, 1960–1965.* Annapolis, MD: Naval Institute Press, 2001.

Ogilvie, Marilyn Bailey. *Philanthropy and Cultural Context-Western Philanthropy in South, East and Southeast Asia in the 20th Century: The Rockefeller Foundation, China, Western Medicine and PUMC.* Indianapolis Center of Philanthropy, 1995.

Oh, John Kie-chiang. *Korea: Democracy on Trial.* Ithaca, NY: Cornell University Press, 1968.

Opler, Morris Edward. *Social Aspects of Technical Assistance in Operation: A Report of a Conference Held Jointly by the United Nations and Unesco.* Paris: UNESCO, 1954.

Ostrower, Gary B. *The United Nations and the United States,* Twayne's International History Series. New York: Twayne Publishers/Simon & Schuster Macmillan, 1998.

Overy, R. J. *The Dictators: Hitler's Germany and Stalin's Russia.* New York: Norton, 2004.

Owens, Edgar, and Robert Shaw. *Development Reconsidered: Bridging the Gap between Government and People.* Lexington, MA: Lexington Books, 1972.

Pach, Chester J. *Arming the Free World: The Origins of the United States Military Assistance Program, 1945-1950.* Chapel Hill: University of North Carolina Press, 1991.

Packenham, Robert A. *Liberal America and the Third World: Political Development Ideas in Foreign Aid and Social Science.* Princeton, NJ: Princeton University Press, 1973.

Packer, George. *The Assassins' Gate: America in Iraq.* 1st ed. New York: Farrar, Straus and Giroux, 2005.

Park, Tae-Gyun. "Change in U.S. Policy Toward South Korea in the Early 1960s." *Korean Studies* 23 (1999): 94–120.

Parmar, Inderjeet. "The Carnegie Corporation and the Mobilization of Opinion in the United States' Rise to Globalism, 1939–1945." *Minerva* 37 (1999): 355–78.

———. " 'To Relate Knowledge to Action.' The Impact of the Rockefeller Foundation on Foreign Policy Thinking During America's Rise to Globalism, 1939–1945." *Minerva* 40 (2002): 235–63.

Paterson, Thomas G. *Meeting the Communist Threat: Truman to Reagan.* New York: Oxford University Press, 1988.

Patterson, James T. *America's Struggle against Poverty, 1900–1994.* Cambridge, MA: Harvard University Press, 1994.

———. *Grand Expectations: The United States, 1945–1974.* New York: Oxford University Press, 1996.

Paxton, Robert O. *The Anatomy of Fascism.* New York: Knopf, 2004.

Pearce, Kimber Charles. *Rostow, Kennedy, and the Rhetoric of Foreign Aid,* Rhetoric and Public Affairs Series. East Lansing: Michigan State University Press, 2001.

Peking United International Famine Relief Committee. *The North China Famine of 1920–1921, with Special Reference to the West Chihli Area. Being the Report of the Peking United International Famine Relief Committee.* Peking: Printed by the Commercial Press Works, 1922.

Pells, Richard H. *Radical Visions and American Dreams: Culture and Social Thought in the Depression Years.* New York: Harper & Row, 1973.

———. *The Liberal Mind in a Conservative Age: American Intellectuals in the 1940s and 1950s.* 2nd ed. Middletown, CT: Wesleyan University Press, 1989.

The Pentagon Papers: The Defense Department History of United States Decisionmaking on Vietnam, Senator Gravel Edition, Boston: Beacon Press, 1971.

Pirages, Dennis. "Scarcity and International Politics." *International Studies Quarterly* 21 (December 1977): 563–67.

Popp, Roland. "An Application of Modernization Theory During the Cold War?: The Case of Pahlavi Iran." *International History Review* 30 (March 2008): 76–98.

Public Affairs Institute. *Bold New Program Series No. 1–8.* Washington, DC, 1950.

Pye, Lucian. "Political Science and the Crisis of Authoritarianism." *American Political Science Review* 84 (March 1990): 3–19.

Rabe, Steven. *Eisenhower in Latin America: The Foreign Policy of Anti-Communism.* Chapel Hill: University of North Carolina Press, 1988.

Race, Jeffrey. *War Comes to Long An: Revolutionary Conflict in a Vietnamese Province.* Berkeley: University of California Press, 1972.

Radosh, Ronald, and ebrary Inc. *Prophets on the Right: Profiles of Conservative Critics of American Globalism.* Cybereditions http://site.ebrary.com/lib/yale/Doc?id=10041217.

Rassweiler, Anne Dickason. *The Generation of Power: The History of Dneprostroi.* New York, Oxford: Oxford University Press, 1988.

Raucher, Alan R. *Paul G. Hoffman: Architect of Foreign Aid.* Lexington: University Press of Kentucky, 1985.

Reagan, Patrick D. *Designing a New America: The Origins of New Deal Planning, 1890–1943.* Amherst: University of Massachusetts Press, 2000.

Reich, Cary. *The Life of Nelson A. Rockefeller: Worlds to Conquer, 1908–1958.* New York: Doubleday, 1996.

Reich, Charles A. *The Greening of America; How the Youth Revolution Is Trying to Make America Livable.* New York: Random House, 1970.

Reintjes, Monique. *Odette Keun: 1888–1978.* Netherlands: M. Reintjes, 2000.

Renda, Mary A. *Taking Haiti: Military Occupation and the Culture of U.S. Imperialism, 1915–1940.* Chapel Hill: University of North Carolina Press, 2001.

Reynolds, David. *From Munich to Pearl Harbor: Roosevelt's America and the Origins of the Second World War.* Chicago: Ivan R. Dee, 2001.

Rhodes, Richard. *The Making of the Atomic Bomb.* New York: Simon & Schuster, 1986.

Rich, Bruce. *Mortgaging the Earth: The World Bank, Environmental Impoverishment, and the Crisis of Development.* Boston: Beacon Press, 1994.

Richardson, Elmo. *Dams, Parks & Politics: Resource Development & Preservation in the Truman-Eisenhower Era.* Lexington: University Press of Kentucky, 1973.

Richardson, Theresa R., and Donald Fisher. *The Development of the Social Sciences in the United States and Canada: The Role of Philanthropy,* Contemporary Studies in Social and Policy Issues in Education. Stamford, CT: Ablex, 1999.

Rieff, David. *A Bed for the Night: Humanitarianism in Crisis.* New York: Simon & Schuster, 2002.

Rist, Gilbert. *The History of Development: From Western Origins to Global Faith.* New York: Zed Books, 1997.

Rivas, Darlene. *Missionary Capitalist: Nelson Rockefeller in Venezuela,* Chapel Hill: University of North Carolina Press, 2002.

Robert R. Nathan Associates, and United Nations Korean Reconstruction Agency. *An Economic Programme for Korean Reconstruction, Prepared for the United Nations Korean Reconstruction Agency.* New York, 1954.

Robertson, Thomas. " 'This Is the American Earth': American Empire, the Cold War, and American Environmentalism." *Diplomatic History* 32 (September 2008): 561–84.

Rodgers, Daniel T. *Atlantic Crossings: Social Politics in a Progressive Age.* Cambridge, MA, London: Belknap Press of Harvard University Press, 1998.

Rodman, Peter W. *More Precious Than Peace: The Cold War and the Struggle for the Third World.* New York: C. Scribner's Sons, 1994.

Rook, Robert. "Race, Water, and Foreign Policy: The Tennessee Valley Authority's Global Agenda Meets 'Jim Crow.'" *Diplomatic History* 28 (January 2004): 55–81.

Rosenberg, Emily S. *Spreading the American Dream: American Economic and Cultural Expansion, 1890–1945.* New York: Hill and Wang, 1982.

Rosenfield, Patricia L., and Blair T. Bower. "Management Strategies for Mitigating Adverse Health Impacts of Water Resource Development Projects." *Progress in Water Technology* 11 (1979): 285–301.

Ross, Dorothy. *The Origins of American Social Science,* Ideas in Context. Cambridge, New York: Cambridge University Press, 1991.

Rostow, W. W. *An American Policy in Asia.* Cambridge: published jointly by the Technology Press of Massachusetts Institute of Technology and Wiley New York, 1955.

———. *The Stages of Economic Growth, a Non-Communist Manifesto.* Cambridge: University Press, 1960.

———. *The Diffusion of Power: An Essay in Recent History.* New York: Macmillan, 1972.

———. *Eisenhower, Kennedy, and Foreign Aid.* 1st ed. Austin: University of Texas Press, 1985.

———. *The United States and the Regional Organization of Asia and the Pacific, 1965–1985.* 1st ed. Austin: University of Texas Press, 1986.

Rotter, Andrew Jon. *The Path to Vietnam: Origins of the American Commitment to Southeast Asia.* Ithaca, NY: Cornell University Press, 1987.

Rusk, Dean, Richard Rusk, and Daniel S. Papp. *As I Saw It.* 1st ed. New York: Norton, 1990.

Russell, Dean. *The TVA Idea.* Irvington-on-Hudson, NY: Foundation for Economic Education, 1949.

Ruttan, Vernon W. *United States Development Assistance Policy: The Domestic Politics of Foreign Economic Aid*, The Johns Hopkins Studies in Development. Baltimore: Johns Hopkins University Press, 1996.

Rydell, Robert W. *All the World's a Fair: Visions of Empire at American International Expositions, 1876–1916*. Chicago: University of Chicago Press, 1984.

Sachs, Jeffrey. *The End of Poverty: Economic Possibilities for Our Time*. New York: Penguin Press, 2005.

———. *Common Wealth: Economics for a Crowded Planet*. New York: Penguin Press, 2008.

Sachs, Wolfgang. "The Archaeology of the Development Idea." *INTERculture* 23 (Fall 1990): 2–37.

———. *The Development Dictionary: A Guide to Knowledge as Power*. London, Atlantic Highlands, NJ: Zed Books, 1992.

Sackley, Nicole. "Passage to Modernity: American Social Scientists, India, and the Pursuit of Development, 1945–1961." Ph.D. Diss. Princeton University, 2004.

Salter, J. A. "The Reconstruction of Hungary." *Journal of the Royal Institute of International Affairs* 3 (July 1924): 190–202.

Schaller, Michael. *The American Occupation of Japan: The Origins of the Cold War in Asia*. New York: Oxford University Press, 1985.

Schivelbusch, Wolfgang. *Three New Deals: Reflections on Roosevelt's America, Mussolini's Italy, and Hitler's Germany, 1933–1939*. 1st ed. New York: Metropolitan Books, 2006.

Schlesinger, Arthur Meier. *The Vital Center: The Politics of Freedom*. Boston: Houghton Mifflin, 1949.

Schulzinger, Robert D. *The Wise Men of Foreign Affairs: The History of the Council on Foreign Relations*. New York: Columbia University Press, 1984.

———. *A Time for War: The United States and Vietnam, 1941–1975*. New York: Oxford University Press, 1997.

Schumacher, E. F. *Small Is Beautiful: A Study of Economics As If People Mattered*. London: Blond and Briggs, 1973.

Schwarz, Jordan A. *The New Dealers: Power Politics in the Age of Roosevelt*. 1st ed. New York: Knopf; distributed by Random House, 1993.

Schyler, R. L. "The Reconstruction of the British Empire." *Political Science Quarterly* 31 (September 1916): 445–52.

Scott, James C. *Seeing Like a State: How Certain Schemes to Improve the Human Condition Have Failed*, Yale Agrarian Studies. New Haven, CT; London: Yale University Press, 1998.

Scudder, Thayer. "The Human Ecology of Big Projects: River Basin Development and Resettlement." *Annual Review of Anthropology* 2 (1973): 45–55.

Sealander, Judith. *Private Wealth and Public Life: Foundation Philanthropy and the Reshaping of American Social Policy from the Progressive Era to the New Deal*. Baltimore: Johns Hopkins University Press, 1997.

Seligman, Edwin Robert Anderson, and Alvin Saunders Johnson. *Encyclopedia of the Social Sciences*. New York: Macmillan, 1935.

Sen, Amartya Kumar. *Poverty and Famines: An Essay on Entitlement and Deprivation*. Oxford, New York: Oxford University Press, 1981.

———. *Development as Freedom*. 1st. ed. New York: Knopf, 1999.

Shapiro, Edward. "The Southern Agrarians and the Tennessee Valley Authority." *American Quarterly* 22 (Winter 1970): 791–806.

Shapiro, Judith. *Mao's War against Nature: Politics and the Environment in Revolutionary China*, Studies in Environment and History. Cambridge, New York: Cambridge University Press, 2001.

Shapley, Deborah. *Promise and Power: The Life and Times of Robert McNamara*. 1st ed. Boston: Little Brown, 1993.

Shenin, Sergei Y. *The United States and the Third World: The Origins of the Postwar Relations and the Point Four Program (1949–1953)*. Commack, NY: Nova Science, 2000.

———. *America's Helping Hand: Paving the Way to Globalization (Eisenhower's Foreign Aid Policy and Politics)*. New York: Nova Science, 2005.

Shotwell, James Thomson, and Raymond Blaine Fosdick. *The Conditions of Enduring Prosperity*. New York: Carnegie Endowment for International Peace, 1931.

Sills, David L., and Robert King Merton. *International Encyclopedia of the Social Sciences*. New York: Macmillan, 1968.

Silverman, Dan P. *Hitler's Economy: Nazi Work Creation Programs, 1933–1936*. Cambridge, MA: Harvard University Press, 1998.

Simpson, Bradley R. *Economists with Guns: Authoritarian Development and U.S.-Indonesian Relations, 1960–1968*. Stanford, CA: Stanford University Press, 2008.

Simpson, Christopher. *Universities and Empire: Money and Politics in the Social Sciences During the Cold War*. New York: New Press, 1998.

Singh, Lalita Prasad. *The Politics of Economic Cooperation in Asia: A Study of Asian International Organizations*. Columbia: University of Missouri Press, 1966.

Skidelsky, Robert Jacob Alexander. *The Road from Serfdom: The Economic and Political Consequences of the End of Communism*. New York: Allen Lane/Penguin Press, 1996.

Sklar, Martin J. *The United States as a Developing Country: Studies in U.S. History in the Progressive Era and the 1920s*. Cambridge: Cambridge University Press, 1992.

Skolnikoff, Eugene B. The International Functional Implications of Future Technology." *Journal of International Affairs* 25 (1971): 274.

———. "Science and Technology: The Implications for International Institutions." *International Organization* 4 (Autumn 1971): 759–75.

———. "International Institutions and the Environmental Crisis: A Look Ahead." *International Organization* 2 (Spring 1972): 469–78.

———. *The Elusive Transformation: Science, Technology, and the Transformation of International Politics*. Princeton, NJ: Princeton University Press, 1993.

Smith, Brian H. *More Than Altruism: The Politics of Private Foreign Aid*. Princeton, NJ: Princeton University Press, 1990.

Snowden, Frank M. *The Conquest of Malaria: Italy, 1900–1962*. New Haven, CT: Yale University Press, 2006.

Soviet Union. *USSR in Construction*. Moscow: State Art Publishing House, various dates.

Spector, Ronald H. *In the Ruins of Empire: The Japanese Surrender and the Battle for Postwar Asia.* 1st ed. New York: Random House, 2007.

Spence, Jonathan D. *To Change China: Western Advisers in China, 1620–1960.* New York: Penguin Books, 1980.

Staley, Eugene. *Foreign Investment and War.* Chicago: University of Chicago Press, 1935.

———. *War and the Private Investor: A Study in the Relations of International Politics and International Private Investment.* Garden City, NY Doubleday, Doran, 1935.

———. "Power Economy versus Welfare Economy." *Annals of the American Academy of Political and Social Science* 198 (July 1938): 9–14.

———. *World Economy in Transition.* New York: Council on Foreign Relations, 1939.

———. *This Shrinking World: World Technology vs. National Politics.* Chicago: World Citizens Association, 1940.

———. "What Types of Economic Planning Are Compatible with Free Institutions?" *Plan Age*, February 1940, 33–50.

———. *Wartime and Peacetime Economic Collaboration.* Princeton, NJ: American Committee for International Studies, 1941.

———. *The Myth of the Continents.* New York: Council on Foreign Relations, 1941.

———. *World Economic Development: Effects on Advanced Industrial Countries.* Montreal: International Labour Office, 1944.

———, ed. *Creating an Industrial Civilization.* New York: Harper, 1952.

———. *The Future of Underdeveloped Countries; Political Implications of Economic Development.* Rev. ed. New York: Harper, 1961.

Stanley, Peter W. *A Nation in the Making: The Philippines and the United States, 1899–1921.* Cambridge, MA: Harvard University Press, 1974.

Staples, Amy L. S. *The Birth of Development: How the World Bank, Food and Agriculture Organization, and World Health Organization Changed the World, 1945–1965.* Kent, OH: Kent State University Press, 2006.

Stephanson, Anders. *Kennan and the Art of Foreign Policy.* Cambridge, MA: Harvard University Press, 1989.

———. *Manifest Destiny: American Expansionism and the Empire of Right.* 1st ed. New York: Hill and Wang, 1995.

Stiglitz, Joseph E. *Globalization and Its Discontents.* 1st ed. New York: Norton, 2002.

Stites, Richard. *Revolutionary Dreams: Utopian Vision and Experimental Life in the Russian Revolution.* New York: Oxford University Press, 1989.

Stone, Peter Bennet. *Did We Save the Earth at Stockholm?* London: Earth Island, 1973.

Strong, Josiah. *Our Country.* Cambridge, MA: Belknap Press of Harvard University Press, 1963.

Strong, Maurice F. *Where on Earth Are We Going?* Toronto: Knopf Canada, 2000.

Stross, Randall E. *The Stubborn Earth: American Agriculturalists on Chinese Soil, 1898–1937.* Berkeley: University of California Press, 1986.

Stueck, William Whitney. *The Road to Confrontation: American Policy toward China and Korea, 1947–1950*. Chapel Hill: University of North Carolina Press, 1981.

———. *The Wedemeyer Mission: American Politics and Foreign Policy during the Cold War*. Athens: University of Georgia Press, 1984.

———. *The Korean War: An International History*, Princeton Studies in International History and Politics. Princeton, NJ: Princeton University Press, 1995.

———. *Rethinking the Korean War: A New Diplomatic and Strategic History*. Princeton, NJ: Princeton University Press, 2002.

Sun, Yat-sen. *The International Development of China*. 2nd ed. New York: Da Capo Press, 1975.

Taffet, Jeffrey F. *Foreign Aid as Foreign Policy: The Alliance for Progress in Latin America*. New York: Routledge, 2007.

Talbert, Roy. *FDR's Utopian: Arthur Morgan of the TVA*, Twentieth-Century America Series. Jackson: University Press of Mississippi, 1987.

Tead, Ordway. "The British Reconstruction." *Political Science Quarterly* 33 (March 1918): 56–76.

Technical Assistance Information Clearing House. "Directory of American Voluntary and Non-Profit Agencies Interested in Technical Assistance." New York: Technical Assistance Information Clearing House, American Council of Voluntary Agencies for Foreign Service, 1960.

Teichova, Alice, Maurice Lévy-Leboyer, and Helga Nussbaum. *Multinational Enterprise in Historical Perspective*. New York: Cambridge University Press, 1986.

Thomson, James C. *While China Faced West: American Reformers in Nationalist China, 1928–1937*. Cambridge, MA: Harvard University Press, 1969.

Thomson, James Claude, Peter W. Stanley, and John Curtis Perry. *Sentimental Imperialists: The American Experience in East Asia*. 1st ed. New York: Harper & Row, 1981.

Tichi, Cecelia. *Shifting Gears: Technology, Literature, Culture in Modernist America*. Chapel Hill: University of North Carolina Press, 1987.

Tignor, Robert L. *W. Arthur Lewis and the Birth of Development Economics*. Princeton, NJ: Princeton University Press, 2006.

Tilly, Charles. *Big Structures, Large Processes, Huge Comparisons*. New York: Russell Sage Foundation, 1984.

Tobey, Ronald C. *Technology as Freedom: The New Deal and the Electrical Modernization of the American Home*. Berkeley: University of California Press, 1996.

Todd, Oliver J. *Two Decades in China*. Peking: Association of Chinese and American Engineers, 1938.

———. *The China That I Knew*. Palo Alto, CA: Todd, 1973

Tomlinson, Edward. *Battle for the Hemisphere: Democracy Versus Totalitarianism in the Other America*. New York: C. Scribner's Sons, 1947.

Truman, Harry S. *Memoirs*. 1st ed. Garden City, NY: Doubleday, 1955.

Tucker, Nancy Bernkopf. *Taiwan, Hong Kong, and the United States, 1945–1992: Uncertain Friendships*. New York: Twayne, 1994.

UNESCO. *Rebuilding Education in the Republic of Korea: Report.* Paris: UNESCO, 1954.

United Nations Department of Economic Affairs. *Measures for the Economic Development of Under-Developed Countries: Report by a Group of Experts Appointed by the Secretary-General of the United Nations.* New York, 1951.

United Nations Environment Programme. *In Defence of the Earth, the Basic Texts on Environment: Founex, Stockholm, Cocoyoc,* Unep Executive Series; 1. Nairobi: United Nations Environment Programme, 1981.

United Nations Office of Public Information. *United Nations Work and Programs for Technical Assistance.* New York: s.n., 1951.

United Nations Relief and Rehabilitation Administration. *UNRRA: The History of the United Nations Relief and Rehabilitation Administration.* New York: Columbia University Press, 1950.

United Nations Relief and Rehabilitation Administration, J. Franklin Ray, and United States Department of State. *UNRRA in China, 1945–1947,* Modern Chinese Economy; 40. New York: Garland, 1980.

United Nations. Secretary-General. *Technical Assistance for Economic Development: Plan for an Expanded Co-Operative Programme through the United Nations and the Specialized Agencies.* Lake Success, 1949.

United States Agency for International Development, and United States Bureau of Reclamation. *To Tame a River.* Washington: U.S. Government Printing Office, 1968.

United States Office of Scientific Research and Development, and Vannevar Bush. *Science, the Endless Frontier. A Report to the President.* Washington, DC: U.S. Government Printing Office, 1945.

United States President (2001–2009: Bush). "The National Security Strategy of the United States of America." White House, http://purl.access.gpo.gov/GPO/LPS67777.

United States President (2001–2009: Bush), and George W. Bush. *The National Security Strategy of the United States of America.* Falls Village, CT: Winterhouse Editions, 2002.

United States President's Scientific Research Board, and John Roy Steelman. *Science and Public Policy: A Report to the President.* Washington, DC: U.S. Government Printing Office, 1947.

Wade, Robert. *Governing the Market: Economic Theory and the Role of Government in East Asian Industrialization.* Princeton, NJ: Princeton University Press, 1990.

Walch, Timothy, and Dwight M. Miller. *Herbert Hoover and Harry S. Truman: A Documentary History.* Worland, WY: High Plains, 1992.

Walker, William O., III. "Crucible for Peace: Herbert Hoover, Modernization, and Economic Growth in Latin America." *Diplomatic History* 30 (Jan. 2006): 83–117.

Wall, Joseph Frazier. *Andrew Carnegie.* New York: Oxford University Press, 1970.

Wallace, Henry Agard. *America Must Choose: The Advantages and Disadvantages of Nationalism, of World Trade, and of a Planned Middle Course.* New York: Foreign Policy Association, 1934.

Ward, Barbara. *The West at Bay.* New York: Norton, 1948.

———. *The Rich Nations and the Poor Nations.* 1st ed. New York: Norton, 1962.

———. *Spaceship Earth*, The George B. Pegram Lectures, No. 6. New York: Columbia University Press, 1966.

Ward, Barbara, and Rene J. Dubos. *Only One Earth: The Care and Maintenance of a Small Planet.* 1st ed. New York: Norton, 1972.

Ward, Barbara, J. D. Runnalls, Lenore D'Anjou, and Commission on International Development. *The Widening Gap: Development in the 1970's: A Report on the Columbia Conference on International Economic Development, Williamsburg, Virginia, and New York, February 15–21, 1970.* New York: Columbia University Press, 1971.

Ward, Diane Raines. *Water Wars: Drought, Flood, Folly, and the Politics of Thirst.* New York: Riverhead Books, 2002.

Warne, William E. *Mission for Peace: Point 4 in Iran.* Bethesda, MD: Ibex, 1999.

Watson, Cynthia Ann. *Nation-Building: A Reference Handbook*, Contemporary World Issues. Santa Barbara, CA: ABC-CLIO, 2004.

Weatherly, Ulysses G. "Haiti: An Experiment in Pragmatism." *American Journal of Sociology* 32 (November 1926): 353–66.

Wei, C. X. George. "The Economic Cooperation Administration, the State Department, and the American Presence in China, 1948–1950." *Pacific Historical Review* 70 (August 2001): 21–53.

Wengert, E. S. "TVA Enlists Local Cooperation." *Public Opinion Quarterly* 1 (April 1937): 97–101.

Westad, Odd Arne. *Brothers in Arms: The Rise and Fall of the Sino-Soviet Alliance, 1945–1963.* Washington, DC, Stanford, CA: Stanford University Press, 1998.

———. *Reviewing the Cold War: Approaches, Interpretations, and Theory.* London, Portland, OR: F. Cass, 2000.

———. "The New International History of the Cold War: Three (Possible) Paradigms." *Diplomatic History* 24 (Fall 2000): 551–65.

———. *The Global Cold War: Third World Interventions and the Making of Our Times.* Cambridge, New York: Cambridge University Press, 2005.

Westbrook, Robert B. *John Dewey and American Democracy.* Ithaca, NY: Cornell University Press, 1991.

White, Gilbert F., Robert William Kates, and Ian Burton. *Selected Writings of Gilbert F. White.* Chicago: University of Chicago Press, 1986.

White, Richard. *The Organic Machine.* New York: Hill and Wang, 1995.

Williamson, John. *Latin American Adjustment: How Much Has Happened.* Washington, DC: Institute for International Economics, 1990.

Wilson, Francis, and Mamphela Ramphele. *Uprooting Poverty: The South African Challenge.* 1st American ed. New York: Norton, 1989.

Winter, J. M. *Dreams of Peace and Freedom: Utopian Moments in the Twentieth Century.* New Haven, CT: Yale University Press, 2006.

Wolf, Charles. *Foreign Aid.* Princeton, NJ: Princeton University Press, 1960.

Woo-Cumings, Meredith. *Race to the Swift: State and Finance in Korean Industrialization*, Studies of the East Asian Institute. New York: Columbia University Press, 1991.

————. *The Developmental State*, Cornell Studies in Political Economy. Ithaca, NY: Cornell University Press, 1999.

Woods, Lawrence Timothy. *Asia-Pacific Diplomacy: Nongovernmental Organizations and International Relations*. Vancouver: UBC Press, 1993.

World Commission on Environment and Development. *Our Common Future*. Oxford, New York: Oxford University Press, 1987.

Worster, Donald. *Rivers of Empire: Water, Aridity, and the Growth of the American West*. New York: Pantheon Books, 1985.

————. *Nature's Economy: A History of Ecological Ideas*. 2nd ed. Studies in Environment and History. Cambridge, New York: Cambridge University Press, 1994.

Wright, Lawrence. *The Looming Tower: Al-Qaeda and the Road to 9/11*. 1st ed. New York: Knopf, 2006.

Yager, Joseph A. *Transforming Agriculture in Taiwan: The Experience of the Joint Commission on Rural Reconstruction*, Food Systems and Agrarian Change. Ithaca, NY: Cornell University Press, 1988.

Yeh, Wen-Hsin. *Becoming Chinese: Passages to Modernity and Beyond*. Berkeley: University of California Press, 2000.

Yergin, Daniel, and Joseph Stanislaw. *The Commanding Heights: The Battle between Government and the Marketplace That Is Remaking the Modern World*. New York: Simon & Schuster, 1998.

Young, Arthur N. *China and the Helping Hand, 1937–1945*, Harvard East Asian Series, 12. Cambridge, MA: Harvard University Press, 1963.

Young, Marilyn Blatt. *The Vietnam Wars, 1945–1990*. 1st ed. New York: HarperCollins, 1991.

Zachary, G. Pascal. *Endless Frontier: Vannevar Bush, Engineer of the American Century*. New York: Free Press, 1997.

Zanasi, Margherita. "Exporting Development: The League of Nations and Republican China." *Comparative Studies in Society and History* 49 (January 2009): 143–69.

Zwayer, Wayland. *Directory of American Voluntary and Non-Profit Agencies Interested in Technical Assistance*. New York: Technical Assistance Information Clearing House, 1960.

INDEX

Note: entries in bold font indicate refrerences to illustrations.